D0765623

THE MACARTHUR NEW TESTAMENT COMMENTARY

ACTS 1-12

John MacArthur, Jr.

MOODY PRESS/CHICAGO

To Alistair Begg, with thanks
for loyal friendship
and kindred spirit
as we contend for the faith

© 1994 by
THE MOODY BIBLE INSTITUTE
OF CHICAGO

ISBN: 0-8024-0759-5

9 10

Printed in the United States of America

Contents

Preface

It continues to be a rewarding divine communion for me to preach expositionally through the New Testament. My goal is always to have deep fellowship with the Lord in the understanding of His Word and out of that experience to explain to His people what a passage means. In the words of Nehemiah 8:8, I strive "to give the sense" of it so they may truly hear God speak and, in so doing, may respond to Him.

Obviously, God's people need to understand Him, which demands knowing His Word of truth (2 Tim. 2:15) and allowing that Word to dwell in us richly (Col. 3:16). The dominant thrust of my ministry, therefore, is to help make God's living Word alive to His people. It is a refreshing adventure.

This New Testament commentary series reflects this objective of explaining and applying Scripture. Some commentaries are primarily linguistic, others are mostly theological, and some are mainly homiletical. This one is basically explanatory, or expository. It is not linguistically technical, but deals with linguistics when this seems helpful to proper interpretation. It is not theologically expansive, but focuses on the major doctrines in each text and on how they relate to the whole of Scripture. It is not primarily homiletical, though each unit of thought is generally treated as one chapter, with a clear outline and logical flow of thought. Most truths are illustrated and applied with other Scripture. After establishing the context of a passage, I have tried to follow closely the writer's development and reasoning.

My prayer is that each reader will fully understand what the Holy Spirit is saying through this part of His Word, so that His revelation may lodge in the minds of believers and bring greater obedience and faithfulness—to the glory of our great God.

Introduction

The book of Acts is the first volume of church history. It records the story of the church from its explosive beginning on the Day of Pentecost to the imprisonment at Rome of its greatest missionary. During those three decades, the church expanded from a small group of Jewish believers gathered in Jerusalem to embrace thousands in dozens of congregations throughout the Roman world. Acts describes how the Spirit of God superintended, controlled, and empowered the expansion of the church. Indeed, the book could well be called "The Acts of the Holy Spirit Through the Apostles."

Acts is a significant book for several reasons. With the epistles, but without Acts, we would have much difficulty understanding the flow of the early history of the church. With it, we have a core history around which to assemble the data in the epistles, enriching our comprehension of them. The book follows first the ministry of Peter, then of Paul. From it we learn principles for discipling believers, building the church, and evangelizing the world.

Although a work of history, not theology, Acts nevertheless emphasizes the doctrinal truths concerning salvation. Jesus of Nazareth is boldly proclaimed as Israel's long-awaited Messiah, and that truth is ably defended from the Old Testament (2:22ff.; 3:12ff.; 4:10ff.; 7:1ff.; 8:26ff.; 13:14ff.; cf. 9:22; 18:5, 24–28; 28:23).

The book of Acts also teaches much about the Holy Spirit, who is mentioned more than fifty times. He regenerates, baptizes, fills, and sanctifies believers. The Holy Spirit is seen choosing missionaries (13:2) and directing their operations (8:29). He presided at the first church council (15:28) and, in short, directed and controlled all operations of the church.

The doctrinal importance of Acts is not limited, however, to its teaching on Jesus Christ and the Holy Spirit. While it does not flow around doctrinal issues, but historical events, it nevertheless touches many theological truths. Donald Guthrie aptly summarizes the theological significance of Acts: "The importance of the book of Acts is in its preservation of the main doctrinal themes presented in apostolic preaching, even if there is no evidence of an attempt to develop a systematized theology" (*New Testament Introduction* [Downers Grove, Ill.: InterVarsity, 1978], 338).

AUTHOR

The unanimous testimony of the early church was that Luke, author of the gospel bearing his name, and the traveling companion and close friend of Paul, wrote Acts. In the second century, the anti-Marcionite prologue to Luke's gospel, the Muratorian Fragment (the earliest extant list of New Testament books), Irenaeus, Clement of Alexandria, and Tertullian all attest to Luke's authorship of Acts. Other church Fathers, such as Origen, Eusebius, and Jerome also attribute Acts to Luke.

The internal evidence for Luke's authorship is equally impressive. That the author of Acts was a traveling companion of the apostle Paul is clear from the so-called "we passages" (16:10–17; 20:5–21:18; 27:1–28:16). In those passages, the writer switches to the first person plural, showing he was present. D. Edmond Hiebert summarizes the significance of that as it relates to the authorship of Acts:

> References to various companions of Paul in these we-sections at once distinguish the author from other of Paul's close companions. Other well-known companions appearing in the Pauline epistles do not fit into the pattern set by these we-sections and can be located elsewhere at one time or another. Of the known close companions of Paul only Titus and Luke are never named in Acts. That Titus is not named is strange, but no one has ever seriously suggested that Titus was the author of Luke-Acts. This leaves only Luke as the probable author, and he is strongly supported by the external evidence. (*An Introduction to the*

> *New Testament: Volume 1: The Gospels and Acts* [Chicago: Moody, 1979], p. 121)

It should be noted too that "although Titus accompanied Paul and Barnabas to Jerusalem and worked in the churches of Corinth, Crete, and Dalmatia, he appears not to have been one of Paul's companions whom the apostle mentions in the greetings of his epistles" (Simon J. Kistemaker, *New Testament Commentary: Acts* [Grand Rapids: Baker, 1990], p. 21). By process of elimination, then, we are left with Luke as author of the "we passages," and therefore of the entire book.

It is also unlikely anyone would have forged a work in Luke's name. If someone were going to attribute a forgery to one of Paul's companions, why would he choose the relatively obscure Luke, mentioned only three times in the New Testament? Would he not choose a more prominent figure?

DATE

There are two schools of thought among evangelical scholars as to when Luke wrote Acts. Some hold he wrote while Paul was still living, probably near the end of his first imprisonment (Acts 28). Others date Acts between the fall of Jerusalem (A.D. 70) and Luke's death (ca. A.D. 85).

The main argument for the later date is Luke's alleged use of Mark as a source for the gospel of Luke. Advocates of this view follow this line of reasoning: Mark was written after Peter's death during Nero's persecution. Luke's gospel could not have been written until after that. And since Acts was written after Luke, it must be dated later still.

Although a discussion of the so-called Synoptic Problem is beyond the scope of this introduction, it should be noted that the priority of Mark has never been established. Serious objections to Luke's dependence on Mark have been raised by competent scholars (cf. Robert L. Thomas and Stanley N. Gundry, eds., *A Harmony of the Gospels* [Chicago: Moody, 1979], 274–79; Eta Linnemann, *Is There a Synoptic Problem?* [Grand Rapids: Baker, 1992]). Unless this theory of Luke's dependence on Mark can be established, the chief argument for a later date for Acts collapses.

There are good reasons for believing Luke wrote Acts during Paul's first Roman imprisonment. They may be summarized as follows:

First, that view best explains the abrupt ending of Acts. Luke stopped writing because he had brought events to the present, and he had no more to relate. Also, Acts ends on a note of triumph, with Paul proclaiming the gospel in Rome unhindered by the Roman authorities. That triumphant ending is difficult to comprehend if Acts were written following Paul's death and the outbreak of the Neronian persecution (F. F. Bruce, "The Acts of the Apostles," in D. Guthrie and J. A. Motyer, eds., *The New Bible Commentary: Revised* [Grand Rapids: Eerdmans, 1978], 968).

Second, the Roman officials in Acts are tolerant of, if not favorable to, Christianity. That was certainly not the case after the outbreak of the Neronian persecution in A.D. 64. Further,

> the only time when the picture of the Roman state's originally friendly attitude toward the Christians would have been worth recalling to people's minds was the time when it was still valid but in danger of being lost. And this means that it was the time of Paul's trial, after he had made an appeal to the court of Caesar. (Johannes Munck, *The Acts of the Apostles* [Garden City, N.Y.: Doubleday, 1973], lii)

Third, Luke does not mention the persecution initiated by Nero. Kistemaker remarks, "If Luke had written Acts in the seventies, he would have done violence to his sense of historical integrity by not reflecting these cruel persecutions instigated by Nero" (*Acts*, 23).

Fourth, there is no mention in Acts of the fall of Jerusalem in A.D. 70. Luke's silence is puzzling if that momentous event had already taken place, especially since "Luke in his gospel centres more attention on Jerusalem than do his fellow synoptists" (Guthrie, *New Testament Introduction*, 340). Similarly, his failure to mention the martyrdom of James, the brother of the Lord (A.D. 62 according to Josephus [*Antiquities* XX, ix, 1]) is strange if he wrote afterward. Luke certainly viewed the martyrdoms of the apostle James and Stephen as worthy of mention. Why not the head of the Jerusalem church?

Fifth, the subject matter of Acts reflects the situation in the early days of the church. Such topics as the conflict between Jews and Gentiles, the inclusion of Gentiles in the church, and the Jewish dietary regulations (Acts 15) lost their urgency after the fall of Jerusalem. Similarly, Acts does not reflect the theological concerns of the latter decades of the first century (Kistemaker, *Acts*, 23).

Sixth, Luke reflects no familiarity with Paul's epistles. That argues that Acts was written before the collection of Pauline epistles was widely circulated in the church.

Finally, and perhaps most significantly, Luke is silent about the further career of Paul. No mention is made in Acts of Paul's travels after his release, his second imprisonment (though Luke was with him then [2 Tim. 4:11]), or his death. Yet Luke devotes more than half of Acts to

Paul's ministry. Why would he not carry that theme through to its triumphant completion if he knew more about the great apostle? These omissions are best explained by the assumption that these events had not yet taken place when Luke wrote.

PURPOSE

Luke states his purpose for writing his two-volume work in the prologue to Luke: "It seemed fitting for me as well, having investigated everything carefully from the beginning, to write it out for you in consecutive order, most excellent Theophilus" (Luke 1:3). Acts was also addressed to Theophilus, continuing where Luke's gospel left off.

Theophilus is unknown, though Luke's address of him as "most excellent" (Luke 1:3) suggests he was a Roman official (cf. Acts 24:3; 26:25). Whether he was a Christian Luke was instructing, or a pagan he was trying to persuade, is also not known. Some have argued that he was Paul's lawyer for his hearing before the emperor, though that also is speculation.

Luke did not write a complete account of the first three decades of the church. He selectively chose those events and persons that suited his inspired purpose. Nevertheless, he was a remarkably accurate historian. Acts shows familiarity with Roman law and the privileges of Roman citizens, gives the correct titles of various provincial rulers, and accurately describes various geographical locations. Such accuracy convinced the nineteenth-century British archaeologist Sir William Ramsay that his earlier doubts about Acts were wrong. He writes,

> I may fairly claim to have entered on this investigation without any prejudice in favour of the conclusion which I shall now attempt to justify to the reader. On the contrary, I began with a mind unfavourable to it, for the ingenuity and apparent completeness of the Tübingen theory [which dated Acts in the second century] had at one time quite convinced me. It did not lie then in my line of life to investigate the subject minutely; but more recently I found myself often brought in contact with the book of *Acts* as an authority for the topography, antiquities, and society of Asia Minor. It was gradually borne in upon me that in various details the narrative showed marvelous truth. (*St. Paul the Traveller and the Roman Citizen* [reprint, Grand Rapids: Baker, 1975], 7–8. Italics in original.)

More recent scholars have confirmed Ramsay's view of the historical reliability of Acts (cf. Guthrie, *New Testament Introduction*, 354–55).

Luke wrote in part to commend Christianity to the Roman world. He directs attention to the high character of the Christians and to the fact that they were law-abiding people. He also relates the favorable treatment given Christians by Roman officials (cf. 18:12ff.; 19:31, 37; 25:25; 26:32; 27:3).

He also makes clear to the Jewish people that the gospel was not their exclusive possession. It was for all people. Nor did the Gentiles first have to become Jews before becoming Christians (Acts 15).

But Luke's primary purpose is to show the spread of Christianity, empowered and energized by the Holy Spirit, throughout the Roman world (1:8).

OUTLINE

I. Jerusalem (1:1–8:4)
  A. The beginning of the church (1:1–2:47)
  B. The expansion of the church (3:1–8:4)
II. Judea and Samaria (8:5–12:25)
  A. The witness to the Samaritans (8:5–25)
  B. The conversion of a Gentile (8:26–40)
  C. The conversion of the apostle to the Gentiles (9:1–31)
  D. The witness to the Gentiles (9:32–12:25)
III. The remotest part of the earth (13:1–28:31)
  A. The first missionary journey (13:1–14:28)
  B. The Jerusalem council (15:1–35)
  C. The second missionary journey (15:36–18:22)
  D. The third missionary journey (18:23–21:16)
  E. The journey to Rome (21:17–28:31)

BIBLIOGRAPHY

Abbott-Smith, G. *A Manual Greek Lexicon of the New Testament.* Edinburgh: T. & T. Clark, 1977.

Barnes, Albert. *Notes on the New Testament: Acts–Romans.* Grand Rapids: Baker, reprint of the 1884–85 edition.

Blaiklock, E. M. *The Acts of the Apostles.* Grand Rapids: Eerdmans, 1975.

Bruce, F. F. "Acts of the Apostles." In vol. 1 of *The International Standard Bible Encyclopedia.* Edited by Geoffrey W. Bromiley. Grand Rapids: Eerdmans, 1989.

_____. "The Acts of the Apostles." In *The New Bible Commentary: Revised*. Edited by D. Guthrie and J. A. Motyer. Grand Rapids: Eerdmans, 1978.

_____. *The Book of the Acts*. Grand Rapids: Eerdmans, 1971.

Dana, H. E., and Julius R. Mantey. *A Manual Grammar of the Greek New Testament*. New York, Macmillan, 1957.

Erdman, Charles R. *The Acts*. Philadelphia: Westminster, 1977.

Gundry, Robert H. *A Survey of the New Testament*. Grand Rapids: Zondervan, 1970.

Guthrie, Donald. *New Testament Introduction*. Downers Grove, Ill.: InterVarsity, 1978.

Harrison, Everett F. *Interpreting Acts: The Expanding Church*. Grand Rapids: Zondervan, 1986.

Hiebert, D. Edmond. *An Introduction to the New Testament: Volume 1: The Gospels and Acts*. Chicago: Moody, 1979.

Kent, Homer A., Jr. *Jerusalem to Rome*. Grand Rapids: Baker, 1992.

Kistemaker, Simon J. *New Testament Commentary: Acts*. Grand Rapids: Baker, 1990.

Lenski, R. C. H. *The Interpretation of the Acts of the Apostles*. Minneapolis: Augsburg, 1961.

Linnemann, Eta. *Is There a Synoptic Problem?* Grand Rapids: Baker, 1992.

Longenecker, Richard N. "The Acts of the Apostles." In vol. 9 of the *Expositor's Bible Commentary*. Edited by Frank E. Gaebelein. Grand Rapids: Zondervan, 1981.

Marshall, I. Howard. *The Acts of the Apostles*. Grand Rapids: Eerdmans, 1984.

Munck, Johannes. *The Acts of the Apostles*. Garden City, N.Y.: Doubleday, 1973.

Polhill, John B. *The New American Commentary: Acts*. Nashville: Broadman, 1992.

Rackham, Richard B. *The Acts of the Apostles*. Grand Rapids: Baker, 1978.

Ramsay, W. M. *St. Paul the Traveller and the Roman Citizen*. Reprint. Grand Rapids: Baker, 1975.

Robertson, A. T. *Acts*. Vol. 3 of *Word Pictures in the New Testament*. Nashville: Broadman, 1930.

Thomas, Robert L., and Stanley N. Gundry, eds. *A Harmony of the Gospels*. Chicago: Moody, 1979.

Resources for Finishing Our Lord's Unfinished Work

1

The first account I composed, Theophilus, about all that Jesus began to do and teach, until the day when He was taken up, after He had by the Holy Spirit given orders to the apostles whom He had chosen. To these He also presented Himself alive, after His suffering, by many convincing proofs, appearing to them over a period of forty days, and speaking of the things concerning the kingdom of God. And gathering them together, He commanded them not to leave Jerusalem, but to wait for what the Father had promised, "Which," He said, "you heard of from Me; for John baptized with water, but you shall be baptized with the Holy Spirit not many days from now." And so when they had come together, they were asking Him, saying, "Lord, is it at this time You are restoring the kingdom to Israel?" He said to them, "It is not for you to know times or epochs which the Father has fixed by His own authority; but you shall receive power when the Holy Spirit has come upon you; and you shall be My witnesses both in Jerusalem, and in all Judea and Samaria, and even to the remotest part of the earth." And after He had said these things, He was lifted up while they were looking on, and a cloud received Him out of their sight. And as they were gazing intently into the sky

while He was departing, behold, two men in white clothing stood beside them; and they also said, "Men of Galilee, why do you stand looking into the sky? This Jesus, who has been taken up from you into heaven, will come in just the same way as you have watched Him go into heaven." (1:1–11)

The work of Jesus Christ is both finished and unfinished. His great work of providing redemption is finished, and nothing may be added to it (cf. John 17:4). His work of ministry and proclamation, however, is not finished. That work He only started. Along with the other gospels, **the first account composed** by Luke for **Theophilus** (the gospel of Luke), records **all that Jesus *began* to do and teach** during His life on earth. The rest of the New Testament describes the continuation of His work by the early church. We are still finishing it until He comes.

Christ's work of redemption is completed, and the church's work of evangelism begins. Acts chronicles the initial stages and features of that unfinished work, and sets the path the church is to follow until the end.

As the book of Acts begins, an important transition takes place. During His ministry on earth, the work of preaching and teaching was done primarily by our Lord Himself as He trained His disciples. Now it is time to pass that responsibility on to the apostles, before He ascends to the Father. The burden of proclaiming repentance and the good news of forgiveness to a lost world will rest squarely on their shoulders. The apostles will also be responsible for teaching the truths of the faith to the church.

From a purely human standpoint the apostles were in no way ready for such a task. There were things they still did not understand. Their faith was weak, as evidenced by our Lord's frequent reprimands of them (cf. Matt. 8:26; 14:31; 16:8; Luke 12:28). Nor had they acquitted themselves well during the traumatic events surrounding Christ's arrest and crucifixion. They had not only failed in public witness but also in private loyalty and in personal faith. Peter, their acknowledged leader, had vehemently and profanely denied even knowing Jesus. His faith and spiritual character were not strong enough to withstand the challenge of a lowly servant girl (Matt. 26:69–70). With the exception of John, all the disciples had fled in fear of their own lives and were nowhere to be found at the crucifixion site. Although Jesus had explicitly predicted His resurrection, the disciples scoffed at the initial reports that His tomb was empty (Luke 24:11). When Jesus appeared to them, He found them cowering behind locked doors for fear of the Jewish authorities (John 20:19). Thomas, not present at that first appearance, refused to believe even the testimony of the other ten apostles (John 20:24–28). Only a second appearance, and the Lord's invitation to touch His crucifixion wounds, cured Thomas of his skepticism.

The apostles themselves obviously lacked the understanding and spiritual power to complete Jesus' unfinished ministry of evangelism and edification. However, in these His last words to them before His ascension, the Lord Jesus Christ reiterates (cf. John 20:22) the promise of the Spirit. He will empower the apostles (and all subsequent believers) with those resources necessary to finish the Savior's unfinished work. They needed the correct message, manifestation, might, mystery, mission, and motive.

THE MESSAGE

The first account I composed, Theophilus, about all that Jesus began to do and teach, until the day when He was taken up, after He had by the Holy Spirit given orders to the apostles whom He had chosen. (1:1–2)

As already noted, **the first account** refers to Luke's gospel, which he **composed** for **Theophilus** (see the Introduction for further details). That **account** was largely concerned with the earthly life and ministry of our Lord, revealing **all that Jesus began to do and teach, until the day when He was taken up.** From the inception of His earthly ministry until His ascension, Jesus had instructed His disciples by both deed and word. His miracles were to strengthen their faith; His parables were to clarify spiritual truth for them; His teaching was to formulate their theology. He revealed to them the truth they would need to carry on His work.

It is axiomatic that those who would carry the message of Christ to the world must know what that message is. There must be an accurate understanding of the content of Christian truth before any ministry can be effective. Such knowledge is foundational to spiritual power and to fulfilling the church's mission. The lack of it is insurmountable and devastating to the evangelistic purpose of God.

The apostle Paul was so concerned about this that it was central to his desire for all believers. In Ephesians 1:18–19a he wrote, "I pray that the eyes of your heart may be enlightened, so that you may know what is the hope of His calling, what are the riches of the glory of His inheritance in the saints, and what is the surpassing greatness of His power toward us who believe."

To the Philippians he wrote, "This I pray, that your love may abound still more and more in real knowledge and all discernment, so that you may approve the things that are excellent, in order to be sincere and blameless until the day of Christ" (Phil. 1:9–10).

Paul's prayer for the Colossians eloquently expresses his longing that all believers be mature in knowledge:

> For this reason also, since the day we heard of it, we have not ceased to pray for you and to ask that you may be filled with the knowledge of His will in all spiritual wisdom and understanding, so that you may walk in a manner worthy of the Lord, to please Him in all respects, bearing fruit in every good work and increasing in the knowledge of God; strengthened with all power, according to His glorious might, for the attaining of all steadfastness and patience. (Col. 1:9–11)

In 2 Timothy 2:15, Paul charged Timothy, "Be diligent to present yourself approved to God as a workman who does not need to be ashamed, handling accurately the word of truth." Then he challenged his son in the faith to teach sound truth to others (cf. 1 Tim. 4:6, 11, 16; 6:2b, 3, 20, 21; 2 Tim. 1:13, 14; 2:2; 3:16, 17; 4:1–4).

The writer of Hebrews rebuked some of his readers' ignorance of the truth: "For though by this time you ought to be teachers, you have need again for someone to teach you the elementary principles of the oracles of God, and you have come to need milk and not solid food" (Heb. 5:12).

Mere factual knowledge, of course, was powerless to save those Hebrews, or anyone else, unless it was believed and appropriated. In Matthew 23:2–3, Jesus warned against imitating the hypocritical Pharisees: "The scribes and the Pharisees have seated themselves in the chair of Moses; therefore all that they tell you, do and observe, but do not do according to their deeds; for they say things, and do not do them." Jesus set the pattern of consistency in behaving and proclaiming because, as Luke observed, He **began** both to **do** as well as to **teach.** He perfectly lived the truth He taught.

Paul admonished believers to "adorn the doctrine" they had been taught by how they lived their lives. He wrote, "Show yourself to be an example of good deeds . . . sound in speech . . . showing all good faith that [you] may adorn the doctrine of God our Savior in every respect" (Titus 2:7, 8, 10). Evangelism is telling people that God saves from sin. What adorns that message, or makes it believable, is a holy life that clearly demonstrates God can save from sin. It is self-defeating to proclaim the message of salvation from sin while living a sinful life. The messenger must manifest the power of the message he is proclaiming. Jesus preached righteousness and lived it perfectly. We have to preach the same message and strive to live it as perfectly as we can.

Two major factors contribute to the church's powerlessness today. First, many are ignorant of biblical truth. Second, those who may know biblical truth all too often fail to live by it. Proclaiming an erroneous message is tragic, yet so is proclaiming the truth but giving scant evidence that one's life has been transformed by it. Such people cannot expect others to be moved by their proclamation. The exemplary nineteenth-century Scottish preacher Robert Murray McCheyne gave the following words of advice to an aspiring young minister:

> Do not forget the culture of the inner man—I mean of the heart. How diligently the cavalry officer keeps his sabre clean and sharp; every stain he rubs off with the greatest care. Remember you are God's sword, His instrument—I trust a chosen vessel unto Him to bear His name. In great measure, according to the purity and perfections of the instrument, will be the success. It is not great talents God blesses so much as great likeness to Jesus. A holy minister is an awful weapon in the hand of God. (Andrew A. Bonar, *Memoirs of McCheyne* [Chicago: Moody, 1978], 95)

Those who would be effective in preaching, teaching, and evangelism must give heed to those words. Sound doctrine supported by holiness of life is essential for all who would minister the Word.

Even after His resurrection, Jesus continued to teach the essential realities of His kingdom **until the day when He was taken up,** a reference to His ascension. (Luke uses this term four times in this chapter, vv. 2, 9, 11, 22.) That day, marking the end of our Lord's earthly ministry, had arrived. As He had predicted, Jesus was about to ascend to the Father (cf. John 6:62; 13:1, 3; 16:28; 17:13; 20:17). During His ministry, He had **given orders** to the apostles **by the Holy Spirit,** who was both the source and the power of His ministry (cf. Matt. 4:1; 12:18, 28; Mark 1:12; Luke 3:22; 4:1, 14, 18). Jesus' ministry in the Spirit's power demonstrated the pattern for believers. They, like the apostles, also are to obey Him (cf. Matt. 28:19–20). The Holy Spirit is the source of power for believers' ministry and enables them to obey their Lord's teaching.

The verb *entellō* (**given orders**) signals a command (cf. Matt. 17:9), emphasizing the force of the truth. It encompasses a series of commands to obey God, as well as threats in light of the consequences of disobedience.

While Jesus instructed thousands of people in His days on earth, His primary and constant learners were **the apostles whom He had chosen.** Equipping them for their foundational ministry was a critical goal of His teaching. Their qualification was simply that the Lord had chosen them for salvation and unique service (cf. John 15:16). He saved, commissioned, equipped, gifted and taught them so that they could be eyewitnesses to the truth and recipients of the revelation of God. They established the message believers are to proclaim.

The importance of this instruction in preparing these men for finishing the Lord's work cannot be overemphasized. Our Lord was building into them the teaching that is later called "the apostles' doctrine" (Acts 2:42)—the organized body of truth that established the church.

The effectiveness of every believer's ministry in large measure depends on a clear and deep knowledge of the Word. No wonder Spurgeon said,

> We might preach 'til our tongue rotted, 'til we exhaust our lungs and die—but never a soul would be converted unless the Holy Spirit uses the Word to convert that soul. So it is blessed to eat into the very heart of the Bible until, at last, you come to talk in scriptural language and your spirit is flavoured with the words of the Lord, so that your blood is Bibline and the very essence of the Bible flows from you. (Partly cited in Richard Ellsworth Day, *The Shadow of the Broad Brim* [Philadelphia: Judson, 1943], 131)

The Manifestation

To these He also presented Himself alive, after His suffering, by many convincing proofs, appearing to them over a period of forty days, and speaking of the things concerning the kingdom of God. (1:3)

The apostles needed not only the proper message but also the confidence to proclaim that message even if it cost their lives. They could hardly have been enthusiastic about proclaiming and facing martyrdom for a dead Christ. They needed to know that He was alive and would fulfill His promise of the kingdom. To secure that necessary confidence, Jesus **presented Himself alive, after His suffering,** to them. He offered them **many convincing proofs** (cf. John 20:30), such as entering a room where the doors were locked (John 20:19), showing them His crucifixion wounds (Luke 24:39), and eating and drinking with them (Luke 24:41–43). Most convincing, though, was His **appearing to them over a period of forty days,** beginning with the day of His resurrection. The Greek text actually reads "through forty days." That affirms that though He was not with them continuously, He did appear in their presence at intervals. Although it is by no means exhaustive, the most extensive summary of those appearances is found in 1 Corinthians 15:5–8.

The end result of these appearances was that the apostles became absolutely convinced of the reality of their Lord's physical resurrection. That assurance gave them the boldness to preach the gospel to the very people who crucified Christ. The transformation of the apostles from fearful, cowering skeptics to bold, powerful witnesses is a potent proof of the resurrection.

There have been many suggestions as to the content of the Lord's teaching during the forty days. The mystical religionists held that He imparted to the apostles the secret knowledge that characterized gnosticism. Many in the early church believed He taught them concerning church order (F. F. Bruce, *The Book of the Acts* [Grand Rapids: Eerdmans, 1971], 33–34). Luke, however, shuts down all such speculations when he reveals that during this time the Lord was **speaking of the things concerning the kingdom of God.** He taught them more truth related to the domain of divine rule over the hearts of believers. That theme, a frequent one during the Lord Jesus Christ's earthly ministry (cf. Matt. 4:23; 9:35; 10:7; 13:1ff.; Mark 1:15; Luke 4:43; 9:2; 17:20ff.; John 3:3ff.), offered further proof to the disciples that it was really He.

The Lord wanted them to know that the crucifixion did not nullify the promised millennial kingdom (cf. Isa. 2:2; 11:6–12; Dan. 2:44; Zech. 14:9). The apostles no doubt had difficulty believing in that kingdom after the death of the King. The resurrection changed all that, and from that time on they proclaimed Jesus Christ as the King over an invisible, spiritual kingdom (cf. Acts 17:7; Col. 1:13; 1 Tim. 1:17; 6:15; 2 Tim. 4:1; 2 Peter 1:11; Rev. 11:15; 12:10; 17:14; 19:16). The kingdom will be manifested in its fullness at the second coming. At that point our Lord will personally reign on earth for a thousand years.

The **kingdom of God** (the realm where God rules, or the sphere of salvation) encompasses much more than the millennial kingdom, however. It has two basic aspects: the universal kingdom, and the mediatorial kingdom (for a detailed discussion of those two aspects see Alva J. McClain, *The Greatness of the Kingdom* [Grand Rapids: Zondervan, 1959]; for a more detailed discussion of the kingdom, see *Matthew 8–15,* MacArthur New Testament Commentary [Chicago: Moody, 1987], 348–51).

The universal kingdom refers to God's sovereign rule over all of His creation. Psalm 103:19 reads, "The Lord has established His throne in the heavens; and His sovereignty rules over all." Other passages that describe the universal kingdom include 1 Chronicles 29:11–12; Psalm 10:16; 29:10; 45:6; 59:13; 145:13; Daniel 4:34; 6:26 (cf. Rom. 13:1–7).

The mediatorial kingdom refers to God's spiritual rule and authority over His people on earth through divinely chosen mediators. Through Adam, then the patriarchs, Moses, Joshua, the judges, prophets, and the kings of Israel and Judah, God revealed His will and mediated His authority to His people. With the end of Israel's monarchy began the times of the Gentiles. During that period, which will last until the second coming of Christ, God mediates His spiritual rule over the hearts of believers through the church (Acts 20:25; Rom. 14:17; Col. 1:13). He does so by means of the Word and the living Christ (Gal. 2:20). The final phase of the mediatorial, spiritual kingdom will dominate the earth in the form of the millennial kingdom, to be set up following Christ's return. During that thousand year period, the Lord Jesus Christ will personally reign on earth, exercising sovereign control over the creation and all men. At the end of the Millennium, with the destruction of all rebels, the spiritual kingdom will be merged with the universal kingdom (1 Cor. 15:24), and they will become the same.

During the church age, then, God mediates His kingdom rule through believers indwelt by the Holy Spirit and obedient to the Word. That is why Peter calls believers "a chosen race, a royal priesthood, a holy nation" (1 Peter 2:9).

Today, Jesus Christ does not manifest Himself physically and visibly to believers. Jesus said to Thomas, "Because you have seen Me, have you believed? Blessed are they who did not see, and yet believed" (John 20:29), while Peter wrote, "Though you have not seen Him, you love Him, and though you do not see Him now, but believe in Him, you greatly rejoice with joy inexpressible and full of glory" (1 Peter 1:8). His manifestation to us is no less real, however (cf. Col. 1:29). Such personal communion with the resurrected and exalted Savior is essential for finishing His unfinished work of ministry.

THE MIGHT

And gathering them together, He commanded them not to leave Jerusalem, but to wait for what the Father had promised, "Which," He said, "you heard of from Me; for John baptized with water, but you shall be baptized with the Holy Spirit not many days from now . . ." but you shall receive power when the Holy Spirit has come upon you; (1:4–5, 8a)

Having received the message, and witnessed the manifestation of the risen Christ, the apostles may have been tempted to assume they were ready to minister in their own strength. To prevent that error Jesus, after **gathering them together, commanded them not to leave Jerusalem** (cf. Luke 24:49). To the apostles, who were no doubt fired with enthusiasm and eager to begin, that must have seemed a strange command. Yet, it illustrates an important point: All the preparation and training that knowledge and experience can bring are useless without the proper might. Power had to accompany truth.

To make certain the apostles were not only motivated but also supernaturally empowered for their mission, Jesus commanded them **to wait for what the Father had promised.** That promise, made repeatedly during the Lord's earthly ministry (cf. Luke 11:13; 24:49; John 7:39; 14:16, 26; 15:26; 16:7; 20:22), was that the Holy Spirit would be sent (cf. Acts 2:33). God's pledge was to be fulfilled just ten days later on the Day of Pentecost.

The apostles, like all believers of all dispensations, knew of and had tasted the working of the Holy Spirit. When Jesus sent them out on a preaching tour, He told them, "It is not you who speak, but it is the Spirit of your Father who speaks in you" (Matt. 10:20; cf. Luke 12:12). In John 14:17, Jesus told the apostles the Holy Spirit "abides with you, and will be in you." Like the other believers in the old economy, they experienced the Spirit's power for salvation and life, as well as for special occasions of ministry. In the new economy, inaugurated at Pentecost, the Spirit would permanently indwell and empower them in a way that was unique.

While this promise of power was primarily for the apostles (as was the promise of revelation and inspiration in John 14:26), it also secondarily forecast the enabling power the Spirit would give to all believers (cf. Acts 8:14–16; 10:44–48; 19:1–7). The general promise was at the heart of the Old Testament prophecies concerning the New Covenant. Ezekiel 36:25–27 records God's promise for all who come into the New Covenant: "Then I will sprinkle clean water on you, and you will be clean; I will cleanse you from all your filthiness and from all your idols. Moreover, I will give you a new heart and put a new spirit within you; and I will remove the heart of stone from your flesh and give you a heart of flesh. And I will put My Spirit within you." There was to come a fullness of the Spirit in some way unique to the New Covenant and for all believers. But there was also a special anointing for the apostles.

A magnificent comparison to this sense of the promise is the baptism of Jesus Christ. Our Lord was obviously in perfect accord and fellowship with the Holy Spirit, yet at the moment of His baptism, Scripture says, "heaven was opened, and the Holy Spirit descended upon Him in bodily form like a dove" (Luke 3:21–22). This was emblematic of the fullness of power He would receive from the Spirit to do His earthly work. One chapter later, Luke records that Jesus was "full of the Holy Spirit" (4:1). When He spoke in the Nazareth synagogue He began by giving testimony to the unusual enabling of the Spirit by saying, "The Spirit of the Lord is upon Me, because He anointed Me to preach the gospel to the poor. He has sent Me to proclaim release to the captives, and recovery of sight to the blind, to set free those who are downtrod-den, to proclaim the favorable year of the Lord" (Luke 4:18–19). Luke 5:17 suggests the same source for His healing power.

Others received such anointing for unusual service, such as Zacharias, the father of John the Baptist, who by that power prophesied (Luke 1:67–79). In all of those cases, the Holy Spirit came in special full-ness to enable unusually powerful ministry to take place.

Jesus further defines the promise of the Father for them as what **you heard of from Me** (cf. John 14:16–21; 15:26; 20:22). Our Lord's next words, **for John baptized with water, but you shall be bap-tized with the Holy Spirit not many days from now,** are reminis-cent of John the Baptist's statement in John 1:33: "He who sent me to baptize in water said to me, 'He upon whom you see the Spirit descend-ing and remaining upon Him, this is the one who baptizes in the Holy Spirit.'" The promise was to be fulfilled, and the disciples would be **baptized with the Holy Spirit, not many days from now**—ten to be exact. Jesus promised that after He departed, He would send the Spirit (John 16:7).

Despite the claims of many, the apostles' and early disciples' ex-perience is not the norm for believers today. They were given unique en-abling of the Holy Spirit for their special duties. They also received the general and common baptism with the Holy Spirit in an uncommon way, subsequent to conversion. All believers since the church began are commanded to be filled with the Spirit (Eph. 5:18) and to walk in the Spirit (Gal. 5:25). Yet these early apostles and believers were told to wait, showing the change that came in the church age. They were in the transitional period associated with the birth of the church. In the pres-ent age, baptism by Christ through the agency of the Holy Spirit takes place for all believers at conversion. At that moment, every believer is placed into the body of Christ (1 Cor. 12:13). At that point the Spirit also takes up His permanent residency in the converted person's soul, so there is no such thing as a Christian who does not yet have the Holy Spirit (Rom. 8:9; cf. 1 Cor. 6:19–20).

The baptism with the Holy Spirit is not a special privilege for some believers, nor are believers challenged and exhorted in Scripture to seek it. It is not even their responsibility to prepare for it by praying, pleading, tarrying, or any other means. The passive voice of the verb translated **be baptized** indicates the baptism by Jesus Christ with the Spirit is entirely a divine activity. It comes, like salvation itself, through grace, not human effort. Titus 3:5–6 says, "He saved us, not on the basis of deeds which we have done in righteousness, but according to His mercy, by the washing of regeneration and renewing by the Holy Spirit, whom He poured out upon us richly through Jesus Christ our Savior." God sovereignly pours out the Holy Spirit on those He saves.

The Spirit's presence, leading, and might were absolutely essential if the apostles were to be effective in continuing the Lord's unfinished work. They had already experienced His saving, guiding, teaching, and miracle-working power. Soon they would **receive** the **power** they needed for ministry after **the Holy Spirit** fell on them.

Power translates *dunamis*, from which the English word "dynamite" derives. All believers have in them spiritual dynamite for use of gifts, service, fellowship, and witness. They need to experience the release of that power in their lives through not grieving the Spirit by sin (Eph. 4:30), and being continually filled and controlled by the Spirit (Eph. 5:18). The latter takes place as believers yield moment by moment control of their lives to Him, and is the same as yielding their minds to the Word (Col. 3:16). The result of being filled with the Spirit is expressed by Paul's prayer in Ephesians 3:16, 20 "that [God] would grant you, according to the riches of His glory, to be strengthened with power through His Spirit in the inner man. . . . Now to Him who is able to do exceeding abundantly beyond all that we ask or think, according to the power that works within us . . ." (For a complete discussion of the filling of the Spirit, see *Ephesians,* MacArthur New Testament Commentary [Chicago: Moody, 1986].)

The Mystery

And so when they had come together, they were asking Him, saying, "Lord, is it at this time You are restoring the kingdom to Israel?" He said to them, "It is not for you to know times or epochs which the Father has fixed by His own authority;" (1:6–7)

A paradoxical component of the resources for continuing the Lord's ministry was something believers don't know and can't find out. The apostles shared the fervent hope of their nation that Messiah would come and take up His earthly kingdom. Often Jesus had taught them prophetically about the future (Matt. 13:40–50; 24, 25; Luke 12:36–40; 17:20–37; 21:5–36). The enthusiastic question **they were asking Him, "Lord, is it at this time You are restoring the kingdom to Israel?"** is thus perfectly understandable. After all, here was the resurrected Messiah speaking with them about His kingdom. They knew of no reason the earthly form of the kingdom could not be set up immediately, since the messianic work signaling the end of the age had arrived. It must be remembered that the interval between the two comings of Messiah was not explicitly taught in the Old Testament. The disciples on the road to Emmaus were greatly disappointed that Jesus had not redeemed Israel and set up the kingdom (Luke 24:21). Further, the apostles knew that

Ezekiel 36 and Joel 2 connected the coming of the kingdom with the outpouring of the Spirit Jesus had just promised. It is understandable that they hoped the arrival of the kingdom was imminent. Surely it was for this kingdom they had hoped since they first joined Jesus. They had experienced a roller coaster ride of hope and doubt which they now felt might be over.

Jesus, however, quickly brings them back to reality. It was not for them **to know times or epochs which the Father has fixed by His own authority.** The Scriptures teach many things about the earthly and glorious reign of Jesus Christ in His kingdom, but not the precise time of its establishment. **Times** (*kairos*) refers to features, characteristics of eras, and events. God, **by His own authority,** has determined all the aspects of the future and the kingdom. But as far as men are concerned, that remains one of "the secret things" that "belong to the Lord our God" (Deut. 29:29). All that believers can know is that the kingdom will be established at the second coming (Matt. 25:21–34). The time of the second coming, however, remains unrevealed (Mark 13:32).

That Jesus does not deny their expectation of a literal, earthly kingdom involving Israel is highly significant. It shows that their understanding of the promised kingdom was correct, except for the time of its coming. If they were mistaken about such a crucial point in His kingdom teaching, His failure to correct them is mystifying and deceptive. A far more likely explanation is that the apostles' expectation of a literal, earthly kingdom mirrored the Lord's own teaching and the plan of God clearly revealed in the Old Testament.

Since the season of His coming cannot be known, and the Lord could return at any moment in the rapture of the church (cf. 1 Thess. 5:2), believers must be continually ready. All must remember the Lord's solemn warning in Mark 13:33–37:

> Take heed, keep on the alert; for you do not know when the appointed time is. It is like a man, away on a journey, who upon leaving his house and putting his slaves in charge, assigning to each one his task, also commanded the doorkeeper to stay on the alert. Therefore, be on the alert—for you do not know when the master of the house is coming, whether in the evening, at midnight, at cockcrowing, or in the morning—lest he come suddenly and find you asleep. And what I say to you I say to all, "Be on the alert!"

Such continual vigilance and anticipation, through all generations of believers who were looking for Jesus to return, has served as true incentive to live with urgency and minister with passion.

The Mission

"you shall be My witnesses both in Jerusalem, and in all Judea and Samaria, and even to the remotest part of the earth." (1:8b)

Rather than engage in useless speculation over the time for the coming of the kingdom, the apostles were to focus on the work at hand. **Witnesses** are those who see something and tell others about it. I once witnessed an attempted murder. When I testified in court, they wanted to know three things: what I saw, heard, and felt. I was reminded of 1 John 1:1–2, where John writes, "What was from the beginning, what we have heard, what we have seen with our eyes, what we beheld and our hands handled, concerning the Word of Life . . . we have seen and bear witness and proclaim to you." A witness for Jesus Christ is simply someone who tells the truth about Him. The apostles, as Peter points out, "were eyewitnesses of His majesty" (2 Peter 1:16).

This was the foremost purpose for which the empowering of the Holy Spirit came. And the early church was so effective that they "upset the world" (Acts 17:6). Jesus commands all believers to be His witness in the Great Commission: "Go therefore and make disciples of all the nations, baptizing them in the name of the Father and the Son and the Holy Spirit, teaching them to observe all that I commanded you; and lo, I am with you always, even to the end of the age" (Matt. 28:19–20).

So many Christians sealed their witness to Christ with their blood that *marturēs* (**witnesses**) came to mean "martyrs." Their blood, as the second-century theologian Tertullian stated, became the seed of the church. Many were drawn to faith in Christ by observing how calmly and joyously Christians met their deaths.

There is a sense in which believers do not even choose whether or not to be **witnesses.** They *are* witnesses, and the only question is how effective their witness is. If the church is to reach the lost world with the good news of the gospel, believers must "sanctify Christ as Lord in [their] hearts, always being ready to make a defense to everyone who asks [them] to give an account for the hope that is in [them]" (1 Peter 3:15). Titus 2 indicates that how Christians live their lives lays the platform of integrity and believability on which effective personal witness is built. In that text, Paul writes that we are to so live "that the word of God may not be dishonored" (v. 5), "that the opponent [of the Christian faith] may be put to shame, having nothing bad to say about us" (v. 8), and "that they may adorn the doctrine of God our Savior in every respect" (v. 10), so that we may make it possible that the saving gospel comes winsomely to all.

Beginning in **Jerusalem,** the apostles carried out the Lord's mandate. Their witness spread beyond there to **all Judea and Samaria** (the neighboring area), and finally **even to the remotest part of the earth.** Verse 8 provides the general outline for the book of Acts. Following that outline, Luke chronicles the irresistible march of Christianity from Jerusalem, into Samaria and then through the Roman world. As the book unfolds, we will move through those three sections of the expansion of the church.

This beginning was to dramatically alter the course of history, and the spread of the gospel message has continued past Acts to reach all the earth. Today, believers continue to have the responsibility for being Christ's witnesses throughout this world. The sphere for witnessing is as extensive as the kingdom—all the world. That was and is the mission for the church until Jesus comes.

The Motive

And after He had said these things, He was lifted up while they were looking on, and a cloud received Him out of their sight. And as they were gazing intently into the sky while He was departing, behold, two men in white clothing stood beside them; and they also said, "Men of Galilee, why do you stand looking into the sky? This Jesus, who has been taken up from you into heaven, will come in just the same way as you have watched Him go into heaven." (1:9–11)

The Lord Jesus Christ was about to depart for heaven to return to His former glory (cf. John 17:1–6). Before doing that, He left the apostles with a final, dramatic moment which provided powerful motivation for carrying on His work. To their amazement, **He was lifted up while they were looking on, and a cloud received Him out of their sight** (cf. vv. 2, 11, 22). Jesus, in His glorious resurrection body, left this world for the realm of heaven to take His place on the throne at God's right hand. Back on the Mount of Olives (Luke 24:50), the shocked apostles **were gazing intently into the sky while He was departing.** To their further consternation, angels, described as **two men in white clothing,** suddenly appeared and **stood beside them.** Such angelic appearances were not unusual (Gen. 18:2; Josh. 5:13–15; Mark 16:5). Two of them confirm the promise of Christ's return as true (cf. John 8:17). These angels asked the bewildered apostles, **"Men of Galilee, why do you stand looking into the sky?"** They are called **men of Galilee** since all the apostles (with the exception of the dead traitor Judas) were from that region. The angels' question, **"why do you stand looking**

into the sky?" indicates more than curiosity at the miracle. The word translated **looking** indicates a long gaze, in this case a transfixed look as if losing someone. The question, then, is a mild rebuke to the apostles. They were not losing Jesus, as they feared. Maybe some of them remembered the vision of Ezekiel, who saw the glory of God depart to heaven from Israel (Ezek. 10:18–19) and feared it was happening again.

The angels went on to say, **"This Jesus, who has been taken up from you into heaven, will come in just the same way as you have watched Him go into heaven."** The promise of Zechariah 14:4 will come to pass, namely that the Messiah will return to the Mount of Olives. The angels stressed that **this** same **Jesus** whom they had watched ascend would one day return **in just the same way as** they had **watched Him go into heaven.** He will return in His glorified body, accompanied with clouds (cf. Dan. 7:13; Matt. 24:30; 26:64; Rev. 1:7; 14:14), just as at His ascension.

This becomes a compelling motive. No one knows when He will come, but everyone must live in anticipation that it could be in their lifetime (cf. Rom. 13:12–14; 2 Peter 3:14–18). The truth that Christ will return provides a powerful motive to serve Him. Paul writes, "We must all appear before the judgment seat of Christ, that each one may be recompensed for his deeds in the body, according to what he has done, whether good or bad" (2 Cor. 5:10). In Revelation 22:12 the Lord Jesus Christ said, "Behold, I am coming quickly, and My reward is with Me, to render to every man according to what he has done." Believers must serve Christ faithfully in light of His imminent return. In Revelation 16:15 Jesus warned, "Behold, I am coming like a thief. Blessed is the one who stays awake and keeps his garments, lest he walk about naked and men see his shame" (cf. 1 John 2:28).

The task of finishing the work that Jesus began, the duty of evangelizing the lost world, is a daunting one. But the Lord in His mercy from the start has provided all the spiritual resources necessary to accomplish that task. It is up to each believer to appropriate those resources and put them to use. "We must work the works of Him who sent [Jesus Christ], as long as it is day; night is coming, when no man can work" (John 9:4).

Replacing the Traitor

2

Then they returned to Jerusalem from the mount called Olivet, which is near Jerusalem, a Sabbath day's journey away. And when they had entered, they went up to the upper room, where they were staying; that is, Peter and John and James and Andrew, Philip and Thomas, Bartholomew and Matthew, James the son of Alphaeus, and Simon the Zealot, and Judas the son of James. These all with one mind were continually devoting themselves to prayer, along with the women, and Mary the mother of Jesus, and with His brothers. And at this time Peter stood up in the midst of the brethren (a gathering of about one hundred and twenty persons was there together), and said, "Brethren, the Scripture had to be fulfilled, which the Holy Spirit foretold by the mouth of David concerning Judas, who became a guide to those who arrested Jesus. For he was counted among us, and received his portion in this ministry. (Now this man acquired a field with the price of his wickedness; and falling headlong, he burst open in the middle and all his bowels gushed out. And it became known to all who were living in Jerusalem; so that in their own language that field was called Hakeldama, that is, Field of Blood.) For it is written in the book of Psalms, 'Let his

homestead be made desolate, and let no man dwell in it'; and, 'His office let another man take.' It is therefore necessary that of the men who have accompanied us all the time that the Lord Jesus went in and out among us—beginning with the baptism of John, until the day that He was taken up from us—one of these should become a witness with us of His resurrection." And they put forward two men, Joseph called Barsabbas (who was also called Justus), and Matthias. And they prayed, and said, "Thou, Lord, who knowest the hearts of all men, show which one of these two Thou hast chosen to occupy this ministry and apostleship from which Judas turned aside to go to his own place." And they drew lots for them, and the lot fell to Matthias; and he was numbered with the eleven apostles. (1:12–26)

It is a marvelous and reassuring truth that our sovereign, omnipotent God works His will through men. His providential control over events takes into consideration all the acts of human wills—even those opposed to Him, such as Haman, Herod, and Judas. Scripture is filled with examples of God's using humans to accomplish His purposes. A graphic illustration of this use can be noted in the unique battle cry of Gideon's army: "A sword for the Lord and for Gideon!" (Judg. 7:20). God involved Gideon actively in effecting His sovereign will. In Exodus, He used a combination of components to part the Red Sea and allow Israel to cross: His own supernatural power, an east wind, and Moses' striking of the waters with a stick.

Even in God's work of redemption, He has called certain men to significant participation. Men have been used throughout the unfolding drama of the kingdom of God. After His earthly ministry, the Lord Jesus Christ chose the apostles to set down His truth and to continue His work of evangelizing the world. In John 15:16, He reminded them, "You did not choose Me, but I chose you, and appointed you" (cf. Luke 6:13; 1 Cor. 12:28; Eph. 4:11). In Acts 10:39–42, Peter described both God's sovereign choice of the apostles, and their mission:

> We are witnesses of all the things [Jesus] did both in the land of the Jews and in Jerusalem. And they also put Him to death by hanging Him on a cross. God raised Him up on the third day, and granted that He should become visible, not to all the people, but to witnesses who were chosen beforehand by God, that is, to us, who ate and drank with Him after He arose from the dead. And He ordered us to preach to the people, and solemnly to testify that this is the One who has been appointed by God as Judge of the living and the dead.

The call to preach is still not a matter of human recruitment but of divine appointment. Paul wrote in Romans 10:14–15, "How then shall they call upon Him in whom they have not believed? And how shall they believe in Him whom they have not heard? And how shall they hear without a preacher? And how shall they preach unless they are sent?" Far too many in our day claim the right to ascend the place of preaching, yet have never been called by Him. They are like the false prophets of Jeremiah's day, of whom the Lord said, "I did not send these prophets, but they ran. I did not speak to them, but they prophesied" (Jer. 23:21; cf. 23:32; 29:31).

As the book of Acts opened, Jesus equipped the apostles with the necessary resources to launch the completion of His unfinished work of gathering the elect for the kingdom. In addition to those resources, He wanted to be sure that the proper men were involved in carrying out that task. Accordingly, a replacement had to be chosen for the dead traitor Judas Iscariot. The passage may be understood by sorting it into three sections: the submission of the disciples, the suicide of a disciple, and the selection of a disciple.

THE SUBMISSION OF THE DISCIPLES

Then they returned to Jerusalem from the mount called Olivet, which is near Jerusalem, a Sabbath day's journey away. And when they had entered, they went up to the upper room, where they were staying; that is, Peter and John and James and Andrew, Philip and Thomas, Bartholomew and Matthew, James the son of Alphaeus, and Simon the Zealot, and Judas the son of James. These all with one mind were continually devoting themselves to prayer, along with the women, and Mary the mother of Jesus, and with His brothers. And at this time Peter stood up in the midst of the brethren (a gathering of about one hundred and twenty persons was there together), and said, (1:12–15)

In His final charge to them before His ascension, Jesus had commanded the apostles to wait in Jerusalem for divine enablement that was to be given them in the coming of the Holy Spirit (Luke 24:49; Acts 1:4). It was necessary for them to wait, because Jesus had made clear that the Spirit could not be given until He returned to the Father (John 16:7). In compliance with their Lord's command, the apostles **returned to Jerusalem from the mount called Olivet, which is near Jerusalem** (the place of His ascension). Luke adds the latter phrase for the benefit of Theophilus, who no doubt was unfamiliar with Palestinian geography. **The mount called Olivet** is the Mount of Olives, which rises to overlook Jerusalem from across the Kidron Valley to the east (cf. Zech. 14:4). More a hill than a mountain, it rises some 400 feet above the floor of the Kidron Valley. That makes it only about 200 feet higher in elevation than Jerusalem itself. It was from the backside of the Mount, near the little village of Bethany, that the Lord ascended (Luke 24:50). That site was probably chosen for its privacy and nearness to Jerusalem.

A **Sabbath day's journey** was the maximum distance one was permitted to travel on the Sabbath under rabbinic law. It was fixed at 2,000 cubits, or about one half to three quarters of a mile (cf. Josh. 3:4). That distance derives, according to tradition, from Israel's encampments during the forty years of wilderness wanderings. The farthest tents were held to have been 2,000 cubits from the tabernacle, although Scripture nowhere specifies that distance. Since work was prohibited on the Sabbath, the farthest anyone would need to travel was the 2,000 cubits to the tabernacle to worship. Consequently, **a Sabbath day's journey** became synonymous with 2,000 cubits.

When the apostles **had entered** Jerusalem, **they went up to the upper room, where they were staying.** Houses commonly had upper rooms, which were used for a variety of purposes. This one must have been part of a large house, since it accommodated 120 people (v. 15). Its exact location is unknown. It was probably where the Last Supper had been celebrated and where Jesus had appeared to them after His resurrection. Some have identified it with the house of John Mark's mother (cf. Acts 12:12), but that identification is uncertain. In any case, it could not have been far from the Eastern Gate of the city. A Sabbath day's journey from the back side of the Mount of Olives would have put the apostles just inside the city walls.

By this time the apostles must have gained a measure of courage from their encounters with the risen Lord. Immediately following the crucifixion, they remained in seclusion behind locked doors (John 20:19). Now, however, they "were continually in the temple, praising God" (Luke 24:53), returning to the upper room for occasional meetings.

The eleven remaining apostles, **Peter and John and James and Andrew, Philip and Thomas, Bartholomew and Matthew, James the son of Alphaeus, and Simon the Zealot, and Judas the son of James** (also known as Thaddeus, cf. Matt. 10:3; Mark 3:18), were joined by others. They included **the women, Mary the mother of Jesus, and His brothers. The women** no doubt included Mary Magdalene, Mary the wife of Clopas, Mary and Martha, and Salome, among others. Jesus' **brothers** were his biological siblings, the natural children of Mary and Joseph. Mark 6:3 gives their names as James, Joses, Judas, and Simon. James and Judas (Jude) figure prominently in the

New Testament. James was the first head of the Jerusalem church (cf. Acts 12:17; 15:13ff.) and author of the epistle that bears his name. Judas wrote the epistle of Jude. They had become believers after their earlier skepticism. In fact, as recently as eight months before this, John 7:5 records that "not even His brothers were believing in Him." Their conversions are not recorded in Scripture, but we can surmise that James was converted when his "half-brother" appeared to him after the resurrection (1 Cor. 15:7). It was perhaps through James's efforts that the rest of the Lord's brothers came to faith in Him. However their conversions took place, they became devoted followers of Christ, whom they acknowledged as Lord, God, and Savior.

Much legend, myth, and faulty dogma have arisen over the centuries in connection with **Mary the mother of Jesus.** In contrast to the inordinate devotion to her in some religious systems, the Bible never exalts her. In fact, this is the last reference to her in Scripture; she does not appear again in Acts, nor in any of the epistles. In Mark 3:31–32, she, along with Jesus' brothers, tried to assume some special privileges based upon their earthly relationship to Him. Jesus replied, "'Who are My mother and My brothers?' And looking about on those who were sitting around Him, He said, 'Behold, My mother and My brothers! For whoever does the will of God, he is My brother and sister and mother'" (Mark 3:33–35). In other words, their earthly, familial relationship to Him gained them no special spiritual recognition or privileges. That truth is applied specifically to Mary in Luke 11:27–28: "And it came about while He said these things, one of the women in the crowd raised her voice, and said to Him, 'Blessed is the womb that bore You, and the breasts at which You nursed.' But He said, 'On the contrary, blessed are those who hear the word of God, and observe it.'"

Mary was a woman of singular virtue, or she would never have been chosen to be the mother of the Lord Jesus Christ. For that role she deserves respect and honor (cf. Luke 1:42). But she was a sinner who exalted God *her* Savior. She referred to herself as a humble bondslave to God, who needed mercy (cf. Luke 1:46–50). To offer prayers to her and elevate her to a role as co-redemptrix with Christ is to go beyond the bounds of Scripture and her own confession. The silence of the epistles, which form the doctrinal core of the New Testament, about Mary is especially significant. If she played the important role in salvation assigned her by the Roman Catholic Church, or if she were to receive prayers as an intercessor between believers and Christ, surely the New Testament would have spelled that out. Nor do such Roman Catholic teachings as her virgin birth and bodily assumption into heaven find any biblical support; they are fabrications.

The unbiblical elevation of Mary has its roots in paganism, some of it dating back to the tower of Babel and Nimrod's wife Semiramis.

She, along with her son Tammuz, formed the basis for the many counterfeit mother-child cults of antiquity. The Roman syncretism of such pagan beliefs with Christianity led Catholicism to unbiblical teaching about Mary. (For a discussion of the relationship of the pagan mother-child cults to Roman Catholic teachings about Mary, see Alexander Hislop, *The Two Babylons* [Neptune, N.J.: Loizeaux, 1959].)

All those gathered in the upper room **with one mind were continually devoting themselves to prayer. With one mind** expresses the spiritual unity that characterized the early fellowship. **Continually devoting** is a strong expression, denoting persistence in prayer. Contrary to the view of some, they were not praying for the baptism with the Holy Spirit. They had not been told to pray for that but to wait for it, and they knew it was coming soon. The coming of the Spirit did not require or depend on their prayers but on God's promise (see the discussion of Acts 2:1–13 in chapter 3). They were praying because they were physically separated from the ascended Jesus, and prayer was their only means of communicating with Him. They may have been asking Him to return soon and in the meantime to grant them all they would need to be faithful. This was the beginning of the pattern of prayer offered in the name of Jesus (cf. John 14:13–14) and thus marks another of the many historical transitions found in the book of Acts.

At some unspecified time during the ten days of fellowship and prayer between the ascension and Pentecost, **Peter stood up in the midst of the brethren** and began to speak. Luke adds the parenthetical note that the **gathering of** believers in the upper room numbered **about one hundred and twenty persons.** From that small nucleus (plus perhaps a few hundred more in Galilee) the Christian church was born. Many pastors would be discouraged with such a small congregation. One such man came to Charles Spurgeon and complained about the small size of his congregation. Spurgeon's devastating reply was that perhaps the man had as many people as he cared to give account for in the day of judgment. The 120 gathered in the upper room were small in number but had counted the cost and were willing to take up the cross and follow their Lord. They believed in Him fully. From this modest beginning, Christianity spread throughout the Roman Empire in an amazingly short time span. In spite of repeated attempts to stamp out the movement, it eventually prevailed and became the dominant force in Western culture for nearly two thousand years.

Instead of launching out on their own, they patiently, submissively waited for the promised Holy Spirit to come and give them the power they needed. Subsequent history testifies to the impact of that patience.

THE SUICIDE OF A DISCIPLE

"Brethren, the Scripture had to be fulfilled, which the Holy Spirit foretold by the mouth of David concerning Judas, who became a guide to those who arrested Jesus. For he was counted among us, and received his portion in this ministry. (Now this man acquired a field with the price of his wickedness; and falling headlong, he burst open in the middle and all his bowels gushed out. And it became known to all who were living in Jerusalem; so that in their own language that field was called Hakeldama, that is, Field of Blood.) For it is written in the book of Psalms, 'Let his homestead be made desolate, and let no man dwell in it'; and, 'His office let another man take.'" (1:15–20)

The joy of those gathered together was tempered by one sad reflection, the tragic hypocrisy and suicide of Judas. As the acknowledged leader of the apostles, Peter took charge. Some were no doubt wondering how the defection of Judas fit into God's plan, or how Jesus' words in Matthew 19:28 were now to be fulfilled. In that passage, He promised the apostles, "You who have followed Me, in the regeneration when the Son of Man will sit on His glorious throne, you also shall sit upon twelve thrones, judging the twelve tribes of Israel." Peter, under the inspiration of the Holy Spirit, acts to allay those doubts and avoid any possible quibbling over who would occupy the twelfth throne.

The **Scripture** refers to the passages quoted in verse 20, already in Peter's mind as he leads up to it. Peter was not offering his own opinion but rather affirming a word from God. As is the case with all predictive Scripture, the prophecies he was about to quote **had to be fulfilled.** God's Word is true, and what He predicts must certainly come to pass. In Psalm 115:3, the psalmist writes, "Our God is in the heavens; He does whatever He pleases." God Himself adds in Isaiah 46:10, "My purpose will be established, and I will accomplish all My good pleasure" (cf. Josh. 23:14; 1 Kings 8:15, 20, 24). Isaiah added that God's word never returns empty but always accomplishes its purpose (55:11).

Peter characterized the Scripture he was about to quote as that **which the Holy Spirit foretold by the mouth of David.** No clearer description of inspiration can be found anywhere in Scripture. The Bible was written when "men moved by the Holy Spirit spoke from God" (2 Peter 1:21). Peter reassured his hearers that despite Judas's treachery in acting as **a guide to those who arrested Jesus,** God's word was being fulfilled. Judas's betrayal was, in fact, crucial to the plan of the Sovereign who predicted it in the Old Testament.

Although **he was counted among** the apostles **and received his portion in** their **ministry,** Judas was obviously never saved. Jesus expressed that fact in John 6, when He told the apostles, 'There are some of you who do not believe.' For Jesus knew from the beginning who they were who did not believe, and who it was that would betray Him. Jesus answered them, 'Did I Myself not choose you, the twelve, and yet one of you is a devil?' Now He meant Judas the son of Simon Iscariot, for he, one of the twelve, was going to betray Him" (John 6:64, 70–71; cf. 17:12). Judas was placed among the apostles because it was essential for him to betray Jesus. God did not force Judas into that betrayal against the man's will. Jesus even said of Judas that it would have been better for him if he had never been born, because of the choice he made (Matt. 26:24; cf. Luke 22:22). Instead He used Judas's evil intent to accomplish His own predetermined purposes (cf. Acts 2:23).

Judas represents the greatest example of wasted opportunity in all of history. He had the rare privilege, given to only twelve men, of living and ministering with Jesus Christ, God incarnate, for more than three years. He had the same convincing, overwhelming opportunity to come to faith in Him as the eleven did. Yet his motives for following Jesus were never anything but selfish. He no doubt shared the common Jewish hope that Messiah would deliver the nation from the yoke of the hated Romans. When it became obvious that was not Jesus' plan, and he would not get the wealth and power he wanted, Judas decided to cut his losses and get out with whatever he could salvage. Betraying the incarnate Son of God to the authorities for a paltry sum seemed a way to gain some compensation. The greed he evidenced by that act was another indicator of his wicked heart. There had been a preview of this avarice when, after Jesus' anointing with costly perfume by Mary, Judas indignantly exclaimed, "Why was this perfume not sold for three hundred denarii, and given to poor people?" (John 12:5). His real concern was evident from John's cutting editorial comment in verse 6: "Now he said this, not because he was concerned about the poor, but because he was a thief, and as he had the money box, he used to pilfer what was put into it." Driven by disappointment and greed, this most tragic of all men squandered inestimable privilege, betrayed the Lord for thirty pieces of silver, and damned his soul to hell.

Judas's tragic life reached a damning climax in his suicide. In a parenthetical statement for Theophilus's benefit and ours, Luke describes the scene: **Now this man acquired a field with the price of his wickedness; and falling headlong, he burst open in the middle and all his bowels gushed out. And it became known to all who were living in Jerusalem; so that in their own language that field was called Hakeldama, that is, Field of Blood.** Judas did not, of course, actually purchase the field in question. But because it was purchased with the money paid to him by the Jewish leaders, Luke refers to Judas as the buyer. Feeling unbearable guilt and remorse (but not genuine repentance) for his betrayal of the innocent Lord, he returned the money he had received to the Jewish authorities (Matt. 27:3–8). They hypocritically refused to keep it, because it was blood money. Instead, **with the price of his wickedness,** the legalistic, but spiritually dead, leaders **acquired a field,** which those **living in Jerusalem** named **Hakeldama (Field of Blood)** since it was purchased with blood money. The traditional site for this field is south of Jerusalem in the Valley of Hinnom, near its intersection with the Kidron Valley. Because the soil there is suitable for use in pottery, Matthew refers to it as the Potter's Field (B. Van Elderen, "Akeldama," in vol. 1 of the *Zondervan Pictorial Encyclopedia of the Bible,* edited by Merrill C. Tenney [Grand Rapids: Zondervan, 1977], 94–95).

Meanwhile, Judas, overwhelmed by his accusing conscience, committed suicide. Matthew records that he hanged himself (Matt. 27:5), whereas Luke here records that **falling headlong, he burst open in the middle and all his bowels gushed out.** Luke's account supplements Matthew's and does not contradict it. Evidently the tree Judas chose overlooked a cliff. Either the rope or the branch broke, or his knot failed to hold under the weight of his body. He then plunged to a gruesome death on the rocks below. The imagined scene is depicted in a relief on a medieval cathedral, in which demons are shown pulling on Judas's legs to hasten his death.

As already noted, Judas's tortured life and death did fulfill Old Testament prophecy. As Peter indicates, Judas's treachery in betrayal, his death, and his replacement were foretold by David in the Psalms. Psalm 55:12–15 clearly predicts the betrayal. Psalm 69:25 is the source of the prediction of his removal from office: **Let his homestead be made desolate, and let no man dwell in it.** Psalm 109:8 promises his replacement: **His office let another man take.** All those quotes are in contexts that point to the time of Messiah's death, and the Holy Spirit clearly affirms that they speak of Judas. Peter is using the most compelling proof, Scripture, to reassure his hearers that Judas's defection, and their choice of his replacement, were all part of God's plan.

The Selection of a Disciple

"It is therefore necessary that of the men who have accompanied us all the time that the Lord Jesus went in and out among us—beginning with the baptism of John, until the day that He was taken up from us—one of these should become a witness with us of His resurrection." And they put forward two men, Joseph called

Barsabbas (who was also called Justus), and Matthias. And they prayed, and said, "Thou, Lord, who knowest the hearts of all men, show which one of these two Thou hast chosen to occupy this ministry and apostleship from which Judas turned aside to go to his own place." And they drew lots for them, and the lot fell to Matthias; and he was numbered with the eleven apostles. (1:16–21)

Some have argued that Peter and the apostles were mistaken to choose a replacement for Judas. Paul, they assume, was really the Lord's choice as the twelfth apostle. Since there are only to be twelve thrones in the kingdom (Matt. 19:28), the twelfth must be for the greatest apostle, Paul. Nothing in this passage, however, indicates that this action is wrong. It is inconceivable that the Lord would allow such a crucial error in such a crucial office at the very beginning of His church. Why would He take pains to provide the apostles with all the proper resources, and then allow them to choose the wrong man? Jesus Christ chose Matthias just as surely as He chose the other eleven. And while Paul was in no way inferior to the twelve, he was not one of their number. By his own testimony he was "in no respect . . . inferior to the most eminent apostles, even though I am a nobody" (2 Cor. 12:11). He was a unique apostle. The mission of the twelve was primarily to the nation of Israel, while he was the apostle sent to the Gentiles (Rom. 11:13).

Peter initiates the selection process by listing the requirements for Judas's successor. He must **have accompanied** the apostles **all the time that the Lord Jesus went in and out among them—beginning with the baptism of John, until the day that He was taken up.** He would have to have witnessed the Lord's entire earthly ministry, from its inception at His baptism to its culmination at the ascension. It should be noted that Paul did not meet that qualification.

The second requirement was that the one selected be **a witness with** the other eleven **of His resurrection.** He must have seen the resurrected Christ, since the resurrection was a central theme of apostolic preaching (cf. Acts 2:24, 32; 3:15; 5:30; 10:40; 13:30, 33, 34, 37). All the apostles were to be personal eyewitnesses of the risen Lord.

Two men met those requirements: **Joseph called Barsabbas (who was also called Justus), and Matthias.** Nothing is known of either individual; they appear nowhere else in Scripture. Knowing that the third qualification for an apostle was to be chosen by the Lord, those gathered **prayed, and said, "Thou, Lord, who knowest the hearts of all men, show which one of these two Thou hast chosen to occupy this ministry and apostleship from which Judas turned aside to go to his own place."** The last phrase is a shocking and sobering statement. Judas, and all others who go to hell, belong there; it is the **place** of their **own** choosing. It belongs to them, and they to it!

The fact that they prayed for the Lord to choose Judas's replacement offers further proof that the choice of Matthias was no mistake. The Lord could have answered their prayers by telling them to wait, then added Paul to the ranks of the twelve, if that had been His plan.

After praying, **they drew lots for them**—an accepted Old Testament method for determining God's will. Proverbs 16:33 says, "The lot is cast into the lap, but its every decision is from the Lord" (cf. Lev. 16:8ff.; Num. 26:55ff.; Josh. 7:14; 1 Sam. 10:20; 14:41ff.; Prov. 18:18). That is the last occurrence in Scripture of this practice, since the coming of the Spirit rendered it unnecessary. The Lord made His choice, **the lot fell to Matthias; and he was numbered with the eleven apostles.** The name **Matthias** means "gift of God," and so he was to the apostles and the church.

With Matthias's selection to replace the traitor Judas, the final preparation for the church was completed; the final resource provided. All was now ready for the birth of the church on the Day of Pentecost.

The Baptism of the Holy Spirit

3

And when the day of Pentecost had come, they were all together in one place. And suddenly there came from heaven a noise like a violent, rushing wind, and it filled the whole house where they were sitting. And there appeared to them tongues as of fire distributing themselves, and they rested on each one of them. And they were all filled with the Holy Spirit and began to speak with other tongues, as the Spirit was giving them utterance. Now there were Jews living in Jerusalem, devout men, from every nation under heaven. And when this sound occurred, the multitude came together, and were bewildered, because they were each one hearing them speak in his own language. And they were amazed and marveled, saying, "Why, are not all these who are speaking Galileans? And how is it that we each hear them in our own language to which we were born? Parthians and Medes and Elamites, and residents of Mesopotamia, Judea and Cappadocia, Pontus and Asia, Phrygia and Pamphylia, Egypt and the districts of Libya around Cyrene, and visitors from Rome, both Jews and proselytes, Cretans and Arabs—we hear them in our own tongues speaking of the mighty deeds of God. And they all continued in amazement and great perplexity, saying to one an-

other, "What does this mean?" But others were mocking and saying, "They are full of sweet wine." (2:1–13)

The second chapter of Acts marks a turning point in the history of God's kingdom. A new phase of His redemptive plan unfolds as the church is born. In chapter 1 the disciples were to wait for the coming of the Holy Spirit; in chapter 2 He comes. In chapter 1 the disciples were equipped; in chapter 2 they are empowered. In chapter 1 they were held back; in chapter 2 they are sent forth. In chapter 1 the Savior ascended; in chapter 2 the Spirit descends. The promises of the Lord Jesus Christ given in chapter 1 (1:5, 8) come to fulfillment, as the believers gathered in the upper room receive the wonderful promise of the Father.

God's eternal redemptive plan began to unfold in human history in the Garden of Eden after man's sin. In Genesis 3:15, He promised a savior, who would one day redeem the human race from the effects of that sin. The unfolding continued throughout the patriarchal age, past the giving of the Mosaic Law, to a small hill outside Jerusalem called Calvary. There the incarnate Son of God gave His life for the sins of the world. After rising victorious over sin and death, He promised to send the Holy Spirit to indwell believers. As we have seen, that event of necessity had to wait until Jesus' ascension to the Father. John 7:37–39 reads,

> Now on the last day, the great day of the feast, Jesus stood and cried out, saying, "If any man is thirsty, let him come to Me and drink. He who believes in Me, as the Scripture said, 'From his innermost being shall flow rivers of living water.'" But this He spoke of the Spirit, whom those who believed in Him were to receive; for the Spirit was not yet given, because Jesus was not yet glorified.

Though the assembling of the redeemed in God's kingdom has gone on since the Fall, the coming of the Spirit marks the beginning of the unique church age. That there would be an intervening age between the two advents of Messiah was not foreseen in the Old Testament. Nor was the unity of Jew and Gentile in one body. Paul called that concept a mystery in Ephesians 3:3–10. The word "church" translates *ekklēsia*, which means "called-out ones." The church is the bride of Christ; the branches of the Vine; the flock of the Good Shepherd; the kingdom of God's dear Son; God's household, consisting of His adopted children; a spiritual temple, of which Jesus Christ is the cornerstone; but, uniquely, the body of Christ.

Within the body, there is a unity, since all are indwelt by Jesus Christ, and all possess the same Spirit (Rom. 8:9). In Galatians 3:28 Paul wrote, "There is neither Jew nor Greek, there is neither slave nor free man, there is neither male nor female; for you are all one in Christ Jesus" (cf. 1 Cor. 12:13).

This passage describes the birth of the church by the coming of the Spirit on the Day of Pentecost. It is summarized in the evidence of the Spirit's coming, the effect of the Spirit's coming, and the explanation of the Spirit's coming.

THE EVIDENCE OF THE SPIRIT'S COMING

And when the day of Pentecost had come, they were all together in one place. And suddenly there came from heaven a noise like a violent, rushing wind, and it filled the whole house where they were sitting. And there appeared to them tongues as of fire distributing themselves, and they rested on each one of them. And they were all filled with the Holy Spirit and began to speak with other tongues, as the Spirit was giving them utterance. (2:1–4)

The events of Christ's life, death, and resurrection, according to Paul, were not held in a quiet corner (Acts 26:26) but out in the open before all the people. The same could be said of the birth of the church. It did not begin in an obscure manner in some out of the way place. Rather, it was born with a startling, dramatic event in the very heart of Jerusalem.

The coming of the **day of Pentecost** found the believers **all together in one place,** undoubtedly the same upper room described in 1:13. As already noted, that room was located just inside the Eastern Gate, probably in the vicinity of the temple. There is no reason to restrict all to the twelve apostles. It encompasses the entire gathering of 120 believers (1:15).

It was on the **day of Pentecost** that God's sovereign timetable called for the Spirit to descend. It should be noted that the Spirit was not induced into coming because the believers prayed, tarried, or met certain spiritual requirements. Luke's account points only to the sovereign timing of God as the cause of the Spirit's descent.

Pentecost means "fiftieth." It is the New Testament name for the Feast of Weeks (Ex. 34:22–23), or Harvest (Ex. 23:16), which was celebrated fifty days after Passover. In post-exilic Judaism, it also celebrated the giving of the Law to Moses. The Spirit's coming on that day was linked to the pattern of feasts in the Old Testament.

God's redemptive New Testament timetable is pictured in the feasts of Leviticus 23. The first great feast mentioned in that chapter is Passover. The killing of the passover lamb pictured the death of Jesus Christ, the ultimate Passover Lamb (1 Cor. 5:7). A second feast was the

Feast of Unleavened Bread, celebrated on the day after Passover. During that feast, an offering of the first fruits of the grain harvest was made. Leviticus 23:15 commands that offering to be made on the day after the sabbath. The Sadducees and Pharisees differed on what that sabbath was. The Sadducees interpreted it as the weekly sabbath, and hence the grain offering would always be on a Sunday. The Pharisees interpreted the sabbath as the first day of the Feast of Unleavened Bread. According to that interpretation, the grain offering would always fall on the same day of the month but not the same day of the week. Until the destruction of the Temple in A.D. 70, the Sadducees' interpretation was normative for Judaism (F. F. Bruce, *The Book of the Acts* [Grand Rapids: Eerdmans, 1971], 53 n. 3). Hence, the day the first fruits were offered would have been on Sunday. That provides an apt picture of the Lord Jesus Christ's resurrection as the "first fruits of those who are asleep" (1 Cor. 15:20).

Fifty days after the first Sunday following Passover, the Feast of Pentecost was celebrated (Lev. 23:15ff.). At Pentecost, another offering of first fruits was made (Lev. 23:20). Completing the cycle of the typical fulfillment of the feasts, the Spirit came on Pentecost as the first fruits of the believers' inheritance (cf. 2 Cor. 5:5; Eph. 1:13–14). Further, those gathered into the church on that day were the first fruits of the full harvest of believers to come. God sent the Spirit on Pentecost, then, following the pattern of Leviticus 23, not in response to any activity of men.

Luke describes this sovereignly designed event by taking us to the upper room, where the believers were gathered. **Suddenly there came from heaven a noise like a violent, rushing wind.** Luke's use of the word **suddenly** emphasizes the element of surprise. Even though the believers knew the Spirit's coming to be imminent (cf. 1:5), they were nevertheless caught by surprise. The same will be true when the Lord returns to earth. Believers will know from the signs that His coming is imminent. Yet He will still come unexpectedly, like a thief in the night (1 Thess. 5:2; cf. Matt. 24:44). Those gathered in the upper room could not have expected the dramatic signs that accompanied the Spirit's coming.

By describing the **noise** as emanating **from heaven,** Luke emphasizes that this was a supernatural action. That it was not a weather phenomenon, a physical **violent, rushing wind** is evident from the use of the term **like.** The supernatural activity of God is so utterly beyond the grasp of humans that the Bible writers have to employ similes to describe His manifestations to men (cf. Ezek. 43:2; Rev. 1:15).

In both Hebrew and Greek, the words for wind and spirit are the same. Wind is frequently used as a picture of the Spirit (cf. Ezek. 37:9ff.; John 3:8). Although the sound of the heavenly wind may have attracted the crowd that soon gathered, the Spirit's presence **filled** only **the whole house where** the believers **were sitting.** They alone received the promised baptism with the Spirit (Acts 1:4–5; 11:15–17). That they were **sitting** offers further proof that they were not praying for the Spirit's coming. Standing and kneeling were the postures for prayer.

After the auditory manifestation of the Spirit's arrival came a visual one (cf. Luke 3:22). **There appeared to them tongues as of fire distributing themselves, and they rested on each one of them.** That these were not flames of literal **fire,** any more than the wind was moving air, is clear from the use of the phrase **as of.**

Some have tried to link the **fire** here with that of Matthew 3:11. As the context of that passage indicates, however, the fire in view there is the fire of eternal judgment (cf. Matt. 3:12). That the **tongues rested on each one of them** shows that all who were present received the Spirit in that moment. It was a uniform, sovereign work of God on all collectively, not something sought individually. At this point, by the baptism with the Spirit, they were all made into one spiritual body—the body of Christ.

Being **filled with the Spirit** must be distinguished from being baptized with the Spirit. The apostle Paul carefully defines the baptism with the Spirit as that act of Christ by which He places believers into His body (Rom. 6:4–6; 1 Cor. 12:13; Gal. 3:27). In contrast to much errant teaching today, the New Testament nowhere commands believers to seek the baptism with the Spirit. It is a sovereign, single, unrepeatable act on God's part, and is no more an experience than are its companions justification and adoption. Although some wrongly view the baptism with the Spirit as the initiation into the ranks of the spiritual elite, nothing could be further from the truth. The purpose of the baptism with the Spirit is not to divide the body of Christ, but to unify it. As Paul wrote to the Corinthians, through the baptism with the Spirit "we were all baptized into one body" (1 Cor. 12:13; cf. Gal. 3:26–27; Eph. 4:4–6).

Unlike the baptism with the Spirit, being filled with the Spirit is an experience and should be continuous. Although filled initially on the Day of Pentecost, Peter was filled again in Acts 4:8. Many of the same people filled with the Spirit in Acts 2 were filled again in Acts 4:31. Acts 6:5 describes Stephen as a man "full of faith and the Holy Spirit," yet Acts 7:55 records his being filled again. Paul was filled with the Spirit in Acts 9:17 and again in Acts 13:9.

While there is no command in Scripture to be baptized with the Spirit, believers are commanded to be filled with the Spirit (Eph. 5:18). The grammatical construction of that passage indicates believers are to be continuously being filled with the Spirit. Those who would be filled with the Spirit must first empty themselves. That involves confession of sin and dying to selfishness and self-will. To be filled with the Spirit is to consciously practice the presence of the Lord Jesus Christ and to have a mind saturated with the Word of God. Colossians 3:16–25 delineates the results of "letting the word of Christ richly dwell" in us. They are the same ones that result from the filling of the Spirit (Eph. 5:19–33). As believers yield the moment by moment decisions of life to His control, they "walk by the Spirit" (Gal. 5:16). (For a further discussion of the filling with the Spirit, see *Ephesians,* MacArthur New Testament Commentary [Chicago: Moody, 1986].) The baptism with the Spirit grants the power that the filling with the Spirit unleashes. (For a further discussion of the difference between the baptism and the filling with the Spirit, see my book *Charismatic Chaos* [Grand Rapids: Zondervan, 1992], 191–93.)

After being **filled with the Spirit,** they **began to speak with other tongues, as the Spirit was giving them utterance.** There has been much dispute in recent years over what it meant **to speak with other tongues.** The text, however, is not ambiguous. Far from being ecstatic speech, the **tongues** spoken on the Day of Pentecost were known languages. The term *glōssa* is the word for languages, and the context allows for no other interpretation (cf. the discussion of verses 8–11 below).

In contrast to much teaching today, being given the ability to speak in languages is associated not with the baptism with the Spirit but here with the filling with the Spirit. Nor is speaking in languages the normal response to being filled with the Spirit. Acts 4:8, 31, 6:5; 7:55; 9:17; and 13:9 all record instances where speaking in tongues did not accompany the filling with the Spirit. Paul taught that the filling of the Spirit should result in many things, such as worship, thankfulness, love, submissiveness, and obedience—but not speaking in tongues (Eph. 5:18ff.).

Paul states the purpose of speaking in languages in 1 Corinthians 14:21–22: they were to be a sign to unbelieving Israel. While that was true on the one hand, on the other they were the links given to show that Jews, Gentiles, and Samaritans were all equal in the church (Acts 15:8–9). The Samaritans received the Holy Spirit in Acts 8:14–19. Although there is no reference to languages, that there was likely that supernatural sign is evident from Simon's reaction (cf. verses 18–19). Acts 10:44–47 describes the receiving of the Spirit by the Gentiles of Cornelius's household. That they spoke in languages convinced the Jewish believers, as well as Peter, that the Gentiles had received the Spirit too (cf. verses 45, 47). The last group to speak in tongues were John the Baptist's disciples whom Paul encountered in Ephesus (Acts 19:1–7). They were among the last remnants of Old Testament saints, now coming to faith in Christ. They were given the ability to speak in languages in order to demonstrate their full equality with Jews, Samaritans, and Gentiles in the church. Each case describes a unique, historical transition. No doctrinal teaching for today can be established from those incidents.

That the true biblical gift of languages no longer exists is clear from the following lines of evidence. First, it was a miraculous gift, and the age of miracles ended with the passing of the apostles (Heb. 2:3–4). It is significant that outside of Acts the miraculous gifts of the Spirit are mentioned only in the early epistle of 1 Corinthians. Later epistles, such as Ephesians, Romans, and 1 Peter, discuss spiritual gifts but make no mention of miraculous ones.

Contrary to much teaching today, the purpose of the gift of languages was not the edification of believers. As noted above, they were a sign of judgment to unbelieving Israel (1 Cor. 14:21–22), showing that the church would encompass people from all nations and languages. The gift of languages was therefore a sign of the transition between the Old and New Covenants—a transition completed nearly two thousand years ago.

Having thus fulfilled its purpose, the gift of languages passed from the scene, just as 1 Corinthians 13:8 said it would. That fact is confirmed by church history. Speaking in tongues was unknown from the close of the apostolic era until the beginning of this century, except in heretical groups. (For a further discussion of speaking in tongues, see my book *Charismatic Chaos* [Grand Rapids: Zondervan, 1992], and *1 Corinthians,* MacArthur New Testament Commentary [Chicago: Moody, 1984].)

Those who spoke the languages at Pentecost did not have to be taught how to do so by reading a book, attending a seminar, or being coached by other people. Nor did they have to develop the gift through repeated practice on their own. Rather, they spoke **as the Spirit was giving them utterance.** He was in total control of the situation. They simply received what He gave.

The evidence of the Spirit's coming was unmistakable. He manifested His presence to the ears, eyes, and mouths of the believers. But it didn't stop there. His coming had a profound effect on the people of Jerusalem as well.

The Effect of the Spirit's Coming

Now there were Jews living in Jerusalem, devout men, from every nation under heaven. And when this sound occurred, the multitude came together, and were bewildered, because they were each one hearing them speak in his own language. And they were amazed and marveled, saying, "Why, are not all these who are speaking Galileans? And how is it that we each hear them in our own language to which we were born? Parthians and Medes and Elamites, and residents of Mesopotamia, Judea and

Cappadocia, Pontus and Asia, Phrygia and Pamphylia, Egypt and the districts of Libya around Cyrene, and visitors from Rome, both Jews and proselytes, Cretans and Arabs—we hear them in our own tongues speaking of the mighty deeds of God. (2:5–11)

Pentecost was one of the three major feasts of the Jewish calendar, and all Hebrew males were expected to celebrate it in Jerusalem. Consequently, **there were Jews living in Jerusalem** at the time of Pentecost, **devout men, from every nation under heaven.** Those who went to the trouble to make the pilgrimage were obviously **devout men.** The phrase **from every nation under heaven** is an idiomatic expression meaning "from many lands," or from all of the nations where Jews had been dispersed.

When they heard the **sound** of the rushing wind (rather than the sounds of the languages), **the multitude came together** in the vicinity of the upper room. What they found when they arrived astonished and **bewildered** them, with **each one hearing his own language** being spoken.

The supernatural signs had their desired effect, and the attention of the crowd was riveted on Peter and the others. What **amazed** them the most was that **all** those who were **speaking** were **Galileans.** That was shocking to the sophisticated city dwellers, who viewed rural Galileans as ignorant and uneducated.

When Philip excitedly told Nathanael that he had found the Messiah, Jesus of Nazareth (a city in Galilee), Nathanael replied in disdain, "Can any good thing come out of Nazareth?" (John 1:45–46). Nicodemus's attempt to defend Jesus met with the scornful reply, "You are not also from Galilee, are you? Search, and see that no prophet arises out of Galilee" (John 7:52).

The sight of the supposedly ignorant Galileans speaking so many languages caused the astonished crowd to exclaim, **how is it that we each hear them in our own language to which we were born?** That this supernatural communication was known human languages, not ecstatic speech, becomes clear as the list of the specific tongues is enumerated. **Parthians** lived in what is modern Iran. They had never been conquered by the Romans and remained their bitter enemies. **Medes,** partners in empire with the Persians in Daniel's time, were now part of the Parthian Empire. **Elamites** lived in what is now southwestern Iran. They, too, were part of the Parthian Empire. The **residents of Mesopotamia** lived between the two great rivers, the Tigris and the Euphrates (**Mesopotamia** means "between the rivers"). Great numbers of Israelites had been deported to that region by the Assyrians and Babylonians. Not all had returned to Palestine at the time of Cyrus's decree (2 Chron. 36:22–23). **Judea** should probably be construed in the broadest sense as all the region once controlled by David and Solomon. That would explain the absence of Syria from the list. **Cappadocia, Pontus and Asia, Phrygia and Pamphylia** were all regions in Asia Minor. They had a large Jewish population, as did **Egypt,** particularly in the city of Alexandria. It was in that city that the Septuagint, the Greek translation of the Old Testament, had been produced. **The districts of Libya around Cyrene** were west of Egypt on the African coast of the Mediterranean Sea. Josephus mentions a Jewish population there. That there were Jews in **Rome,** as well as Gentile **proselytes,** is obvious from the Emperor Claudius's expulsion of them some years later (Acts 18:2). **Cretans** were from the island of Crete, off the southern coast of Greece. **Arabs** were Jews living in the kingdom of the Nabatean Arabs, located south of Damascus (cf. Gal. 1:17).

The content of these languages is identified by Luke as **speaking of the mighty deeds of God.** Such rehearsal was an essential element of Jewish life and worship. Exodus 15:11 says, "Who is like Thee among the gods, O Lord? Who is like Thee, majestic in holiness, awesome in praises, working wonders?" (cf. Isa. 25:1). Such praise was also a frequent theme of the book of Psalms. Psalm 40:5 reads, "Many, O Lord my God, are the wonders which Thou hast done," while Psalm 77:11 adds, "I shall remember the deeds of the Lord; surely I will remember Thy wonders of old" (cf. Pss. 26:7; 78:4; 89:5; 96:3; 107:8, 21; 111:4).

Having used the sound of the wind to gather the crowd, the Spirit now convinces them that these believers in Jesus Christ were devoted to praising the one true God. Blasphemers, as many thought them to be, could not be extolling the greatness of God. All that recitation of what God had done prepared the way for Peter's proclamation of the gospel beginning in verse 14. The good news of salvation in Jesus Christ was the climax toward which the Holy Spirit was building.

THE EXPLANATION OF THE SPIRIT'S COMING

And they all continued in amazement and great perplexity, saying to one another, "What does this mean?" But others were mocking and saying, "They are full of sweet wine." (2:12–13)

As is regularly the case when God's truth is presented, some in the crowd accepted it, while others rejected. The former **continued in amazement and great perplexity, saying to one another, "What does this mean?"** They would soon understand when Peter proclaimed the gospel in his sermon.

At the same time the **others were mocking and saying, "they are full of sweet wine."** Like the Pharisees who heard Jesus' claims and saw the confirming miracles, but concluded He was of the devil (Matt. 12:24ff.), these scoffers rejected the evidence that this was a work of God. Instead, they proposed the ridiculous hypothesis that the apostles were **full of sweet wine.** They tried to explain away the miracle of speaking in languages as a drunken frolic. Tragically, their skepticism was to harden into full-fledged opposition toward the message and the messengers (cf. 4:7ff.; 5:17–18, 40; 7:58–60). However, no amount of opposition could stop the work of God that began at Pentecost.

The First Christian Sermon—part 1 The Introduction: Explaining Pentecost

4

But Peter, taking his stand with the eleven, raised his voice and declared to them: "Men of Judea, and all you who live in Jerusalem, let this be known to you, and give heed to my words. For these men are not drunk, as you suppose, for it is only the third hour of the day; but this is what was spoken of through the prophet Joel: 'And it shall be in the last days,' God says, 'That I will pour forth of My Spirit and they shall prophesy. And I will grant wonders in the sky above, and signs on the earth beneath, blood, and fire, and vapor of smoke. The sun shall be turned into darkness, and the moon into blood, before the great and glorious day of the Lord shall come. And it shall be, that everyone who calls on the name of the Lord shall be saved.'" (2:14–21)

In an effort to appeal to people's interest, the church today emphasizes a great many different programs, methods, and approaches. Small group activities, sharing, and "culturally relevant" worship services, emphasizing music and drama, have become increasingly popular. Secular psychology, management techniques, and advertising strategies have all made significant inroads into the life of the church.

Seminars on everything from how to have a good marriage to how to handle money abound.

Not all of those things may be harmful. Some, in their proper place, may even be helpful. But what has too often been sacrificed in the flurry of activities and programs is the priority of preaching. While some moderns may bid it good riddance, such has not been the attitude of the church through history, starting with the early church. The first event of church history, following the coming of the Spirit, was Peter's sermon. It led to 3,000 conversions and launched the church. The book of Acts is largely the record of apostolic preaching. Preaching has always remained central to the church's mission.

Acts 4:2 records the displeasure of the Jewish officials that the apostles "were teaching the people and proclaiming in Jesus the resurrection from the dead." Undaunted, "every day, in the temple and from house to house, they kept right on teaching and preaching Jesus as the Christ" (Acts 5:42). After the first great persecution of the church broke out, "those who had been scattered went about preaching the word" (Acts 8:4). Acts 8 also records the preaching of Philip (vv. 5, 12), and Peter and John (v. 25) to the Samaritans, and Philip to the Ethiopian eunuch (v. 35). It also describes the further preaching ministry of Philip (v. 40).

After his conversion, Paul immediately "began to proclaim Jesus in the synagogues, saying, 'He is the Son of God'" (Acts 9:20). Acts 11:20 describes the ministry of the "men of Cyprus and Cyrene, who came to Antioch and began speaking to the Greeks also, preaching the Lord Jesus." All the way to the very last verse, Acts records how the early church "continued to preach the gospel" (Acts 14:7; cf. 10:42; 13:5, 32; 14:15, 21; 15:35; 16:10; 17:3, 13; 20:25; 28:31).

The early church's emphasis on preaching reflected that of our Lord. At the very outset of His ministry, "Jesus began to preach and say, 'Repent, for the kingdom of heaven is at hand'" (Matt. 4:17). Mark records that "after John [the Baptist] had been taken into custody, Jesus came into Galilee, preaching the gospel of God" (Mark 1:14). In Luke 4:43 Jesus said, "I must preach the kingdom of God to the other cities also, for I was sent for this purpose." Throughout His ministry, Jesus continued to preach and teach (cf. Matt. 11:1; Mark 1:38–39; Luke 8:1; 20:1). Luke 4:16–21 gives us insight into the Lord's view of His ministry:

> And He came to Nazareth, where He had been brought up; and as was His custom, He entered the synagogue on the Sabbath, and stood up to read. And the book of the prophet Isaiah was handed to Him. And He opened the book, and found the place where it was written, "The Spirit of the Lord is upon Me, because He anointed Me to preach the gospel to the poor. He has sent Me to proclaim release to the captives, and re-

covery of sight to the blind, to set free those who are downtrodden, to proclaim the favorable year of the Lord." And He closed the book, and gave it back to the attendant, and sat down; and the eyes of all in the synagogue were fixed upon Him. And He began to say to them, "Today this Scripture has been fulfilled in your hearing."

Preaching or proclaiming is mentioned three times in the passage from Isaiah that Jesus read. That clearly shows the importance of preaching in His ministry. Jesus instructed His disciples, "As you go, preach" (Matt. 10:7), and at the end said, "Go into all the world and preach" (Mark 16:15). This call to preach is best summed up in the words of Paul in 1 Corinthians 1:17–25:

> For Christ did not send me to baptize, but to preach the gospel, not in cleverness of speech, that the cross of Christ should not be made void. For the word of the cross is to those who are perishing foolishness, but to us who are being saved it is the power of God. For it is written, "I will destroy the wisdom of the wise, and the cleverness of the clever I will set aside." Where is the wise man? Where is the scribe? Where is the debater of this age? Has not God made foolish the wisdom of the world? For since in the wisdom of God the world through its wisdom did not come to know God, God was well-pleased through the foolishness of the message preached to save those who believe. For indeed Jews ask for signs, and Greeks search for wisdom; but we preach Christ crucified, to Jews a stumbling block, and to Gentiles foolishness, but to those who are the called, both Jews and Greeks, Christ the power of God and the wisdom of God. Because the foolishness of God is wiser than men, and the weakness of God is stronger than men.

Preaching has rightly held that central place in the life of the true church throughout the ages. The Reformation, which recovered the faith, was initiated and spread largely through the revival of preaching by men like Luther, Calvin, Zwingli, and Knox. At the very core of the great strength of seventeenth-century Puritanism was its emphasis on sound biblical preaching. The Great Awakening of the eighteenth century was led through preaching by men such as George Whitefield, John Wesley, and Jonathan Edwards. The nineteenth century saw great evangelists, such as D. L. Moody, and great preachers, such as Charles Spurgeon, Joseph Parker, and Alexander Maclaren.

A godly man, gifted by the Spirit to preach the Word, has no equal in the presentation of God's truth. It is the God-ordained method for evangelism and edification. The weakness of the contemporary church is largely due to the decline in powerful biblical preaching. Paul set the standard in bold relief when he said,

And when I came to you, brethren, I did not come with superiority of speech or of wisdom, proclaiming to you the testimony of God. For I determined to know nothing among you except Jesus Christ, and Him crucified. And I was with you in weakness and in fear and in much trembling. And my message and my preaching were not in persuasive words of wisdom, but in demonstration of the Spirit and of power, that your faith should not rest on the wisdom of men, but on the power of God. (1 Cor. 2:1–5)

The apostle was inspired by God to ask the question, "How shall they hear without a preacher?" Then he affirmed the nobility of the preacher when he quoted from Isaiah 52:7: "How beautiful are the feet of those who bring glad tidings of good things!" (Rom. 10:14–15).

The content of biblical preaching can be summed up in two Greek words: *kērugma* and *didachē*. *Kērugma* derives from the verb *kērussō*, which means "to proclaim," or "to announce a proclamation." The noun *kērugma* refers to the content of a proclamation. At least five elements made up the New Testament *kērugma*. First, it presented Jesus as the fulfillment of Old Testament prophecy. Second, it described Him as God in human flesh. Third, it focused on His life and work, especially His death and resurrection. Fourth, it spoke of His second coming. Finally, it declared that salvation was only through faith in Him, and that those who rejected Him as Lord and Savior would be eternally damned.

In addition to *kērugma*, or proclamation, true biblical preaching must also contain *didachē*, or teaching. *Didachē*, from which the English word "didactic" derives, refers to the doctrinal content within the preaching of the *kērugma*. The epistles are largely composed of this theology of salvation that provides the depth and breadth and height of preaching. True preaching is proclaiming the great truths and undergirding them with the richness of the supernatural and profound wisdom revealed throughout Scripture, particularly the New Testament. There is no such thing as genuine biblical preaching that is devoid of doctrinal content.

The book of Acts frequently records that men were persuaded to believe and be redeemed by apostolic preaching. After Paul and Silas preached in the synagogue in Thessalonica, "some of them were persuaded and joined Paul and Silas" (Acts 17:4). In Corinth, Paul "was reasoning in the synagogue every Sabbath and trying to persuade Jews and Greeks" (Acts 18:4). After arriving in Ephesus, Paul "entered the synagogue and continued speaking out boldly for three months, reasoning and persuading them about the kingdom of God" (Acts 19:8). Even while imprisoned at Rome, Paul kept up his ministry of preaching and persuading men:

And when they had set a day for him, they came to him at his lodging in large numbers; and he was explaining to them by solemnly testifying about the kingdom of God, and trying to persuade them concerning Jesus, from both the Law of Moses and from the Prophets, from morning until evening. And some were being persuaded by the things spoken, but others would not believe. (Acts 28:23–24)

The use of the term "persuaded" suggests the apostolic preaching had both a logical flow and doctrinal content. And Paul affirmed that saving faith comes by hearing a message about Christ (Rom. 10:17).

Before launching into the main body of his sermon, Peter discusses what is immediately on the people's minds—the phenomena of Pentecost. He begins by giving a refutation of the scurrilous charge of drunkenness. Then he offers an explanation of Pentecost based on Old Testament prophecy.

THE REFUTATION

But Peter, taking his stand with the eleven, raised his voice and declared to them: "Men of Judea, and all you who live in Jerusalem, let this be known to you, and give heed to my words. For these men are not drunk, as you suppose, for it is only the third hour of the day; (2:14–15)

Peter had been the acknowledged leader and often the spokesman for the apostles during Christ's earthly ministry. In all four lists of apostles, his name is first (Matt. 10:2–4; Mark 3:16–19; Luke 6:14–16; Acts 1:13). He now continues in that role, **taking his stand,** along **with the eleven** other apostles, facing the crowd. The **eleven** included Matthias, chosen earlier to replace the traitor Judas and complete the ranks of the twelve. As eyewitnesses of the resurrected Christ themselves, they supported Peter.

Peter **raised his voice** so the huge crowd could hear him. The verb translated **declared** also appears in 2:4. Here, as there, it refers to a Spirit-inspired utterance. Peter probably spoke in Aramaic, the vernacular language of Palestine and thus familiar to his hearers, who included the **men of Judea** (the residents of Jerusalem), and **all who live in Jerusalem** (the multitudes who had flocked there to celebrate Pentecost). The Semitic expression **let this be known to you, and give heed to my words** expresses Peter's confidence and boldness. There is no hesitation or equivocation in his heart. Commentator Albert Barnes observes,

> Peter did not intimate that this was a doubtful matter, or one that could not be explained. His address was respectful, yet firm. He proceeded calmly to *show* them their error. When the enemies of religion deride us or the gospel, we should answer them kindly and respectfully, yet firmly. We should *reason* with them coolly, and convince them of their error, Proverbs 15:1. In this case Peter acted on the principle which he afterward enjoined on all, 1 Peter 3:15, "Be ready always to give an answer to every man that asketh you a reason of the hope that is in you, with meekness and fear." (*Notes on the New Testament: Acts–Romans* [Grand Rapids: Baker, reprint of the 1884–85 edition], 29–30. Italics in original.)

Obviously a Spirit-filled Peter was a very different man than the one who cringed before a lowly servant girl and denied his Lord on three occasions.

Every good sermon begins with an introduction that grabs the hearers' attention. In this case, the Holy Spirit had already provided a dramatic introduction. The sound like a mighty wind and the miracle of languages had arrested the attention of the crowd. They were amazed and confused and wanted an explanation. Before giving that explanation, Peter refutes the false charge that the disciples were **drunk** (cf. v. 13). He dismisses the accusation as absurd, since it was **only the third hour of the day.** The **third hour,** reckoned from sunrise, was 9:00 A.M. Even those who were drunkards were not inebriated that early in the day. That was especially true on a festival day such as Pentecost. So universal was that reality that Peter's appeal to it was enough to refute the charge of drunkenness.

THE EXPLANATION

but this is what was spoken of through the prophet Joel: 'And it shall be in the last days,' God says, 'That I will pour forth of My Spirit upon all mankind; and your sons and your daughters shall prophesy, and your young men shall see visions, and your old men shall dream dreams; even upon My bondslaves, both men and women, I will in those days pour forth of My Spirit and they shall prophesy. And I will grant wonders in the sky above, and signs on the earth beneath, blood, and fire, and vapor of smoke. The sun shall be turned into darkness, and the moon into blood, before the great and glorious day of the Lord shall come. And it shall be, that everyone who calls on the name of the Lord shall be saved.' (2:16–21)

What transpired on the Day of Pentecost was not a drunken aberration. Rather, as Peter now demonstrates, it was connected to **what was spoken of through the prophet Joel** (cf. Joel 2:28–32).

The term **the last days** is a common Old Testament expression (cf. Isa. 2:2; Jer. 23:20; 49:39; Ezek. 38:16; Hos. 3:5; Micah 4:1). It denotes the time when Messiah would come to set up His kingdom. That there would be two comings of Messiah, separated by a long intervening period, was not clearly understood in the Old Testament. The two comings, however, can be inferred from the two purposes for Messiah's coming set forth in the Old Testament. On the one hand, the Old Testament teaches that Messiah would come as the Suffering Servant, to die for the sins of the world (Isa. 53). On the other hand, it also teaches that Messiah would come in glory to set up His kingdom (Isa. 9:6).

The first coming of Christ ushered in **the last days.** First John 2:18 says, "Children, it is the last hour." Peter writes that Christ "has appeared in these last times for the sake of you" (1 Peter 1:20). The writer of Hebrews informs us that God "in these last days has spoken to us in His Son" (Heb. 1:2), and "now once at the consummation of the ages [Christ] has been manifested to put away sin by the sacrifice of Himself" (9:26). **The last days** have thus lasted nearly two thousand years. During that time, God has graciously called Gentiles to salvation and chastened Israel for her unbelief.

The complete fulfillment of Joel's prophecy awaits the coming of the millennial kingdom. On the Day of Pentecost, and indeed throughout the church age, God has given both a preview and a sample of the power the Spirit will release in the kingdom. Believers in the present age have a foretaste of kingdom life. In the millennial kingdom, God **will pour forth of [His] Spirit upon all mankind,** since all who enter the kingdom will be redeemed. (See Matt. 24:29–25:46 for the evidence that only redeemed people will enter the Millennium.) During the church age, God pours His Spirit into believers (cf. Titus 3:5–6). In the kingdom there will be perfect peace (Isa. 9:7); peace rules now in the hearts of believers. In the kingdom, Christ will reign (Luke 1:33); He reigns now in the hearts of His people. In the kingdom, Christ will judge all men (Acts 17:31; 2 Tim. 4:1); now He judges His people through the Spirit's convicting ministry in their lives. What will ultimately come to full fruition in the kingdom began to be seen at Pentecost.

Obviously, however, not all the components of Joel's prophecy are prefigured in the church age. It is not until the **Spirit** is poured out **upon all mankind** in the kingdom, Peter says, that **your sons and your daughters shall prophesy, and your young men shall see visions, and your old men shall dream dreams.** It is then, God says, that **even upon My bondslaves, both men and women, I will in those days pour forth of My Spirit and they shall prophesy.** It is

only **in those days** (the millennial kingdom) that such extensive prophesying will take place. The nature of the prophesying, dreams, and visions that will take place remains a mystery. Prophecy was exercised in
the early church (cf. Acts 21:8–11) and continues in a nonrevelatory
sense throughout this age. (For a discussion of the cessation of the sign
gifts, see my book *Charismatic Chaos* [Grand Rapids: Zondervan,
1992].)

Nor did the **wonders in the sky above, and signs on the
earth beneath** occur at Pentecost. There was no **blood, fire,** or **vapor
of smoke.** The **sun** was not **turned into darkness,** nor **the moon
into blood.** Those events are associated with the coming of **the great
and glorious day of the Lord.**

The **day of the Lord** may refer to any time God acts in judgment
(cf. Isa. 13:6ff; Ezek. 30:2ff; Joel 1:15; 2:1–11; 3:14; Amos 5:18–20; Obad.
15; Zeph. 1:14–18). In this passage, however, the ultimate day of the
Lord associated with the second coming of Christ is in view (cf. 1 Thess.
5:2; 2 Thess. 2:2). That is clear from the details of Joel's prophecy. The
signs in the earth and heavens Joel mentions are connected elsewhere
in Scripture with the events surrounding Christ's second coming. The
book of Revelation associates blood with that time:

> And I looked, and behold, an ashen horse; and he who sat on it had
> the name Death; and Hades was following with him. And authority was
> given to them over a fourth of the earth, to kill with sword and with
> famine and with pestilence and by the wild beasts of the earth. (6:8)
>
> And the first sounded, and there came hail and fire, mixed with blood,
> and they were thrown to the earth; and a third of the earth was burned
> up, and a third of the trees were burned up, and all the green grass was
> burned up. And the second angel sounded, and something like a great
> mountain burning with fire was thrown into the sea; and a third of the
> sea became blood. (8:7–8)
>
> And the four angels, who had been prepared for the hour and day and
> month and year, were released, so that they might kill a third of man-
> kind. (9:15)
>
> And the wine press was trodden outside the city, and blood came out
> from the wine press, up to the horses' bridles, for a distance of two
> hundred miles. (14:20)
>
> And the second angel poured out his bowl into the sea, and it became
> blood like that of a dead man; and every living thing in the sea died.
> (16:3)

Revelation also mentions fire in connection with the time surrounding
Christ's second coming:

> And the angel took the censer; and he filled it with the fire of the altar and threw it to the earth; and there followed peals of thunder and sounds and flashes of lightning and an earthquake. (8:5)
>
> And the first sounded, and there came hail and fire, mixed with blood, and they were thrown to the earth; and a third of the earth was burned up, and a third of the trees were burned up, and all the green grass was burned up. (8:7)
>
> And the second angel sounded, and something like a great mountain burning with fire was thrown into the sea; and a third of the sea became blood. (8:8)
>
> And the third angel sounded, and a great star fell from heaven, burning like a torch, and it fell on a third of the rivers and on the springs of waters. (8:10)

Finally, Revelation mentions smoke at that time:

> And he opened the bottomless pit; and smoke went up out of the pit, like the smoke of a great furnace; and the sun and the air were darkened by the smoke of the pit. And out of the smoke came forth locusts upon the earth; and power was given them, as the scorpions of the earth have power. And this is how I saw in the vision the horses and those who sat on them: the riders had breastplates the color of fire and of hyacinth and of brimstone; and the heads of the horses are like the heads of lions; and out of their mouths proceed fire and smoke and brimstone. A third of mankind was killed by these three plagues, by the fire and the smoke and the brimstone, which proceeded out of their mouths. (9:2–3, 17–18)
>
> And the kings of the earth, who committed acts of immorality and lived sensuously with her, will weep and lament over her when they see the smoke of her burning. (18:9; cf. 18:18)

In Matthew 24:29–30, the Lord Jesus Christ described the changes in the sun, moon, and stars that would accompany His second coming:

> But immediately after the tribulation of those days the sun will be darkened, and the moon will not give its light, and the stars will fall from the sky, and the powers of the heavens will be shaken, and then the sign of the Son of Man will appear in the sky, and then all the tribes of the earth will mourn, and they will see the Son of Man coming on the clouds of the sky with power and great glory.

Some of those cosmic disturbances had been prefigured by the events surrounding Christ's death on the cross (cf. Luke 23:44–45).

After hearing Peter quote Joel's terrifying description of the day of the Lord, the crowd would naturally want to know how to avoid being caught in that time of terror and devastation. Peter then delivers the climax of his quote from Joel: **And it shall be, that everyone who calls on the name of the Lord shall be saved.** There is salvation for those who turn to the Savior. In the main body of his sermon, Peter describes to his hearers exactly who that Savior is and what He requires for salvation.

The First Christian Sermon—part 2 The Theme: Proclaiming the Risen Lord

5

Men of Israel, listen to these words: Jesus the Nazarene, a man attested to you by God with miracles and wonders and signs which God performed through Him in your midst, just as you yourselves know—this Man, delivered up by the predetermined plan and foreknowledge of God, you nailed to a cross by the hands of godless men and put Him to death. And God raised Him up again, putting an end to the agony of death, since it was impossible for Him to be held in its power. For David says of Him, "I was always beholding the Lord in my presence; for He is at my right hand, that I may not be shaken. Therefore my heart was glad and my tongue exulted; moreover my flesh also will abide in hope; because Thou wilt not abandon my soul to Hades, nor allow Thy Holy One to undergo decay. Thou hast made known to me the ways of life; Thou wilt make me full of gladness with Thy presence." Brethren, I may confidently say to you regarding the patriarch David that he both died and was buried, and his tomb is with us to this day. And so, because he was a prophet, and knew that God had sworn to him with an oath to seat one of his descendants upon his throne, he looked ahead and spoke of the resurrection of the Christ, that He was neither abandoned to Ha-

des, nor did His flesh suffer decay. This Jesus God raised up again, to which we are all witnesses. Therefore having been exalted to the right hand of God, and having received from the Father the promise of the Holy Spirit, He has poured forth this which you both see and hear. For it was not David who ascended into heaven, but he himself says: "The Lord said to my Lord, sit at My right hand, until I make Thine enemies a footstool for Thy feet." Therefore let all the house of Israel know for certain that God has made Him both Lord and Christ—this Jesus whom you crucified. (2:22–36)

Ever since God's covenant with Abraham, in which He promised to bless all nations through Abraham's seed (Gen. 12:1ff.; cf. Gal. 3:16), the Jewish people have longed for messianic times. They believe that when Messiah comes all wrongs will be made right, and He will lead them to victory over their enemies and usher in the blessings of His promised kingdom.

Viewed in that context of intense Jewish expectation, Peter's announcement that the last days, a name for messianic times, had already begun (2:16–21) was shocking. That startling claim, made by the apostle in the introduction to his sermon on the Day of Pentecost, directed his hearers logically into his sermon's theme. For if the messianic times had indeed begun, then Messiah must have come. That is precisely the thesis Peter develops in the main body of his sermon. He presents the truth that Israel's long-awaited Messiah has come in the person of Jesus of Nazareth.

It is difficult for twentieth-century readers to appreciate how profoundly disturbing that claim was to the Jews. Messiah was the central figure in Jewish thought. Of Him God had revealed, "The scepter shall not depart from Judah, nor the ruler's staff from between his feet, until Shiloh comes, and to him shall be the obedience of the peoples" (Gen. 49:10). Of Him the psalmist warned, "Do homage to the Son, lest He become angry, and you perish in the way, for His wrath may soon be kindled" (Ps. 2:12). He was the great descendant of David, of whom God said, "I will establish the throne of his kingdom forever" (2 Sam. 7:13; cf. Luke 1:31–33).

In light of that, for Peter to boldly proclaim Jesus of Nazareth as the Messiah had to both shock and outrage his listeners. After all, less than two months earlier they had executed Jesus for claiming to be the Messiah. Now his upstart followers were making that same claim on His behalf. To the Jewish mind, there could be no greater expression of blasphemy.

That same antipathy toward Jesus Christ persists in our own day. I'll never forget the time when, as a young man, I visited the office of a local rabbi. We had a pleasant discussion until I asked him what he thought of Jesus Christ. He brought his fist crashing down on his desk and glared at me. Pointing his finger at me he said vehemently, "Don't ever mention that name in my presence again!"

For Peter to proclaim Jesus as Israel's Messiah was to raise the most dynamic, powerful and forceful issue possible. By so doing, Peter showed a boldness and courage that he had previously lacked. That is once again evidence of the transforming power of Pentecost in his life.

Knowing that his hearers would demand compelling evidence before accepting such an audacious claim, Peter proceeds to provide it. Having explained the miracle of Pentecost in his introduction, he now launches into his theme, namely that Jesus of Nazareth is the divine Messiah. Peter establishes Jesus's credentials by demonstrating how His life, death, resurrection, and exaltation prove Him to be the Messiah. As his sermon unfolds, Peter flows through those four elements in chronological order. In keeping with apostolic custom, however, he focuses primarily on the resurrection of Christ (cf. Acts 3:15; 5:30; 10:40; 13:30, 33, 34, 37).

THE LIFE OF CHRIST

Men of Israel, listen to these words: Jesus the Nazarene, a man attested to you by God with miracles and wonders and signs which God performed through Him in your midst, just as you yourselves know— (2:22)

As he did at the beginning of his sermon (cf. 2:14), Peter boldly challenged the **men of Israel** present to **listen to** his **words.** His boldness was predicated on two undeniable truths: God had worked miracles through Jesus, and they had seen them. That salvation was being offered to Israel despite their unbelief and rejection of the Lord Jesus Christ is a testimony to the magnanimity of God's grace.

Jesus the Nazarene was the name by which our Lord was commonly known during His earthly ministry (Matt. 21:11; Mark 10:47; 14:67; 16:6; Luke 24:19; John 18:5, 7). It identified Him with His hometown of Nazareth; in fact, the phrase is sometimes translated "Jesus of Nazareth." It was the name on the inscription on His cross (John 19:19). Peter used it several other times in Acts (3:6; 4:10; 10:38), as did Paul (26:9). It was even used in derision by some (cf. John 1:46), thus Peter's use of it constitutes a mild rebuke. This name for our Lord reflects His wonderful condescension in leaving the glory of heaven to live in a humble Galilean village.

Peter further describes Jesus as **a man attested** to them **by God** (cf. John 5:32–37; 8:18). *Apodeiknumi* (**attested**) has various shades of meaning. It is used in 1 Corinthians 4:9 to speak of exhibiting something. In Acts 25:7 it conveys the idea of proof. Second Thessalonians 2:4 uses it in the sense of proclamation to high office. All those shades of meaning are applicable to Jesus. He was exhibited as God in human flesh, and that was confirmed by "many convincing proofs" (Acts 1:3). Finally, God "highly exalted Him, and bestowed on Him the name which is above every name" (Phil. 2:9). There is no higher office than that of Messiah, God's anointed King.

Peter describes the means by which God **attested** Jesus as **miracles and wonders and signs.** The many miracles performed by our Lord provide overwhelming evidence that He is who He claimed to be. From His miraculous birth to His miraculous resurrection, to all the miracles He performed during His earthly ministry, the miraculous element was central in our Lord's life. Nicodemus no doubt spoke for many when he exclaimed, "Rabbi, we know that You have come from God as a teacher; for no one can do these signs that You do unless God is with him" (John 3:2).

It should come as no surprise if the God Who supernaturally created the universe should choose at times to supernaturally intervene in it. Yet it is the claim of miracles that many in our culture find most objectionable in biblical Christianity. The many attempts by rationalistic critics to invent the "historical" (that is, nonmiraculous) Jesus have inevitably ended in frustration. If the miracles are removed from His life, there is very little left.

Many would agree with the eighteenth-century British philosopher David Hume, who rejected the possibility of miracles. Hume argued that since the laws of nature are uniform, and a miracle is by definition a violation of the laws of nature, miracles are impossible. There is a fatal flaw in Hume's argument, however. C. S. Lewis writes,

> Now of course we must agree with Hume that if there is absolutely "uniform experience" against miracles, if in other words they have never happened, why then they never have. Unfortunately we know the experience against them to be uniform only if we know that all the reports of them are false. And we can know all the reports to be false only if we know already that miracles have never occurred. In fact, we are arguing in a circle. (C. S. Lewis, *Miracles* [New York: Macmillan, 1972], 105; for a defense of the possibility of miracles, see also Norman L. Geisler, *Miracles and Modern Thought* [Grand Rapids: Zondervan, 1982]).

Miracles, wonders, and **signs** all describe God's miraculous works. **Miracles** is from *dunamis,* a term that describes the powerful, supernatural character of the works. **Wonders** is the plural form of *teras.* It describes the marveling that takes place in the mind of the one who witnesses a miracle. **Signs** derives from *sēmeion* and gives the intent of God's miraculous works: to point to spiritual truth. It should be noted that "throughout Acts the term 'wonders' only occurs in conjunction with 'signs,' a testimony to the fact that mere marvels have no value in themselves except as they point beyond themselves to the divine power behind them and so lead to faith" (John B. Polhill, *The New American Commentary: Acts* [Nashville: Broadman, 1992], 112).

The miracles of our Lord were thus mighty manifestations of God's power designed to get people's attention and point them to spiritual truth. For example in John 6 Jesus followed the miracle of the feeding of the multitude by offering Himself as the bread of life. Similarly, He used the miracle of Lazarus's resurrection to illustrate the spiritual truth that He is the resurrection and the life (John 11:25).

Jesus did not do His miracles on His own; **God performed** them **through Him** (John 5:17–20, 30, 36; 8:28; 14:10). They showed both His deity and the Father's approval of Him (Matt. 11:1–6; Luke 7:20–23; John 3:2; 6:14). Peter repeatedly emphasizes God's involvement in Christ's life, death, and resurrection (vv. 23, 24, 32, 33, 36). He drives home the point that ample evidence reveals that Jesus Christ was no impostor but was indeed God's chosen Messiah.

The miracles God performed through Jesus Christ, Peter reminds them, were done **in your midst, just as you yourselves know.** They could not claim ignorance. Their rejection of Jesus was not based on lack of information but on hatred and love of sin.

That hatred appears in many passages. In John 10:37–38, Jesus said, "If I do not do the works of My Father, do not believe Me; but if I do them, though you do not believe Me, believe the works, that you may know and understand that the Father is in Me, and I in the Father." What was the response? "Therefore they were seeking again to seize Him, and He eluded their grasp" (v. 39). Note that, although they rejected His claims, they did not deny the works He did.

After Jesus' resurrection of Lazarus, "some of the [crowd who had witnessed the raising of Lazarus] went away to the Pharisees, and told them the things which Jesus had done. Therefore the chief priests and the Pharisees convened a council, and were saying, 'What are we doing? For this man is performing many signs'" (John 11:46–47). Even His most bitter enemies did not deny His miracles. Their response, however, was to plot His death (vv. 48–53).

At the triumphal entry, "the multitude who were with Him when He called Lazarus out of the tomb, and raised him from the dead, were bearing Him witness. For this cause also the multitude went and met Him, because they heard that He had performed this sign" (John 12:17–18). A few days later, this same multitude cried out before Pilate, "Let Him be crucified" (Matt. 27:22–23).

Perhaps the clearest statement of this truth comes from our Lord's words in John 15:24–25: "If I had not done among them the works which no one else did, they would not have sin; but now they have both seen and hated Me and My Father as well. But they have done this in order that the word may be fulfilled that is written in their Law, 'They hated Me without a cause.'"

The evidence from Jesus' life and works that He was the Messiah of God was conclusive and undeniable. But because "men loved darkness rather than the light; for their deeds were evil" (John 3:19), they committed the greatest sin that can be committed—they rejected Jesus Christ.

The Death of Christ

this Man, delivered up by the predetermined plan and foreknowledge of God, you nailed to a cross by the hands of godless men and put Him to death. (2:23)

Peter's emphatic use of the phrase **this Man** brings out the stark contrast between his hearers' evaluation of Jesus and God's. The very One whom God had honored as Messiah, they had rejected and crucified.

In this verse Peter answers an objection that would arise in the minds of his listeners. If Jesus was the Messiah, why was He a victim? Why did He not use His power to avoid the cross? Peter's reply to this unspoken objection is that Jesus was no victim (John 10:17–18; 19:10–11); rather, He was **delivered up by the predetermined plan and foreknowledge of God.**

Ekdotos (**delivered up**) appears only here in the New Testament. It describes those surrendered to their enemies, or betrayed. God gave His Son to be the Savior of the world, which entailed delivering Him to His enemies. By the design of God, Jesus was betrayed by Judas into the hands of the Jewish leaders, who handed Him over to the Romans for execution.

Predetermined is from *horizō,* from which we get our English word "horizon." It means "to mark out with a boundary," or "to determine." **Plan** is from *boulomai* and refers to God's will, design, or purpose. Taken together they indicate that Jesus Christ was delivered to death because God planned and ordained it (Acts 4:27–28; 13:27–29) from all eternity (2 Tim. 1:9; Rev. 13:8).

Foreknowledge translates *prognōsis,* an important and often misunderstood New Testament word. It means far more than knowing beforehand what will happen. Significantly, the word appears here in the instrumental dative case. That shows that it was the means by which Christ's deliverance to His enemies took place. Yet, mere knowledge cannot perform such an act. Foreordination can act, however, and that is the New Testament meaning of *prognōsis:*

> *Proginoskein* and *prognōsis* in the New Testament . . . do not denote simple intellectual foresight or prescience, the mere taking knowledge of something beforehand, but rather a selective knowledge which regards one with favor and makes one an object of love, and thus approaches the idea of foreordination, Acts 2:23 (comp. 4:28); Rom. 8:29; 11:2; 1 Peter 1:2. These passages simply lose their meaning, if the words be taken in the sense of simply taking knowledge of one in advance, for God foreknows all men in that sense. Even Arminians feel constrained to give the words a more determinative meaning, namely, to foreknow one with absolute assurance in a certain state or condition. This includes the absolute certainty of that future state, and for that very reason comes very close to the idea of predestination. (L. Berkhof, *Systematic Theology* [Grand Rapids: Eerdmans, 1976], 112)

The idea that God saw in advance that Israel would reject and crucify Christ and worked that into His eternal plan is a implicit denial both of His sovereignty and omniscience (cf. Berkhof, *Systematic Theology,* 68).

Peter strongly emphasizes the point that Jesus was delivered to death by God's eternal plan. That being the case, His death in no way contradicted His messianic claims.

That Jesus Christ was delivered to death by God's predetermined plan, however, does not absolve those who put Him to death of their guilt. Peter goes on to indict them because they nailed Jesus **to a cross . . . and put Him to death.** They were the instigators of Jesus' execution, which **by the hands of godless** (literally, "lawless") Romans was carried out.

God used evil men to accomplish His purpose, yet never violated their will or removed their culpability by doing so. Peter thus presents the total sovereignty of God alongside the complete responsibility of man. That apparently paradoxical truth is affirmed throughout Scripture and is illustrated in Luke 22:22. Speaking of His betrayer there, our Lord said, "The Son of Man is going as it has been determined; but woe to that man through whom He is betrayed!" Men are responsible not for God's plans but for their own sins.

The heinous sin of rejecting Jesus Christ was the blackest moment in Israel's history. Far from casting doubt on His messianic credentials, however, that betrayal was part of God's eternal plan. And though Peter does not develop the thought here, the Old Testament clearly teaches that Messiah had to die (cf. Ps. 22; Isa. 53). The death of Jesus Christ, no less than His life, confirmed that He was the Messiah.

THE RESURRECTION OF CHRIST

And God raised Him up again, putting an end to the agony of death, since it was impossible for Him to be held in its power. For David says of Him, "I was always beholding the Lord in my presence; for He is at my right hand, that I may not be shaken. Therefore my heart was glad and my tongue exulted; moreover my flesh also will abide in hope; because Thou wilt not abandon my soul to Hades, nor allow Thy Holy One to undergo decay. Thou hast made known to me the ways of life; Thou wilt make me full of gladness with Thy presence." Brethren, I may confidently say to you regarding the patriarch David that he both died and was buried, and his tomb is with us to this day. And so, because he was a prophet, and knew that God had sworn to him with an oath to seat one of his descendants upon his throne, he looked ahead and spoke of the resurrection of the Christ, that He was neither abandoned to Hades, nor did His flesh suffer decay. This Jesus God raised up again, to which we are all witnesses. (2:24–32)

As already noted, the resurrection of Jesus Christ was not only the central theme of apostolic preaching but also is without question the climax of redemptive history. It proves beyond doubt the deity of Jesus Christ and establishes His messianic credentials. It is also the guarantee of our own resurrection (John 14:19; Rom. 6:4–5; 1 Cor. 6:14; 15:16–23). The resurrection is the crowning proof that God accepted the sacrifice of Jesus Christ (cf. Rom. 4:25). Without it, His death becomes the heroic death of a noble martyr, the pathetic death of a madman, or the execution of a fraud.

The greatest proof that Jesus is the Messiah, then, is not His teaching, His miracles, or even His death. It is His resurrection. That becomes the main theme of Peter's sermon. After spending one verse each on Christ's life and death, he spends nine verses on His resurrection.

Verses 23 and 24 form one connected thought. Israel rejected and crucified her Messiah, but **God raised Him up again.** Peter forcefully drives home the point that they were guilty of opposing God—despite their boasts to the contrary (Rom. 2:17–20). That tactic was frequently employed in Acts (cf. 3:14–15; 10:39–40; 13:27–30).

By raising Jesus, God put **an end to the agony of death** for Him. **Agony** translates *ōdinas,* which literally means "birth pangs." Like the pain of a woman in labor, the pain of death for Jesus was temporary and resulted in something glorious—the resurrection.

God delivered Jesus from death **since it was impossible for Him to be held in its power.** Death was powerless to hold Him for several reasons. First, death could not hold Him because of divine power. Jesus was "the resurrection and the life" (John 11:25), who died "that through death He might render powerless him who had the power of death, that is, the devil" (Heb. 2:14). Second, death could not hold Him because of divine promise. John 2:18–22 records the following dialogue:

> The Jews therefore answered and said to Him, "What sign do You show to us, seeing that You do these things?" Jesus answered and said to them, "Destroy this temple, and in three days I will raise it up." The Jews therefore said, "It took forty-six years to build this temple, and will You raise it up in three days?" But He was speaking of the temple of His body. When therefore He was raised from the dead, His disciples remembered that He said this; and they believed the Scripture, and the word which Jesus had spoken.

"Thus it is written," our Lord told the disciples, "that the Christ should suffer and rise again from the dead the third day" (Luke 24:46). Finally, death could not hold Him because of divine purpose. God has designed that His people be with Him for all eternity. In order to do that, they need to go through death and out the other side. Jesus had to go first to make the way (cf. 1 Cor. 15:16–26). Because He lives, His people will live forever (John 14:19).

To further confirm that the resurrection was God's plan for the Messiah, Peter quotes a prophetic passage from Psalm 16:8–11. Although written by **David,** the passage is prophetically Messiah speaking in the first person (cf. Ps. 22). It describes Messiah's confident trust in God as He looked to the cross. His declaration **I was always beholding the Lord in my presence** is the key to that trust. Jesus kept His focus on God no matter what trials came His way. He knew that because God was at His **right hand,** He would **not be shaken.** The **right hand** symbolizes protection. In a wedding ceremony, the bridegroom stands to the right of the bride. In the ancient world, a bodyguard stood on the right side of the one he was protecting. In that position he could cover him with his shield and still have his right arm free to fight.

Because of His confidence in God's protection, Messiah could say **my heart was glad and my tongue exulted.** Even the prospect of the cross could not dampen Christ's joy. As the writer of Hebrews puts it, "Jesus . . . for the joy set before Him endured the cross" (Heb. 12:2). **Moreover,** another reason for Messiah's joy was His confidence that His **flesh also** would **abide in hope. Flesh** here refers to the physical body. *Kataskēnoō* (**abide**) literally means "to pitch a tent." It expresses Messiah's certainty that He could commit His body to the grave with the confident **hope** that it would be raised to life again.

The next statement from Psalm 16 gives the reason for Messiah's confidence: **because Thou wilt not abandon my soul to Hades. Hades** is the New Testament equivalent of the Old Testament term "Sheol." Although it can refer specifically to hell (Matt. 11:23), Peter uses it here in its more general sense of the abode of the dead. The phrase expresses Christ's confidence that He would not remain a captive in the realm of death. Nor would God **allow** His **Holy One** (a messianic title; cf. Mark 1:24; Luke 4:34; John 6:69) **to undergo decay.** During its three days in the tomb, our Lord's body experienced no corruption. The significance of this verse will be seen shortly.

Peter's quote of verse 11 of Psalm 16 has puzzled some commentators, since it doesn't appear to advance his argument. The phrase **the ways of life** (the Hebrew text of Psalm 16:11 uses the singular "path of life"), however, can be interpreted as a reference to the resurrection. It would thus have the sense of "the path to resurrection life." The context strongly implies such an interpretation. As a result of the resurrection, Messiah would be **full of gladness** as He experienced God's **presence.**

Peter now comes to the crux of his argument. Addressing them once again as **brethren,** he **confidently** reminds them that **the patriarch David both died and was buried.** In fact, his **tomb** provided visible evidence that he had not fulfilled the prophecy of Psalm 16. David spoke as a **prophet,** however, not of himself. He **knew that God had sworn to him with an oath to seat one of his descendants upon his throne.** That promise is recorded in 2 Samuel 7:11–16:

> The Lord also declares to you that the Lord will make a house for you. When your days are complete and you lie down with your fathers, I will raise up your descendant after you, who will come forth from you, and I will establish his kingdom. He shall build a house for My name, and I will establish the throne of his kingdom forever. I will be a father to him and he will be a son to Me; when he commits iniquity, I will correct him with the rod of men and the strokes of the sons of men, but My lovingkindness shall not depart from him, as I took it away from Saul, whom I removed from before you. And your house and your kingdom shall endure before Me forever; your throne shall be established forever.

David, then, **looked ahead and spoke of the resurrection of the Christ,** who, in contrast to David, **was neither abandoned to Hades, nor did His flesh suffer decay.**

Peter's argument from Psalm 16 can be summarized as follows: The psalm speaks of a resurrection. Since David, however, was not resurrected, it cannot speak of him. Thus, David speaks in the psalm of the Messiah. Hence, Messiah will rise from the dead. Peter now delivers his powerful conclusion: **This Jesus God raised up again, to which we are all witnesses.** The argument is conclusive: Jesus of Nazareth is the Messiah.

THE EXALTATION OF CHRIST

Therefore having been exalted to the right hand of God, and having received from the Father the promise of the Holy Spirit, He has poured forth this which you both see and hear. For it was not David who ascended into heaven, but he himself says: "The Lord said to my Lord, sit at My right hand, until I make Thine enemies a footstool for Thy feet." Therefore let all the house of Israel know for certain that God has made Him both Lord and Christ— this Jesus whom you crucified. (2:33-36)

Not only did Jesus rise from the dead, but he also was **exalted** to the place of honor, glory, and power (cf. Phil. 2:9–11) at the **right hand of God** (cf. Mark 16:19; Luke 22:69; Acts 5:31; 7:55–56; Rom. 8:34; Col. 3:1; Heb. 10:12; 12:2; 1 Peter 3:22). From that exalted position, Peter says, Jesus, **having received from the Father the promise of the Holy Spirit, has poured forth this which you both see and hear.** Peter now brings his listeners full circle back to the phenomena of Pentecost. He tells them that what they had just seen resulted from God's promise to send the Spirit to inaugurate the messianic age (Joel 2:28–29). Now that Christ was risen and glorified, God fulfilled that promise (cf. John 7:39).

Peter then quotes from another Davidic psalm, Psalm 110, to prove from His ascension and exaltation that Jesus Christ is the Messiah. Once again, the psalm could not be referring to David, since **it was not David who ascended into heaven.** In fact, David **himself says** in that psalm, **"The Lord said to my Lord, sit at My right hand, until I make Thine enemies a footstool for Thy feet."** Placing one's enemies under one's feet was a figure of speech denoting their abject submission (cf. Josh. 10:24–25). David was not exalted to God's right hand, but Jesus was (Acts 1:9–11). The proof of that was the outpouring of the Spirit that the crowd had just witnessed.

Peter has provided overwhelming evidence from Jesus' life, death, resurrection, and exaltation that He is indeed Israel's long-awaited Messiah. He now draws his sermon to a powerful conclusion with these ringing words: **Therefore let all the house of Israel know for certain that God has made Him both Lord and Christ—this Jesus whom you crucified.** *Asphalōs* (**for certain**) speaks of that which is known beyond a doubt. The same Jesus whom God attested as Messiah through His life, death, resurrection, and exaltation was the same **Jesus whom** they had **crucified.** The verdict was in, and they were on the wrong side, guilty of opposing God and rejecting their Messiah. As Peter was later to put it, "He is the stone which was rejected by you, the builders, but which became the very corner stone" (Acts 4:11).

The First Christian Sermon—part 3 The Appeal and Results

6

Now when they heard this, they were pierced to the heart, and said to Peter and the rest of the apostles, "Brethren, what shall we do?" And Peter said to them, "Repent, and let each of you be baptized in the name of Jesus Christ for the forgiveness of your sins; and you shall receive the gift of the Holy Spirit. For the promise is for you and your children, and for all who are far off, as many as the Lord our God shall call to Himself." And with many other words he solemnly testified and kept on exhorting them, saying, "Be saved from this perverse generation!" So then, those who had received his word were baptized; and there were added that day about three thousand souls. (2:37–41)

The most momentous question anyone can ask is the question, "What must I do to be saved?" A wrong answer to that question, no matter how correct a person's beliefs may be in other areas, is the path to eternal tragedy.

Knowing how vitally important a correct answer is to this question, Satan has made his greatest efforts to confuse the issue. The result has been a plethora of wrong answers. Although ostensibly based on the Bible, each is in fact a perversion of biblical truth.

The legalist, for example, argues that salvation comes through a works-righteousness system. He may cite James 2:21 as a proof text: "Was not Abraham our father justified by works, when he offered up Isaac his son on the altar?" Such a misuse of that verse ignores the context in which it appears (James 2:14-26). It also is directly contradicted by the apostle Paul's words in Romans 4:2-3: "For if Abraham was justified by works, he has something to boast about; but not before God. For what does the Scripture say? 'And Abraham believed God, and it was reckoned to him as righteousness'" (cf. Gal. 3:6-9). And Paul emphatically rejects any idea of salvation through keeping the law in Romans 3:20, "By the works of the Law no flesh will be justified in His sight."

The moralist takes a slightly different tack. He believes that as long as his good deeds outweigh his bad ones in God's scales he will be all right for eternity. As proof, he may cite John 5:28-29, "An hour is coming, in which all who are in the tombs shall hear His voice, and shall come forth; those who did the good deeds to a resurrection of life, those who committed the evil deeds to a resurrection of judgment." That verse, however, merely states that a redeemed life will be characterized by good works, an unredeemed one by their absence. Further, the moralist will carefully avoid any discussion of such passages as Ephesians 2:8-9 ("For by grace you have been saved through faith; and that not of yourselves, it is the gift of God; not as a result of works, that no one should boast"), Romans 3:12 ("There is none righteous, not even one"), and Romans 3:23 ("All have sinned and fall short of the glory of God").

Some of Peter's Jewish listeners would have argued for salvation based on racial heritage. To such people, John the Baptist gave the following warning: "Do not suppose that you can say to yourselves, 'We have Abraham for our father'; for I say to you, that God is able from these stones to raise up children to Abraham. And the axe is already laid at the root of the trees; every tree therefore that does not bear good fruit is cut down and thrown into the fire" (Matt. 3:9-10). The truth is that "they are not all Israel who are descended from Israel" (Rom. 9:6).

The universalist rests his false hopes on a misinterpretation of passages such as Romans 5:18, "So then as through one transgression there resulted condemnation to all men, even so through one act of righteousness there resulted justification of life to all men." He ignores our Lord's solemn warning to "enter by the narrow gate; for the gate is wide, and the way is broad that leads to destruction, and many are those who enter by it" (Matt. 7:13).

The ritualist also appeals to Scripture to validate his notion that salvation comes through observing rituals. Verse 38 of the present passage is often cited in support of the ritualist viewpoint: "Repent, and let each of you be baptized in the name of Jesus Christ for the forgiveness of your sins." Ritualists ignore the biblical truth that salvation comes not through rituals but through faith in Jesus Christ. They fail to understand that "with the heart man believes, resulting in righteousness, and with the mouth he confesses, resulting in salvation" (Rom. 10:10).

Sadly, all of those aberrant views have legions of followers in our day. That shows that any position can be proven from the Bible by misinterpreting or taking passages out of context and failing to compare Scripture with Scripture.

Unlike the purveyors of false teaching, Peter gives the correct answer to the question of how to be saved. He wraps up his sermon with an appeal to his listeners. The passage then concludes by giving the results of Peter's sermon.

The Appeal

Now when they heard this, they were pierced to the heart, and said to Peter and the rest of the apostles, "Brethren, what shall we do?" And Peter said to them, "Repent, and let each of you be baptized in the name of Jesus Christ for the forgiveness of your sins; and you shall receive the gift of the Holy Spirit. For the promise is for you and your children, and for all who are far off, as many as the Lord our God shall call to Himself." And with many other words he solemnly testified and kept on exhorting them, saying, "Be saved from this perverse generation!" (2:37–40)

Peter's conclusion to the main body of his sermon was devastating. He charged his listeners with rejecting and executing their Messiah—the very One whom God had made both Lord and Christ (v. 36). **When they heard this**—Peter's statement in verse 36—**they were pierced to the heart.** *Katanussō* (**pierced**) appears only here in the New Testament. It means "to pierce," or "to stab," and thus depicts something sudden and unexpected. Stunned by their inability to evade the indictment that they were guilty of heinous behavior before God, they were overcome by grief and remorse.

There were several reasons for their anguish. First, as already noted, was the realization that they had executed their Messiah. The One for whom they had longed for centuries, the One who was the hope of all their personal and national promises, had finally come. Instead of welcoming Him, however, they rejected Him and handed Him over to their bitter and hated enemies, the Romans, for execution.

Second, they themselves had done it. It would have been bad enough to learn that Messiah had been killed. Far worse was the knowledge of their own complicity in the crime. That no doubt produced in them a deep sense of guilt. They could not imagine a greater sin than killing their Messiah.

A third cause for their anguish was fear of Messiah's wrath. Peter had announced to them in no uncertain terms that the same Jesus they had crucified was now alive (vv. 24, 31, 32). Worse still, he had quoted to them a passage from Psalm 110 that spoke of the vanquishing of Messiah's enemies. What greater enemies of God existed than those who killed His Messiah?

Finally, they were devastated by the understanding that what they had done could not be undone.

Overwhelmed with anguish, despair, remorse, and guilt, they **said to Peter and the rest of the apostles, "Brethren, what shall we do?"** They sought desperately for a way to make right what they had done, and avoid Messiah's wrath. They were at the same point Paul was when he cried out on the Damascus road, "What shall I do, Lord?" (Acts 22:10). Their words are reminiscent of those of the Philippian jailer, who asked Paul and Silas, "Sirs, what must I do to be saved?" (Acts 16:30). Their state of mind illustrates perfectly that of the convicted sinner. They had a deep sense of their own guilt, and a panicky fear of God's wrath. They had a strong desire to be saved from that wrath, and a willingness to submit to God's will. Such conviction of sin is a part of every genuine conversion.

The book of Zechariah illustrates that truth. Zechariah 12:10 describes the first step in the restoration of Israel—conviction of sin: "And I will pour out on the house of David and on the inhabitants of Jerusalem, the Spirit of grace and of supplication, so that they will look on Me whom they have pierced; and they will mourn for Him, as one mourns for an only son, and they will weep bitterly over Him, like the bitter weeping over a first-born." Only after that conviction does the cleansing of sin described in Zechariah 13:1 take place: "In that day a fountain will be opened for the house of David and for the inhabitants of Jerusalem, for sin and for impurity." Conviction is the key used by the Holy Spirit to open the heart to salvation.

An indictment for sin is an essential part of any gospel presentation. People need to be convicted of sin before they will see the need for a savior. No matter how morally upright they may be, all unbelievers are guilty of the vile sins of rebellion against God (cf. Acts 17:30) and rejection of Jesus Christ (John 16:8–9). Genuine conviction is produced by the Spirit of God, in conjunction with the Word of God, which is "living and active and sharper than any two-edged sword, and piercing as far as the division of soul and spirit, of both joints and marrow, and able to judge the thoughts and intentions of the heart" (Heb. 4:12).

The Holy Spirit, through Peter's powerful preaching, had brought them to the point of desperation. Peter now answers their question with the only correct answer: **repent.** *Metanoeō* (**repent**) is a rich New Testament term. It speaks of a change of purpose, of turning from sin to God (1 Thess. 1:9). It is an essential component of a genuine conversion. Both John the Baptist (Matt. 3:2) and the Lord Jesus Christ (Matt. 4:17) called for repentance. It is an oft-repeated theme in Acts (3:19; 5:31; 8:22; 11:18; 17:30; 20:21; 26:20).

Although Peter's hearers feared God's judgment, true repentance involves more than fear of consequences. Commentator Albert Barnes rightly notes that "false repentance dreads the *consequences* of sin; true repentance dreads *sin itself*" (*Barnes' Notes on the New Testament: Acts-Romans* [1884–85; reprint, Grand Rapids: Baker, n.d.], 52. Emphasis in original). True repentance hates sin for what it is—an affront to God. Knowing that sin is evil and that God hates it motivates the truly repentant person to forsake it. Genuine repentance thus forsakes sin and turns in total commitment to Jesus Christ. (For a discussion of repentance, see my books *The Gospel According to Jesus*, rev. ed. [Grand Rapids: Zondervan, 1994], and *Faith Works* [Dallas: Word, 1993].)

It is difficult for modern readers to grasp the magnitude of the change facing Peter's Jewish hearers. They were part of a unique community, with a rich cultural and religious history. Despite long years of subjugation to Rome, they were fiercely nationalistic. The nation had rejected Jesus as a blasphemer and executed Him. Now Peter calls on them to turn their back on all that and embrace Jesus as their Messiah.

By calling on **each** of them to **be baptized in the name of Jesus Christ** Peter does not allow for any "secret disciples" (cf. Matt. 10:32–33). Baptism would mark a public break with Judaism and identification with Jesus Christ. Such a drastic public act would help weed out any conversions which were not genuine. In sharp contrast to many modern gospel presentations, Peter made accepting Christ difficult, not easy. By so doing, he followed the example of our Lord Himself (Luke 14:26–33; 18:18–27). Baptism was always **in the name of Jesus Christ.** That was the crucial identification, and the cost was high for such a confession.

The meaning of Peter's statement that baptism is **for the forgiveness of sins** has been much disputed. Those who teach baptismal regeneration—the false teaching that baptism is necessary for salvation—see this verse as a primary proof text for their view.

That view ignores the immediate context of the passage. As already noted, baptism would be a dramatic step for Peter's hearers. By publicly identifying themselves as followers of Jesus of Nazareth, they risked becoming outcasts in their society (cf. John 9:22). Peter calls upon them to prove the genuineness of their repentance by submitting to public baptism. In much the same way, our Lord called upon the rich young ruler to prove the genuineness of his repentance by parting with his wealth (Luke 18:18–27). Surely, however, no one would argue from the latter passage that giving away one's possessions is necessary for salvation. Salvation is not a matter of either water or economics. True repentance, however, will inevitably manifest itself in total submission to the Lord's will.

Second, such teaching violates the important hermeneutical principle known as *analogia Scriptura* (the analogy of Scripture). That principle states that no passage, when correctly interpreted, will teach something contradictory to the rest of Scripture. And the rest of Scripture unmistakably teaches that salvation is solely by faith (cf. John 1:12; 3:16; Acts 16:31; Rom. 3:21–30; 4:5; 10:9–10; Phil. 3:9; Gal. 2:16).

Third, after condemning the ritualistic religion of the scribes and Pharisees, our Lord would hardly have instituted one of His own. F. F. Bruce remarks, "It is against the whole genius of Biblical religion to suppose that the outward rite [of baptism] had any value except in so far as it was accompanied by true repentance within" (*The Book of the Acts* [Grand Rapids: Eerdmans, 1971], 77).

Fourth, this interpretation is not true to the facts of Scripture. Throughout the book of Acts, forgiveness is linked to repentance, not baptism (cf. 3:19; 5:31; 26:20). In addition, the Bible records that some who were baptized were not saved (Acts 8:13; 21–23), while some were saved with no mention of their being baptized (Luke 7:37–50; Matt. 9:2; Luke 18:13–14). The story of the conversion of Cornelius and his friends very clearly shows the relationship of baptism to salvation. It was only after they were saved, as shown by their receiving the Holy Spirit (Acts 10:44–46), that they were baptized (vv. 47–48). Indeed, it was because they had received the Spirit (and hence were saved) that Peter ordered them to be baptized (v. 47). That passage clearly shows that baptism follows salvation; it does not cause it.

In 1 Corinthians 15:1–4, the apostle Paul summarizes the gospel he preached and by which the Corinthians had been saved. There is no mention of baptism. Further, in 1 Corinthians 1:14–16, Paul rejoiced that he had baptized none of the Corinthians except Crispus, Gaius, and the household of Stephanas. That statement is inexplicable if baptism is necessary for salvation. Paul would then in effect be saying he was thankful that only those few were saved under his ministry. The apostle clearly distinguishes baptism from the gospel in 1 Corinthians 1:17, where he says that "Christ did not send me to baptize, but to preach the gospel." How could Paul have made such a statement if baptism was necessary for salvation?

While the preposition *eis* (**for**) can mean "for the purpose of," it can also mean "because of," or "on the occasion of" (A. T. Robertson,

Word Pictures in the New Testament [Grand Rapids: Baker, reprint of the 1930 edition], 3:35–36; H. E. Dana and J. R. Mantey, *A Manual Grammar of the Greek New Testament* [Toronto: Macmillan, 1957], 104). The latter is clearly its meaning in Matthew 12:41, which says that the people of Nineveh repented because of the preaching of Jonah.

The order is clear. Repentance is for forgiveness. Baptism follows that forgiveness; it does not cause it (cf. 8:12, 34–39; 10:34–48; 16:31–33). It is the public sign or symbol of what has taken place on the inside. It is an important step of obedience for all believers, and should closely follow conversion. In fact, in the early church it was inseparable from salvation, so that Paul referred to salvation as being related to "one Lord, one faith, one baptism" (Eph. 4:5).

Complete **forgiveness of sins** is the blessed joy and privilege of every believer. That glorious truth fills the pages of the New Testament. In Matthew 26:28, our Lord said, "This is My blood of the covenant, which is poured out for many for forgiveness of sins." In Luke 24:47, He reminded the disciples that "repentance for forgiveness of sins should be proclaimed in His name to all the nations, beginning from Jerusalem." Therefore, "in Him we have redemption through His blood, the forgiveness of our trespasses, according to the riches of His grace" (Eph. 1:7). Paul wrote to the Colossians that "when you were dead in your transgressions and the uncircumcision of your flesh, He made you alive together with Him, having forgiven us all our transgressions" (Col. 2:13). The apostle John says simply, "Little children, your sins are forgiven you for His name's sake" (1 John 2:12. See also Acts 5:31; 10:43; 13:38; 26:18; Rom. 4:7; Eph. 4:32; Col. 1:14; 1 John 1:9.)

Salvation would not only bring them forgiveness, but they would also **receive the gift of the Holy Spirit.** For this they had been waiting; the gift of the Spirit, according to Joel 2:28–29, would mark the beginning of messianic times.

Dōrea (**gift**) refers to that which is free and unmerited. Contrary to much contemporary teaching, Peter attached no condition to receiving the Spirit except repentance. Nor did he promise that any supernatural phenomena would accompany their reception of the Spirit. It should be noted as well that the gift of the Spirit does not come through water baptism (Acts 10:47).

The marvelous gift of the Holy Spirit was not merely for those in Peter's audience that day. **The promise** of the Holy Spirit, Peter informs them, **is for you and your children, and for all who are far off.** They and their children, the nation of Israel, would receive the Spirit, as the Old Testament promised (Isa. 44:3; Ezek. 36:27; 37:14; Joel 2:28–29). They would share that blessing, however, with those **who are far off**—the Gentiles (cf. Eph. 2:11–13).

Peter's description of those who would receive the Spirit as those whom **the Lord our God shall call to Himself** describes God's sovereignty at work in salvation. It presents the necessary balance to his statement in verse 21 that "everyone who calls on the name of the Lord shall be saved." A biblical view of salvation does not exclude either human responsibility or divine sovereignty, but allows them to remain in tension. We must resist the attempt to harmonize what Scripture does not, content in the knowledge that there is no ultimate contradiction in God's mind.

Luke adds that **with many other words** Peter **solemnly testified and kept on exhorting them, saying, "Be saved from this perverse generation!"** Luke has given us only a synopsis of Peter's sermon, which obviously lasted far longer than the few minutes it takes to read this passage. It is likely as well that Peter engaged in a dialogue with the crowd following his sermon, as the statement **kept on exhorting** indicates. The gist of his exhortation was that they should **be saved from this perverse generation** through repentance and faith in Christ. **Perverse** translates *skolios,* which means "bent," or "crooked," and hence evil and unrighteous.

Peter's condemnation echoed that of our Lord. In Matthew 12:39 and 16:4, He described them as an "evil and adulterous generation." In Matthew 12:45 He referred to them as "this evil generation," while in Luke 11:29 He commented that "this generation is a wicked generation." In Mark 9:19 He condemned them as an "unbelieving generation," while Matthew 17:17 and Luke 9:41 add the word "perverted" to "unbelieving." Finally, in Mark 8:38, Jesus denounced them as an "adulterous and sinful generation."

Many thousands from that generation were to perish during the Jewish revolt, culminating in the destruction of Jerusalem in A.D. 70. Peter's appeal for immediate response was timely.

THE RESULTS

So then, those who had received his word were baptized; and there were added that day about three thousand souls. (2:41)

As already noted, much present day evangelism seeks to make coming to Christ as easy as possible. Many today would be appalled that Peter made the cost of coming to Christ so high. How could he expect them to turn their backs publicly on their culture? How could he ask them to risk becoming outcasts among their families and society? How could he demand that they accept as Messiah the very One their leaders had rejected and executed? They would no doubt predict that the results of Peter's sermon would be minimal.

Such was not the case, however. **Those who had received his word** accepted the conditions and **were baptized.** Further, they amounted to more than an insignificant handful; **there were added** to the church **that day about three thousand souls.** That a precise number was recorded suggests that they kept track of those who were saved and baptized.

The First Christian Fellowship

7

And they were continually devoting themselves to the apostles' teaching and to fellowship, to the breaking of bread and to prayer. And everyone kept feeling a sense of awe; and many wonders and signs were taking place through the apostles. And all those who had believed were together, and had all things in common; and they began selling their property and possessions, and were sharing them with all, as anyone might have need. And day by day continuing with one mind in the temple, and breaking bread from house to house, they were taking their meals together with gladness and sincerity of heart, praising God, and having favor with all the people. And the Lord was adding to their number day by day those who were being saved. (2:42–47)

The epistles of the New Testament shape the doctrine for the life of the church. Acts traces the application of that doctrine in the history of the early church. This passage describes the historical outworking of God's ideal in the first local church. It describes the new-born church in its prime, when it possessed a purity of devotion to the risen Lord unmatched in succeeding generations.

In this brief cameo of life in the early church, three distinguishing dimensions emerge that reveal this to be a remarkable assembly. They manifested spiritual duties and spiritual attitudes, and the result was spiritual impact.

SPIRITUAL DUTIES

And they were continually devoting themselves to the apostles' teaching and to fellowship, to the breaking of bread and to prayer. (2:42)

This was really a church, nothing more and nothing less. Its life was completely defined by the devotion to those spiritual duties which make up the unique identity of the church. Nothing outside the living Lord, the Spirit, and the Word define life for the church. This church, though not having any cultural elements of success, no worldly strategies, was still endowed with every necessary component for accomplishing the purposes of its Lord. The church will still be effective in bringing sinners to Christ when it manifests the same key elements of spiritual duty that marked this first fellowship.

IT WAS A SAVED CHURCH

they were continually devoting themselves (2:42a)

The three thousand who confessed faith in Christ and were baptized in verse 41 are the **they** who showed the genuineness of their faith by continuing. Despite the hate, ridicule, and persecution they suffered, they remained faithful. That is a mark of genuine salvation. Jesus said in John 8:31, "If you abide in My word, then you are truly disciples of Mine." The true branch will abide in the vine (John 15:1–4). The good seed will not wither and die under persecution (Matt. 13:3–9, 21). In contrast, the apostle John writes of false believers, "They went out from us, but they were not really of us; for if they had been of us, they would have remained with us; but they went out, in order that it might be shown that they all are not of us" (1 John 2:19).

That the church should be composed of saved individuals seems axiomatic. Sadly, however, many churches today are made up largely of unsaved individuals. Amazingly, some even try to design a church where non-Christians can feel comfortable. This can't be the goal in a church that is devoted to holiness and righteousness in all areas of life. Such a church will be unpopular with sinners. In this first fellowship, all the professors were possessors.

That is not to say that unbelievers are not welcome to attend the preaching of the truth and the worship. They are welcome to hear the gospel preached and the Word of God expounded. They are welcome to hear the prayers of confession, the anthems of praise, and the calls to holiness. They are welcome to witness the corporate love and devotion of the church to Jesus Christ and the eternal God. All of that should make them uncomfortable with their spiritual condition. Membership and service in the church, however, are restricted to believers. God's people and Satan's people cannot work together to achieve God's goals. "Do not be bound together with unbelievers," Paul warned the Corinthians, "for what partnership have righteousness and lawlessness, or what fellowship has light with darkness? Or what harmony has Christ with Belial, or what has a believer in common with an unbeliever?" (2 Cor. 6:14–15).

Paul commended the Thessalonians in terms that leave no doubt that they were saved:

> Paul and Silvanus and Timothy to the church of the Thessalonians in God the Father and the Lord Jesus Christ: Grace to you and peace. We give thanks to God always for all of you, making mention of you in our prayers; constantly bearing in mind your work of faith and labor of love and steadfastness of hope in our Lord Jesus Christ in the presence of our God and Father, knowing, brethren beloved by God, His choice of you; for our gospel did not come to you in word only, but also in power and in the Holy Spirit and with full conviction; just as you know what kind of men we proved to be among you for your sake. You also became imitators of us and of the Lord, having received the word in much tribulation with the joy of the Holy Spirit, so that you became an example to all the believers in Macedonia and in Achaia. For the word of the Lord has sounded forth from you, not only in Macedonia and Achaia, but also in every place your faith toward God has gone forth, so that we have no need to say anything. For they themselves report about us what kind of a reception we had with you, and how you turned to God from idols to serve a living and true God, and to wait for His Son from heaven, whom He raised from the dead, that is Jesus, who delivers us from the wrath to come. (1 Thess. 1:1–10)

In that passage, Paul described the people in the Thessalonian church as in the Father, Christ (v. 1), and the Holy Spirit (v. 5). He noted that they possessed the great triad of Christian virtues, faith, hope, and love (v. 3). He was confident of God's choice of them for salvation (v. 4). They were imitators of Paul and Christ (v. 6), so much so that they were an example to the other believers in their region (vv. 7–9). Clearly it was a congregation of saved people.

Conversely, the Lord Jesus Christ rebuked the church at Pergamum for allowing itself to be infiltrated by unbelievers, thus being influenced by Satan:

> But I have a few things against you, because you have there some who hold the teaching of Balaam, who kept teaching Balak to put a stumbling block before the sons of Israel, to eat things sacrificed to idols, and to commit acts of immorality. Thus you also have some who in the same way hold the teaching of the Nicolaitans. Repent therefore; or else I am coming to you quickly, and I will make war against them with the sword of My mouth. (Rev. 2:14–16)

They had those who compromised with the world, as Balaam and Balak caused Israel to intermingle with Moab. The error of the Nicolaitans apparently involved sexual immorality. Christ's stern rebuke of them shows His concern for the purity of the church.

To fail to exclude unbelievers from the fellowship of the church is a grave error. Only disunity and dissension can result when those who serve Christ try to work in harmony with those who serve Satan. Additionally, to design the activities of the church to appeal to unbelievers, or to allow them to play a major role in the life of the church, is to give them a false sense of security. The result for them may be eternal tragedy. The church must reach out in love to those who do not know Christ. It must never, however, let them feel that they are a part of the fellowship until they come to faith in Christ. And no evangelistic purpose should ever be undertaken that alters what the church is by divine design—an assembly of saved worshipers pursuing holiness and spiritual service.

The first fellowship passed the initial test of spiritual duty; it encompassed only those who knew and loved Jesus Christ. Luke later points out that while many were drawn by the Lord to salvation, unbelievers were actually afraid to go near the church in Jerusalem because sin was being dealt with so severely (Acts 5:13–14).

IT WAS A SCRIPTURAL CHURCH

to the apostles' teaching (2:42b)

The content for the church is clearly to be revealed truth. God designed the church to be a place where His Word is proclaimed and explained. Paul mandates such a priority all through the Pastoral Epistles, where he described the ongoing process to Timothy when he wrote, "The things which you have heard from me in the presence of many witnesses, these entrust to faithful men, who will be able to teach others also" (2 Tim. 2:2).

A commitment to **the apostles' teaching** is foundational to the growth and spiritual health of every church. Peter wrote, "Like newborn babes, long for the pure milk of the word, that by it you may grow in respect to salvation" (1 Peter 2:2). To the Romans Paul wrote, "Do not be conformed to this world, but be transformed by the renewing of your mind, that you may prove what the will of God is, that which is good and acceptable and perfect" (Rom. 12:2).

Paul's letters to his protégés Timothy and Titus also reflect the priority of preaching the Word. "In pointing out these things to the brethren, you will be a good servant of Christ Jesus, constantly nourished on the words of the faith and of the sound doctrine which you have been following" (1 Tim. 4:6). "Prescribe and teach these things" (1 Tim. 4:11). "Until I come, give attention to the public reading of Scripture, to exhortation and teaching" (1 Tim. 4:13). "Pay close attention to yourself and to your teaching; persevere in these things; for as you do this you will insure salvation both for yourself and for those who hear you" (1 Tim. 4:16). "I solemnly charge you in the presence of God and of Christ Jesus, who is to judge the living and the dead, and by His appearing and His kingdom: preach the word; be ready in season and out of season; reprove, rebuke, exhort, with great patience and instruction" (2 Tim. 4:1–2). An elder must be one who holds "fast the faithful word which is in accordance with the teaching, that he may be able both to exhort in sound doctrine and to refute those who contradict" (Titus 1:9).

A believer should count it a wasted day when he does not learn something new from, or is not more deeply enriched, by the truth of God's Word. The early church sat under the teaching ministry of the apostles, whose **teaching,** now written on the pages of the New Testament Scriptures, is to be taught by all pastors.

Scripture is food for the believer's growth and power—and there is no other. The church today ignores the exposition and application of Scripture at its peril, as the warning of Hosea to Israel suggests: "My people are destroyed for lack of knowledge" (Hos. 4:6). The church cannot operate on truth it is not taught; believers cannot function on principles they have not learned. The most noble are still those who search the Scriptures daily (cf. Acts 17:11). They contain **the apostles' teaching.**

IT WAS A FELLOWSHIPPING CHURCH

and to fellowship (2:42c)

Fellowship is the spiritual duty of believers to stimulate each other to holiness and faithfulness. It is most specifically expressed through the "one anothers" of the New Testament (cf. Rom. 12:10, 16; 13:8; 14:19; 15:5, 7, 14; 16:16; Gal. 5:13; Eph. 4:2, 25, 32; 5:21; Phil. 2:3; Col. 3:9, 13, 16; 1 Thess. 4:9, 18, 5:11, 13; Heb. 3:13; 1 Peter 1:22; 4:9, 10; 5:5, etc.). The basic meaning of *koinōnia* (**fellowship**) is "partner-ship," or "sharing." Those who receive Jesus Christ become partners with Him and with all other believers (1 John 1:3). That fellowship is permanent, because our shared eternal life is forever. The joy associated with it, however, may be lost through sinful neglect of its duties.

For a Christian to fail to participate in the life of a local church is inexcusable. In fact, those who choose to isolate themselves are disobedient to the direct command of Scripture. Hebrews 10:24–25 charges believers to "consider how to stimulate one another to love and good deeds, not forsaking our own assembling together, as is the habit of some, but encouraging one another; and all the more, as you see the day drawing near." The Bible does not envision the Christian life as one lived apart from other believers. All members of the universal church, the body of Christ, are to be actively and intimately involved in local assemblies.

IT WAS A CHRIST-CENTERED CHURCH

to the breaking of bread (2:42d)

Their fellowship was symbolized by obedience to the spiritual duty of **the breaking of bread,** a reference to the celebration of the Lord's Supper, or Communion. This duty is not optional, since our Lord commanded it of every believer (cf. 1 Cor. 11:24–29). In Communion, all believers meet on common ground at the foot of the cross (Eph. 2:16; Col. 1:20), since all are sinners saved by the grace of God in Christ. Communion acknowledges the wondrous work of the Lord Jesus on the cross. Communion further exemplifies the unity of believers, since in it all partake together symbolically of the same Lord (Eph. 4:5). Paul wrote in 1 Corinthians 10:16–17, "Is not the cup of blessing which we bless a sharing in the blood of Christ? Is not the bread which we break a sharing in the body of Christ? Since there is one bread, we who are many are one body; for we all partake of the one bread."

Communion calls for self-examination and purging of sin, thus purifying the church. Nothing is more vital to the church's ongoing, regular confrontation of sins in the lives of its people than the thoughtful expression of devotion to the remembrance of the cross. (For an indepth discussion of the Lord's Table, see *1 Corinthians,* MacArthur New Testament Commentary [Chicago: Moody, 1984], 265ff.)

IT WAS A PRAYING CHURCH

to prayer (2:42e)

The first fellowship was eagerly and persistently engaged in the critical duty of prayer. Prayer is the slender nerve that moves the muscles of omnipotence. Understanding the sense of loss His disciples were feeling as they anticipated His leaving, the Lord Jesus Christ had promised in John 14:13–14 that "whatever you ask in My name, that will I do, that the Father may be glorified in the Son. If you ask Me anything in My name, I will do it." The early church took that promise as the source of God's provision for all their needs, and they relentlessly pursued divine help. The **prayer** in view here is not only that of individual believers but of the church corporately (cf. 1:14, 24; 4:24–31).

Sadly, prayer is much neglected in the church today. Programs, concerts, entertainment, or the testimonies of the rich and famous draw large crowds. Prayer meetings, on the other hand, attract only the faithful few. That is undoubtedly the reason for much of the weakness in the contemporary church. Unlike the early church, we have forgotten the Bible's commands to pray at all times (Luke 18:1; Eph. 6:11), and to be devoted to prayer (Rom. 12:12; Col. 4:2).

The first fellowship knew the critical importance of pursuing spiritual duties. They knew the church must be made up of saved individuals, devoted to studying the Word, fellowship, breaking of bread, and prayer. Those elements are the unique expressions of the life of the church. They are the means of grace by which the church becomes what God wants it to be.

SPIRITUAL CHARACTER

And everyone kept feeling a sense of awe; and many wonders and signs were taking place through the apostles. And all those who had believed were together, and had all things in common; and they began selling their property and possessions, and were

sharing them with all, as anyone might have need. And day by day continuing with one mind in the temple, and breaking bread from house to house, they were taking their meals together with gladness and sincerity of heart, praising God (2:43–47a)

A church that fulfills the spiritual duties will find that those duties produce spiritual character. Four aspects of the first fellowship's character may be discerned in this passage.

IT WAS AN AWE-INSPIRING CHURCH

And everyone kept feeling a sense of awe (2:43a)

Phobos (**awe**) refers to fear or holy terror related to the sense of divine presence, to the attitude of reverence. It describes the feeling produced when one realizes God is at hand. It is used in Acts 5:5 and 11 to describe the reaction to the deaths of Ananias and Sapphira. In Acts 19:17 it depicts the reaction of the citizens of Ephesus to the attack on some Jewish exorcists by a demon-possessed man. Luke 7:16 uses it to portray the reaction to our Lord's raising of the widow's son. The life of this first fellowship was so genuine and spiritually powerful that **everyone,** whether inside or outside the church, **kept feeling a sense of awe.** They weren't awed by the church because of its buildings, programs, or anything reflecting human ability, but by the supernatural character of its life. Such an effect should be produced when the spiritual gifts are properly operative (1 Cor. 14:24, 25).

IT WAS A MIRACULOUS CHURCH

and many wonders and signs were taking place through the apostles. (2:43b)

One reason for the awe the first fellowship inspired was the **many wonders and signs** performed by the **apostles** (cf. Mark 16:20; Heb. 2:4). Some of those miracles are described in the succeeding chapters (cf. 3:1–10; 5:12, 15–16; 9:32–35, 40–42). As noted in the discussion of Acts 2:22 in chapter 5, **wonders and signs** were designed to attract attention and point to spiritual truth. The response to Peter's healing of the paralyzed man in Lydda (Acts 9:32–34) shows that purpose clearly. The people of that region, after witnessing the healing, "turned to the Lord" (Acts 9:35). Peter's raising of Dorcas elicited the same response in Joppa (Acts 9:42).

Our Lord did His miracles for the same reason. In John 14:10–12 He said,

> Do you not believe that I am in the Father, and the Father is in Me? The words that I say to you I do not speak on My own initiative, but the Father abiding in Me does His works. Believe Me that I am in the Father, and the Father in Me; otherwise believe on account of the works themselves. Truly, truly, I say to you, he who believes in Me, the works that I do shall he do also; and greater works than these shall he do; because I go to the Father.

The ability to perform miracles was not given to all, but was limited to the apostles and their close associates (such as Philip; cf. Acts 8:13). The writer of Hebrews said,

> How shall we escape if we neglect so great a salvation? After it was at the first spoken through the Lord, it was confirmed to us by those who heard, God also bearing witness with them, both by signs and wonders and by various miracles and by gifts of the Holy Spirit according to His own will. (Heb. 2:3–4; cf. 2 Cor. 12:12)

God attended the preaching of the apostles with miracles to confirm that they were indeed His messengers. With the passing of the apostolic age, and the completion of the canon of Scripture, the need for such confirmatory signs ended. Today we can determine who speaks for God by comparing their teaching with God's revelation in Scripture.

Although the sign gift of miracles is no longer extant, God still performs miracles in response to the prayers of His people. They are not, however, public signs like those in the apostolic era. The greatest of all miracles God performs today is the transformation of rebellious sinners into His beloved children, who are becoming like His Son. Such miracles occur in the life of the church that is committed to the fulfillment of its spiritual duties.

IT WAS A SHARING CHURCH

And all those who had believed were together, and had all things in common; and they began selling their property and possessions, and were sharing them with all, as anyone might have need. And day by day continuing with one mind in the temple, and breaking bread from house to house, they were taking their meals together (2:44–46a)

In these early days, before strife and divisions affected the church, **all those who had believed were together.** They possessed not only a spiritual unity but also a practical oneness. That they **had all things in common** does not, as some imagine, indicate communal living. The first Christian fellowship was not a commune, nor does the passage offer support for such a notion. The family, not the commune, is the basic social unit in God's design.

Such sharing and mutual meeting of the needs of pilgrims was a long-standing tradition in Israel during the great religious feasts. The inns could not accommodate the vast influx of people to Jerusalem during those feast times. As a result, the common people opened their homes and shared their resources with the visitors. Many members of the early church were such pilgrims, saved while visiting Jerusalem for the feast of Pentecost. They now stayed to be a part of the new work of God. It was only basic Christian love for those who lived in the city to share with them. Additionally, some in the fellowship had no doubt lost their livelihoods due to their profession of faith in Christ. The rest of the fellowship met their needs. And others were just the poor believers who always needed help.

That this was not a primitive form of communism is evident from the imperfect tense (denoting continuous past action) of the verbs translated **selling and sharing** (cf. 4:34). They did not at any point sell everything and pool the proceeds into a common pot. Such a principle for Christian living would have obviated the responsibility of each believer to give in response to the Spirit's prompting (cf. 1 Cor. 16:1–2). Further, it is clear from verse 46 that individuals still owned homes. What actually happened was that personal property was sold **as anyone might have need.** It was an indication of immense generosity, as people gave not only their present cash or goods, but also their future in acts of sacrificial love to those in need. And it is clear from Peter's words to Ananias in Acts 5:4 that such selling was purely voluntary. Ananias and Sapphira sinned not by refusing to part with their possessions but by lying to the Holy Spirit. Finally, in no other church described in Acts was this pattern of selling property repeated. Second Corinthians 8:13–14 describes a similar kind of generosity to the Jerusalem poor.

Sharing was not limited to material things but included spiritual benefits and ministry as well. **Day by day** they continued **with one mind** to meet in **the temple.** They went to the Temple for the hours of prayer (cf. 3:1), and, no doubt, to witness. They had every right to continue to use the Temple, since Jesus had claimed it as His Father's house. They are still found going to the Temple in Acts 21:26 and probably continued until it was destroyed in A.D. 70. Nor had the hostility of the Jewish leaders reached the point where the believers were put out of the Temple. The phrase **with one mind** again expresses the unity the first fellowship experienced.

Their times of fellowship were not limited to the Temple, however. They also **were breaking bread from house to house,** and **taking their meals together. Breaking bread** refers to the Communion service, the **taking** of **meals together** to the love feast that accompanied the Lord's Supper. They modeled the principles laid down by Peter, "Be hospitable to one another without complaint" (1 Peter 4:9), and Paul, "At this present time your abundance being a supply for their want, that their abundance also may become a supply for your want, that there may be equality; as it is written, 'He who gathered much did not have too much, and he who gathered little had no lack'" (2 Cor. 8:14–15). The apostle John extends this command to all believers:

> We know love by this, that He laid down His life for us; and we ought to lay down our lives for the brethren. But whoever has the world's goods, and beholds his brother in need and closes his heart against him, how does the love of God abide in him? Little children, let us not love with word or with tongue, but in deed and truth. (1 John 3:16–18)

IT WAS A JOYFUL CHURCH

with gladness and sincerity of heart, praising God (2:46b–47a)

It comes as no surprise that a unified, miraculous, sharing church was also a joyful church. *Agalliasis* (**gladness**) is the noun form of the verb *agalliaō,* which means "to rejoice." One of the key reasons for that joy was the **sincerity of heart** they manifested. *Apheloftēs* (**sincerity**) appears only here in the New Testament. It literally means "simplicity" and derives from a root word meaning "free from rocks," or "smooth" (A. T. Robertson, *Word Pictures in the New Testament* [1930; reprint, Grand Rapids: Baker, n.d.], 3:39–40). There were no stones of selfishness in their hearts.

Praising God also produced joy. To praise God is to recite His wonderful works and attributes. The goal of the first fellowship was to exalt the Lord, and that produced true happiness. Those who glorify themselves and seek the preeminence will never know lasting joy. Joy comes to those who give God glory. Paul expressed that truth to the Philippians when he wrote, "If therefore there is any encouragement in Christ, if there is any consolation of love, if there is any fellowship of the Spirit, if any affection and compassion, make my joy complete by being of the same mind, maintaining the same love, united in spirit, intent on one purpose" (Phil. 2:1–2).

SPIRITUAL IMPACT

and having favor with all the people. And the Lord was adding to their number day by day those who were being saved. (2:47b)

The dynamic corporate life and spiritual character of the church had great impact. Two features of that impact appear in this verse.

THEY WERE AN ATTRACTIVE CHURCH

and having favor with all the people (2:47b)

Their duties and character granted them **favor with all the people.** They were still going to the Temple and being open about their faith, so that all could see and experience their transformed lives. Later came the intense persecution by the Jews. They proved true the words of Jesus in John 13:35, "By this all men will know that you are My disciples, if you have love for one another." Their unity was an answer to our Lord's high priestly prayer "that they may all be one; even as Thou, Father, art in Me, and I in Thee, that they also may be in Us; that the world may believe that Thou didst send Me" (John 17:21).

Some of the reasons the early church found favor with the common people can be discerned from the apology written by the philosopher Aristides early in the second century:

Now the Christians, O King, by going about and seeking, have found the truth. For they know and trust in God, the Maker of heaven and earth, who has no fellow. From him they received those commandments which they have engraved on their minds, and which they observe in the hope and expectation of the world to come.

For this reason they do not commit adultery or immorality; they do not bear false witness, or embezzle, nor do they covet what is not theirs. They honor father and mother, and do good to those who are their neighbors. Whenever they are judges, they judge uprightly. They do not worship idols made in the image of man. Whatever they do not wish that others should do to them, they in turn do not do; and they do not eat the food sacrificed to idols.

Those who oppress them they exhort and make them their friends. They do good to their enemies. Their wives, O King, are pure as virgins, and their daughters are modest. Their men abstain from all unlawful sexual contact and from impurity, in the hope of recompense that is to come in another world.

As for their bondmen and bondwomen, and their children, if there are any, they persuade them to become Christians; and when they have done so, they call them brethren without distinction.

They refuse to worship strange gods; and they go their way in all humility and cheerfulness. Falsehood is not found among them. They love one another; the widow's needs are not ignored, and they rescue the orphan from the person who does him violence. He who has gives to him who has not, ungrudgingly and without boasting. When the Christians find a stranger, they bring him to their homes and rejoice over him as a true brother. They do not call brothers those who are bound by blood ties alone, but those who are brethren after the Spirit and in God.

When one of their poor passes away from the world, each provides for his burial according to his ability. If they hear of any of their number who are imprisoned or oppressed for the name of the Messiah, they all provide for his needs, and if it is possible to redeem him, they set him free.

If they find poverty in their midst, and they do not have spare food, they fast two or three days in order that the needy might be supplied with the necessities. They observe scrupulously the commandments of their Messiah, living honestly and soberly as the Lord their God ordered them. Every morning and every hour they praise and thank God for his goodness to them; and for their food and drink they offer thanksgiving.

If any righteous person of their number passes away from the world, they rejoice and thank God, and escort his body as if he were setting out from one place to another nearby. When a child is born to one of them, they praise God. If it dies in infancy, they thank God the more, as for one who has passed through the world without sins. But if one of them dies in his iniquity or in his sins, they grieve bitterly and sorrow as over one who is about to meet his doom.

Such, O King, is the commandment given to the Christians, and such is their conduct. (*The Apology of Aristides*, translated by Rendel Harris [London: Cambridge, 1893])

With all of that virtue to commend them it is small wonder they were an attractive church.

THEY WERE A GROWING CHURCH

And the Lord was adding to their number day by day those who were being saved. (2:47c)

Effective evangelism was the ultimate impact of the first fellowship's spiritual duties and character. That **the Lord was adding** to the church **those who were being saved** reminds one that God is sovereign in salvation (cf. 5:14). The imperfect tense of the verb translated **was adding,** along with the phrase **day by day,** indicates that people were continually being saved as they observed the daily conduct of the believers. So unified, joyful, and Spirit-filled were they that their very existence was a powerful testimony to the truth of the gospel. True evangelism flows from the life of a healthy church.

This brief glimpse of the first fellowship gives valuable insight into what makes a healthy, growing church worthy of the name. The proper devotion to the duties of the Spirit produces the proper character, which in turn produces a powerful and saving impact on sinners.

A Miracle to Confirm the Word

8

Now Peter and John were going up to the temple at the ninth hour, the hour of prayer. And a certain man who had been lame from his mother's womb was being carried along, whom they used to set down every day at the gate of the temple which is called Beautiful, in order to beg alms of those who were entering the temple. And when he saw Peter and John about to go into the temple, he began asking to receive alms. And Peter, along with John, fixed his gaze upon him and said, "Look at us!" And he began to give them his attention, expecting to receive something from them. But Peter said, "I do not possess silver and gold, but what I do have I give to you: In the name of Jesus Christ the Nazarene—walk!" And seizing him by the right hand, he raised him up; and immediately his feet and his ankles were strengthened. And with a leap, he stood upright and began to walk; and he entered the temple with them, walking and leaping and praising God. And all the people saw him walking and praising God; and they were taking note of him as being the one who used to sit at the Beautiful Gate of the temple to beg alms, and they were filled with wonder and amazement at what had happened to him. And while he was clinging to Peter and John, all

the people ran together to them at the so-called portico of Solomon, full of amazement. (3:1–10)

The Bible warns repeatedly of the ever-present danger of heretical false teachers. Because they claim to represent God, yet misrepresent His truth, they do great harm. Jesus described these preachers in Matthew 7:15 as "ravenous wolves" and warned that "many false prophets will arise, and will mislead many" (Matt. 24:11). Some will be exceedingly dangerous, showing "great signs and wonders, so as to mislead, if possible, even the elect" (Matt. 24:24).

The apostle Paul called false teachers "savage wolves" (Acts 20:29), "rebellious men, empty talkers and deceivers" (Titus 1:10). He warned the Corinthians to beware of them, calling them "false apostles, deceitful workers, disguising themselves as apostles of Christ" (2 Cor. 11:13). They are those who "fall away from the faith, paying attention to deceitful spirits and doctrines of demons" (1 Tim. 4:1), who "oppose the truth, men of depraved mind, rejected as regards the faith" (2 Tim. 3:8).

Perhaps the most scathing denunciation of heretical preachers comes from the pen of the apostle Peter. It needs to be read in full.

But false prophets also arose among the people, just as there will also be false teachers among you, who will secretly introduce destructive heresies, even denying the Master who bought them, bringing swift destruction upon themselves. And many will follow their sensuality, and because of them the way of the truth will be maligned; and in their greed they will exploit you with false words; their judgment from long ago is not idle, and their destruction is not asleep. For if God did not spare angels when they sinned, but cast them into hell and committed them to pits of darkness, reserved for judgment; and did not spare the ancient world, but preserved Noah, a preacher of righteousness, with seven others, when He brought a flood upon the world of the ungodly; and if He condemned the cities of Sodom and Gomorrah to destruction by reducing them to ashes, having made them an example to those who would live ungodly thereafter; and if He rescued righteous Lot, oppressed by the sensual conduct of unprincipled men (for by what he saw and heard that righteous man, while living among them, felt his righteous soul tormented day after day with their lawless deeds), then the Lord knows how to rescue the godly from temptation, and to keep the unrighteous under punishment for the day of judgment, and especially those who indulge the flesh in its corrupt desires and despise authority. Daring, self-willed, they do not tremble when they revile angelic majesties, whereas angels who are greater in might and power do not bring a reviling judgment against them before the Lord. But these, like unreasoning animals, born as creatures of instinct to be captured and killed, reviling where they have no knowledge, will in the destruction of those creatures also be destroyed, suffering wrong as the wages of doing wrong. They count it a pleasure to revel in the daytime. They are stains and blemishes, reveling in their deceptions, as they carouse with you, having eyes full of adultery and that never cease from sin, enticing unstable souls, having a heart trained in greed, accursed children; forsaking the right way they have gone astray, having followed the way of Balaam, the son of Beor, who loved the wages of unrighteousness, but he received a rebuke for his own transgression; for a dumb donkey, speaking with a voice of a man, restrained the madness of the prophet. These are springs without water, and mists driven by a storm, for whom the black darkness has been reserved. For speaking out arrogant words of vanity they entice by fleshly desires, by sensuality, those who barely escape from the ones who live in error, promising them freedom while they themselves are slaves of corruption; for by what a man is overcome, by this he is enslaved. For if after they have escaped the defilements of the world by the knowledge of the Lord and Savior Jesus Christ, they are again entangled in them and are overcome, the last state has become worse for them than the first. For it would be better for them not to have known the way of righteousness, than having known it, to turn away from the holy commandment delivered to them. (2 Peter 2:1–21; cf. Jude 4–16)

The danger posed by such liars makes it imperative that there be a way to distinguish them from those who speak truth from God. The apostle John recognized that need for discernment when he warned believers, "Do not believe every spirit, but test the spirits to see whether they are from God; because many false prophets have gone out into the world" (1 John 4:1).

The Lord Jesus Christ recognized the responsibility for God's messengers to have His teaching accredited by His works. He said of His own ministry, "the works that I do in My Father's name, these bear witness of Me" (John 10:25), and, "If I do not do the works of My Father, do not believe Me; but if I do them, though you do not believe Me, believe the works, that you may know and understand that the Father is in Me, and I in the Father" (John 10:37–38). He challenged Philip to "believe Me that I am in the Father, and the Father in Me; otherwise believe on account of the works themselves" (John 14:11). The works that He did corroborated the words that He said. Nicodemus recognized that when he said, "Rabbi, we know that You have come from God as a teacher; for no one can do these signs that You do unless God is with him" (John 3:2).

The Lord granted that His spokesmen in the early church, the apostles and prophets, also be accredited by miracles. Paul wrote to the Corinthians, "The signs of a true apostle were performed among you with all perseverance, by signs and wonders and miracles" (2 Cor. 12:12). The writer of Hebrews added, "How shall we escape if we neglect so great a salvation? After it was at the first spoken through the Lord, it was confirmed to us by those who heard, God also bearing witness with them, both by signs and wonders and by various miracles and by gifts of the Holy Spirit according to His own will" (Heb. 2:3–4). As noted in the discussion of Acts 2:43 in chapter 7, however, such miraculous accreditation is no longer necessary. We can determine who speaks for God by comparing their teaching with Scripture.

The miraculous sign gifts included the gift of healing (cf. Matt. 10:1) exercised in this passage. This is one of many healings done by the apostles (cf. Acts 2:43), selected for its impact and connection to Peter's inspired sermon. Unfortunately, there is much confusion about that gift. Many today claim to possess or have access to that gift. Their so-called healings run the gamut from psychological ploys to outright fakes to demonic activity. A biblical understanding of the apostolic healing ministry includes the following points:

First, as noted above, many alleged healings are fraudulent. Over the years, faith healers have been exposed as charlatans. Apparent healings result from mind manipulation or a kind of hypnosis, stemming from a strong belief in an authority figure. When that figure tells people they are healed, their emotions may temporarily override their physical symptoms. Such "healings," needless to say, are short-lived.

A related category of "healings" involves cures of psychosomatic illnesses. Since such imagined diseases can produce symptomatic illnesses having no physical, organic cause, their cure is not an illustration of the gift of healing. Jesus and the apostles healed those afflicted with physical ailments, such as blindness, deafness, and paralysis, and organic diseases, such as leprosy. The cure of those conditions, and others like them, however, is beyond the reach of contemporary faith healers.

Second, Satan and his demonic hosts can produce counterfeit healings. They do so not only in false religions but also under the guise of Christianity. The Lord Jesus Christ warned that "false Christs and false prophets will arise, and will show signs and wonders, in order, if possible, to lead the elect astray" (Mark 13:22). The apostle Paul echoed that warning, relating it specifically to the coming man of sin. He described him as the "one whose coming is in accord with the activity of Satan, with all power and signs and false wonders" (2 Thess. 2:9). Jesus warned that "many will say to Me on that day, 'Lord, Lord, did we not prophesy in Your name, and in Your name cast out demons, and in Your name perform many miracles?' And then I will declare to them, 'I never knew you; depart from Me, you who practice lawlessness,'" (Matt. 7:22–23). God is not involved in, nor does He approve of, everything done in His name. Still less does He desire testimony from demonic sources. Our Lord refused to allow the demons to disclose His true identity (Luke 4:41), and Paul refused to allow a demon-possessed girl even to testify to the truth that he and Silas were God's servants (Acts 16:16–18).

Believers must constantly be aware of the danger of satanic deception. Paul warned the Corinthians of that when he wrote regarding some of the false teachers of his day:

> For such men are false apostles, deceitful workers, disguising themselves as apostles of Christ. And no wonder, for even Satan disguises himself as an angel of light. Therefore it is not surprising if his servants also disguise themselves as servants of righteousness; whose end shall be according to their deeds. (2 Cor. 11:13–15)

Satan is perhaps even more dangerous in his subtlety as a wolf in sheep's clothing than as a roaring lion.

Third, contrary to the teaching of many today, the early church was not a miracle-working church. Rather, they were a church with miracle-working apostles. The gift of healing in the early church was limited to the apostles and their close associates in ministry. When they disappeared, so did the gift of healing.

Fourth, in every recorded instance of the gift of healing in Acts, it is unbelievers who are healed (3:1–11; 5:15–16; 8:7; 19:11–12; 28:8). (Whether or not Aeneas [Acts 9:33–34] was a believer is difficult to determine due to the brevity of the passage. However the description of him as "a certain man," rather than a believer or disciple [cf. Acts 9:36] suggests he was an unbeliever.) That miraculous healing was an utterly uncommon occurrence in the early church is clear from the stir Peter's healing of Aeneas caused. If healings were common, what would be so sensational about one more? Yet Peter's healing of Aeneas caused all who lived in that region to turn to the Lord (Acts 9:35).

Further evidence that the gift of healing was not used on behalf of the church comes from the passages that mention sick believers. Paul did not heal Trophimus but left him sick at Miletus (2 Tim. 4:20). Nor did he advise Timothy to go to the local healer for his medical problems. Instead, he told him to take wine for his illness (1 Tim. 5:23).

Does that mean God no longer heals? Of course not! God may choose to heal today in response to the prayers of His children, when that is consistent with His will. But that is a far cry from the miraculous, supernatural healing ability given the apostles on behalf of non-Christians. They were the foundation of the church (Eph. 2:20), but they have passed from the scene. With them went the miraculous gifts that were uniquely associated with them (2 Cor. 12:12). It is an unfounded assumption without biblical support that healings should be expected as commonplace in the church. Never in all history has there been a time of such healing power as exhibited by Christ and the apostles. There is no time before or since when God manifested such prolific healing miracles. It was rare before the ministry of the Lord and the apostles and equally, if not more, rare since. (For a detailed discussion of healing, see my book *Charismatic Chaos* [Grand Rapids: Zondervan, 1992], and Richard Mayhue, *The Healing Promise* [Eugene, Oreg.: Harvest House, 1994].)

In Acts 3:1–10, the Holy Spirit selects one of the "many wonders and signs" mentioned in 2:43 as an illustration. This astounding miracle of healing a man lame from birth gathers a curious crowd and prepares them to hear Peter's sermon. It also confirms that Peter and John represent God. The record of the lame man unfolds in three events: the scene, the sign, and the sequel.

THE SCENE

Now Peter and John were going up to the temple at the ninth hour, the hour of prayer. And a certain man who had been lame from his mother's womb was being carried along, whom they used to set down every day at the gate of the temple which is called Beautiful, in order to beg alms of those who were entering the temple. And when he saw Peter and John about to go into the temple, he began asking to receive alms. (3:1–3)

The gospels and Acts reveal that **Peter** and **John** were closely associated. According to Luke 5:10, they were partners in a fishing business before their call as disciples. With John's brother James, they made up the inner circle of the twelve (cf. Matt. 17:1; Mark 5:37; 9:2; 13:3; 14:33; Luke 8:51; 9:28). Jesus entrusted them with making preparations for the Passover meal (Luke 22:8). They alone of the twelve followed Jesus to the high priest's house after His arrest (John 18:15ff.). Peter and John were the first of the disciples to visit the tomb after the resurrection (John 20:2ff.). The early chapters of Acts often find them traveling and ministering together (cf. 4:13, 19; 8:14).

The imperfect tense of the verb translated **were going up** suggests it was their custom to go to the temple frequently (cf. 2:46). The **ninth hour, the hour of prayer** would be three in the afternoon according to the Jewish reckoning, which counted the hours from sunrise. Psalm 55:17 mentions the three hours of prayer, the other two being in the morning (the third hour) and at noon (the sixth hour). The ninth hour was also the time of the evening sacrifice, when the daily temple crowds would be at their peak.

On their way into the temple, the two apostles encountered **a certain man who had been lame from his mother's womb.** Crippled from birth, his case was hopeless; his affliction was not one the doctors of his day could cure. The imperfect tense of the verb translated **was being carried along,** together with the phrase **set down every day** indicates it was his daily routine to beg at that location.

The gate of the temple which is called Beautiful was the perfect site **to beg alms of those who were entering the temple.** Beggars in Palestine favored three locations: the houses of the rich (cf. Luke 14:1–2; 16:19–21), main highways (cf. Mark 10:46), and the temple. Of the three, the temple was the best site. Not only did crowds throng the temple daily, but they also came to impress God with their piety. One way to do that was to give alms to the poor. Further, the temple treasury was where people gave their offerings to the Lord. They would therefore be in the frame of mind to give money when they came to the temple. The **Beautiful** Gate, inside the temple mount area on the eastern side, separated the Court of the Gentiles from the Court of the Women. Like the other gates, it was large and ornate. According to the Jewish historian Josephus, it was made of Corinthian brass, and was so large it took twenty men to close it (*Wars* V.V.3, VI.V.3).

The lame man was strategically placed at the gate for maximum effect, and spotting **Peter and John about to go into the temple, he began asking to receive alms.** He expected mercy in the form of money, little realizing he was about to receive the greater mercy of healing and salvation.

THE SIGN

And Peter, along with John, fixed his gaze upon him and said, "Look at us!" And he began to give them his attention, expecting to receive something from them. But Peter said, "I do not possess silver and gold, but what I do have I give to you: In the name of Jesus Christ the Nazarene—walk!" And seizing him by the right hand, he raised him up; and immediately his feet and his ankles were strengthened. And with a leap, he stood upright and began to walk; and he entered the temple with them, walking and leaping (3:4–8a)

Four aspects of this miracle are noteworthy: it was unexpected, it was done in the name of the Lord Jesus Christ, it was instantaneous, and it was complete.

IT WAS UNEXPECTED

And Peter, along with John, fixed his gaze upon him and said, "Look at us!" And he began to give them his attention, expecting to receive something from them. But Peter said, "I do not possess silver and gold, but what I do have I give to you: (3:4–6a)

In response to the beggar's cries for alms, **Peter** and **John fixed** their **gaze upon him.** *Atenizō* **(fixed his gaze upon)** is the same word used in 1:10 to describe the apostles' intense gaze at the ascending Lord. The two apostles focused their attention on the unhappy cripple, commanding him, **"Look at us!"** With eager anticipation, the beggar **began to give them his attention, expecting to receive something from them.** He was expecting, of course, to receive money. Peter's reply, **"I do not possess silver and gold, but what I do have I give to you,"** was totally unexpected. The beggar no doubt wondered what these men could give him that would be more valuable than money. He was soon to find out.

Like all of God's works, this miracle was based on God's sovereign will. There were hundreds of other beggars in Jerusalem, many of them undoubtedly crippled as well. But it was this man that God sovereignly chose to receive healing. Expecting only some money to help momentarily ease his desperate situation, the beggar instead received far more than he would have ever dreamed possible.

IT WAS DONE IN THE NAME OF JESUS CHRIST

In the name of Jesus Christ the Nazarene—walk! (3:6b)

The beggar had little reason to believe in Jesus Christ. Jesus had not changed his plight, and He had been executed as a blasphemer. He therefore must have found Peter's use of His name perplexing. **In the name of** means by virtue of Christ's character, authority, and power. As noted in the discussion of Acts 2:22 in chapter 5, **Jesus Christ the Nazarene** was the common designation of our Lord during His earthly ministry. It describes Him as Jesus, the Messiah from Nazareth. To do something in the name of Jesus Christ is to act consistent with His will; to do what He would do if He were here, to act in His authority and with His delegated power. Peter had seen the Lord heal countless times. Now, acting on behalf of His Lord with the power delegated to him (cf. Matt. 10:1), he commands the beggar to **walk.**

IT WAS INSTANTANEOUS

And seizing him by the right hand, he raised him up; and immediately his feet and his ankles were strengthened. (3:7)

The beggar's confusion did not last long. **Seizing him by the right hand, Peter raised him up; and immediately his feet and ankles were strengthened.** The genuine gift of healing, in contrast to the alleged healings of today, resulted in immediate cures. Our Lord's healings were instantaneous (cf. Matt. 8:13; Mark 5:29; Luke 5:13; 17:14; John 5:9); there was no gradual process involved. Scripture knows nothing of "progressive healings." The beggar did not even need to be taught how to walk. He received his coordination and balance instantly.

IT WAS COMPLETE

And with a leap, he stood upright and began to walk; and he entered the temple with them, walking and leaping (3:8a)

Peter did not have to manhandle the beggar to get him on his feet. As soon as he felt the strength surge through his feet and ankles, **with a leap he stood upright and began to walk.** His symptoms were completely gone. Peter and John did not have to support him as he limped along. Instead, **he entered the temple with them, walking and leaping.** His joy and excitement knew no bounds. Mere walking was not enough for him, he also had to leap. Like a child with a new toy he could not resist using his new-found ability.

The four characteristics of this miracle provide a checklist to screen all alleged miraculous healings. A healing that fits the true biblical pattern will stem from God's sovereign choice, it will be done to glorify Jesus Christ, it will be instantaneous, and it will be complete. Needless to say, the so-called instances of healing claimed by modern "healers" do not meet those criteria.

THE SEQUEL

and praising God. And all the people saw him walking and praising God; and they were taking note of him as being the one who used to sit at the Beautiful Gate of the temple to beg alms, and they were filled with wonder and amazement at what had happened to him. And while he was clinging to Peter and John, all

**the people ran together to them at the so-called portico of Solo-
mon, full of amazement.** (8b–11)

There were three results of the miraculous healing of the lame
beggar. First was joy to the beggar himself, which he expressed by
praising God. The sedate, stately ritual of the evening sacrifice was
suddenly shattered by his loud cries of joy and praise. It is God's desire
that all His children experience joy. Jesus said, "These things I have
spoken to you, that My joy may be in you, and that your joy may be made
full" (John 15:11; cf. 16:24).

A second result was praise and worship toward God. Mere participation in a religious service does not in itself guarantee true worship.
The most genuine worship of God likely to have taken place that day in
the temple was the praise of the beggar.

Third, the miracle was a testimony to the people. The beggar's
outburst of praise caused shock and amazement on the part of the
crowd. **All the people** there in the temple **saw him walking and
praising God.** His was a very public testimony. Recognizing **him as
being the one who used to sit at the Beautiful Gate of the temple
to beg alms,** the crowd was **filled with wonder and amazement at
what had happened to him.** That a miracle had taken place was undeniable. They had seen the beggar sitting at the Beautiful Gate for
many years, so everyone knew his condition. Even the Jewish leaders
did not deny that a miracle had taken place. In Acts 4:16, they said,
"What shall we do with these men? For the fact that a noteworthy miracle has taken place through them is apparent to all who live in Jerusalem, and we cannot deny it."

As noted in the discussion of Acts 2:22 in chapter 5, God designed miracles to act as signs to attract attention and point people to
divine truth. This healing did both. It certainly drew the attention of the
crowd, who **ran together to them at the so-called portico of Solomon, full of amazement.** And had they remembered their Old Testament, they would have known that healings were to mark the beginning
of messianic times. Isaiah said of that age, "Then the lame will leap like
a deer" (Isa. 35:6).

As He had for Peter's first sermon on the Day of Pentecost, God
provided the introduction. Amazed at the miraculous healing of the
lame man, a large crowd gathered at the **portico of Solomon,** the
porch surrounding the Court of the Gentiles (the same location where
Jesus had given the discourse on the Good Shepherd [John 10:23]). The
man who had been healed stood with the apostles, **clinging to Peter
and John.** He was living proof that a miracle had taken place. The
stage was set for Peter to preach Christ.

Peter's Powerful Sermon— part 1
Peter Preaches Christ

9

But when Peter saw this, he replied to the people, "Men of Israel, why do you marvel at this, or why do you gaze at us, as if by our own power or piety we had made him walk? The God of Abraham, Isaac, and Jacob, the God of our fathers, has glorified His servant Jesus, the one whom you delivered up, and disowned in the presence of Pilate, when he had decided to release Him. But you disowned the Holy and Righteous One, and asked for a murderer to be granted to you, but put to death the Prince of life, the one whom God raised from the dead, a fact to which we are witnesses. And on the basis of faith in His name, it is the name of Jesus which has strengthened this man whom you see and know; and the faith which comes through Him has given him this perfect health in the presence of you all. And now, brethren, I know that you acted in ignorance, just as your rulers did also. But the things which God announced beforehand by the mouth of all the prophets, that His Christ should suffer, He has thus fulfilled." (3:12–18)

The early preachers were supremely concerned with exalting the name of Jesus Christ. It was in that name that they baptized (Acts 2:38) and healed (Acts 3:6, 16; 4:10). Even the church's opponents recognized how central the name of Jesus was in apostolic preaching (Acts 5:40). Philip preached the name of Jesus (Acts 8:12), as did Paul (Acts 9:27). The Jerusalem council commended Barnabas and Paul as "men who have risked their lives for the name of our Lord Jesus Christ" (Acts 15:26), and Paul expressed his willingness to die for that name (Acts 21:13).

The Bible refers to our Lord by many names—by some estimates more than 200. They include such familiar ones as Alpha and Omega (Rev. 22:13), Beloved (Eph. 1:6), Bread of Life (John 6:48), Bright and morning star (Rev. 22:16), Firstborn from the dead (Col. 1:18), Holy One (Acts 2:27), Immanuel (Isa. 7:14), Lamb (Rev. 5:6), Light of the world (John 8:12), Lion of the tribe of Judah (Rev. 5:5); Lord (John 13:13), Lord of lords (Rev. 17:14), Lord of the Sabbath (Matt. 12:8), Man of sorrows (Isa. 53:3), Mighty God (Isa. 9:6), Prince of peace (Isa. 9:6), Righteous Judge (2 Tim. 4:8), Root of David (Rev. 5:5), Savior (Luke 2:11), Servant (Acts 3:13), Shepherd (John 10:11), Son of God (Mark 1:1), Son of Man (John 5:27), and Word of God (John 1:1; Rev. 19:13). But of all the names of our Lord, the most common is Jesus, which appears more than 800 times in the New Testament.

By whatever name He is called, the testimony of Scripture is that Jesus Christ is the only person who can provide salvation. All spiritual blessings come through His name, including adoption as God's children (John 1:12), salvation (Acts 4:12), forgiveness of sins (Acts 10:43), answered prayer (John 14:13–14), and the Holy Spirit (John 14:26). It is at His name that every knee will bow (Phil. 2:10). Believers are to do everything in His name (Col. 3:17), so that His name will be glorified (2 Thess. 1:12). Those who name His name must turn away from sin (2 Tim. 2:19).

Peter was the first to preach in the name of Jesus, and all who truly preach the gospel stand in the tradition deriving from him. On the Day of Pentecost, against the backdrop of the Spirit's coming, he preached the first sermon in the church's history. The theme of that sermon was Jesus Christ.

As He did for Peter's first sermon, the Holy Spirit provided a dramatic introduction for his second one. Peter and John's healing of a man crippled from birth drew a large crowd. He stood with the apostles on Solomon's portico in the temple, a living illustration that God's power rested on them. **When Peter saw** that the crowd had gathered, he began his sermon. **Replied** is from *apokrinomai,* a word often used to mark the beginning of a discourse (cf. Matt. 11:25; 12:38; 17:4; 22:1; Mark 10:24; 11:14; 14:48; Luke 14:3; John 5:19; Acts 10:46). It does not necessarily refer to answering a question. Whether the crowd asked Peter questions is unknown, but their confusion and desire for an explanation of the miracle were obvious.

Before launching into his theme, Peter first asks two questions. By so doing he cleared up any confusion the crowd may have had about the source of the healing. He prefaces those questions by addressing the crowd as **men of Israel,** a courteous title emphasizing their identity as the covenant people (cf. v. 25). His first question, **why do you marvel at this,** is a mild rebuke. As the covenant people, they knew God to be a miracle-working God. Miracles had played an important role in their history. More recently, they had witnessed the miracles performed by Jesus to demonstrate that He was the Messiah, God's Son. That God should work another miracle through the apostles should come as no surprise to them.

Peter then asks them **why do you gaze at us, as if by our own power or piety we had made him walk?** They should have known that two Galilean fishermen had neither the **power** nor the **piety** to perform such a feat on their own. The crowd's dilemma was that while they acknowledged God alone as having the power to do miracles, they had denied that Jesus was God, and that His followers had divine power granted by God. So they were left with no explanation for what they had just seen.

Peter directs attention away from himself and John to Jesus Christ. He makes clear that it was His power that effected the healing (3:6).

So Peter takes as the theme of his sermon the matchless name of Jesus Christ. He presents five of the many names of our Lord, all of which have messianic implications. As he did in his first sermon, Peter presents Jesus as the Messiah, approved by God, yet rejected by the people. By so doing, he again stresses to them that they were in the disastrous condition of being at odds with God. Peter describes his Master as Servant, Jesus, Holy and Righteous One, Prince of Life, and Christ.

SERVANT

The God of Abraham, Isaac, and Jacob, the God of our fathers, has glorified His servant (3:13a)

Since his message was directed mainly to Israelites, Peter chooses a familiar Jewish description of God. The depiction of God as **the God of Abraham, Isaac, and Jacob, the God of our fathers** stresses again His covenant faithfulness to Israel. This description seems to have been employed on significant occasions (cf. Ex. 3:6, 15, 16; 1 Kings 18:36; 1 Chron. 29:18; 2 Chron. 30:6; Matt. 22:32; Acts 7:32). By using it, Peter claims continuity with the Old Testament prophets, since he is declaring the same God they preached and the Messiah they promised.

Peter proclaims that the God of the covenant, the God of the patriarchs and the prophets, **has glorified His servant.** *Pais* (**servant**) is an unusual title for our Lord, appearing only here, verse 26, Acts 4:27, 30; and Matthew 12:18. It describes Jesus as God's personal representative or ambassador.

Servant, however, was a familiar Old Testament designation of Messiah (Isa. 42:1, 19; 49:5–7). It receives its fullest exposition in the familiar passage in Isaiah 52:13–53:12:

> Behold, My servant will prosper, He will be high and lifted up, and greatly exalted. Just as many were astonished at you, My people, so His appearance was marred more than any man, and His form more than the sons of men. Thus He will sprinkle many nations, kings will shut their mouths on account of Him; for what had not been told them they will see, and what they had not heard they will understand. Who has believed our message? And to whom has the arm of the Lord been revealed? For He grew up before Him like a tender shoot, and like a root out of parched ground; He has no stately form or majesty that we should look upon Him, nor appearance that we should be attracted to Him. He was despised and forsaken of men, a man of sorrows, and acquainted with grief; and like one from whom men hide their face, He was despised, and we did not esteem Him. Surely our griefs He Himself bore, and our sorrows He carried; yet we ourselves esteemed Him stricken, smitten of God, and afflicted. But He was pierced through for our transgressions, He was crushed for our iniquities; the chastening for our well-being fell upon Him, and by His scourging we are healed. All of us like sheep have gone astray, each of us has turned to his own way; but the Lord has caused the iniquity of us all to fall on Him. He was oppressed and He was afflicted, yet He did not open His mouth; like a lamb that is led to slaughter, and like a sheep that is silent before its shearers, so He did not open His mouth. By oppression and judgment He was taken away; and as for His generation, who considered that He was cut off out of the land of the living, for the transgression of my people to whom the stroke was due? His grave was assigned with wicked men, yet He was with a rich man in His death, because He had done no violence, nor was there any deceit in His mouth. But the Lord was pleased to crush Him, putting Him to grief; if He would render Himself as a guilt offering, He will see His offspring, He will prolong His days, and the good pleasure of the Lord will prosper in His hand. As a result of the anguish of His soul, He will see it and be satisfied; by His knowledge the Righteous One, My Servant, will justify the many, as He will bear their iniquities. Therefore, I will allot Him a portion with the great, and He will divide the booty with the strong; because He poured out Himself to death, and was numbered with the transgressors; yet He Himself bore the sin of many, and interceded for the transgressors.

That passage depicts Messiah as the suffering Servant, obedient even to the point of death.

Matthew identifies Jesus as the Servant of Isaiah's prophecy as in 12:18–21 he quotes Isaiah 42:1–4 and applies it to Him:

> Behold, My Servant whom I have chosen; My Beloved in whom My soul is well-pleased; I will put My Spirit upon Him, and He shall proclaim justice to the Gentiles. He will not quarrel, nor cry out; nor will anyone hear His voice in the streets. A battered reed He will not break off, and a smoldering wick He will not put out, until He leads justice to victory. And in His name the Gentiles will hope.

Jesus said of Himself, "The Son of Man did not come to be served, but to serve" (Matt. 20:28). In John 6:38 He said, "I have come down from heaven, not to do My own will, but the will of Him who sent Me." In John 8:28 He added, "I do nothing on My own initiative, but I speak these things as the Father taught Me." John 13:1–7 gives a beautiful example of our Lord's humble service:

> Now before the Feast of the Passover, Jesus knowing that His hour had come that He should depart out of this world to the Father, having loved His own who were in the world, He loved them to the end. And during supper, the devil having already put into the heart of Judas Iscariot, the son of Simon, to betray Him, Jesus, knowing that the Father had given all things into His hands, and that He had come forth from God, and was going back to God, rose from supper, and laid aside His garments; and taking a towel, He girded Himself about. Then He poured water into the basin, and began to wash the disciples' feet, and to wipe them with the towel with which He was girded. And so He came to Simon Peter. He said to Him, "Lord, do You wash my feet?" Jesus answered and said to him, "What I do you do not realize now, but you shall understand hereafter."

When His suffering was over, God **glorified** Jesus, exalting Him to the position of honor at His right hand (Acts 2:33; 5:31; Phil. 2:9–11; Heb. 7:26).

JESUS

Jesus, the one whom you delivered up, and disowned in the presence of Pilate, when he had decided to release Him. (3:13b)

Jesus is the Greek form of the Hebrew name *Joshua,* meaning "the Lord is salvation." As already noted, it is the most common name of our Lord in the New Testament. It was first revealed to Joseph when the angel told him, "You shall call His name Jesus, for it is He who will save His people from their sins" (Matt. 1:21). Commenting on that verse, Charles Spurgeon said,

> The angel spake to Joseph the name in a dream: that name so soft and sweet that it breaks no man's rest, but rather yields a peace unrivalled, the peace of God. With such a dream Joseph's sleep was more blessed than his waking. The name has evermore this power, for, to those who know it, it unveils a glory brighter than dreams have ever imagined. (*The Metropolitan Tabernacle Pulpit*, vol. XXIV [London: Passmore & Alabaster, 1879], 518)

There have been many false views of Jesus throughout history, from noble example to political revolutionary. Yet to imagine a Jesus who was not the Savior is as foolish as to imagine a Shakespeare who was not a writer, or a Rembrandt who was not a painter. His name is Jesus not because He is our example, guide, leader, or friend, though He is all those things. His name is Jesus because He is our savior.

Instead of welcoming Him, the nation rejected Him. "He came to His own, and those who were His own did not receive Him" (John 1:11). They were looking for a political or military deliverer to throw off the hated yoke of Rome. Because they "loved the darkness rather than the light; for their deeds were evil" (John 3:19), they were not prepared to accept One Who came to confront their sin and deliver them from it.

Accordingly, the same Jesus whom God glorified they **delivered up, and disowned in the presence of Pilate, when he had decided to release Him.** Pilate was well aware that the crucifixion was a blatant injustice. He declared Jesus innocent no less than six times (Luke 23:4, 16, 22; John 18:38; 19:4, 6) and repeatedly sought to release Him (Luke 23:13–22). Even his wife recognized Jesus' innocence (Matt. 27:19). As a Roman, he came from a people with a strong tradition of justice (cf. Acts 16:37–38; 22:25–29; 25:16). To condemn a man he believed innocent went against that tradition. Yet Pilate had no choice. The Jewish leaders had him backed into a corner. They had already complained to Rome and put his position in jeopardy. Another complaint would probably have cost him his place as governor.

Peter boldly confronts his hearers with the enormity of their sin in executing their Messiah. All truly biblical preaching must follow his example and render men guilty before God. That is the necessary foundation of the gospel message. Only those who see themselves as sinners will recognize their need for a Savior and comprehend the work of Jesus.

HOLY AND RIGHTEOUS ONE

But you disowned the Holy and Righteous One, and asked for a murderer to be granted to you, (3:14)

To emphasize their guilt, Peter repeats the charge that they **disowned** Jesus, **the Holy and Righteous One** before Pilate. Worse, they **asked for a murderer to be granted** to them.

Hagios (**Holy**) means to be separated to God. Jesus is not only holy by nature but separated to God to do His will. Holy One is also a messianic title. Psalm 16:10, a messianic passage quoted by Peter in his sermon on the Day of Pentecost, reads, "For Thou wilt not abandon my soul to Sheol; neither wilt Thou allow Thy Holy One to undergo decay." Speaking for the rest of the disciples, Peter said, "We have believed and have come to know that You are the Holy One of God" (John 6:69). Even the demons knew the truth that Jesus was the Holy One (Luke 4:34). Israel's guilt in rejecting Him was both monumental and inexcusable and placed them in open rebellion against God.

Dikaios (**Righteous**) carries the idea of being innocent of any crime. Faced with the choice between Jesus, their innocent Messiah, and the guilty **murderer** Barabbas, they chose the latter. "Barabbas" means "son of father," an interesting earthly contrast to Jesus, who was the "Son of the Father" in heaven. Even pagans, such as Pilate's wife (Matt. 27:19) and a Roman centurion (Luke 23:47), recognized what Israel could not—that Jesus was innocent and righteous. Peter's indictment of them was devastatingly direct.

PRINCE OF LIFE

but put to death the Prince of life, the one whom God raised from the dead, a fact to which we are witnesses. And on the basis of faith in His name, it is the name of Jesus which has strengthened this man whom you see and know; and the faith which comes through Him has given him this perfect health in the presence of you all. And now, brethren, I know that you acted in ignorance, just as your rulers did also. (3:15–17)

Peter has been presenting a series of paradoxes. Although Jesus was a servant, God exalted Him. He was their deliverer, yet the nation delivered him to Pilate. They rejected the Holy and Righteous One in favor of an unholy, unjust murderer. Now he comes to the greatest paradox of all. They **put to death the Prince of life,** while asking for the release of one who took life.

Prince of life translates *archēgos.* It refers to the originator, pioneer, or beginner of something. Hebrews 2:10 uses it in the phrase "author of salvation." In Hebrews 12:2 it describes Jesus as the "author" of faith. Here Peter uses it to describe Jesus as the originator of life. That is a claim of deity for Jesus, since Psalm 36:9 describes God as the "fountain of life."

The New Testament repeatedly describes Jesus as the source of life. In the prologue to his gospel, John writes, "In Him was life, and the life was the light of men" (John 1:4). In his first epistle, he adds, "God has given us eternal life, and this life is in His Son" (1 John 5:11). Speaking of Jesus later in that chapter John wrote "This is the true God and eternal life" (1 John 5:20).

Jesus also claimed to be the source of life. In John 5:26 He said, "Just as the Father has life in Himself, even so He gave to the Son also to have life in Himself." He declared to Martha, "I am the resurrection and the life; he who believes in Me shall live even if he dies" (John 11:25), while in John 14:6 He says simply, "I am the way, and the truth, and the life."

The preaching does not end with the death of the Prince of life, however. In true apostolic fashion, Peter adds the ringing note of the resurrection. Jesus, the Prince of life, was **the one whom God raised from the dead.** That was **a fact to which** Peter and the apostles were **witnesses** (cf. 1 Cor. 15:3–7). Peter's audacious claim is powerful evidence for the resurrection. If Jesus had not risen from the dead, that claim would have been easy to disprove. Had the Jewish leaders been able to produce Jesus' dead body, the church would have been stillborn. But they could not and did not. The apostles' testimony was undeniable.

Peter forcefully brings home the point that the Jews were open enemies of the God they professed to love, the very One they had come to the temple to worship. The One whom God had exalted, they had delivered up, disowned, and executed.

Their guilt was enormous, but their murder was unsuccessful. Not only was Jesus alive, but the miracle was also done **on the basis of faith in His name.** The faith in view here is not that of the beggar but of Peter and John. Although occasionally the faith of the one healed is noted (cf. Acts 14:19), the New Testament gift of healing operated through the faith of the healer, rather than the one healed. To tell those who are not healed that it is because they lack the faith to be healed is another misrepresentation of the biblical nature of apostolic healing. As in verse 12, Peter, in spite of his strong faith in the risen Christ, refuses to take credit for the healing. **It is the name of Jesus,** he tells them, **which**

has strengthened this man whom you see and know; and the faith which comes through Him has given him this perfect health in the presence of you all. The healed beggar was living proof that the nation's evaluation of Jesus was wrong.

Verse 17 marks a transition in Peter's sermon. He first convicted them of rejecting and executing their Messiah. Then, beginning with verse 19, he proclaimed the necessity of repentance. In between, in verses 17–18, Peter offers them hope. By addressing them as **brethren,** he identifies with them as fellow Jews and places himself on their level, showing his love and concern for them.

Peter offers them the possibility of forgiveness because they had **acted in ignorance** (cf. Acts 13:27). He may be alluding to the Old Testament distinction between willful sins and sins done in ignorance (Num. 15:22–31). Jesus prayed for those who crucified Him, saying "Father, forgive them; for they do not know what they are doing" (Luke 23:34). Paul wrote that if the rulers had understood who Jesus was, "they would not have crucified the Lord of glory" (1 Cor. 2:8). Their ignorance was certainly inexcusable, since the evidence that Jesus was the Messiah was clear from the Old Testament, the words and works of Jesus, and His death and resurrection. Yet, none of them were beyond the reach of God's grace, if they would repent and turn to Christ. Even the rulers who incited the people to cry for the death of their Messiah are indicted for the less heinous motive of ignorance. There is a note of mercy in the fact that Peter focuses on the blindness and ignorance of the unregenerate (cf. 2 Cor. 4:3–4).

CHRIST

But the things which God announced beforehand by the mouth of all the prophets, that His Christ should suffer, He has thus fulfilled. (3:18)

Peter reassures his hearers that their rejection and execution of the Messiah had not thwarted God's plan. The crucifixion, so unthinkable to them as happening to the true Messiah, did not at all alter God's program, nor did it disqualify Jesus as the Messiah. **God** had **announced beforehand by the mouth of all the prophets that His Christ should suffer,** and those prophecies had now been **fulfilled.** The Old Testament foresaw Christ's death in such passages as Isaiah 53, Psalm 22, and Zechariah 12:10. Even the nation's rejection of Him had been predicted (Isa. 53:3). God used their evil intentions to fulfill His own purposes (cf. Acts 2:23; Gen. 50:20).

Peter portrays our Lord as Servant, Jesus (Savior), Holy and Righteous One, Prince of Life, and Christ (Messiah; John 1:41; 4:25). He convicts his hearers of disowning, denying, and executing Him. They must have been wondering, as did the crowd on the Day of Pentecost, "What shall we do?" (Acts 2:37). In the second part of his sermon, Peter gives them the answer. His sermon is a classic example of how to present the gospel. Before the good news of salvation in Christ must come the bad news that men are sinners.

Peter's Powerful Sermon— part 2 The Necessity of Repentance

10

Repent therefore and return, that your sins may be wiped away, in order that times of refreshing may come from the presence of the Lord; and that He may send Jesus, the Christ appointed for you, whom heaven must receive until the period of restoration of all things about which God spoke by the mouth of His holy prophets from ancient time. Moses said, "The Lord God shall raise up for you a prophet like me from your brethren; to Him you shall give heed in everything He says to you. And it shall be that every soul that does not heed that prophet shall be utterly destroyed from among the people." And likewise, all the prophets who have spoken, from Samuel and his successors onward, also announced these days. It is you who are the sons of the prophets, and of the covenant which God made with your fathers, saying to Abraham, "And in your seed all the families of the earth shall be blessed." For you first, God raised up His Servant, and sent Him to bless you by turning every one of you from your wicked ways. (3:19–26)

Throughout redemptive history, God's spokesmen have called sinners to repentance. God told Jeremiah to say to rebellious Israel,

"Thus says the Lord, 'Do men fall and not get up again? Does one turn away and not repent? Why then has this people, Jerusalem, turned away in continual apostasy? They hold fast to deceit, they refuse to return'" (Jer. 8:4–5). He commanded Ezekiel, "Therefore say to the house of Israel, 'Thus says the Lord God, "Repent and turn away from your idols, and turn your faces away from all your abominations"'" (Ezek. 14:6). Second Kings 17:13 summarizes the sad history of God's dealings with Israel in the Old Testament: "Yet the Lord warned Israel and Judah, through all His prophets and every seer, saying, 'Turn from your evil ways and keep My commandments, My statutes according to all the law which I commanded your fathers, and which I sent to you through My servants the prophets.'" The primary ministry of the prophets was to bring Israel to repentance. Yet the nation refused to heed them, and suffered the terrible consequences of destruction and captivity.

Nor did the message change in the New Testament. Matthew 3:1–2 relates that "John the Baptist came, preaching in the wilderness of Judea, saying, 'Repent, for the kingdom of heaven is at hand.'" According to Matthew 4:17, "From that time [of John the Baptist's imprisonment] Jesus began to preach and say, 'Repent, for the kingdom of heaven is at hand.'"

Repentance was also the command of apostolic preaching. In his sermon on the Day of Pentecost, Peter commanded his hearers to "repent, and let each of you be baptized in the name of Jesus Christ for the forgiveness of your sins" (Acts 2:38). Paul characterized his ministry in Ephesus as one of "solemnly testifying to both Jews and Greeks of repentance toward God and faith in our Lord Jesus Christ" (Acts 20:21). In his defense before Agrippa he said, "I did not prove disobedient to the heavenly vision, but kept declaring both to those of Damascus first, and also at Jerusalem and then throughout all the region of Judea, and even to the Gentiles, that they should repent and turn to God, performing deeds appropriate to repentance" (Acts 26:19–20).

As he draws his sermon to a conclusion, Peter continues in that tradition and calls his hearers to repentance. They needed to repent, for they had rejected their Messiah and were in rebellion against God. In the first part of his sermon, Peter convicted them of their guilt. He now offers them hope, reassuring them that it is not too late to repent. If they do so, they will receive the promised covenant blessings.

Repentance is a key New Testament term. The literal meaning of *metanoeō* (**repent**) is "to change one's mind or purpose." Repentance involves far more than a mere intellectual decision. It is a change of mind that issues in a change of behavior. Peter's use of *epistrephō* (**return**), a word used frequently in the New Testament to speak of sinners turning to God (Luke 1:16–17; Acts 9:35; 11:21; 14:15; 15:19; 26:18, 20; 2 Cor. 3:16; 1 Thess. 1:9; 1 Peter 2:25), reinforces that meaning.

In the parable of the two sons, the Lord Jesus Christ gave an illustration of true repentance:

> But what do you think? A man had two sons, and he came to the first and said, "Son, go work today in the vineyard." And he answered and said, "I will, sir"; and he did not go. And he came to the second and said the same thing. But he answered and said, "I will not"; yet he afterward regretted it and went. Which of the two did the will of his father? They said, "The latter." Jesus said to them, "Truly I say to you that the tax-gatherers and harlots will get into the kingdom of God before you." (Matt. 21:28–31)

Note that the second son not only changed his mind but also followed that decision with a change in his behavior. John the Baptist demanded that anyone claiming to have repented validate such a confession with the evidence of a changed life (Matt. 3:6–8). That is the nature of true repentance.

God's design for men is that they repent (Acts 17:30). To accomplish that purpose, He uses at least four prompters. First, the knowledge of God's revealed truth should cause men to repent. In Matthew 11:21–24, Jesus sharply rebuked the cities of Chorazin, Bethsaida, and Capernaum for refusing to repent:

> Woe to you, Chorazin! Woe to you, Bethsaida! For if the miracles had occurred in Tyre and Sidon which occurred in you, they would have repented long ago in sackcloth and ashes. Nevertheless I say to you, it shall be more tolerable for Tyre and Sidon in the day of judgment, than for you. And you, Capernaum, will not be exalted to heaven, will you? You shall descend to Hades; for if the miracles had occurred in Sodom which occurred in you, it would have remained to this day. Nevertheless I say to you that it shall be more tolerable for the land of Sodom in the day of judgment, than for you.

Luke 16:30–31 illustrates the sufficiency of the Word to cause repentance: "But [the rich man in Hades] said, 'No, Father Abraham, but if someone goes to them from the dead, they will repent!' But he said to him, 'If they do not listen to Moses and the Prophets, neither will they be persuaded if someone rises from the dead.'"

The apostle John defined his purpose in writing his gospel in these words: "Many other signs therefore Jesus also performed in the presence of the disciples, which are not written in this book; but these have been written that you may believe that Jesus is the Christ, the Son of God; and that believing you may have life in His name" (John 20:30–31).

God has given men all the evidence they need to arrive at the proper conclusion about Jesus Christ. Those who refuse to repent are without excuse.

Second, God uses sorrow for sin to lead men to repentance. In 2 Corinthians 7:9–10 Paul wrote,

> I now rejoice, not that you were made sorrowful, but that you were made sorrowful to the point of repentance; for you were made sorrowful according to the will of God, in order that you might not suffer loss in anything through us. For the sorrow that is according to the will of God produces a repentance without regret, leading to salvation; but the sorrow of the world produces death.

Sorrow or regret for sin, however, must not be confused with genuine repentance. Judas "felt remorse" over his betrayal of Jesus, yet never repented. It is possible to have sorrow for sin without repentance, just as it is possible to have knowledge without repentance.

Third, God's goodness and kindness are to motivate men to repentance. In Romans 2:4, Paul rebukes Israel for missing that point: "Do you think lightly of the riches of His kindness and forbearance and patience, not knowing that the kindness of God leads you to repentance?" God, in common grace, blesses men with good things to enjoy. Jesus said in Matthew 5:45 that "He causes His sun to rise on the evil and the good, and sends rain on the righteous and the unrighteous." This common grace should lead people to penitence.

A final motivation to repentance is fear of final judgment. The apostle Paul warned the pagan Athenians that "having overlooked the times of ignorance, God is now declaring to men that all everywhere should repent, because He has fixed a day in which He will judge the world in righteousness through a Man whom He has appointed, having furnished proof to all men by raising Him from the dead" (Acts 17:30–31). The sobering reality of coming judgment should cause any rational person to repent and turn to God for forgiveness. There is no other way of escape.

In the first part of his sermon Peter gave his hearers abundant evidence that Israel had reached the wrong conclusion about Jesus Christ. Then he called on them to repent and reverse their verdict concerning Jesus Christ and place their faith in Him. To help persuade them, he gives them promised results if they repent: God will forgive their sin, the kingdom will come, Messiah will return, judgment will be avoided, and blessing will be realized.

GOD WILL FORGIVE THEIR SIN

that your sins may be wiped away, (3:19b)

Peter's words no doubt reminded the crowd of David's cry in Psalm 51:9, "Hide Thy face from my sins, and blot out all my iniquities." The legalism of first-century Judaism, like any works-righteousness system, could not bring about forgiveness. It served only to "weigh men down with burdens hard to bear" (Luke 11:46). The glorious truth is that God has graciously provided for men what they could never obtain on their own. In Isaiah 43:25 God says, "I, even I, am the one who wipes out your transgressions for My own sake; and I will not remember your sins," while in Isaiah 44:22 He adds, "I have wiped out your transgressions like a thick cloud, and your sins like a heavy mist" (cf. Num. 14:18; Pss. 65:3; 85:2; 86:5; 130:3–4).

There is only one way to receive God's forgiveness—through faith in His Son Jesus Christ. Peter boldly proclaimed to the Sanhedrin that "[Jesus] is the one whom God exalted to His right hand as a Prince and a Savior, to grant repentance to Israel, and forgiveness of sins" (Acts 5:31). It is "through His name [that] everyone who believes in Him receives forgiveness of sins" (Acts 10:43). "In Him," Paul wrote to the Ephesians, "we have redemption through His blood, the forgiveness of our trespasses, according to the riches of His grace" (Eph. 1:7; cf. Col. 1:14). In Ephesians 4:32 he added, "God in Christ . . . has forgiven you." The sacrificial death of Jesus Christ accomplished what the Levitical system was unable to, since "it is impossible for the blood of bulls and goats to take away sins" (Heb. 10:4).

Exaleiphō (**wiped away**) pictures the wiping of ink off a document (cf. Col. 2:14). Unlike modern ink, ink in the ancient world had no acid content. Consequently, it did not bite into the papyrus or vellum used for documents. Instead, it remained on the surface where it could easily be wiped away by a damp sponge. God does far more than merely cross out believers' sins, He wipes them away completely. They are gone beyond the possibility of review or recall. Even their horrible sin of rejecting and executing their Messiah was not indelible and could be wiped away.

Those who place their faith in Christ are united with Him in His death and resurrection (Rom. 6:4–5). Consequently, God has "canceled out the certificate of debt consisting of decrees against us and which was hostile to us; and He has taken it out of the way, having nailed it to the cross" (Col. 2:14). As a result there is eternally "no condemnation for those who are in Christ Jesus" (Rom. 8:1).

Forgiveness produces joy and relief from guilt. Horatio Spafford expressed that reality beautifully in his classic hymn "It Is Well with My Soul." In it he penned the following familiar words:

> My sin, O, the bliss of this glorious thought,
> My sin not in part but the whole
> Is nailed to the cross and I bear it no more,
> Praise the Lord, praise the Lord, O my soul!

Those words find their echo in every redeemed heart.

THE KINGDOM WILL COME

in order that times of refreshing may come from the presence of the Lord; (3:19c)

Repentance would not only bring the individual blessing of forgiveness of sin, but ultimately collective blessing also. The phrase **times of refreshing** refers to the millennial kingdom. For generations, Israel had waited anxiously for that kingdom. They longed to see Messiah reign personally on the earth and to have their enemies vanquished. The prophets had spoken of a glorious period of rest for the people who had known little peace over the centuries. Tragically, when the King came to offer that kingdom, they rejected Him. And, as Peter points out, it is impossible to have the kingdom without accepting the King.

Kairos (**times**) points to a fixed, set, or predetermined time. Jesus used it in Acts 1:7 to answer the disciples' query about the restoration of the kingdom. He told them, "It is not for you to know times or epochs which the Father has fixed by His own authority." God's sovereign determination of the time of the kingdom encompasses Israel's repentance. It is only when "all Israel [is] saved" that "the Deliverer will come from Zion" (Rom. 11:26).

The kingdom will be a time of much needed **refreshing** for Israel. Ezekiel said it would be a time of "showers of blessing" (34:26). Isaiah saw the kingdom as a time when God "will pour water on him that is thirsty" (44:3 KJV). Joel 2 gives a description of the coming of the kingdom, even referring to it as a time of satisfaction (2:26). No people in history have been so ill-treated as the Jewish people. Over the centuries they have endured invasions, deportations, persecutions, and pogroms. All that has culminated in our century in the insane attempt of the Nazis to exterminate them altogether. Although they are back in their own land, their enemies give them no rest. The rest offered by God in the kingdom will fulfill their hearts' desire.

The kingdom will be a golden age of blessing for Israel (and believing Gentiles), surpassing even the time of David and Solomon's reigns. Isaiah 11:6–10 describes the peaceful rest of the kingdom in these familiar words:

> And the wolf will dwell with the lamb, and the leopard will lie down with the kid, and the calf and the young lion and the fatling together; and a little boy will lead them. Also the cow and the bear will graze; their young will lie down together; and the lion will eat straw like the ox. And the nursing child will play by the hole of the cobra, and the weaned child will put his hand on the viper's den. They will not hurt or destroy in all My holy mountain, for the earth will be full of the knowledge of the Lord as the waters cover the sea. Then it will come about in that day that the nations will resort to the root of Jesse, who will stand as a signal for the peoples; and His resting place will be glorious.

Isaiah 35:1–10 adds,

> The wilderness and the desert will be glad, and the Arabah will rejoice and blossom; like the crocus it will blossom profusely and rejoice with rejoicing and shout of joy. The glory of Lebanon will be given to it, the majesty of Carmel and Sharon. They will see the glory of the Lord, the majesty of our God. Encourage the exhausted, and strengthen the feeble. Say to those with anxious heart, "Take courage, fear not. Behold, your God will come with vengeance; the recompense of God will come, but He will save you." Then the eyes of the blind will be opened, and the ears of the deaf will be unstopped. Then the lame will leap like a deer, and the tongue of the dumb will shout for joy. For waters will break forth in the wilderness and streams in the Arabah. And the scorched land will become a pool, and the thirsty ground springs of water; in the haunt of jackals, its resting place, grass becomes reeds and rushes. And a highway will be there, a roadway, and it will be called the Highway of Holiness. The unclean will not travel on it, but it will be for him who walks that way, and fools will not wander on it. No lion will be there, nor will any vicious beast go up on it; these will not be found there. But the redeemed will walk there, and the ransomed of the Lord will return, and come with joyful shouting to Zion, with everlasting joy upon their heads. They will find gladness and joy, and sorrow and sighing will flee away.

The kingdom will not come about through human efforts, but will **come from the presence of the Lord.** He will bring it to pass according to His own sovereign will. Revelation 5 presents the scene in heaven when the Lamb, the Lord Jesus Christ, takes the title deed to the universe. The unfolding of that scroll (chapters 6–19) describes His method of retaking of what is rightfully His from the usurper, culminating in the coming of the kingdom (Rev. 20:4–6).

Peter thus placed the responsibility for the delay in the coming of the kingdom squarely on their shoulders. It was their lack of repentance that, humanly speaking, postponed the kingdom. God, through Peter, gave them the opportunity to repent of that sin. Sadly, though a few individuals responded, the nation as a whole continued to spurn God's gracious offer. There was nothing left for them except the fulfillment of the Lord's sorrowful prophecy of Luke 19:41–44:

> And when He approached, He saw the city [Jerusalem] and wept over it, saying, "If you had known in this day, even you, the things which make for peace! But now they have been hidden from your eyes. For the days shall come upon you when your enemies will throw up a bank before you, and surround you, and hem you in on every side, and will level you to the ground and your children within you, and they will not leave in you one stone upon another, because you did not recognize the time of your visitation."

The first devastating divine judgment for Israel's rejection fell upon them in A.D. 70 when the Romans sacked Jerusalem, destroyed the temple, and killed more than one million Jews.

Peter's hearers paid a fearful price in time and eternity for their rejection of God's repeated calls for repentance. But "God has not rejected His people whom He foreknew" (Rom. 11:2). The kingdom, though delayed at least two thousand years, will yet come when Israel is converted. Zechariah 12:10–13:1; 14:1ff. prophesy the day of salvation for the Jews and the subsequent coming of the King and His kingdom.

MESSIAH WILL RETURN

and that He may send Jesus, the Christ appointed for you, whom heaven must receive until the period of restoration of all things about which God spoke by the mouth of His holy prophets from ancient time. (3:20–21)

As already noted, it is a truism that there can be no kingdom without the King. Peter told the crowd that if they would reverse the verdict of Passover evening, God would **send Jesus, the Christ appoint-**

ed for them. Our Lord expressed that truth in Matthew 23:39 when He said to the unbelieving city of Jerusalem, "From now on you shall not see Me until you say, 'Blessed is He who comes in the name of the Lord!'" He will not return until after repentant Israel acknowledges Him as their Messiah (Rom. 11:26; Zech. 12:10–14:9).

Some may have wondered why, if Jesus were the Messiah, He did not remain and set up His kingdom. In reply, Peter reiterates the truth that in God's sovereign timetable the millennial kingdom follows the nation's repentance. Until that time, Jesus will remain in **heaven.**

The period of restoration of all things is another name for the future earthly reign of Christ, the millennial kingdom. It is reminiscent of our Lord's description of the kingdom as the "regeneration" (Matt. 19:28). It is then that the apostles' question in Acts 1:6 will be answered (cf. Mark 9:12). The kingdom will be marked by peace, joy, holiness, the revelation of God's glory, comfort, justice, knowledge of the Lord, health, prosperity, and freedom from oppression. The universe will be dramatically altered in its physical form (Joel 2:30, 31; 3:14–16; Rev. 16:1–21) as the curse on man and his world is reversed.

The truths Peter proclaimed were not new; God had spoken of them **by the mouth of His holy prophets from ancient time.** The Old Testament prophets spoke repeatedly of Messiah's earthly kingdom. Joel 2:25 even refers to it as a time of restoration. That God spoke through the prophets proves their teachings were not human speculation but divine revelation (cf. 2 Peter 1:21). No clearer biblical statement of the inspiration of Old Testament Scripture can be found.

JUDGMENT WILL BE AVOIDED

Moses said, "The Lord God shall raise up for you a prophet like me from your brethren; to Him you shall give heed in everything He says to you. And it shall be that every soul that does not heed that prophet shall be utterly destroyed from among the people." And likewise, all the prophets who have spoken, from Samuel and his successors onward, also announced these days. (3:22–24)

As an example of a prophet through whom God spoke, Peter cites Moses—Israel's first and greatest prophet. In Deuteronomy 18:15, quoted here by Peter, Moses spoke of the coming Messiah: **The Lord God shall raise up for you a prophet like me from your brethren; to Him you shall give heed in everything He says to you.** The prophet like Moses was generally regarded by the Jews as the Messiah (cf. John 1:21, 25; 6:14; 7:40). Commenting on Deuteronomy 18 the Midrash Rabbath said,

> As was the former redeemer so shall the latter redeemer be. While of the former it is said (Ex. 4:20) "And Moses took his wife and his sons and set them upon an ass," so of the latter: for it says (Zech. 9:9) "He is lowly and riding on an ass." And while the former redeemer brought down manna (Ex. 16:4) "Behold I will rain bread from heaven for you," so the latter redeemer shall bring down manna.

Moses also warned of the consequences of rejecting the Messiah. In Deuteronomy 18:19, also quoted by Peter, Moses cautioned, **And it shall be that every soul that does not heed that prophet shall be utterly destroyed from among the people.** Rejection of the Messiah would result in loss of the covenant blessings. That was the perilous condition in which Peter's hearers found themselves. Those who persist in rejecting Jesus Christ, whether Jew or Gentile, will forfeit God's promised blessings. They will **be utterly destroyed from among the people**—killed and damned.

Not only Moses, but also **all the prophets who have spoken, from Samuel and his successors onward, also announced these days.** That **Samuel** was a prophet is clear from 1 Samuel 3:20: "And all Israel from Dan even to Beersheba knew that Samuel was confirmed as a prophet of the Lord." While he made no recorded prophecy of the Messiah, "Samuel was the prophet who anointed David as king and spoke of the establishment of his kingdom (1 Sam. 13:14; 15:28; 16:13; 28:17), and the promises made to David found their highest fulfillment in Jesus" (F. F. Bruce, *The Book of the Acts* [Grand Rapids: Eerdmans, 1971] 93). Second Samuel 7:10ff. is the record of the great promise of God to David concerning Messiah and His eternal kingdom.

But Peter's audience was carrying on a sad tradition of their ancestors—refusing to heed their prophets. In Matthew 23:37 Jesus lamented, "O Jerusalem, Jerusalem, who kills the prophets and stones those who are sent to her! How often I wanted to gather your children together, the way a hen gathers her chicks under her wings, and you were unwilling."

Jesus fulfilled numerous Old Testament prophecies, leaving the nation without excuse. To the unbelieving Jews Jesus said, "You search the Scriptures, because you think that in them you have eternal life; and it is these that bear witness of Me" (John 5:39). Luke 24:25–27 records His rebuke of two of His followers: "And He said to them, 'O foolish men and slow of heart to believe in all that the prophets have spoken! Was it not necessary for the Christ to suffer these things and to enter into

His glory?' And beginning with Moses and with all the prophets, He explained to them the things concerning Himself in all the Scriptures." Israel's problem was moral, not intellectual; they lacked repentance, not information.

BLESSING WILL BE REALIZED

It is you who are the sons of the prophets, and of the covenant which God made with your fathers, saying to Abraham, "And in your seed all the families of the earth shall be blessed." For you first, God raised up His Servant, and sent Him to bless you by turning every one of you from your wicked ways. (3:25–26)

Peter closes on a hopeful note. In spite of their sin of rejecting the Messiah, they were still the sons of the prophets, and of the covenant. The apostle Paul expressed that truth in Romans 9:3–5:

> For I could wish that I myself were accursed, separated from Christ for the sake of my brethren, my kinsmen according to the flesh, who are Israelites, to whom belongs the adoption as sons and the glory and the covenants and the giving of the Law and the temple service and the promises, whose are the fathers, and from whom is the Christ according to the flesh, who is over all, God blessed forever. Amen.

They were heirs of all the promised covenant blessings—more so than any other generation, since in their lifetime Messiah had come. God's covenant with **Abraham** found its ultimate fulfillment in Jesus Christ. He is the **seed** of Abraham in whom **all the families of the earth shall be blessed.** That blessing was still available. The leaders had made their choice when they killed Jesus. These people now faced theirs.

Because of God's grace, mercy, and love for Israel, He did not permanently reject them even when they rejected His Son (Rom. 11:2). It was for them **first** that **God raised up His Servant and sent Him to bless them.** By preaching the gospel to the Jewish people first, Peter and the apostles were obeying the mandate of their Lord. In Luke 24:47, He told them that "repentance for forgiveness of sins should be proclaimed in His name to all the nations, beginning from Jerusalem." In His last conversation with them before His ascension, He repeated that command: "But you shall receive power when the Holy Spirit has come upon you; and you shall be My witnesses both in Jerusalem, and in all Judea and Samaria, and even to the remotest part of the earth" (Acts

1:8). Even Paul, the apostle to the Gentiles, acknowledged that the gospel was "the power of God for salvation to everyone who believes, to the Jew first and also to the Greek" (Rom. 1:16).

All the rich blessings of salvation and all the covenant promises were available. Peter's hearers could only obtain them, however, by **turning** from their **wicked ways.** Repentance was the key that unlocked everything. Peter had clearly shown that the claims of Jesus were consistent with Old Testament prophecy, so that it was a compelling case for his hearers to respond in repentance and belief. Tragically, most of Peter's audience refused to repent. Like their fathers before them, they hardened their hearts and failed to enter God's rest (Heb. 3:8; 4:3). As a result, within the lifetime of many in the audience the nation would be destroyed. And those who refused to turn from their sins would find themselves "cast out into the outer darkness" (Matt. 8:12), where they will "pay the penalty of eternal destruction, away from the presence of the Lord and from the glory of His power" (2 Thess. 1:9).

Such a fate awaits all those in every age and place who refuse to repent and receive God's gracious offer of salvation in Jesus Christ.

How to Handle Persecution

11

And as they were speaking to the people, the priests and the captain of the temple guard, and the Sadducees, came upon them, being greatly disturbed because they were teaching the people and proclaiming in Jesus the resurrection from the dead. And they laid hands on them, and put them in jail until the next day, for it was already evening. But many of those who had heard the message believed; and the number of the men came to be about five thousand. And it came about on the next day, that their rulers and elders and scribes were gathered together in Jerusalem; and Annas the high priest was there, and Caiaphas and John and Alexander, and all who were of high-priestly descent. And when they had placed them in the center, they began to inquire, "By what power, or in what name, have you done this?" Then Peter, filled with the Holy Spirit, said to them, "Rulers and elders of the people, if we are on trial today for a benefit done to a sick man, as to how this man has been made well, let it be known to all of you, and to all the people of Israel, that by the name of Jesus Christ the Nazarene, whom you crucified, whom God raised from the dead—by this name this man stands here before you in good health. He is the stone which was rejected by you, the builders, but which became the very corner stone. And there is salvation in no one else; for there is no other name under heaven that has been given among men, by which we must be saved." Now as they observed the confidence of Peter and John, and understood that they were uneducated and untrained men, they were marveling, and began to recognize them as having been with Jesus. And seeing the man who had been healed standing with them, they had nothing to say in reply. But when they had ordered them to go aside out of the Council, they began to confer with one another, saying, "What shall we do with these men? For the fact that a noteworthy miracle has taken place through them is apparent to all who live in Jerusalem, and we cannot deny it. But in order that it may not spread any further among the people, let us warn them to speak no more to any man in this name." And when they had summoned them, they commanded them not to speak or teach at all in the name of Jesus. But Peter and John answered and said to them, "Whether it is right in the sight of God to give heed to you rather than to God, you be the judge; for we cannot stop speaking what we have seen and heard." And when they had threatened them further, they let them go (finding no basis on which they might punish them) on account of the people, because they were all glorifying God for what had happened; for the man was more than forty years old on whom this miracle of healing had been performed. And when they had been released, they went to their own companions, and reported all that the chief priests and the elders had said to them. And when they heard this, they lifted their voices to God with one accord and said, "O Lord, it is Thou who didst make the heaven and the earth and the sea, and all that is in them, who by the Holy Spirit, through the mouth of our father David Thy servant, didst say, 'Why did the Gentiles rage, and the peoples devise futile things? The kings of the earth took their stand, and the rulers were gathered together against the Lord, and against His Christ.' For truly in this city there were gathered together against Thy holy servant Jesus, whom Thou didst anoint, both Herod and Pontius Pilate, along with the Gentiles and the peoples of Israel, to do whatever Thy hand and Thy purpose predestined to occur. And now, Lord, take note of their threats, and grant that Thy bond-servants may speak Thy word with all confidence, while Thou dost extend Thy hand to heal, and signs and wonders take place through the name of Thy holy servant Jesus." And when they had prayed, the place where they had gathered together was shaken, and they were all filled with the Holy Spirit, and began to speak the word of God with boldness. (4:1–31)

Throughout its history the church of Jesus Christ has faced persecution. During the Roman persecutions of the first three centuries, for example, Christians were thrown to wild animals, crucified, turned into human torches, and tortured in all the cruel ways evil men could devise. Uncounted thousands of martyrs met their deaths with a calmness and serenity that unnerved their tormenters. So, according to tradition, did all the apostles except John.

Far from destroying the church, however, persecution merely served to purify and strengthen it. It matures the church the way trials mature individual believers. After surviving three centuries of violent attacks the church emerged as the dominant force in the Roman empire. In the words of the church Father Tertullian, "The blood of the martyrs is the seed of the church."

In modern times the church (at least in the West) has rarely faced physical persecution. Satan's attacks have become much more subtle—the type of attack detailed, for example, in C. S. Lewis's *The Screwtape Letters.* Instead of threatening the body, Satan's persecutions today aim at the ego. They threaten our selfish pride, need for acceptance, or status. Satan has largely destroyed the spiritual effectiveness of the church without having to kill the individual believers in it. In fact, letting believers live self-centered, complacent, indolent, worldly lives is more effective in keeping people from being attracted to the Christian faith than killing them. Martyrs are respected for the strength of their character; compromisers are despised.

The first opposition to the church did not take long to arise, and it came from the same Jewish leaders who had executed Jesus. Acts chapters 4, 5, 7, 8, and 12 record those persecutions.

That the church should face persecution came as no surprise, since the Lord Jesus Christ warned His followers to expect it. In John 15:18–20 He said,

> If the world hates you, you know that it has hated Me before it hated you. If you were of the world, the world would love its own; but because you are not of the world, but I chose you out of the world, therefore the world hates you. Remember the word that I said to you, "A slave is not greater than his master." If they persecuted Me, they will also persecute you; if they kept My word, they will keep yours also.

In John 16:2 He warned, "They will make you outcasts from the synagogue, but an hour is coming for everyone who kills you to think that he is offering service to God."

The apostles also taught the certainty of persecution. Paul wrote to Timothy, "Indeed, all who desire to live godly in Christ Jesus will be persecuted" (2 Tim. 3:12). Peter added, "For you have been called for this purpose, since Christ also suffered for you, leaving you an example for you to follow in His steps" (1 Peter 2:21). Those Christians who live godly, Christ-centered lives will inevitably come into conflict with the satanic world system. And the day may soon come when believers will be physically persecuted, tortured, or even martyred, as the world escalates its hatred of the true gospel.

Acts chapter 4 records the first outbreak of persecution against the church. Verses 1–31 can be simply divided into two sections: the persecution manifest and the persecution met.

THE PERSECUTION MANIFEST

And as they were speaking to the people, the priests and the captain of the temple guard, and the Sadducees, came upon them, being greatly disturbed because they were teaching the people and proclaiming in Jesus the resurrection from the dead. And they laid hands on them, and put them in jail until the next day, for it was already evening. But many of those who had heard the message believed; and the number of the men came to be about five thousand. (4:1–4)

Luke's use of the plural pronoun **they** suggests both Peter and John **were speaking to the people.** Perhaps in the aftermath of the healing and Peter's sermon both apostles were dialoguing with the crowd. Before they were finished speaking, however, the temple authorities arrived on the scene to arrest them. The **priests** were the ordinary priests conducting the evening sacrifice. They were divided into twenty-four courses and were chosen by lot to serve at a given time. They had eagerly anticipated their week to minister and were no doubt upset at the disturbance Peter and John had caused.

The captain of the temple guard was the chief of the temple police force, which was composed of Levites. He was second in rank only to the high priest and was responsible for maintaining order in the temple grounds. The Romans gave the right to police the temple to the Jews, and this *stratēgos* (a word meaning commander, or general) ranked next to the high priest in authority.

The **Sadducees** were one of the four sects that made up first-century Judaism, along with their archrivals the Pharisees, the Essenes, and the Zealots. Although small in number, they were highly influential. They were the dominant religious and political force in Israel, since the high priests through that period were all Sadducees. The Sadducees were mostly aristocratic, wealthy landowners. To protect their political position and wealth, they firmly opposed any overt opposition to Rome. John 11:47–48 highlights their concerns: "Therefore the chief priests [Sadducees] and the Pharisees convened a council, and were saying, 'What are we doing? For this man is performing many signs. If we let Him go on like this, all men will believe in Him, and the Romans will come and take away both our place and our nation.'" Then the high priest, a Sadducee, gave a solution in keeping with the Sadducees' philosophy: "But a certain one of them, Caiaphas, who was high priest that year, said to them, 'You know nothing at all, nor do you take into account that it is expedient for you that one man should die for the people, and that the whole nation should not perish.'" (John 11:49–50).

The religion of the Sadducees was largely one of social custom. They believed only the written law, rejecting the oral tradition so vital to the Pharisees. They did not believe in the resurrection of the body, or in any future rewards or punishments. In contrast to the Pharisees, they denied the existence of angels and the spirit world (Acts 23:8). Finally, they rejected predestination and the sovereignty of God, believing man to be the master of his own destiny. These theological liberals were the first to persecute the church.

Ephistēmi (**came upon**) has the idea of coming upon suddenly, sometimes with hostile intent (cf. Acts 6:12). The authorities were **greatly disturbed** with the apostles for several reasons. First, they were annoyed that they **were teaching the people** at all. They had no reputation as teachers, no sanction, no credentials, yet had gathered a huge crowd and stirred up a major commotion. That was intolerable to the leaders since Peter and John were "uneducated and untrained" (v. 13); that is, they had not undergone rabbinic training. Worse, they were from Galilee, from which nothing good could be expected (John 1:46; 7:41, 52). Commentator Albert Barnes writes, "They were offended that unlearned Galileans, in no way connected with the priestly office, and unauthorized by *them,* should presume to set themselves up as religious teachers" (*Barnes' Notes on the New Testament: Acts–Romans* [reprint of the 1884–85 edition; Grand Rapids: Baker], 74). That Peter and John were doing so in the temple, the heart of the Sadducees' domain, was especially galling.

But the major source of irritation was Peter and John's **proclaiming in Jesus the resurrection from the dead.** The Jewish leaders had executed Jesus as a blasphemer, and now the apostles were boldly **proclaiming** Him as the resurrected Messiah. They no doubt viewed that as a direct attack on their authority. Nor were the Sadducees pleased that the apostles were preaching **the resurrection from the dead.** As already noted, they rejected the idea of a general resurrection. If Jesus had risen, they were exposed as heretics. Further, the idea of a general resurrection was an apocalyptic concept with all sorts of messianic overtones. Messianic ideas among the Jews of that day meant revolt, overthrow of the foreign overlords, and restoration of the Davidic kingdom. . . . The notes of Peter's sermon alarmed them: resurrection, Author of life, a new Moses. These were revolutionary ideas. The movement must not spread. It must be nipped in the bud. (John B. Polhill, *The New American Commentary: Acts* [Nashville: Broadman, 1992], 140)

Unable to tolerate the apostles' preaching, the authorities **laid hands on them, and put them in jail until the next day.** By now several hours had passed since Peter and John entered the temple, and **it was already evening.** Peter's sermon must have been much longer than what is recorded in chapter 3, since he began it soon after the ninth hour (3:1). The fact that it was evening meant it was too late to convene the Sanhedrin for a trial that day, and Jewish law did not permit trials at night (though that regulation was ignored in the case of Jesus). Peter and John were detained in jail overnight for trial the next day before the very Sanhedrin that had judged their Lord.

Imprisoning the apostles, however, did not nullify the effect of their preaching. **Many of those who had heard the message believed; and the number of the men came to be about five thousand.** As was to prove the case repeatedly through the centuries, persecution led to the expansion of the church. **Five thousand** represents the cumulative **number of the men** in the Jerusalem congregation, not those added at this time. This is the last mention of a specific number in Acts; from this time on the church grew too fast to keep an accurate count. Luke does, however, note the church's continued growth (5:14; 6:7; 9:31; 12:24; 16:5; 19:20; 28:31).

THE PERSECUTION MET

And it came about on the next day, that their rulers and elders and scribes were gathered together in Jerusalem; and Annas the high priest was there, and Caiaphas and John and Alexander, and all who were of high-priestly descent. And when they had placed them in the center, they began to inquire, "By what power, or in what name, have you done this?" Then Peter, filled with the Holy Spirit, said to them, "Rulers and elders of the people, if we are on trial today for a benefit done to a sick man, as to how this man has been made well, let it be known to all of you, and to all the people of Israel, that by the name of Jesus Christ the Nazarene, whom you crucified, whom God raised from the dead

—by this name this man stands here before you in good health. He is the stone which was rejected by you, the builders, but which became the very corner stone. And there is salvation in no one else; for there is no other name under heaven that has been given among men, by which we must be saved." Now as they observed the confidence of Peter and John, and understood that they were uneducated and untrained men, they were marveling, and began to recognize them as having been with Jesus. And seeing the man who had been healed standing with them, they had nothing to say in reply. But when they had ordered them to go aside out of the Council, they began to confer with one another, saying, "What shall we do with these men? For the fact that a noteworthy miracle has taken place through them is apparent to all who live in Jerusalem, and we cannot deny it. But in order that it may not spread any further among the people, let us warn them to speak no more to any man in this name." And when they had summoned them, they commanded them not to speak or teach at all in the name of Jesus. But Peter and John answered and said to them, "Whether it is right in the sight of God to give heed to you rather than to God, you be the judge; for we cannot stop speaking what we have seen and heard." And when they had threatened them further, they let them go (finding no basis on which they might punish them) on account of the people, because they were all glorifying God for what had happened; for the man was more than forty years old on whom this miracle of healing had been performed. And when they had been released, they went to their own companions, and reported all that the chief priests and the elders had said to them. And when they heard this, they lifted their voices to God with one accord and said, "O Lord, it is Thou who didst make the heaven and the earth and the sea, and all that is in them, who by the Holy Spirit, through the mouth of our father David Thy servant, didst say, 'Why did the Gentiles rage, and the peoples devise futile things? The kings of the earth took their stand, and the rulers were gathered together against the Lord, and against His Christ.' For truly in this city there were gathered together against Thy holy servant Jesus, whom Thou didst anoint, both Herod and Pontius Pilate, along with the Gentiles and the peoples of Israel, to do whatever Thy hand and Thy purpose predestined to occur. And now, Lord, take note of their threats, and grant that Thy bond-servants may speak Thy word with all confidence, while Thou dost extend Thy hand to heal, and signs and wonders take place through the name of Thy holy servant Jesus." And when they had prayed, the place where they had gathered together was shaken, and they

were all filled with the Holy Spirit, and began to speak the word of God with boldness. (4:5–31)

This section records the church's reaction to the initial outbreak of persecution. From that response believers can learn seven principles for handling persecution in all times and places.

And it came about on the next day, that their rulers and elders and scribes were gathered together in Jerusalem; and Annas the high priest was there, and Caiaphas and John and Alexander, and all who were of high-priestly descent. And when they had placed them in the center, they began to inquire, "By what power, or in what name, have you done this?" (4:5–7)

Peter and John offered no resistance during their arrest (v. 3), nor did they resist when arraigned before the Sanhedrin (cf. 1 Peter 2:18–24). They quietly submitted, knowing that God controlled their circumstances. Persecution gave them an opportunity they would never otherwise have had—to preach to the Sanhedrin.

The **rulers** (also called chief priests) represented the twenty-four priestly orders. Together with the **elders** (family heads and heads of tribes) **and scribes** (law experts, mostly Pharisees), they made up the Sanhedrin. The next morning, they **were gathered together in Jerusalem.** The Sanhedrin was the ruling body of the nation (under the ultimate authority of the Romans) and also its supreme court. It had seventy-one members, including the high priest. At the time of this incident it was dominated by the Sadducees. **Annas** was not the current **high priest,** having been deposed by the Romans in favor of his son-in-law **Caiaphas.** He still bore the title of high priest, just as ex-presidents of the United States are still called president. Although not officially serving as high priest, Annas was the real power behind the scenes. Five of his sons, one of his sons-in-law (Caiaphas), and one of his grandsons all served as high priests. The identification of **John** and **Alexander** is uncertain. Some manuscripts read "Jonathan" instead of **John,** and Annas had a son named Jonathan, who later replaced Caiaphas as high priest. Nothing further is known of **Alexander. All who were of high-priestly descent** may refer generally to those of the elite families from which the high priests were drawn, or specifically to members of Annas's family.

The Sanhedrin met in a place called the Hall of Hewn Stone, possibly within the temple area. Having **placed** the apostles **in the**

center of the semicircle in which they sat, they began the formal questioning process. Homer Kent, Jr., points out that

> the Mosaic Law specified that whenever someone performed a miracle and used it as the basis for teaching, he was to be examined, and if the teaching were used to lead men away from the God of their fathers, the nation was responsible to stone him (Deut. 13:1–5). On the other hand, if his message was doctrinally sound, the miracle-worker was to be accepted as coming with a message from God. (*Jerusalem to Rome* [Grand Rapids: Baker, 1992], 45–46)

The Sanhedrin demanded to know **by what power, or in what name** the apostles had healed the lame man. A **name** represented authority. The question implied Peter and John were rebels, since the Sanhedrin had not granted them authority to act. Whatever their motive for asking, the question provided an opening for Peter to preach to them.

BE FILLED WITH THE SPIRIT

Then Peter, filled with the Holy Spirit, (4:8a)

There was one essential prerequisite for Peter's powerful defense. He faced persecution triumphantly because he was **filled with the Holy Spirit** (cf. Acts 2:4; 13:9). The Lord Jesus Christ had told the disciples that "when they bring you before the synagogues and the rulers and the authorities, do not become anxious about how or what you should speak in your defense, or what you should say; for the Holy Spirit will teach you in that very hour what you ought to say" (Luke 12:11–12). All Christian ministry and witness depends on the filling of the Holy Spirit (see the discussion of the filling of the Spirit in *Ephesians,* MacArthur New Testament Commentary [Chicago: Moody, 1986]). The passive voice of the verb translated **filled** shows Peter's yieldedness to the Spirit's control. He did not become filled by lengthy prayer or an emotional experience. The filling of the Spirit occurs when the believer walks in obedience to the Word and Spirit (cf. Eph. 5:18; Col. 3:16). Yielding to His control releases His power in the believer's life.

This principle is foundational to all the rest; yieldedness to the Holy Spirit is the key to successfully handling persecution. Because Peter was Spirit-filled, persecution merely drove him closer to the Lord. Lack of being filled with the Spirit is the reason the church today has difficulty facing opposition.

A Spirit-filled, uncompromising church will be uncomfortable in the world, since it will be a rebuke to it. It will, however, be a powerful, victorious church. Peter and John confronted the world head on, with a boldness and eloquence that caused their opponents to marvel (cf. v. 13). They were victorious because they were Spirit-filled.

BE AGGRESSIVE IN SEIZING OPPORTUNITIES

Peter . . . said to them, "Rulers and elders of the people, if we are on trial today for a benefit done to a sick man, as to how this man has been made well, let it be known to all of you, and to all the people of Israel, that by the name of Jesus Christ the Nazarene, whom you crucified, whom God raised from the dead—by this name this man stands here before you in good health. He is the stone which was rejected by you, the builders, but which became the very corner stone. And there is salvation in no one else; for there is no other name under heaven that has been given among men, by which we must be saved." Now as they observed the confidence of Peter and John, and understood that they were uneducated and untrained men, they were marveling, and began to recognize them as having been with Jesus. (4:8–13)

Instead of being frightened into silence or compromise, Peter displayed great courage and went on the offensive. Submission is not cowardice. He began by indicting them for the incongruity of putting him and John **on trial . . . for a benefit done to a sick man.** He thus turned the tables on the Sanhedrin and subtly accused them of injustice—certainly it couldn't be wrong to heal a lame man.

Since they had demanded to know **as to how this man has been made well,** by what name (or authority) the apostles performed the miracle, Peter told them. He desired them and **all the people of Israel** to know that **by the name of Jesus Christ the Nazarene**—whom they **crucified,** but **God raised from the dead**—the beggar stood before them **in good health.** In the very citadel of the Sanhedrin's power Peter put his judges on trial by proclaiming the truth about the living Christ to those responsible for His execution. By pointing out that they executed Jesus but God raised Him up, Peter showed them to be the enemies of God. That approach was frequently employed in Acts (cf. 2:23–24; 3:14–15; 10:39–40; 13:27–30). Peter refused to compromise the gospel by deleting what would offend the Sanhedrin. He spoke courageously because he was devoted to the truth and entrusted the outcome to his Lord. That is an example for all persecuted believers to follow.

One of the most formidable barriers to the Sanhedrin's acceptance of Jesus as Messiah was that He could not prevent Himself from being killed. That did not fit their conception of the Messiah as a political and military deliverer. As he had done on the day of Pentecost, Peter turned to the Old Testament Scriptures to build his case. He quoted Psalm 118:22, applying it to their rejection of Jesus Christ (cf. Mark 12:10–11; 1 Peter 2:4, 6–8). Peter was not leading the Jews away from God but preaching the very truth of the Old Testament as fulfilled in Jesus. He was **the stone which was rejected by** them, **the builders** or spiritual leaders of the nation. Although they rejected Jesus, God made Him **the very corner stone** through His resurrection and exaltation. Again, Peter puts them in opposition to God—they rejected Jesus, but God gave Him the place of preeminence. He is the cornerstone of God's spiritual temple, the church (Eph. 2:19–22). They were the ones leading the people away from God.

In verse 12 Peter gives what amounts to a direct invitation to the Sanhedrin to repent and embrace Jesus Christ to be saved. He had already declared that the healing of the lame beggar had been done in Jesus' name. Now he goes further and proclaims that **there is salvation in no one else; for there is no other name under heaven that has been given among men, by which we must be saved. Saved** is a form of the same verb (*sōzō*) used in verse 9 to describe the healing of the lame man. Not only was Jesus the source of physical healing, but He is also the only source of spiritual healing. Deliverance from the devastating effects of sin comes only through Jesus Christ. Peter did not invent that truth; he is merely echoing his Master. In John 14:6 Jesus declared, "I am the way, and the truth, and the life; no one comes to the Father, but through Me." This same exclusivity is claimed by our Lord in John 10:7–8 when He said, "Truly, truly, I say to you, I am the door of the sheep. All who came before me are thieves and robbers."

The exclusivism of Christianity goes against the grain of our religiously pluralistic society. A chapel built at the North Pole in February 1959 by the men of Operation Deep Freeze 4 typifies the prevalent attitude today toward religious belief. The structure contained an altar, over which was hung a picture of Jesus, a crucifix, a star of David, and a lotus leaf (representing the Buddha). On the wall of the chapel was an inscription that read "Now it can be said that the earth turns on the point of faith."

Christians preach an exclusive Christ in an inclusive age. Because of that, we are often accused of being narrow-minded, even intolerant. Many paths, it is said, lead to the top of the mountain of religious enlightenment. How dare we insist that ours is the only one? In reality, however, there are only two religious paths: the broad way of works salvation leading to destruction, and the narrow way of faith in the only

Savior leading to eternal life (Matt. 7:13–14). Religious people are on either one or the other. Sadly, the Sanhedrin and all who followed them
were on the broad road to hell.

Peter's impassioned plea failed to soften the hardened hearts of
the Sanhedrin. Yet it was not without some effect. They could not help
being impressed with **the confidence of Peter and John.** They were
amazed that **uneducated** (in the rabbinical schools) **and untrained
men** (not professional theologians; laymen) could argue so effectively
from the Scriptures. That two Galilean fishermen powerfully and successfully argued their case before the elite Jewish supreme court was
shocking, so that **they were marveling.** The explanation slowly
dawned on the Sanhedrin, as they **began to recognize them as having been with Jesus.** No doubt it came back to their memories that the
two apostles had been with Jesus in the temple and at His trial (John
18:15–18).

What triggered the Sanhedrin's recognition was the realization
that the apostles were doing what Jesus did. Like the apostles, Jesus
had boldly and fearlessly confronted the Jewish leaders with His authority and truth (cf. Matt. 7:28–29). He, too, had no formal rabbinic training
(cf. John 7:15–16). Yet in His sure handling of the Old Testament Scriptures He had no equal (cf. John 7:46). Jesus had performed many miracles during His earthly ministry. Peter and John were on trial largely
because of a miracle they had performed.

The attempt by the Sanhedrin to suppress the apostles' teaching
had given them a priceless opportunity. They boldly seized it and proclaimed the gospel to the highest officials of the nation. That is how to
handle persecution—face it with the boldest proclamation of the truth.

BE OBEDIENT TO GOD AT ALL COSTS

**And seeing the man who had been healed standing with them,
they had nothing to say in reply. But when they had ordered them
to go aside out of the Council, they began to confer with one another, saying, "What shall we do with these men? For the fact
that a noteworthy miracle has taken place through them is apparent to all who live in Jerusalem, and we cannot deny it. But in
order that it may not spread any further among the people, let us
warn them to speak no more to any man in this name." And when
they had summoned them, they commanded them not to speak
or teach at all in the name of Jesus. But Peter and John answered
and said to them, "Whether it is right in the sight of God to give
heed to you rather than to God, you be the judge; for we cannot
stop speaking what we have seen and heard." And when they had**

threatened them further, they let them go (finding no basis on which they might punish them) on account of the people, because they were all glorifying God for what had happened; for the man was more than forty years old on whom this miracle of healing had been performed. (4:14–22)

The unexpected boldness of Peter and John, and the presence of the healed man standing with them, put the Sanhedrin in an impossible position. **Seeing the man who had been healed standing with** the apostles, **they** (for the moment) **had nothing to say in reply.** Peter's convincing defense that he was, in fact, leading people to God, not away from Him, was unanswerable. The promise of Jesus to His apostles to give them "utterance and wisdom which none of your opponents will be able to resist or refute" (Luke 21:15) had been fulfilled.

Having **ordered** Peter and John **to go aside out of the Council,** the members of the Sanhedrin **began to confer with one another.** Peter had completely turned the tables on them, and now court was recessed while they considered what to **do with these men.** The question was not an easy one to answer. Peter and John had broken no laws and had ably defended themselves from the Old Testament Scriptures. Further, to punish them would be risky, in light of **the fact that a noteworthy miracle** had **taken place through them** and was **apparent to all who live in Jerusalem.** The reality of the power of the risen Lord had spread through the whole city. Even they could not **deny it.** Sadly, though they could not deny it, neither were they willing to accept it. They were a living illustration of our Lord's words in John 3:19 that "the light is come into the world, and men loved the darkness rather than the light; for their deeds were evil." Such is the blindness of sin; they knew the truth, yet refused to accept it, just as they had rejected the truth of the resurrection (Matt. 28:11–15).

The Sanhedrin was reliving its worst nightmare. They had executed Jesus for claiming to be the Messiah. Undaunted by that, His followers were going everywhere repeating those claims. Worse, they were proclaiming with irrefutable proof that He had risen from the dead. And they had performed a **noteworthy miracle** to authenticate their claim to represent God. The Sanhedrin felt compelled to take action **in order that** this teaching **may not spread any further among the people.** They had to stop the incriminating truth that they had executed their Messiah. Accordingly, they decided to try to intimidate the apostles into silence by warning them **to speak no more to any man in this name.**

Because of that decision, they summoned Peter and John back into the courtroom and **commanded them not to speak or teach at all in the name of Jesus.** Ironically, the early believers had to be commanded to be quiet, while many modern ones have to be commanded to speak. This was an important crossroads in the history of the church. Had the apostles acquiesced to the Sanhedrin's demand, all subsequent church history would have been radically different. Everything hinged on their willingness to obey God at all costs—even their lives.

Peter and John did not vacillate but immediately **answered** that they would refuse to obey the Sanhedrin's command. They appealed to a higher court by asking the question of **whether it is right in the sight of God to give heed to men rather than to God** before the supreme court of Israel (cf. Acts 5:29). Which court is higher? By such an appeal to the divine judge the apostles impaled the Sanhedrin on the horns of a dilemma. They certainly did not want Peter and John to continue to speak, yet they could hardly tell them to obey men instead of God. Peter again indicted them for being the enemies of the God they professed to represent.

It is a clearly biblical principle that believers are to obey their government. Peter himself taught such obedience in 1 Peter 2:13–17 (cf. Rom. 13:1–7). The reaction of Peter and John, however, marks the limits of that obedience. They would gladly obey if they could do so without disobeying their sovereign Lord. But when God's commands conflict with those of the government, the government must be disobeyed. The actions of the Hebrew midwives (Ex. 1:15–17) and Daniel (Dan. 6:4–10) further illustrate that obligation.

Although Peter and John refused to obey the Sanhedrin, they nevertheless treated them with respect. They did not argue with them, nor pretend to submit and then go and disobey. Instead, they carefully and respectfully explained that they could not **stop speaking.** Like Paul, who exclaimed, "Woe is me if I do not preach the gospel" (1 Cor. 9:16), they were compelled to speak.

The content of their message, what they had **seen and heard,** stresses that they were eyewitnesses of Jesus' life, death, and, especially, His resurrection (cf. 1 John 1:1, 3). One obvious way for the Sanhedrin to escape their dilemma would have been to deny that Jesus rose from the dead. That they never attempted to do so provides powerful evidence for Jesus' resurrection. F. F. Bruce comments,

> It is particularly striking that neither on this nor on any subsequent occasion (so far as our information goes) did the Sanhedrin take any serious action to disprove the apostles' central affirmation—the resurrection of Jesus. Had it seemed possible to refute them on this point, how readily would the Sanhedrin have seized the opportunity! Had they succeeded, how quickly and completely the new movement would have collapsed! (*The Book of the Acts* [Grand Rapids: Eerdmans, 1971], 102)

The Sanhedrin was cornered; they had run out of options. Having **threatened** the apostles **further they let them go,** since they could find no legitimate **basis on which they might punish them.** It was not a commitment to justice that caused them to free the apostles so much as practical politics. They feared the reaction of the **people, all** of whom **were glorifying God for what had happened; for the man was more than forty years old on whom this miracle of healing had been performed.** He had the birth defect for all forty of those years, and everyone knew him because he sat at the site of the temple daily (Acts 3:2). The healing was undeniable and powerful. Modern claimers of apostolic healing power leave crippling birth defects alone.

In the midst of persecution, Peter and John remained obedient to God. Like them, no bribes or threats should cause us to be unfaithful to our Lord. Later, in his first letter, Peter wrote from experience as well as inspiration,

> And who is there to harm you if you prove zealous for what is good? But even if you should suffer for the sake of righteousness, you are blessed. And do not fear their intimidation, and do not be troubled, but sanctify Christ as Lord in your hearts, always being ready to make a defense to everyone who asks you to give an account for the hope that is in you. (1 Peter 3:13–15)

BE COMMITTED TO FELLOWSHIP

And when they had been released, they went to their own companions, and reported all that the chief priests and the elders had said to them. (4:23)

It is noteworthy that the first thing Peter and John did after being **released** was to go to **their own companions.** That group should not be limited to the other apostles, nor expanded to include the entire church (since there was no building where all 5,000 men, plus women and children, could have gathered). It may have been some or all of the original group that met in the upper room (cf. 1:13–15). They **reported all that the chief priests and the elders had said to them** and no doubt received comfort and encouragement from the others. A primary benefit of persecution is that it results in greater solidarity. Persecuted believers naturally draw together for mutual support. Acts 4:32–35 describes the unity that resulted from this initial outbreak of opposition. Perhaps one reason for the disunity in today's church is the lack of external pressure. And the false unity being attempted through compromise and indifference toward true doctrine only compounds the problem by moving the church ever further from the true unity that comes out of confrontation by the truth. If we confronted the world system more aggressively, the resulting opposition would drive us closer together and enrich our mutual dependence. That real unity marked the early believers.

BE THANKFUL

And when they heard this, they lifted their voices to God with one accord and said, "O Lord, it is Thou who didst make the heaven and the earth and the sea, and all that is in them, who by the Holy Spirit, through the mouth of our father David Thy servant, didst say, 'Why did the Gentiles rage, and the peoples devise futile things? The kings of the earth took their stand, and the rulers were gathered together against the Lord, and against His Christ.' For truly in this city there were gathered together against Thy holy servant Jesus, whom Thou didst anoint, both Herod and Pontius Pilate, along with the Gentiles and the peoples of Israel, to do whatever Thy hand and Thy purpose predestined to occur." (4:24–28)

Peter and John returned not in a state of fear and dejection but of exhilaration. They had preached to the Sanhedrin and had been granted the privilege of suffering for their Lord (cf. Acts 5:41). When the rest **heard** their report, **they lifted their voices to God with one accord and said, "O Lord, it is Thou who didst make the heaven and the earth and the sea, and all that is in them."** *Despotēs* (**Lord**) is an uncommon title for God in the New Testament, appearing only five other times (Luke 2:29; 2 Tim. 2:21; 2 Peter 2:1; Jude 4; Rev. 6:10). It is the word from which our English word "despot" derives, and denotes an absolute master. Faced with opposition, they took comfort in God's sovereignty. All their suffering was in His will. Being the Creator of everything, He is in complete control of all events. Confidence in the absolute rulership and might of God was enough to sustain them.

They derived further comfort from the knowledge that such opposition had been foreseen in the Old Testament. The **Holy Spirit,** speaking **through the mouth of . . . David** in Psalm 2:1–2, spoke of the opposition Christ (and by implication His followers) would face: **Why did the Gentiles rage, and the peoples devise futile things? The kings of the earth took their stand, and the rulers were gathered together against the Lord, and against His Christ.** They had witnessed the initial fulfillment of that prophecy in the **city** of Jerusalem. The final fulfillment is presented in Revelation 17:9–14 and sets the stage for His second coming revealed in Revelation 19:11–21. Those opposed to God's purposes had **gathered together against** God's **holy servant Jesus,** whom God had anointed as His servant. They included **Herod and Pontius Pilate, along with the Gentiles and the people of Israel.** All they had accomplished, however, was **to do whatever** God's **hand and . . . purpose predestined to occur. Predestined** is from *proorizō* (Rom. 8:29–30; 1 Cor. 2:7; Eph. 1:5, 11) and means "to determine beforehand." It reminds us that God is the supreme historian who wrote all history before it ever began. Having done their worst, they merely succeeded in fulfilling God's eternal plan (cf. Acts 2:23). As the psalmist expressed it, "The wrath of man shall praise Thee" (Ps. 76:10).

BE DESIROUS OF GREATER BOLDNESS

"And now, Lord, take note of their threats, and grant that Thy bond-servants may speak Thy word with all confidence, while Thou dost extend Thy hand to heal, and signs and wonders take place through the name of Thy holy servant Jesus." And when they had prayed, the place where they had gathered together was shaken, and they were all filled with the Holy Spirit, and began to speak the word of God with boldness. (4:29–31)

How far those gathered together were from being intimidated by the Sanhedrin's threats is seen in the conclusion of their prayer. After asking the **Lord** to **take note of** those **threats** to register their guilt and to protect the threatened preachers, their praise turns to petition as they request that God enable His **bond-servants** to **speak** His **word with all confidence.** Their description of themselves as **bond-servants** refers back to the use of *despotēs* in verse 24 to describe God. They asked not for protection or a place to hide but for even more courage to boldly proclaim God's truth—the very thing they had been ordered not to do. They also requested that God would continue to **heal** and perform **signs and wonders through the name of** His **holy servant Jesus** to confirm His gospel.

God's answer was not long in coming. **When they had prayed, the place where they had gathered together** (perhaps the upper room, Acts 1:13) **was shaken, and they were all filled with the Holy Spirit** (for the third time), **and began to speak the word of God with boldness.** As on the Day of Pentecost, there was a physical manifestation of the Spirit's presence, a shaking. God granted them the fullness of the Spirit for the **boldness** they desired. As in Acts 4:8, the filling of the Spirit does not involve speaking in foreign languages but speaking in their own language the gospel with power. After the first coming of the

Spirit at Pentecost when the rest of the believers were also filled, the miracle of languages disappeared and the filling is for power in speaking the truth from God. So it is in Acts 13:9 with Paul. It should be noted that the miracle of languages will appear again in the case of the entrance into the church of the Samaritans (Acts 8:17–18), Gentiles (Acts 10:44–46), and the disciples of John the Baptist (Acts 19:6).

The church had successfully faced its initial trial of opposition. Instead of succumbing to the temptation to compromise the gospel, it became even bolder. The persecution also served to draw the congregation closer together and to their Lord. In what was to become a recurring theme in church history, opposition only made the church grow stronger. As He had with Joseph (Gen. 50:20), God took the evil intentions of men and used them for His own purposes.

Sins of
the Saints

12

And the congregation of those who believed were of one heart and soul; and not one of them claimed that anything belonging to him was his own; but all things were common property to them. And with great power the apostles were giving witness to the resurrection of the Lord Jesus, and abundant grace was upon them all. For there was not a needy person among them, for all who were owners of land or houses would sell them and bring the proceeds of the sales, and lay them at the apostles' feet; and they would be distributed to each, as any had need. And Joseph, a Levite of Cyprian birth, who was also called Barnabas by the apostles (which translated means, Son of Encouragement), and who owned a tract of land, sold it and brought the money and laid it at the apostles' feet. But a certain man named Ananias, with his wife Sapphira, sold a piece of property, and kept back some of the price for himself, with his wife's full knowledge, and bringing a portion of it, he laid it at the apostles' feet. But Peter said, "Ananias, why has Satan filled your heart to lie to the Holy Spirit, and to keep back some of the price of the land? While it remained unsold, did it not remain your own? And after it was sold, was it not under your control? Why is it that you have conceived this deed in your heart? You have not lied to men, but to God." And as he heard these words, Ananias fell down and breathed his last; and great fear came upon all who heard of it. And the young men arose and covered him up, and after carrying him out, they buried him. Now there elapsed an interval of about three hours, and his wife came in, not knowing what had happened. And Peter responded to her, "Tell me whether you sold the land for such and such a price?" And she said, "Yes, that was the price." Then Peter said to her, "Why is it that you have agreed together to put the Spirit of the Lord to the test? Behold, the feet of those who have buried your husband are at the door, and they shall carry you out as well." And she fell immediately at his feet, and breathed her last; and the young men came in and found her dead, and they carried her out and buried her beside her husband. And great fear came upon the whole church, and upon all who heard of these things. (4:32–5:11)

The Bible is brutally honest in its recording of redemptive history. It records the blemishes and faults of God's people as well as their strengths. Moses' righteous defiance of Pharaoh appears but so does his unrighteous defiance of God that barred him from entering the Promised Land. David's glorious victories grace the pages of Scripture. But along with them, the Bible tells of his abject cowardice before the Philistine king of Gath. The Psalms reveal David the saint; in 2 Samuel 12 Nathan the prophet confronts David the adulterer and murderer. Proverbs records the heights of Solomon's wisdom; Ecclesiastes the depths of his folly. The inspired record never glosses over the truth, though it may be painful and ugly.

So far in Acts, Luke's portrayal of the church has been totally positive. From its dramatic birth on the Day of Pentecost to its joyous, dynamic fellowship and explosive growth, the faithful writer has portrayed the church in all its pristine beauty, freshness, and vitality. Even Satan's attempt to thwart the church through the external pressure applied to its leaders was a failure.

Such a picture is not complete, however. No church is perfect, since all are made up of sinners, and the early church was no exception. This section of Acts chronicles a negative milestone in the church's history: the first recorded instance of sin. Of all the firsts in Acts, this is certainly the saddest.

Satan's purpose is to oppose the work of God. In doing that he is living up to his name, which means "adversary." Where God is at work, he will be active. His initial attack on the church, the persecution of the apostles by the Sanhedrin, backfired. Not only did it fail to silence the apostles, but also Acts 4:4 records that "many of those who had heard the message believed; and the number of the men came to be about five thousand." Further, it gave Peter and John the opportunity to preach the gospel to the Sanhedrin. Faced with that defeat, Satan changed his tactics. Realizing that external pressure only tended to fan the flames, he decided to get at the base of the fire. To do so, he infiltrated the church to attack it with corruption from within. Through the centuries, that tactic has proven to be far more effective than external persecution.

The sins of the saints were a greater burden to Paul than all the opposition he faced from unbelievers. In 2 Corinthians 11:23–27, he catalogs a horrifying list of the physical persecutions he had endured:

> Are they servants of Christ? (I speak as if insane) I more so; in far more labors, in far more imprisonments, beaten times without number, often in danger of death. Five times I received from the Jews thirty-nine lashes. Three times I was beaten with rods, once I was stoned, three times I was shipwrecked, a night and a day I have spent in the deep. I have been on frequent journeys, in dangers from rivers, dangers from robbers, dangers from my countrymen, dangers from the Gentiles, dangers in the city, dangers in the wilderness, dangers on the sea, dangers among false brethren; I have been in labor and hardship, through many sleepless nights, in hunger and thirst, often without food, in cold and exposure.

All that paled into insignificance, however, in light of his burden for the churches: "Apart from such external things, there is the daily pressure upon me of concern for all the churches. Who is weak without my being weak? Who is led into sin without my intense concern?" (2 Cor. 11:28–29).

Paul expressed that "intense concern" when he urged the Romans to

> keep your eye on those who cause dissensions and hindrances contrary to the teaching which you learned, and turn away from them. For such men are slaves, not of our Lord Christ but of their own appetites; and by their smooth and flattering speech they deceive the hearts of the unsuspecting. (Rom. 16:17–18)

He lamented that the Galatians were "so quickly deserting Him who called [them] by the grace of Christ, for a different gospel; which is really not another," and warned them of "some who are disturbing you, and want to distort the gospel of Christ" (Gal. 1:6–7). To the Philippians he wrote, "If therefore there is any encouragement in Christ, if there is any consolation of love, if there is any fellowship of the Spirit, if any affection and compassion, make my joy complete by being of the same mind, maintaining the same love, united in spirit, intent on one purpose" (Phil. 2:1–2).

The greatest burden any pastor carries, the thing that grieves his heart the most, is the sin of his people. Peter was the first to have to deal with that problem, one every succeeding pastor has faced. Acts 5:1–11 records how he handled it. Before showing us the ugliness of the impurity of the church, however, Luke provides a backdrop with a last look at the purity of the church in 4:32–37. This background makes the sin appear all the more vivid, showing that a church at its noblest and purest is only one act away from spiritual tragedy. The passage thus falls into two sections: the sharing of the saints and the sins of the saints.

THE SHARING OF THE SAINTS

And the congregation of those who believed were of one heart and soul; and not one of them claimed that anything belonging to him was his own; but all things were common property to them. And with great power the apostles were giving witness to the resurrection of the Lord Jesus, and abundant grace was upon them all. For there was not a needy person among them, for all who were owners of land or houses would sell them and bring the proceeds of the sales, and lay them at the apostles' feet; and they would be distributed to each, as any had need. And Joseph, a Levite of Cyprian birth, who was also called Barnabas by the apostles (which translated means, Son of Encouragement), and who owned a tract of land, sold it and brought the money and laid it at the apostles' feet. (4:32–37)

This concise passage forms the positive backdrop against which the negative portrait of sin in the church is portrayed. From it four features emerge that illustrate the richness of the fellowship and sharing experienced in the early church.

SPIRITUAL PARTICIPATION

And the congregation of those who believed were of one heart and soul; (4:32a)

The congregation of those who believed had grown so rapidly that they were no longer numbered. That startling growth was the direct result of the action recorded in verse 31, when those who were "filled with the Holy Spirit . . . began to speak the word of God with boldness." The unity of the believers, who **were of one heart and soul,** was also a powerful testimony. Jesus said in John 13:35, "By this all men will know that you are My disciples, if you have love for one another." In His high-priestly prayer, Jesus prayed that "they may all be one; even as Thou, Father, art in Me, and I in Thee, that they also may be in Us; that the world may believe that Thou didst send Me" (John 17:21). The first fellowship was an answer to that prayer both in position and practice.

The basis of their shared life was twofold. First, they were preoccupied with ministering to each other. So intent were they on meeting each other's needs that they had no concern for gratifying their own desires. Theirs was a humility stemming from seeing themselves in relation to Jesus Christ, and others as more important than themselves (Phil. 2:3). Second, they were focused beyond themselves to reaching the lost world with the truth of the gospel. That left them little time to bother with trivial personal matters. Their unity stemmed from focusing on those priorities Jesus had left them: selflessly loving each other, and reaching the lost world.

STRONG PREACHING

And with great power the apostles were giving witness to the resurrection of the Lord Jesus, and abundant grace was upon them all. (4:33)

The **great power** of the apostles came from the filling of the Spirit (Acts 1:8). It was in His power that they **were giving witness to the resurrection**—the very thing the Sanhedrin had forbidden them to do. The imperfect tense of the verb translated **were giving** shows that was their continual practice. As Peter expressed it to the Sanhedrin, "We cannot stop speaking what we have seen and heard" (Acts 4:20). Like Paul, they felt keenly their obligation to proclaim the gospel (cf. Rom. 1:14–15).

As noted in chapters 2 and 5 of this commentary, **the resurrection of the Lord Jesus** was the major emphasis of apostolic preaching (cf. Acts 2:24, 32; 3:15; 5:30; 10:40; 13:30, 33, 34, 37). Although they knew that such an emphasis greatly offended the Jewish authorities, the apostles never suppressed the truth to avoid that offense. Such an uncompromising attitude stands in stark contrast to the church's practice today. In the name of "contextualization" (a more palatable term for worldliness), the gospel message is stripped of anything deemed offensive. But unbelievers *must* be offended at the point of their sin, or they will never come to Christ. In Romans 9:33, Paul applied to Jesus Christ the words of Isaiah (cf. Isa. 8:14; 28:16): "Behold, I lay in Zion a stone of stumbling and a rock of offense, and he who believes in Him will not be disappointed." Peter also quotes Isaiah and adds that those who stumble do so "because they are disobedient to the word" (1 Peter 2:8). Unbelievers' very existence is an affront to God; certainly we must risk affronting them to let them know that.

Because of the apostles' powerful preaching, **abundant grace was upon them all. Grace** (favor) can be understood in two ways. First, as in 2:47, it can refer to the approval of the people. Although the leaders opposed them, the common people had not yet turned against them. On the contrary, they were impressed by the believers' love and unity. Second, and more important, the early church had God's favor. A fellowship characterized by loving unity and evangelistic zeal receives God's blessings.

SHARING PRACTICALLY

and not one of them claimed that anything belonging to him was his own; but all things were common property to them. . . . For there was not a needy person among them, for all who were owners of land or houses would sell them and bring the proceeds of the sales, and lay them at the apostles' feet; and they would be distributed to each, as any had need. (4:32b, 34–35)

The loving, unselfish unity of the early church found a practical expression in the sharing of material possessions. **Not one of them claimed that anything belonging to him was his own; but all things were common property to them.** The phrase **not one of them** shows that this attitude was characteristic of everyone inclusively. They all understood that everything they had belonged to God, and they possessed it in trust for Him. Since all belonged to God, when someone had a need, they were obligated to use the divine resources to meet that need. A very practical test of a Christian's love is how much he or she is willing to sacrifice financially. James asks, "If a brother or sister is without clothing and in need of daily food, and one of you says to them, 'Go in peace, be warmed and be filled,' and yet do not give them what is necessary for their body, what use is that?" (James 2:15–16). The apostle John expressed it even more bluntly: "But whoever has the world's goods, and beholds his brother in need and closes his heart against him, how does the love of God abide in him?" (1 John 3:17).

Second Corinthians 8 demonstrates the sacrificial spirit of the poor believers in Macedonia:

> Now, brethren, we wish to make known to you the grace of God which has been given in the churches of Macedonia, that in a great ordeal of affliction their abundance of joy and their deep poverty overflowed in the wealth of their liberality. For I testify that according to their ability, and beyond their ability they gave of their own accord, begging us with much entreaty for the favor of participation in the support of the saints, and this, not as we had expected, but they first gave themselves to the Lord and to us by the will of God. (vv. 1–5)

The result of this practical demonstration of love in Jerusalem was that **there was not a needy person among them.** As noted in the discussion of Acts 2:44–46 in chapter 7, thousands of pilgrims flocked into Jerusalem on the Day of Pentecost. Undoubtedly, many in the early church came from the ranks of those pilgrims. They understandably decided to remain in Jerusalem under the apostles' teaching rather than return home. Further, some believers who lived in Jerusalem no doubt lost their jobs because of their faith. That the church met all these needs showed the depth of believers' love for each other. Such care and sharing was a powerful testimony to their community.

More specifically, Luke reports that to meet the needs of others, **all who were owners of land or houses would sell them and bring the proceeds of the sales, and lay them at the apostles' feet.** Selling houses and land was far more sacrificial than sharing part of one's income. It meant liquidating capital assets that could be irreplaceable, thus reducing one's personal security. Some have seen in this passage a primitive form of communism or communal living. As noted in the discussion of Acts 2:44–46 in chapter 7, however, that is not true. As in 2:45, the imperfect tense of the verbs indicates continuous action. They did not at any point pool all their possessions. Also, it is clear from Acts 12:12 that individual believers still owned houses. Further, Peter's words to Ananias in 5:4 show that such selling of property was strictly voluntary. The singling out of Barnabas also implies that the selling was voluntary. If it were compulsory there would have been nothing commendatory about his actions. Finally, Acts does not record that any other church followed this pattern of selling property.

The proceeds **would be distributed to each, as any had need.** That was done by the apostles, who (at least temporarily, cf. 6:1ff.) were in charge of distributing funds to the poor. The imperfect verb denotes the continuous nature of the distribution. It was a continuous way of life for those with property periodically to sell it as needed on behalf of others.

This passage illustrates an important pattern concerning giving in the local church. The donations are to be placed in the control of the spiritual teachers, who are then responsible before God for their use. Too often, people want to give only if they can specify how the money is to be used. That kind of self-serving giving fails to understand the delegated spiritual authority of God-ordained leaders and may often merely seek the applause of men. Giving is to be so selfless that Jesus said in Matthew 6:3–4, "When you give alms, do not let your left hand know what your right hand is doing." Then He added, "Your Father who sees in secret will repay you."

A SAMPLE PERSON

And Joseph, a Levite of Cyprian birth, who was also called Barnabas by the apostles (which translated means, Son of Encouragement), and who owned a tract of land, sold it and brought the money and laid it at the apostles' feet. (4:36–37)

Luke now singles out one man as an example from among those who were donating property. **Joseph,** better known as **Barnabas,** becomes a prominent figure in Acts. He introduced Paul to the suspicious Jerusalem congregation, reassuring them that his conversion was genuine (Acts 9:26–27). In Acts 11:22–24, he undertook a mission to minister to the Greek converts in Antioch. He was Paul's personal companion during the early years of the great apostle's ministry. He accompanied him to Jerusalem with the contributions sent from Antioch to help the poor there (Acts 11:30). After serving alongside him as one of the copastors in Antioch (Acts 13:1), he accompanied Paul on his first missionary journey (Acts 13:2ff.). At the conclusion of that journey, Barnabas and Paul represented the Antioch church at the crucial Jerusalem council (Acts 15). Sadly, his close association with Paul ended in the dispute over taking John Mark on the second missionary journey (Acts 15:36–41).

Because this is the first time Barnabas appears in Acts, Luke provides some background information on him. He was a **Levite,** a member of the priestly tribe. Not all those connected with the temple were enemies of Jesus and the apostles. Like Paul, he was not a native of the land of Israel, but was **of Cyprian birth.** The fact that he was from the island of Cyprus may indicate why the first missionary trip with Paul began with that island. He was given the name **Barnabas** by the apostles, **which translated,** Luke notes, **means Son of Encouragement.** He was related to Mark (Col. 4:10), and his sister's house was the meeting place of the Jerusalem church (Acts 12:12). Despite his falling out with Paul, he certainly lived up to his name. Luke describes him in Acts 11:24 as "a good man, and full of the Holy Spirit and faith."

How it was possible for a **Levite** to have **owned a tract of land** is not stated. The Old Testament prohibited the Levites from owning property (Num. 18:20, 24; Deut. 10:9), though they did own houses (Lev. 25:32–33). That prohibition was apparently not enforced in New Testament times. Whether the property Barnabas sold was located in Palestine or his native Cyprus is also not stated.

Luke is not concerned with how he obtained the property or where it was located. What is important is the loving heart of Barnabas, who **sold** the land **and brought the money and laid it at the apostles' feet.** He gave out of a pure love, not to call attention to himself but for the simple blessedness of giving (cf. Acts 20:35). He represents many others who also gave sacrificially and is an example for us to follow.

The Sins of the Saints

But a certain man named Ananias, with his wife Sapphira, sold a piece of property, and kept back some of the price for himself, with his wife's full knowledge, and bringing a portion of it, he laid it at the apostles' feet. But Peter said, "Ananias, why has Satan filled your heart to lie to the Holy Spirit, and to keep back some of the price of the land? While it remained unsold, did it not remain your own? And after it was sold, was it not under your control? Why is it that you have conceived this deed in your heart? You have not lied to men, but to God." And as he heard these words, Ananias fell down and breathed his last; and great fear came upon all who heard of it. And the young men arose and covered him up, and after carrying him out, they buried him. Now there elapsed an interval of about three hours, and his wife came in, not knowing what had happened. And Peter responded to her, "Tell me whether you sold the land for such and such a price?" And she said, "Yes, that was the price." Then Peter said to her, "Why is it that you have agreed together to put the Spirit of the Lord to the test? Behold, the feet of those who have buried your husband are at the door, and they shall carry you out as well." And she fell immediately at his feet, and breathed her last; and the young men came in and found her dead, and they carried her out and buried her beside her husband. And great fear came upon the whole church, and upon all who heard of these things. (5:1–11)

The beauty of the sacrificial, selfless giving of the early church was marred by the ugly sins of deceit and self-glory. The story of Ananias and Sapphira is to Acts what the story of Achan is to the book of Joshua. Both incidents interrupted the victorious progress of the people of God. The drama unfolds in four scenes: sinful pretense, spiritual perception, swift punishment, and solemn purging.

SPIRITUAL PRETENSE

But a certain man named Ananias, with his wife Sapphira, sold a piece of property, and kept back some of the price for himself, with his wife's full knowledge, and bringing a portion of it, he laid it at the apostles' feet. (5:1–2)

But introduces a sharp contrast between the actions of Barnabas and those of **Ananias** and **his wife Sapphira.** They, too, **sold a piece of property.** Unlike Barnabas, however, Ananias **kept back some of the price for himself, with his wife's full knowledge.** They saw an opportunity to make a double profit: They would gain spiritual prestige and still make some money on the side. Withholding part of the money for their own use was not a sin, as Peter clearly states in verse 4. Nowhere were the believers commanded to give everything. Their giving, like all New Testament giving, was voluntary (cf. 2 Cor. 9:7). The overt sin was lying, by publicly pretending to have given all the proceeds of the sale of their property. That sin was but the outward manifestation, however. The deeper, more devastating sin was hypocrisy based on a desire for spiritual status. They desired the approval of men for their sacrificial act and to be thought of as members of those most spiritually noble.

No sin drew a sharper rebuke from our Lord than hypocrisy. In the Sermon on the Mount He warned His disciples:

> Beware of practicing your righteousness before men to be noticed by them; otherwise you have no reward with your Father who is in heaven. When therefore you give alms, do not sound a trumpet before you, as the hypocrites do in the synagogues and in the streets, that they may be honored by men. Truly I say to you, they have their reward in full. But when you give alms, do not let your left hand know what your right hand is doing that your alms may be in secret; and your Father who sees in secret will repay you. And when you pray, you are not to be as the hypocrites; for they love to stand and pray in the synagogues and on the street corners, in order to be seen by men. Truly I say to you, they have their reward in full. But you, when you pray, go into your in-

ner room, and when you have shut your door, pray to your Father who is in secret, and your Father who sees in secret will repay you. And whenever you fast, do not put on a gloomy face as the hypocrites do, for they neglect their appearance in order to be seen fasting by men. Truly I say to you, they have their reward in full. But you, when you fast, anoint your head, and wash your face so that you may not be seen fasting by men, but by your Father who is in secret; and your Father who sees in secret will repay you. (Matt. 6:1–6, 16–18)

He repeatedly denounced the hypocrisy of the scribes and Pharisees (Matt. 15:7; 22:18; 23:13–36) and warned His disciples against its influence (Luke 12:1). He also warned that hell would be populated by hypocrites (Matt. 24:51).

None are so ugly in God's sight as those who flaunt a spiritual beauty they do not possess. Ananias and Sapphira were nothing more than sinning saints feigning spirituality. Any sin against the fellowship of believers is a sin against Christ (1 Cor. 8:12). Their offering was an affront to God and their execution God's work to keep the church pure.

Some have questioned whether or not they were true believers. It is best to see them as genuine Christians for several reasons. First, they were included in the "congregation of those who believed" in Acts 4:32. Second, they were involved with the Holy Spirit, thus indicating a relationship to Him. Third, if they were not Christians, what lesson about sin did this give to teach all the rest who were true believers? Fourth, Satan can become personally involved with believers (cf. Matt. 16:21–23; Eph. 6:12; 1 Peter 5:8–9). Finally, death can be divine chastening for a believer (1 Cor. 11:30–32; 1 John 5:16).

SPIRITUAL PERCEPTION

But Peter said, "Ananias, why has Satan filled your heart to lie to the Holy Spirit, and to keep back some of the price of the land? While it remained unsold, did it not remain your own? And after it was sold, was it not under your control? Why is it that you have conceived this deed in your heart? You have not lied to men, but to God." (5:3–4)

The deceit of Ananias and Sapphira did not fool Peter. Guided by the Holy Spirit, he saw through their hypocrisy. Ananias, no doubt expecting the accolades of the people for his gift, must have been stunned by Peter's words.

In contrast to the Spirit-filled giving of Barnabas, that of Ananias was satanically inspired. **Satan filled** his **heart to lie to the Holy**

Spirit, and to keep back some of the price of the land. As already noted, to withhold part of the proceeds was not a sin. To **lie to the Holy Spirit,** however, was. And the tragedy is that it was completely unnecessary. While the land **remained unsold,** Peter reminds him, **did it not remain your own? And after it was sold, was it not under your control?** Ananias was under no compulsion to sell his property or to donate the entire amount of the sale.

Peter's next question was a stern rebuke to Ananias: **Why is it that you have conceived this deed in your heart?** Whereas he was surely strongly tempted by Satan (v. 3), the responsibility for the sin rested on Ananias. He had the freedom to do what he wanted to with his property and chose to be deceitful. His sin, as already noted, originated in his own selfish hypocrisy. The Bible nowhere places the blame for a Christian's sin on Satan.

This passage teaches two vitally important truths about the Holy Spirit. First, it affirms that He is a person, not an influence or impersonal force, since He can be lied to. Second, verse 3 says Ananias lied to the Holy Spirit, while verse 4 says that he lied to God, a clear affirmation of the deity of the Holy Spirit.

SWIFT PUNISHMENT

And as he heard these words, Ananias fell down and breathed his last; and great fear came upon all who heard of it. And the young men arose and covered him up, and after carrying him out, they buried him. Now there elapsed an interval of about three hours, and his wife came in, not knowing what had happened. And Peter responded to her, "Tell me whether you sold the land for such and such a price?" And she said, "Yes, that was the price." Then Peter said to her, "Why is it that you have agreed together to put the Spirit of the Lord to the test? Behold, the feet of those who have buried your husband are at the door, and they shall carry you out as well." And she fell immediately at his feet, and breathed her last; and the young men came in and found her dead, and they carried her out and buried her beside her husband. (5:5–10)

God moved quickly to remove this spiritual cancer from the body. **As he heard** Peter's **words, Ananias fell down and breathed his last; and great fear came upon all who heard of it.** The ultimate cause of Ananias's death was God's judgment. The physical cause was perhaps a heart attack, brought on by the terrifying realization of his embarrassing guilt and his shameful exposure. English history records a similar incident, when the Dean of St. Paul's cathedral died of terror after King Edward I gave him an angry look (F. F. Bruce, *The Book of the Acts* [Grand Rapids: Eerdmans, 1971], 114). In this case, however, it was divine judgment, not fear of Peter, that killed Ananias. It is a sobering truth that God sometimes takes the lives of sinning believers. Death is God's ultimate form of physical discipline for sinning believers. He wants His church pure (cf. 2 Cor. 11:2; Eph. 5:27).

After Ananias's death, **the young men** of the congregation **arose and covered him up, and after carrying him out** of the city, **they buried him.** Due to the hot climate of Palestine, it was customary for burial to take place the same day. That was especially prescribed for someone who died because of divine judgment (cf. Deut. 21:22–23).

The second act of the tragedy was about to take place. An **interval of about three hours** elapsed (indicating something of the length of church gatherings in those days) during which the young men buried Ananias. After that much time had elapsed, Sapphira **came in, not knowing what had happened** to her husband. Giving her one last opportunity to repent, **Peter** asked, **"Tell me whether you sold the land for such and such a price?"** As planned before with her husband, she chose to continue the deception, replying, **"Yes, that was the price."**

As he had for her husband, Peter then pronounced judgment on her. **"Why is it,"** he lamented, **"that you have agreed together to put the Spirit of the Lord to the test?"** Peter exposed the conspiracy and the folly of testing holy God's reaction to sin. **"Behold, the feet of those who have buried your husband are at the door, and they shall carry you out as well."** God's judgment fell on her equally swiftly, and **she fell immediately at his feet, and breathed her last; and the young men,** having just returned from burying Ananias, **came in and found her dead, and they carried her out and buried her beside her husband.** So ended Ananias and Sapphira's short-lived and foolish attempt to deceive the Holy Spirit and test God's patience with iniquity.

The action of God was meant to impress upon the church the seriousness of the sins of the saints. It had that effect, as the next verse records.

SOLEMN PURGING

And great fear came upon the whole church, and upon all who heard of these things. (5:11)

One benefit of church discipline is that it deters others from sinning (cf. 1 Tim. 5:19–20). No doubt much self-examination took place following the deaths of Ananias and Sapphira. Their deaths caused **great fear,** not only among **the whole church** but also **upon all who heard of these things.** God's strong desire for a pure church, and His willingness to take drastic steps to achieve that desire, were obvious for all to see. It was time, as Peter was later to write, "for judgment to begin with the household of God; and if it begins with us first, what will be the outcome for those who do not obey the gospel of God?" (1 Peter 4:17). Perhaps Peter remembered this incident when he was inspired to write from Psalm 34, "Let him who means to love life and see good days refrain his tongue from evil and his lips from speaking guile" (1 Peter 3:10).

The Early Church Pattern for Evangelism

13

And at the hands of the apostles many signs and wonders were taking place among the people; and they were all with one accord in Solomon's portico. But none of the rest dared to associate with them; however, the people held them in high esteem. And all the more believers in the Lord, multitudes of men and women, were constantly added to their number; to such an extent that they even carried the sick out into the streets, and laid them on cots and pallets, so that when Peter came by, at least his shadow might fall on any one of them. And also the people from the cities in the vicinity of Jerusalem were coming together, bringing people who were sick or afflicted with unclean spirits; and they were all being healed. But the high priest rose up, along with all his associates (that is the sect of the Sadducees), and they were filled with jealousy; and they laid hands on the apostles, and put them in a public jail. But an angel of the Lord during the night opened the gates of the prison, and taking them out he said, "Go your way, stand and speak to the people in the temple the whole message of this Life." And upon hearing this, they entered into the temple about daybreak, and began to teach. Now when the high priest and his associates had come, they called the Council together, even all the Senate of the sons of Israel, and sent orders to the prison house for them to be brought. But the officers who came did not find them in the prison; and they returned, and reported back, saying, "We found the prison house locked quite securely and the guards standing at the doors; but when we had opened up, we found no one inside." Now when the captain of the temple guard and the chief priests heard these words, they were greatly perplexed about them as to what would come of this. But someone came and reported to them, "Behold, the men whom you put in prison are standing in the temple and teaching the people!" Then the captain went along with the officers and proceeded to bring them back without violence (for they were afraid of the people, lest they should be stoned). And when they had brought them, they stood them before the Council. And the high priest questioned them, saying, "We gave you strict orders not to continue teaching in this name, and behold, you have filled Jerusalem with your teaching, and intend to bring this man's blood upon us." But Peter and the apostles answered and said, "We must obey God rather than men. The God of our fathers raised up Jesus, whom you had put to death by hanging Him on a cross. He is the one whom God exalted to His right hand as a Prince and a Savior, to grant repentance to Israel, and forgiveness of sins. And we are witnesses of these things; and so is the Holy Spirit, whom God has given to those who obey Him." But when they heard this, they were cut to the quick and were intending to slay them. But a certain Pharisee named Gamaliel, a teacher of the Law, respected by all the people, stood up in the Council and gave orders to put the men outside for a short time. And he said to them, "Men of Israel, take care what you propose to do with these men. For some time ago Theudas rose up, claiming to be somebody; and a group of about four hundred men joined up with him. And he was slain; and all who followed him were dispersed and came to nothing. After this man Judas of Galilee rose up in the days of the census, and drew away some people after him, he too perished, and all those who followed him were scattered. And so in the present case, I say to you, stay away from these men and let them alone, for if this plan or action should be of men, it will be overthrown; but if it is of God, you will not be able to overthrow them; or else you may even be found fighting against God." And they took his advice; and after calling the apostles in, they flogged them and ordered them to speak no more in the name of Jesus, and then released them. So they went on their way from the presence of the Council, rejoicing that they had been considered worthy to

suffer shame for His name. And every day, in the temple and from house to house, they kept right on teaching and preaching Jesus as the Christ. (5:12–42)

A perennial problem the church of Jesus Christ faces is a lack of focus on its mission. Widespread confusion exists over what that primary mission should be. Some argue that the church should lead the crusade for social justice for the poor and downtrodden. Others see it as a political force to help change the culture. Still others view their church as a private club, where they can socialize with their friends.

On a more biblical note, the church's goal is to mature the saints through the preaching of the Word, fellowship, and discipleship. It also meets to praise and worship God. Those are important goals, and should mark every church. Yet none of them is the church's primary goal here on earth. Indeed, every one of them could be better accomplished in heaven.

What is the primary goal of the church? Our Lord answered that question by charging us to "go therefore and make disciples of all the nations, baptizing them in the name of the Father and the Son and the Holy Spirit, teaching them to observe all that I commanded you" (Matt. 28:19–20). The church's primary goal is evangelism. It is to carry on the work begun by the Lord Jesus Christ, whose mission was "to seek and to save that which was lost" (Luke 19:10). That is the only duty of the church that can't be better done in heaven.

The early church understood its purpose clearly. The believers never lost sight of their calling to be Christ's witnesses "both in Judea and Samaria, and even to the remotest part of the earth" (Acts 1:8). Their zeal and effectiveness resulted in explosive growth. On the day of Pentecost, the birthday of the church, "there were added that day about three thousand souls" (Acts 2:41). In the days following Pentecost, "the Lord was adding to their number day by day those who were being saved" (Acts 2:47). By the conclusion of Peter's second sermon, the number of men in the church had risen to 5,000 (Acts 4:4). As noted in the discussion of Acts 4:1–4 in chapter 11, that is the last specific number of believers recorded in Acts; from that time on the church grew too rapidly to keep count. Acts 5:14 speaks of "multitudes of men and women" being added to the church, while Acts 6:7 adds that "the number of disciples continued to increase greatly in Jerusalem." Acts 9:31 says that "the church throughout all Judea and Galilee and Samaria enjoyed peace, being built up; and, going on in the fear of the Lord and in the comfort of the Holy Spirit, it continued to increase." Acts 11:21 speaks of "a large number who believed [and] turned to the Lord" in Antioch, while verse 24 records that "considerable numbers were brought to the Lord" through Barnabas's ministry in that city.

What did the church do to contribute to this remarkable growth? How did the church expand so rapidly despite the determined opposition of the Jewish authorities? Acts 5:12–42 presents five keys to the effective evangelism of the early church: purity, power, persecution, persistence, and productivity.

PURITY

They were all with one accord in Solomon's portico. But none of the rest dared to associate with them; however, the people held them in high esteem. And all the more believers in the Lord, multitudes of men and women, were constantly added to their number; (5:12b–14)

To be useful to the Lord, an individual must be pure (cf. 2 Tim. 2:19–21). No one stated that truth any more clearly than the noble nineteenth-century Scottish pastor and evangelist Robert Murray McCheyne. He gave the following sage advice to a young man entering the ministry:

> Do not forget the culture of the inner man—I mean of the heart. How diligently the cavalry officer keeps his sabre clean and sharp; every stain he rubs off with the greatest care. Remember you are God's sword, His instrument—I trust a chosen vessel unto Him to bear His name. In great measure, according to the purity and perfections of the instrument, will be the success. It is not great talents God blesses so much as great likeness to Jesus. A holy minister is an awful weapon in the hands of God. (Andrew A. Bonar, ed., *Memoirs of McCheyne* [reprint, Chicago: Moody, 1978], p. 95)

What is true of believers individually is also true of the church collectively. The church that would reach the world must be pure; it must be a church that deals with sin. God displayed the importance He places on the purity of His church by His dramatic judgment of Ananias and Sapphira (5:1–11). While God may still intervene directly in the lives of sinning Christians (1 Cor. 11:30), disciplining sinning believers is the responsibility of each congregation.

Sadly, church discipline is practically an ignored duty today. It has fallen prey to the unbiblical notion that loving people and building up their self-esteem means tolerating their sin. Biblical love, however, seeks the well-being of others. Since the goal of discipline is to deal with sin, which is harmful, love and discipline are not mutually exclusive (cf. Prov. 27:6). It is because God loves believers that He chastens them (Heb. 12:5–6).

The importance of confronting sin in the church is expressed in many New Testament injunctions. In Luke 17:3, the Lord Jesus Christ commanded, "If your brother sins, rebuke him." Paul put Hymenaeus and Alexander out of the Ephesian church because of their blasphemies (1 Tim. 1:20). He commanded the Corinthians to remove from their fellowship a man guilty of gross sexual immorality (1 Cor. 5:1–7). He instructed his young protégé Titus to "reprove [believers] severely that they may be sound in the faith" (Titus 1:13). Even church leaders are not exempt from public rebuke (1 Tim. 5:20; cf. Gal. 2:11–14).

The most extensive teaching on how to exercise church discipline comes from our Lord Himself:

> If your brother sins, go and reprove him in private; if he listens to you, you have won your brother. But if he does not listen to you, take one or two more with you, so that by the mouth of two or three witnesses every fact may be confirmed. And if he refuses to listen to them, tell it to the church; and if he refuses to listen even to the church, let him be to you as a Gentile and a tax-gatherer. Truly I say to you, whatever you shall bind on earth shall be bound in heaven; and whatever you loose on earth shall be loosed in heaven. Again I say to you, that if two of you agree on earth about anything that they may ask, it shall be done for them by My Father who is in heaven. For where two or three have gathered together in My name, there I am in their midst. (Matt. 18:15–20)

The church pays a steep price for disobeying the Lord's clear teaching on this matter. The impure, worldly church that is the inevitable result of the absence of confrontive holiness will not be an effective witness for Jesus Christ. Disciplining of sinning saints is not an option but an obligation.

Verses 12b–14 form a parenthesis. The thought begun in the first half of verse 12 resumes in verse 15. The subject of the parenthetical thought is the purity of the church. Now that the sin of Ananias and Sapphira had been dealt with, the church was again in **one accord. Solomon's portico** lay along the eastern side of the temple, facing the Court of the Gentiles. It was the site of Peter's second sermon (3:11ff.) and one of our Lord's discourses (John 10:23ff.). It had become a favorite gathering place for the believers, who met there daily for prayer and worship.

Luke then presents the paradoxical truth that **none of the rest** (unbelievers) **dared to associate** with the believers, though **the people held them in high esteem.** They had great respect for the followers of Jesus and their devotion to their beliefs. Surely they also respected the power of God displayed through them. But to balance the respect that might lead them to join was the fear that sin would be severely judged. The swift judgment of Ananias and Sapphira kept the half-hearted and uncommitted from joining the Christians (cf. 5:5, 11). The practice of sternly dealing with sin helps maintain a pure church. People do not rush to join a church that will expose their sin. Discipline is thus an essential key to evangelism, because it purifies the church and keeps the shallow and merely curious away. It is startling to see churches today that will purposely not make sin an issue so as to attract the shallow and curious.

Many pastors fear that the practice of church discipline will drive people away and ruin their churches. It will drive away those who love their sin, but attract those who hate it and seek repentance and righteousness. Despite the strict discipline imposed by God so that unbelievers feared to associate with the church, **all the more believers in the Lord were constantly added to** the exploding church. In fact, there were so many that they lost count. Luke could only describe them **as multitudes of men and women.** The means of this growth was purity.

Uncompromising commitment to holiness characterized these believers—not the fearful commitment of self-righteous legalism but one springing out of love for the Lord. They were a fearful group, and that kept those who loved their sin away, and those who wanted forgiveness for sin near. That stands in sharp contrast to the masses of uncommitted, even unsaved, people that feel comfortable in the church today. The failure of churches to preach holy living, and to discipline those who don't live that way, allows sinners and hypocrites to remain in the church, convoluting its direction, sapping its power, robbing it of purity and marring its testimony. Men may build their churches with a tolerance for sin, but the Lord builds His among people who love holiness and hate and expose sin.

Jesus demands a high level of commitment from those who would follow Him. In Luke 9:57–62 He had the following dialogue with some would-be followers:

> And as they were going along the road, someone said to Him, "I will follow You wherever You go." And Jesus said to him, "The foxes have holes, and the birds of the air have nests, but the Son of Man has nowhere to lay His head." And He said to another, "Follow Me." But he said, "Permit me first to go and bury my father." But He said to him, "Allow the dead to bury their own dead; but as for you, go and proclaim everywhere the kingdom of God." And another also said, "I will follow You, Lord; but first permit me to say good-bye to those at

home." But Jesus said to him, "No one, after putting his hand to the plow and looking back, is fit for the kingdom of God."

In Matthew 10:32–39 He added,

> Everyone therefore who shall confess Me before men, I will also confess him before My Father who is in heaven. But whoever shall deny Me before men, I will also deny him before My Father who is in heaven. Do not think that I came to bring peace on the earth; I did not come to bring peace, but a sword. For I came to set a man against his father, and a daughter against her mother, and a daughter-in-law against her mother-in-law; and a man's enemies will be the members of his household. He who loves father or mother more than Me is not worthy of Me; and he who loves son or daughter more than Me is not worthy of Me. And he who does not take his cross and follow after Me is not worthy of Me. He who has found his life shall lose it, and he who has lost his life for My sake shall find it.

The Lord Jesus Christ wants total commitment. Only those who are willing to forsake all, including sin, and lose their lives in submission to Him, are worthy to be His followers. A church made up of such people will be a pure church, with a powerful testimony to the world.

POWER

And at the hands of the apostles many signs and wonders were taking place among the people . . . to such an extent that they even carried the sick out into the streets, and laid them on cots and pallets, so that when Peter came by, at least his shadow might fall on any one of them. And also the people from the cities in the vicinity of Jerusalem were coming together, bringing people who were sick or afflicted with unclean spirits; and they were all being healed. (5:12a, 15–16)

As already noted, verse 15 resumes the thought begun in the first half of verse 12. The parenthesis, describing the purity of the church, is foundational to this section. The early church was a growing church because it was a pure church. They were a clean channel through which the power of God could flow.

As discussed in chapters 5, 7, and 8 of this commentary, **signs and wonders** were designed to point men to spiritual truth. They also confirmed the apostles' claim to be God's messengers. With the passing of the apostles from the scene and the completion of the canon of Scripture, the need for miracles vanished. They were not intended to be an ongoing part of the life of the church but a unique ministry of the apostles. In fact, in 2 Corinthians 12:12, Paul wrote, "The signs of a true apostle were performed among you with all perseverance, by signs and wonders and miracles." In keeping with that unique ministry, Luke carefully notes that it was **at the hands of the apostles that the many signs and wonders were taking place among the people.** As noted in the discussion of Acts 3:1–10 in chapter 8, the early church was not a miracle-working church—it was a church with miracle-working apostles.

The outpouring of miracles was an answer to their prayer that God would "grant that Thy bond-servants may speak Thy word with all confidence, while Thou dost extend Thy hand to heal, and signs and wonders take place through the name of Thy holy servant Jesus" (Acts 4:29–30). God did not answer that prayer, however, until the church was pure.

The apostles carried on their widespread, public healing ministry **to such an extent that** people **even carried the sick out into the streets, and laid them on cots and pallets. Cots** (*klinariōn*) refers to small beds or couches, whereas **pallets** (*krabattōn*) describes the straw mattresses commonly used by the poor. Luke's use of these two terms implies that both rich and poor sought healing from the apostles. Far from being skeptical about the apostles' healing power, they were so aware of their potency over disease that they hoped **that when Peter came by, at least his shadow might fall on any one of them** and heal them. That was not mere superstition but reflected the belief he had divine power and that his shadow might carry the power of healing. The Bible does not say that Peter's shadow actually healed anyone, merely that the people believed it might.

The stir caused by the massive number of the apostles' healings was not limited to Jerusalem. Additional **people from the cities in the vicinity of Jerusalem were coming together, bringing people who were sick or afflicted with unclean spirits; and they were all being healed.** This is the first record of the church's influence spreading beyond Jerusalem. They were beginning to fulfill the Lord's charge to be His witnesses not only in Jerusalem but also "in all Judea and Samaria, and even to the remotest part of the earth" (Acts 1:8).

PERSECUTION

But the high priest rose up, along with all his associates (that is the sect of the Sadducees), and they were filled with jealousy;

and they laid hands on the apostles, and put them in a public jail. But an angel of the Lord during the night opened the gates of the prison, and taking them out he said, "Go your way, stand and speak to the people in the temple the whole message of this Life." And upon hearing this, they entered into the temple about daybreak, and began to teach. Now when the high priest and his associates had come, they called the Council together, even all the Senate of the sons of Israel, and sent orders to the prison house for them to be brought. But the officers who came did not find them in the prison; and they returned, and reported back, saying, "We found the prison house locked quite securely and the guards standing at the doors; but when we had opened up, we found no one inside." Now when the captain of the temple guard and the chief priests heard these words, they were greatly perplexed about them as to what would come of this. But someone came and reported to them, "Behold, the men whom you put in prison are standing in the temple and teaching the people!" Then the captain went along with the officers and proceeded to bring them back without violence (for they were afraid of the people, lest they should be stoned). And when they had brought them, they stood them before the Council. And the high priest questioned them, saying, "We gave you strict orders not to continue teaching in this name, and behold, you have filled Jerusalem with your teaching, and intend to bring this man's blood upon us." (5:12–28)

A pure, powerful church will inevitably provoke a hostile reaction from the satanic world system. Successful Christians and churches will make waves, and the world and Satan will retaliate with persecution. "Indeed," Paul wrote to Timothy, "all who desire to live godly in Christ Jesus will be persecuted" (2 Tim. 3:12). Reflecting on the persecution he had faced during his ministry, Peter wrote, "If when you do what is right and suffer for it you patiently endure it, this finds favor with God" (1 Peter 2:20); "for it is better, if God should will it so, that you suffer for doing what is right rather than for doing what is wrong" (1 Peter 3:17); "if you are reviled for the name of Christ, you are blessed, because the Spirit of glory and of God rests upon you" (1 Peter 4:14). In the Beatitudes, Jesus said,

> Blessed are those who have been persecuted for the sake of righteousness, for theirs is the kingdom of heaven. Blessed are you when men cast insults at you, and persecute you, and say all kinds of evil against you falsely, on account of Me. Rejoice, and be glad, for your reward in

heaven is great, for so they persecuted the prophets who were before you (Matt. 5:10–12; cf. John 15:17–20).

We are "heirs of God and fellow heirs with Christ," wrote Paul to the Romans, "if indeed we suffer with Him in order that we may also be glorified with Him" (Rom. 8:17).

It comes as no surprise, then, that the power and effectiveness of the church resulted in bitter opposition. Alarmed by the continuing rapid spread of the gospel and the church, and the prevailing of its influence, **the high priest rose up, along with all his associates (that is the sect of the Sadducees), and they were filled with jealousy.** The **high priest** could refer to Annas (cf. 4:6) or to Caiaphas, who was in office until A.D. 36. As were all the high priests of that time, he was a member of **the sect of the Sadducees.** They **were filled with jealousy** at the church's popularity with the people (cf. 5:13). Further, as noted in the discussion of Acts 4:1–4 in chapter 11, they were committed to maintaining the status quo. They sought at all costs to avoid provoking a reaction from the Romans that would cost them their privileged leadership position. While the Pharisees led the opposition to Jesus in the gospels, the Sadducees were the chief opponents of the early church.

The Sadducees' jealousy did not remain idle. The rise of a new religious sect in Jerusalem, the very seat of their power, would threaten to erode their hold on the people. This sect above all, which believed the very man they had murdered was alive from the dead and the power behind the amazing and prolific miracles, could not be tolerated. Their leadership was in a fragile state, religiously and politically, since there was also the danger that the turmoil created in the city would cause the Romans to take action. Compelled by the gravity of the situation, **they laid hands on the apostles** (this time all twelve), **and put them in a public jail,** which held the common prisoners. After all the miracles they had seen, it is hard to understand how they felt prison bars would restrain the power of God. Throughout Acts, imprisonment would prove to be no obstacle to the Lord (cf. 12:3–11; 16:23ff.).

Again, Satan's opposition backfired, providing opportunity for God to display His power. **An angel of the Lord during the night opened the gates of the prison** and freed the apostles. God's use of an angel to free them was especially ironic, since the Sadducees denied the existence of angels. After releasing them, the angel commanded them to **go your way, stand and speak to the people in the temple the whole message of this Life.** They were freed not to hide, but to boldly return to the temple and continue to preach. The **whole message of this Life** refers to the gospel (cf. Phil. 2:16; 1 John 1:1–4). The good news we proclaim is that Jesus Christ came into the world to give abundant and eternal life to the spiritually dead (cf. John 1:4; 11:25; 14:6; 1 John 5:20).

Although the angel's command may have seemed incredible, even reckless, the apostles did not argue. **Upon hearing his** words, **they entered into the temple about daybreak, and began to teach.** Before the Sadducees were even aware that they had been released they were back preaching. They chose to boldly obey and leave the consequences to God. Theirs was a defiant courage, and they did not hesitate to put their lives at risk.

Meanwhile, **when the high priest and his associates** had gathered, **they called the Council together, even all the Senate of the sons of Israel.** The morning after the apostles' imprisonment, the Sanhedrin (Council and Senate both refer to this body) convened to decide what to do about the apostolic prisoners. Accordingly, they **sent orders to the prison house for them to be brought** before them.

To their shock and consternation, however, **the officers** (Levites of the temple police) sent to retrieve the apostles **did not find them in the prison.** Instead they reported finding **the prison house locked quite securely and the guards standing at the doors; but when** they **opened up,** they **found no one inside.** Everything was as it should have been with one exception—the prisoners were gone!

Not surprisingly, **when the captain of the temple guard and the chief priests heard these words, they were greatly perplexed about them as to what would come of this.** Already at their wit's end as to how to stop the spread of Christianity, the harried Jewish authorities wondered what was going to happen next. As their efforts proved futile, their panic and alarm mounted. The apostles were openly flaunting their authority. They were powerless to stop the spread of what to them was the worst heresy imaginable and the greatest threat to their own credibility. People from all over the region were thronging Jerusalem to witness firsthand the miracles done by the apostles—miracles the Sanhedrin still refused to believe.

At the moment of their deliberation, **someone came and reported to them** news of the apostles' escape and shocking defiance of their authority: **Behold, the men whom you put in prison are standing in the temple and teaching the people!** Had the apostles gone into hiding after their escape it would have been bad enough. That they had the audacity to go right back into the temple and resume preaching was the ultimate act of insolence.

The **captain** of the temple police led his **officers** to the temple and **proceeded to bring** the willing apostles **back without violence.** By now the Sanhedrin was ready to resort to the most drastic measures in dealing with the gospel preachers, but **they were afraid of the people, lest they should be stoned.** The apostles' popularity and credibility with the people forced the authorities to proceed with uneasy caution. As with their prior arrests, the apostles offered no resistance (cf. 4:1–3; 5:18). They were content to submit to whatever God had in store for them. As noted in the discussion of Acts 4:5–7 in chapter 11, submission is one of the principles for handling persecution.

Having returned to the Sanhedrin with the apostles in tow, **they stood them before the Council.** The stage was set for the apostles' second sermon to the Sanhedrin. The **high priest** opened the proceedings by reminding the apostles that the Sanhedrin had given them **strict orders not to continue teaching in this name.** That was the first indictment brought against the apostles: they had disregarded the orders of the Sanhedrin. Instead, as the rulers reluctantly acknowledged, they had **filled Jerusalem with** their **teaching.**

Even worse was the second indictment, that the apostles **intend to bring this man's blood upon us.** Interestingly, the high priest could not bring himself to mention Jesus' name, calling Him **this man.** That charge was also true; Peter and the rest had boldly indicted the Jewish leaders for their role in Jesus' death (cf. 2:23, 36; 3:15; 4:10–11). The high priest conveniently forgot, however, that he and his associates had said to Pilate, "His blood be on us and on our children!" (Matt. 27:25). They were only getting what they had asked Pilate to give them.

Conspicuously absent from the high priest's charges is any mention of the apostles' escape from prison. Since the Sanhedrin could not explain that miracle, they simply acknowledged it and ignored it. Their minds made up, they had no wish to be confused by the facts. They "loved the darkness rather than the light; for their deeds were evil" (John 3:19).

PERSISTENCE

But Peter and the apostles answered and said, "We must obey God rather than men. The God of our fathers raised up Jesus, whom you had put to death by hanging Him on a cross. He is the one whom God exalted to His right hand as a Prince and a Savior, to grant repentance to Israel, and forgiveness of sins. And we are witnesses of these things; and so is the Holy Spirit, whom God has given to those who obey Him." (5:29–32)

If the Sanhedrin expected the apostles to be cowed by their accusations, they were mistaken. **Peter,** speaking for the rest of **the apostles, answered** that they **must obey God rather than men.** As in 4:19, he placed the Sanhedrin in opposition to God. He reinforced that point by noting **that the God of our fathers raised up Jesus, whom**

you had put to death by hanging Him on a cross. They had executed Jesus, but God raised Him (cf. 2:23–24, 36; 3:13–15; 4:10). Peter persistently, fearlessly repeated the offense for which the Sanhedrin had
just indicted the apostles (cf. 5:28). *Diacheirizō* (**put to death**) appears
only here and in Acts 26:21. It means "to put to death with one's own
hands." Far from backing off, Peter intensifies his accusation of the Sanhedrin. He had previously charged the Jewish authorities with responsibility for Jesus' death (2:23–24, 36; 3:13–15; 4:10). Now he insists they
are as guilty as if they had killed Him with their own hands. They had
not merely put the Messiah to death, but to the shameful death of **hanging Him on a cross** (cf. Deut. 21:23).

The One they despised and executed is the very **one whom
God exalted to** the place of honor at **His right hand as a Prince and
a Savior.** As noted in the discussion of Acts 3:15 in chapter 9, *archēgos*
(**Prince**) refers to the originator or pioneer of something (cf. its use in
Heb. 2:10 and 12:2). Here it describes Jesus as the source of eternal life
(cf. Acts 3:15) and is closely connected with the term **Savior.** He came
to grant repentance to Israel, and forgiveness of sins. Repentance
from sin is an integral part of saving faith, not a human work added to it.
The apostles' claims to be **witnesses** to and proclaimers of the momentous events of Christ's life, death, and resurrection were never disputed
by their opponents. And not only were they witnesses, but **so is the
Holy Spirit, whom God has given to those who obey Him.** Two interesting points are made here. First, the saved are described as **those
who obey Him.** They are characterized by obedience (cf. Romans 1:5;
Heb. 5:9), which is synonymous with saving faith. The verb used is
peitharcheō, which means "to obey one in authority." Salvation is sur-
rendering in obedience to the authority of Jesus Christ as Lord. Second,
the Holy Spirit is given to every saved person at salvation (cf. Acts 2:4;
Rom. 8:9; 1 Cor. 6:19, 20; 12:13). So Peter makes obeying God and the
gift of the Holy Spirit synonymous with saving faith.

PRODUCTIVITY

**But when they heard this, they were cut to the quick and were in-
tending to slay them. But a certain Pharisee named Gamaliel, a
teacher of the Law, respected by all the people, stood up in the
Council and gave orders to put the men outside for a short time.
And he said to them, "Men of Israel, take care what you propose
to do with these men. For some time ago Theudas rose up, claiming to be somebody; and a group of about four hundred men
joined up with him. And he was slain; and all who followed him
were dispersed and came to nothing. After this man Judas of Ga-**

lilee rose up in the days of the census, and drew away some people after him, he too perished, and all those who followed him were scattered. And so in the present case, I say to you, stay away from these men and let them alone, for if this plan or action should be of men, it will be overthrown; but if it is of God, you will not be able to overthrow them; or else you may even be found fighting against God." And they took his advice; and after calling the apostles in, they flogged them and ordered them to speak no more in the name of Jesus, and then released them. So they went on their way from the presence of the Council, rejoicing that they had been considered worthy to suffer shame for His name. And every day, in the temple and from house to house, they kept right on teaching and preaching Jesus as the Christ. (5:33–42)

The concluding verses of this chapter give the productive results of the evangelism of the pure, powerful, persecuted, persistent church. Although to some it was brief, Peter's sermon to the Sanhedrin was powerful and convicting. He charged them with rejecting and executing their Messiah, and hence being in rebellion against God. He did not play on their emotions or soften the confrontation, but presented the truth. Conviction that leads to salvation can only take place when the Spirit of God (cf. John 16:7–11) uses the facts of the Word of God to produce repentance in a person's heart and mind.

To convicting preaching there are but three possible reactions: violent hostility, tolerant indecision, or saving acceptance. This passage illustrates them all.

VIOLENT HOSTILITY

But when they heard this, they were cut to the quick and were intending to slay them. (5:33)

Convicting preaching will inevitably provoke a violent reaction from those hardened in sin. When the authorities **heard** Peter's bold presentation, they heard it as blasphemy and **they were cut to the quick.** *Diaprio* (**cut to the quick**) appears only here and in Acts 7:54. It literally refers to cutting something in two—an apt metaphor to describe the power of the Word of God (Heb. 4:12). Instead of yielding to the truth, the authorities hardened their hearts. As they had done to Jesus (cf. John 5:16; 7:32; 8:59; 10:31; 11:57) in spite of the abundant evidence, they rejected the apostles' teaching and violently opposed them as blasphemers.

The high priest and his fellow Sadducees were enraged with the apostles for several reasons. The apostles had denied their doctrine by proclaiming the resurrection. They had defied the Sanhedrin's authority by preaching after they had ordered them to stop. By charging the Sanhedrin with executing the Messiah, the apostles assaulted their spirituality. Finally, by winning large numbers of converts they threatened the Sadducees' domination of the people. They had had enough and **were intending to slay** the troubling apostles.

The apostle Paul would later face the same reaction. Acts 9:22–23 records that after his conversion he "kept increasing in strength and confounding the Jews who lived at Damascus by proving that this Jesus is the Christ. And when many days had elapsed, the Jews plotted together to do away with him." "The wicked plots against the righteous," wrote David, "and gnashes at him with his teeth. The wicked have drawn the sword and bent their bow . . . to slay those who are upright in conduct. The wicked spies upon the righteous, and seeks to kill him" (Ps. 37:12, 14, 32). In Matthew 23:34, Jesus said, "I am sending you prophets and wise men and scribes; some of them you will kill and crucify, and some of them you will scourge in your synagogues, and persecute from city to city." In verse 37 He lamented, "O Jerusalem, Jerusalem, who kills the prophets and stones those who are sent to her!"

Our gospel presentations must be definitive enough that the world must take note, even if they reject our message. If the gospel we preach is not convicting enough to make some men angry, is it convicting enough to bring them salvation?

TOLERANT INDECISION

But a certain Pharisee named Gamaliel, a teacher of the Law, respected by all the people, stood up in the Council and gave orders to put the men outside for a short time. And he said to them, "Men of Israel, take care what you propose to do with these men. For some time ago Theudas rose up, claiming to be somebody; and a group of about four hundred men joined up with him. And he was slain; and all who followed him were dispersed and came to nothing. After this man Judas of Galilee rose up in the days of the census, and drew away some people after him, he too perished, and all those who followed him were scattered. And so in the present case, I say to you, stay away from these men and let them alone, for if this plan or action should be of men, it will be overthrown; but if it is of God, you will not be able to overthrow them; or else you may even be found fighting against God." And they took his advice; and after calling the apostles in, they

flogged them and ordered them to speak no more in the name of Jesus, and then released them. (5:34–40)

Some react to a convicting presentation of the gospel not with open hostility, but with indifference. Such a one was **a certain Pharisee named Gamaliel, a teacher of the Law.** He was easily the most prominent rabbi of that time and one of the greatest of all antiquity. He was the grandson of another prominent rabbi, Hillel, and his successor as leader of the liberal wing of the Pharisees. Gamaliel was one of the few honored with the title *rabban,* instead of the usual title "rabbi" (F. F. Bruce, *The Book of the Acts* [Grand Rapids: Eerdmans, 1971], 124 n. 44). How highly he was **respected by all the people** may be seen in the following quotation from the *Mishna*: "When Rabban Gamaliel the Elder died, the glory of the Law ceased and purity and abstinence died" (cited in John B. Polhill, *The New American Commentary: Acts* [Nashville: Broadman, 1992], 171). His most famous student was the apostle Paul (Acts 22:3).

Gamaliel **stood up in the Council and gave orders to put** the apostles **outside for a short time.** He then warned his fellow members of the Sanhedrin, **Men of Israel, take care what you propose to do with these men.** Unlike the Sadducees, the Pharisees accepted both the miraculous and the sovereignty of God. Gamaliel's counsel reflects his belief that God was in control of events. He then offers two illustrations before driving home his main point.

Many critical scholars view Luke's reference to **Theudas** as a gross historical blunder. The only other reference to a Theudas from this period is in Josephus's *Antiquities.* Josephus, however, dates Theudas's revolt at around A.D. 44, a decade after Gamaliel's speech. Further, Gamaliel's speech as recorded by Luke places Theudas's revolt before that of Judas's. Luke, however, does not present a garbled version of Josephus's account, as many charge. *Antiquities* was not written until many years after Luke wrote Acts, so Luke could not have borrowed from it. The details Luke gives about Theudas's revolt differ markedly from Josephus's account. Josephus suggests, for example, that he had a far larger following than a mere **four hundred men.** Since Theudas was a common name, it is most likely that two different people are in view. That an otherwise unknown Theudas should have led a revolt in the early years of the first century is entirely possible, since Josephus spoke of "innumerable tumults and insurrections that arose in Judea following the death of Herod the Great (4 B.C.)" (Polhill, *Acts,* 173). Josephus writes of 2,000 who were crucified for revolting before the enrollment in A.D. 6 (*Antiquities* XVII.10.4, 10).

No such controversy surrounds the identification of Gamaliel's second example, **Judas of Galilee.** He led a revolt against the **census** ordered by Quirinius (A.D. 6–7). (For evidence that this was not the same census referred to in Luke 2 see Gleason L. Archer, *Encyclopedia of Bible Difficulties* [Grand Rapids: Zondervan, 1982], 365–66.) The Zealots, to which Jesus' disciple Simon had belonged, trace their origin to him (Archer, p. 378). Like Theudas, **he too perished, and all those who followed him were scattered.**

Gamaliel then gets to his point. **In the present case,** involving the apostles, he cautions his fellow members to **stay away from these men and let them alone.** He urges the Council to adopt a "wait and see" policy, since **if this plan or action should be of men, it will be overthrown,** like those of Theudas and Judas. On the other hand, he warns, **if it is of God, you will not be able to overthrow them; or else you may even be found fighting against God,** something Peter had already indicted them for, and something they were supposed to be trying the apostles for doing. The Sanhedrin **took his advice; and after calling the apostles in, they flogged them and ordered them to speak no more in the name of Jesus, and then released them.**

While Gamaliel's counsel seemed wise to the Sanhedrin, the notion that whatever succeeds has God's blessing is false. Cults and false religions in our day have millions of followers. And what more evidence did he need to convince him beyond the empty tomb of Jesus and the miracles performed by the apostles? The word to all such fence sitters is "Now is the acceptable time, behold, now is the day of salvation" (2 Cor. 6:2; cf. Heb. 3:7; 4:7). Gamaliel was a pragmatist—a poor substitute for being a good biblical scholar. Such lethargy on his part is not commendable in light of what he knew of the Scripture and what he knew of the work of Jesus and the power of the apostles in His name.

The flogging was criminally unjust and done to frighten them. It usually involved a beating of forty lashes, less one to avoid violating the legal limit (Deut. 25:3). Apparently Gamaliel had no problem with the whipping, again revealing his indifference.

SAVING ACCEPTANCE

So they went on their way from the presence of the Council, rejoicing that they had been considered worthy to suffer shame for His name. And every day, in the temple and from house to house, they kept right on teaching and preaching Jesus as the Christ. (5:41–42)

The apostles typify those who accept the gospel message. Far from being embittered or disillusioned at their suffering, **they went on their way from the presence of the Council, rejoicing that they**

had been considered worthy to suffer shame for His name (cf. Gal. 6:17; Col. 1:24). That they were persecuted for Christ's sake showed that they possessed the Holy Spirit (1 Peter 4:13).

Undaunted by the Council's actions, **every day, in the temple and from house to house, they kept right on teaching and preaching Jesus as the Christ.** Theirs was a battle-tested faith, unlike the false faith that wilts under persecution (Matt. 13:20–21).

The early church understood the pattern for effective evangelism. By consistently practicing that pattern, they turned their world upside down (cf. Acts 17:6). At the very time they were experiencing the most furious opposition, and some tolerant indecision, their number was constantly increasing (Acts 6:1). As Paul told the Corinthians, such preachers "are a fragrance of Christ to God among those who are being saved and among those who are perishing; to the one an aroma from death to death, to the other an aroma from life to life" (2 Cor. 2:15–16).

Spiritual Organization

14

Now at this time while the disciples were increasing in number, a complaint arose on the part of the Hellenistic Jews against the native Hebrews, because their widows were being overlooked in the daily serving of food. And the twelve summoned the congregation of the disciples and said, "It is not desirable for us to neglect the word of God in order to serve tables. But select from among you, brethren, seven men of good reputation, full of the Spirit and of wisdom, whom we may put in charge of this task. But we will devote ourselves to prayer, and to the ministry of the word." And the statement found approval with the whole congregation; and they chose Stephen, a man full of faith and of the Holy Spirit, and Philip, Prochorus, Nicanor, Timon, Parmenas and Nicolas, a proselyte from Antioch. And these they brought before the apostles; and after praying, they laid their hands on them. And the word of God kept on spreading; and the number of the disciples continued to increase greatly in Jerusalem, and a great many of the priests were becoming obedient to the faith. (6:1–7)

Christians, someone once said, become very unchristian when they get organized. That remark crystallizes one side of the long-running debate over church polity. One extreme, affirming the power of Christ in His church, would agree with that sentiment. Its proponents argue that the church should reject formal organization or structure and just flow with the Spirit. Whatever is organized, they insist, cannot be from God. Some would even reject the concept of church membership. Such a loose, unorganized model of the church, however, underestimates the strength of the flesh and is inconsistent with the character of God (cf. 1 Cor. 14:33). All creation reflects the highly organized nature of its Creator. Nor is it consistent with the thoughtful New Testament teaching on how the church is to function.

Others would structure the church like a Fortune 500 corporation, complete with detailed organizational charts, job descriptions, boards, committees, and subcommittees. The Holy Spirit, they hope, will operate within the rigid framework they have constructed. They will reject any bold, new proposals because "We've never done it that way before." These people tend to underestimate the strength of the new nature and the power of the Spirit.

Both extremes are wrong; the church is neither a highly contrived corporation nor a loose commune, but an organism. It has both an organic unity and an operative life principle, since all members are connected to its living Head, the Lord Jesus Christ. Yet just as living organisms require structure and organization to function, so does the church.

The early church set the example of a living, interdependent organism. Their unity and power gave them a testimony that swept Jerusalem. Multitudes had come to faith in Jesus Christ. No persecution or opposition from the Jewish authorities could stop the spread of the gospel. The believers' love for each other, expressed in the sharing of material goods, had made a profound impact on the community. As a result, even unbelievers held the church in high regard (5:13).

The church's explosive growth had brought with it the need for further organization. It was already somewhat organized. They knew (at least early on) the number of converts (2:41) and members (4:4). Someone must have been keeping count. They met together in specific places at specific times. The believers also met for meals in private homes. Money and goods were collected by the apostles and distributed to those in need. Sin had to be dealt with. All those activities also demanded some level of organization. The church became further structured as its life and growth demanded.

That illustrates an important principle: Biblical church organization always responds to needs and to what the Spirit is already doing. To organize a program and then expect the Holy Spirit to get involved in it is to put the cart before the horse. We dare not try to force the Spirit to fit our mold. Organization is never an end in itself but only a means to facilitate what the Lord is doing in His church.

In Acts chapter 6 the church faced its first serious organizational crisis. To eliminate a potentially divisive problem required further organization. From this first organizational meeting four features stand out: the reason, the requirements, the roster, and the results.

The Reason

Now at this time while the disciples were increasing in number, a complaint arose on the part of the Hellenistic Jews against the native Hebrews, because their widows were being overlooked in the daily serving of food. And the twelve summoned the congregation of the disciples and said, "It is not desirable for us to neglect the word of God in order to serve tables. . . . But we will devote ourselves to prayer, and to the ministry of the word." (6:1–2, 4)

At the very **time** that **the disciples were increasing in number** another problem arose. It was related to their rapid growth. Just how large the church had become is not known, since they no longer kept an accurate count. The last figure given, 5,000 (4:4), apparently included only the men. To that figure must be added the women and youths and those who had joined the church since then (cf. 5:14). There must have been more than 20,000 in the Jerusalem church at this point.

Without means of mass communication, the leadership and administrative problems associated with such a large congregation were enormous. Merely to meet their spiritual needs and to deal with sin would have been a daunting task, let alone caring for their physical needs. Not only did the size of the church create problems, but also its explosive growth left little time to adjust. As a result, the apostles could no longer handle the entire load of caring for the congregation. Further organization was needed.

There was another reason for the church to organize. They had fulfilled the first part of the Lord's four-part charge to them (1:8). They had saturated Jerusalem with the gospel message (5:28) and even begun to reach out to the surrounding region (5:16). Now they were poised to evangelize Samaria and the Gentile world. To do so successfully required further planning and structuring of the assembly.

In a congregation of that size, it was inevitable that someone's needs would be overlooked. It comes as no surprise to learn that **a**

complaint arose on the part of the Hellenistic Jews against the native Hebrews, because their widows were being overlooked in the daily serving of food. Here was an issue that Satan could use with devastating force against the church. He had already attacked it through persecution (4:1–31; 5:17–41). That, however, had merely caused the church to grow faster (4:4). Next, he had sought to cripple it by introducing sin into the body (5:1–11). God stepped in quickly and judged Ananias and Sapphira, and again Satan's attack failed ignominiously. As with persecution, it only made the church's number increase (5:14). The purified church was even more effective in spreading the gospel.

Having failed to stop the church through persecution or corruption, Satan tried a third tactic. He sought to create dissension within the church. A church racked by internal conflict finds its message lost in conflict, its energy dissipated. And a church thus focused on itself will find it difficult to reach out to the lost world. Before the church could evangelize the Gentile world, they would have to deal with any division within their ranks. That was the need that spurred the church to further organization.

The **Hellenistic Jews** were those of the Diaspora. Unlike the **native** or Palestinian **Hebrews,** their native language was Greek, not Aramaic or Hebrew. They used the Septuagint instead of the Hebrew Scriptures. While remaining loyal to Judaism, they had absorbed some of the Greek culture that surrounded them. That made them suspect to the Palestinian Jews, especially the Pharisees. "According to the Talmud, Pharisaism made little secret of its contempt for Hellenists . . . they were frequently categorized by the native-born and assumedly more scrupulous populace of Jerusalem as second-class Israelites" (Richard N. Longenecker, "The Acts of the Apostles," in Frank E. Gaebelein, ed., *The Expositor's Bible Commentary*, vol. 9 [Grand Rapids: Zondervan, 1981], 329). Some of that racial and cultural hostility carried over into the church.

Many of the Hellenists had been in Jerusalem for Passover and Pentecost. After their conversion, they decided to remain there under the apostles' teaching. Others were older people who had returned to Palestine to live out their lives. They were a minority in the church, which helps explain why their needs were overlooked.

As often happens, matters came to a head over a seemingly insignificant issue. The Hellenists complained that **their widows were being overlooked in the daily serving of food.** Care of widows was traditional in Jewish society (cf. Deut. 14:29; 16:11; 24:19–21; 26:12). Paul later defined it as the responsibility of the church (1 Tim. 5:3ff.). Given the natural dichotomy between the Hellenists and native Palestinians, this issue could easily have split the church. Certainly the fact that the Hellenist Jews spoke of **their widows** collectively indicates they felt the neglect was deliberate.

The Hellenists' **complaint** eventually came to the attention of **the twelve.** Luke uses that term to describe the apostles only here in Acts, though he uses it six times in his gospel. Recognizing the legitimacy of the Hellenists' grievance, they **summoned the congregation of the disciples** to seek a solution. While the apostles recognized the problem, they did not have the time to handle it. It was **not desirable for** the apostles **to neglect the word of God in order to serve tables.** It may be helpful to note that the word for tables, *trapeza,* can mean "a table or counter of a money changer," or "money matters," as well as an eating table (cf. such use in Matt. 21:12; Luke 19:23). To involve themselves in the details of serving meals and handling money matters would take them away from their calling. Instead, they would **devote** themselves **to prayer, and to the ministry of the word.** The apostles knew their priority was praying, preaching, teaching, and studying the Word. They would let nothing, however pressing, distract them from those duties. They said, in effect, "You serve the tables and we will serve the Word." Paul was concerned that the needs of the poor be met (Rom. 15:26; 2 Cor. 8–9), but never wanted to be distracted by the details (1 Cor. 16:1–4).

Many in the ministry today have left the emphasis on prayer and the Word of God. They are so involved in the administrative details of their church that they have little time left for intercession and study. Yet pastors are given to the church "for the equipping of the saints for the work of service, to the building up of the body of Christ" (Eph. 4:12). Their calling is to mature the saints so they can do the work of the ministry. By neglecting that calling, they doom their congregations to languish in spiritual infancy. Programs are no substitute for the power of God and His Word. Those whom God has called to the ministry of prayer and the Word must make it their priority.

Prayer and **the ministry of the word** are inseparably linked. Prayer must permeate a pastor's sermon preparation, or his sermons will be superficial and dry. He must also pray constantly that his people will apply the truths he teaches them. The man of God must also pray that he would be a pure channel through which God's truth can flow to his congregation. (For a discussion of the relationship of prayer to preaching, see James E. Rosscup, "The Priority of Prayer and Expository Preaching," in John F. MacArthur, Jr., *Rediscovering Expository Preaching* [Dallas: Word, 1992].)

The greatest proclaimer of God's Word who ever lived, the apostle Paul, was a man devoted to prayer. He assured the Romans that "God, whom I serve in my spirit in the preaching of the gospel of His Son, is my witness as to how unceasingly I make mention of you always in my prayers" (Rom. 1:9–10). He told the Ephesians "[I] do not cease giving thanks for you, while making mention of you in my prayers (Eph. 1:16). To the Philippians he wrote, "I thank my God in all my remembrance of you, always offering prayer with joy in my every prayer for you all" (Phil. 1:3–4). Paul also prayed constantly for the Colossian church: "For this reason also, since the day we heard of it, we have not ceased to pray for you and to ask that you may be filled with the knowledge of His will in all spiritual wisdom and understanding" (Col. 1:9). Paul's passion for the Word was equaled only by his devotion to prayer.

The apostles' pledge to devote themselves to their ministry set the pattern for all to follow. The ministry demands total commitment, everything a man has to give. There is no substitute for hard work and discipline. A young man once said to the gifted expository preacher of God's Word Donald Grey Barnhouse, "I'd give the world to be able to teach the Bible like you." Looking him straight in the eye Dr. Barnhouse replied, "Good, because that's exactly what it will cost you."

Again, Paul serves as an appropriate model of the commitment to the Word that the ministry demands. In his farewell speech to the Ephesian elders he said,

> You yourselves know, from the first day that I set foot in Asia, how I was with you the whole time, serving the Lord with all humility and with tears and with trials which came upon me through the plots of the Jews; how I did not shrink from declaring to you anything that was profitable, and teaching you publicly and from house to house, solemnly testifying to both Jews and Greeks of repentance toward God and faith in our Lord Jesus Christ. (Acts 20:18–21)

Acts 19:9–10 describes Paul's ministry at Ephesus: "But when some were becoming hardened and disobedient, speaking evil of the Way before the multitude, he withdrew from them and took away the disciples, reasoning daily in the school of Tyrannus. And this took place for two years, so that all who lived in Asia heard the word of the Lord, both Jews and Greeks." Imprisoned in Rome, he nevertheless "was solemnly testifying [to the Jews of Rome] about the kingdom of God, and trying to persuade them concerning Jesus, from both the Law of Moses and from the Prophets, from morning until evening" (Acts 28:23). That continued for two years (28:30–31).

Paul expressed his personal philosophy of ministry in the following words:

> If I preach the gospel, I have nothing to boast of, for I am under compulsion; for woe is me if I do not preach the gospel. For if I do this vol-

untarily, I have a reward; but if against my will, I have a stewardship entrusted to me. Therefore I run in such a way, as not without aim; I box in such a way, as not beating the air; but I buffet my body and make it my slave, lest possibly, after I have preached to others, I myself should be disqualified. (1 Cor. 9:16–17, 26–27)

From his dramatic conversion on the Damascus Road to the day a Roman executioner ended his life, Paul gave himself totally to the ministry. There is no other way. Every minister of Jesus Christ must give heed to Paul's exhortation to Timothy:

Prescribe and teach these things. Let no one look down on your youthfulness, but rather in speech, conduct, love, faith and purity, show yourself an example of those who believe. Until I come, give attention to the public reading of Scripture, to exhortation and teaching. Do not neglect the spiritual gift within you, which was bestowed upon you through prophetic utterance with the laying on of hands by the presbytery. Take pains with these things; be absorbed in them, so that your progress may be evident to all. (1 Tim. 4:11–15)

The devotion that Paul demanded of his young protégé is the same devotion the Lord Jesus Christ demands of all who serve Him.

THE REQUIREMENTS

But select from among you, brethren, seven men of good reputation, full of the Spirit and of wisdom, whom we may put in charge of this task. (6:3)

While the apostles had to remain faithful to their priorities, the problem of distributing the food and money equitably remained. That important ministry needed oversight, and others would have to be found to do that. Accordingly, the apostles commanded the believers to **select** from their own ranks **seven men.** The word translated **select** is from the verb *episkeptomai,* meaning "to oversee," or "to supervise." The congregation was to look over the men who were respected and present their choices to the apostles. They would make the final decision regarding their appointment to the task, as indicated by the words **whom we may put in charge of this task.**

This brief verse lists five required characteristics for those appointed to church ministry. First, those who would lead the church must be men. Women certainly have vital roles to fill (cf. Titus 2:3–5). In the early church, such women as Dorcas, Lydia, Phoebe, Priscilla, and Philip's daughters were greatly used by God. Nevertheless, God's design for the church is that men assume the leadership roles (1 Cor. 11:3, 8, 9; 14:34; 1 Tim. 2:11–12).

A second requirement is that they be **from among you.** That indicates more than the obvious truth that those who lead the church must be believers. Churches should seek to develop their leadership from within their own ranks. By hiring pastors away from other churches, they often overlook the gifted men God has raised up in their own congregations. A church committed to the ministry of edifying and equipping its members will not have to look elsewhere for its leaders.

A third requirement for leaders is that they be men **of good reputation.** They must be men of integrity, above reproach, as is required of elders and deacons in 1 Timothy 3 and Titus 1. Servants must set an example of godliness for their people to follow. And they must be qualified spiritually regardless of their position in the world or their human ability. To have a **good reputation** was essential for these seven, since they would be entrusted with large sums of money to purchase the food to be distributed.

Those who would lead the church must also be **full of the Spirit.** They must be fully yielded to His control in every area of their lives. Such men were Stephen (Acts 6:5) and Barnabas (Acts 11:24).

A final requirement is that they possess **wisdom.** They must have biblical and theological knowledge, and the practical wisdom to apply biblical truth to the situations of everyday life. They must be men of sober, righteous judgment. First Chronicles 12:32 describes some wise leaders of Israel as "men who understood the times, with knowledge of what Israel should do." Such men does God call to serve His church.

The question arises as to whether these seven can be properly viewed as the first official deacons. They performed some functions of the later deacons, and forms of the Greek word *diakonos* (deacon) are used to describe their ministry (vv. 1–2). Yet to view them in terms of a formal office is anachronistic. Of the seven, only Stephen and Philip appear elsewhere in Scripture, but they are never called deacons. Indeed, Stephen's later ministry was clearly that of an evangelist, as was Philip's (Acts 21:8). While Acts later refers to elders (14:23; 20:17), there is no mention of deacons. That is strange, if the office of deacon began in Acts 6. Further, all seven had Greek names, implying that they may have been Hellenists. It seems unlikely, however, that a permanent order of deacons for the Jerusalem church would include no native Palestinian Jews.

There are important principles in this passage for the continuing life of the church. Here we see that the congregation is to nominate certain spiritually qualified men to serve, with the final appointment resting with those already in position as teachers and spiritual leaders. Still, it seems best to see the selection of these seven as the Jerusalem church's response to a temporary crisis. It should be noted that the Greek word group from which our English word "deacon" derives denotes service in general. *Diakonos, diakoneō,* and *diakonia* are used throughout the New Testament in a general, nonspecific way (cf. Luke 4:39; 10:40; 17:8; 22:27; John 2:5, 9; 12:2; Rom. 13:3–4; 15:25; 2 Cor. 8:3–4). Thus their use in Acts 6 does not imply that the seven held the office of a deacon. Significantly, when the church at Antioch later sent famine relief to the Jerusalem church, no mention is made of deacons (Acts 11:29–30). Instead, the relief was sent to the elders. Stephen and Philip certainly did not continue long in this role, since both became evangelists. And persecution would shortly scatter the Jerusalem congregation (Acts 8:1), ending the ministry of the other five. God raised them for a brief period of ministry, to handle a crisis. The continuing unity of the church shows the effectiveness of their ministry.

THE ROSTER

And the statement found approval with the whole congregation; and they chose Stephen, a man full of faith and of the Holy Spirit, and Philip, Prochorus, Nicanor, Timon, Parmenas and Nicolas, a proselyte from Antioch. And these they brought before the apostles; and after praying, they laid their hands on them. (6:5–6)

The apostles' plan **found approval with the whole congregation,** and seven men were appointed to the ministry. That all seven bore Greek names suggests all were Hellenists. If true, it was a demonstration of the loving unity of the church. Since the Hellenists felt slighted, the church decided to appoint seven from among them to rectify the situation. A split was thus avoided, and again Satan's attack was thwarted.

Stephen was to play a pivotal role in the spread of the gospel beyond Jerusalem. It was the persecution connected with his martyrdom that propelled the church out of Jerusalem (Acts 8:1). The commendation of him as **a man full of faith and of the Holy Spirit** reveals his character.

Philip also plays a prominent role in Acts. He took the gospel to the Samaritans (8:4–25), and to the Ethiopian eunuch (8:26–40). Four of his daughters became prophetesses (21:8).

Nothing definite is known about the remaining five men. Some early traditions connect **Prochorus** with John the apostle, possibly as his amanuensis when he wrote his gospel. According to those traditions, he later became bishop of Nicomedia and was martyred in Antioch (John B. Polhill, *The New American Commentary: Acts* [Nashville: Broadman, 1992], p. 182).

All that is known for certain about **Nicolas** is that he was a **proselyte** (a Gentile convert to Judaism) from **Antioch.** Some of the church Fathers associated him with the heretical group known as the Nicolaitans (Rev. 2:6, 15). But there is no evidence, apart from the similarity in the names, to connect him with that group. And as Lenski rightly observes, "It ought to be understood that decidedly more evidence is required in a matter of so serious a charge" (R. C. H. Lenski, *The Interpretation of the Acts of the Apostles* [Minneapolis: Augsburg, 1961], 246).

The congregation **brought** the seven **before the apostles; and after praying, they laid their hands on them.** This first occasion in the New Testament of laying on of hands signified the identification and affirmation of the church with these men, and the support of their ministry. Elders, deacons, and all who served in the early church were ordained this way (cf. Acts 13:3; 1 Tim. 4:14; 5:22; 2 Tim. 1:6).

All though little is known about most of these men, they played a crucial role in the foundational history of the church. But for them, either the apostles' priorities would have been compromised, or the church may have split. Either would have been disastrous.

THE RESULTS

And the word of God kept on spreading; and the number of the disciples continued to increase greatly in Jerusalem, and a great many of the priests were becoming obedient to the faith. (6:7)

As already noted, the organization of the church freed the apostles to devote themselves to prayer and the Word. It also avoided a church split. Luke closes this section, as he has before, by noting the development of the church. **The word of God kept on spreading** from the church as a direct result of the freeing of the apostles to carry out their primary ministry, and also of the church's unity. As the Word continued to spread, **the number of the disciples continued to increase greatly in Jerusalem. Greatly,** like the general reference to multitudes (5:14), shows that there were so many new converts being added that they lost count of the exact number. Astonishingly, **a great many of the priests were becoming obedient to the faith.** These were, of course, not the chief priests or members of the Sanhedrin, but a very large number of the rank and file priests who ministered in the temple. Perhaps this dramatic impact of the gospel on the priests accounts for the opposition that soon arose against Stephen.

The church today needs organization for the same reasons as the first fellowship. Pastors must be freed to focus on the preaching of the Word and prayer. Better organization can help meet the needs of all members and thus avoid conflict. And a unified, well-taught church will be a powerful witness to the lost world.

The Man with the Face of an Angel

15

And Stephen, full of grace and power, was performing great wonders and signs among the people. But some men from what was called the Synagogue of the Freedmen, including both Cyrenians and Alexandrians, and some from Cilicia and Asia, rose up and argued with Stephen. And yet they were unable to cope with the wisdom and the Spirit with which he was speaking. Then they secretly induced men to say, "We have heard him speak blasphemous words against Moses and against God." And they stirred up the people, the elders and the scribes, and they came upon him and dragged him away, and brought him before the Council. And they put forward false witnesses who said, "This man incessantly speaks against this holy place, and the Law; for we have heard him say that this Nazarene, Jesus, will destroy this place and alter the customs which Moses handed down to us." And fixing their gaze on him, all who were sitting in the Council saw his face like the face of an angel. (6:8–15)

This passage marks a transition in the book of Acts. Up to this point, Peter has been the dominating figure, fulfilling his calling by taking the gospel to the circumcised (Gal. 2:7). Another figure of major importance looms on the horizon: the apostle Paul, who is introduced at the end of chapter 7. Following Paul's conversion, recorded in chapter 9, Peter begins to fade from the scene. Chapters 10 and 11 record his ministry to Cornelius, and chapter 12 his second miraculous release from prison. But from chapter 13 to the end of the book, the record focuses on Paul. Peter's only appearance in that section is at the Jerusalem council (Acts 15).

Bridging the gap between those two giants is Stephen. Peter ministered primarily to the Jewish people, and Paul primarily to the Gentiles. Stephen's brief ministry was mainly to Jews from Gentile lands. Peter ministered in Jerusalem, Paul throughout the Roman Empire. Stephen's ministry was the catalyst that catapulted the church out of Jerusalem into the rest of the world (8:1).

Stephen was in many ways a forerunner to Paul. He boldly confronted the synagogues of foreign Jews in Jerusalem, possibly even entering them to debate their members (6:9). When he entered a new city to minister, Paul would habitually go first to a synagogue (17:2). Like Paul, Stephen encountered fierce opposition, even to the point of physical persecution (7:54–60; cf. 2 Cor. 11:23–25). Truly, the mantle of Stephen fell on his Hellenistic countryman Saul of Tarsus. It is even possible that Paul's first exposure to the gospel came through Stephen (7:58; 8:1). His death must have left an indelible impression on Paul.

Stephen was thus a key figure in the early history of the church. But apart from his historical role, he was significant because of his character. He was proof that the impact of a man's life and ministry has nothing necessarily to do with length. His ministry, though brief, was essential to God's plan for world evangelism. He showed that the efforts of one courageous person, though of short duration, can have far-reaching effects.

Stephen's selfless, fearless proclamation of the gospel led him to pay the ultimate price for his commitment. He was the first Christian martyr, as the people who had favored the believers (5:13) were manipulated to turn hostile. His death triggered the first in a long series of persecutions that have challenged the church throughout its history. When Stephen died, the church grieved loudly (8:2) because he was so vital a preacher and so deeply loved. Yet he did not die before accomplishing the mission God laid out for him. Nor was his ministry any less significant because no list of converts is recorded. Certainly he had many. In God's economy, some plant, some water, and others harvest (1 Cor. 3:6). A rich harvest resulted from the seeds Stephen planted.

That the world failed to recognize Stephen's greatness comes as no surprise. The world measures success by popularity, prestige, or material wealth and thus fails to understand true greatness. After all, they killed Jesus, beheaded Paul, executed Peter, and persecuted the church. Although the people judged Stephen a blasphemer and killed him, he was one of the noblest and most powerful men who ever lived. It is no exaggeration to place him on a par with the likes of Abraham, Moses, Elijah, David, John the Baptist, and the apostles.

One proof of Stephen's virtue appeared in the previous passage. Out of the thousands of men in the Jerusalem church, he was one of the seven chosen to oversee the distribution of food. Indeed, his was the first name mentioned. His choosing reveals the high esteem the church had for him. They approved him for the highest duty they could. Only the apostles were loftier, and they were not chosen by the church, but by the Lord Himself.

Acts 6:8–15 presents three further evidences of Stephen's spiritual nobility: his character, his courage, and his countenance.

HIS CHARACTER

And Stephen, full of grace and power, was performing great wonders and signs among the people. (6:8)

Verse 5 described Stephen as "full of faith and of the Holy Spirit." **Full** both there and in verse 8 translates *plērēs,* which means "to be filled up." Stephen was totally controlled by faith, the Holy Spirit, grace, and power. His sermon before the Sanhedrin reveals the content of his faith. He believed that God ruled history (7:1–51), and was confident of God's sovereign control of his life. He could say with Paul, "If we live, we live for the Lord, or if we die, we die for the Lord; therefore whether we live or die, we are the Lord's" (Rom. 14:8). Stephen saw Jesus as the fulfillment of messianic prophecy (7:52) and believed He had risen and been exalted to the right hand of the Father (7:55–56). His confident trust in Jesus' care for him allowed him to face death calmly (7:59–60). Finally, he believed in the Holy Spirit (7:51).

Sadly, many Christians today could not be described as full of faith. Like the father of the demon-possessed boy healed by Jesus, their cry is "I do believe; help my unbelief" (Mark 9:24). While trusting God for their eternal destiny, they find it difficult to trust Him with the concerns of their everyday life. Stephen, however, was not like that. He trusted God fully and concentrated on doing what God wanted him to do. The consequences he gladly left in God's hands.

Not only was Stephen full of faith but also of the Holy Spirit (cf. 7:55). That is the privilege of every believer (Eph. 5:18). To be full of faith is to trust God; to be filled with the Spirit is to obey fully His will. Stephen believed God and submitted to the leading of the empowering, purifying Holy Spirit. Those two realities epitomize the strength of the Christian life. In the words of the beloved hymn,

> Trust and obey,
> For there's no other way
> To be happy in Jesus,
> But to trust and obey.

A third spiritual reality, flowing from trust and obedience, that characterized Stephen was **grace.** Because Stephen trusted God, and walked in the fullness of the Spirit, he was given the grace to face persecution, even death. Neither fear nor hatred controlled him, only trust and submission. He could be gracious even at the point of death because of his confident trust in God and resignation to the divine purpose. Having committed himself fully into God's hands (7:59), he was willing to endure anything in the strength of enabling grace. God's grace also flowed out of his life to others. Perhaps that was one reason the church chose him to minister to widows. Stephen was even gracious toward his executioners, praying for their forgiveness as their stones crushed out his life (7:60).

The only way a believer can live like Stephen is by dying to his sinful self. Those busy looking out for their own interests will have little time or inclination to abandon themselves and experience the grace Stephen experienced.

Finally, Stephen was full of **power.** That was a direct result of his being filled with the Spirit (cf. Acts 1:8). That he **was performing great wonders and signs among the people** suggests he was far more than simply a deacon. Instead, his deeds of power show his close link with the apostles. In the New Testament church only the apostles, Stephen, Philip (Acts 8:6–7), and Barnabas (15:12) performed miracles. The imperfect tense of *poieō* (**was performing**) shows Stephen was continually doing those mighty works, no doubt with the same impact as the apostles (5:12–14).

Taken together, verses 5 and 8 give both the Godward and manward sides of Christian character. A man full of faith toward God, and yielded to the Spirit's control, will be gracious toward others and manifest great spiritual power.

That a righteous man will do righteous deeds is a basic New Testament principle. Paul teaches repeatedly that all Christian joy and usefulness, all power and gracious service, flow out of faith and obedience. For example in Colossians 3, Paul gave the Colossians the following practical injunctions: "But now you also, put them all aside: anger, wrath, malice, slander, and abusive speech from your mouth. Do not lie to one another" (Col. 3:8–9a). They were to do those things because they had "laid aside the old self with its evil practices, and . . . put on the new self who is being renewed to a true knowledge according to the image of the One who created him" (vv. 9b–10). As "those who [had] been chosen of God" and were therefore "holy and beloved" (3:12a), they were to "put on a heart of compassion, kindness, humility, gentleness and patience; bearing with one another, and forgiving each other, whoever has a complaint against anyone; just as the Lord forgave you, so also should you. And beyond all these things put on love, which is the perfect bond of unity" (vv. 12b–14). Paul also expressed that principle to the Ephesians:

> I, therefore, the prisoner of the Lord, entreat you to walk in a manner worthy of the calling with which you have been called, with all humility and gentleness, with patience, showing forbearance to one another in love, being diligent to preserve the unity of the Spirit in the bond of peace. (4:1–3)
>
> This I say therefore, and affirm together with the Lord, that you walk no longer just as the Gentiles also walk, in the futility of their mind, being darkened in their understanding, excluded from the life of God, because of the ignorance that is in them, because of the hardness of their heart; and they, having become callous, have given themselves over to sensuality, for the practice of every kind of impurity with greediness. But you did not learn Christ in this way, if indeed you have heard Him and have been taught in Him, just as truth is in Jesus, that, in reference to your former manner of life, you lay aside the old self, which is being corrupted in accordance with the lusts of deceit, and that you be renewed in the spirit of your mind, and put on the new self, which in the likeness of God has been created in righteousness and holiness of the truth. Therefore, laying aside falsehood, speak truth, each one of you, with his neighbor, for we are members of one another. Be angry, and yet do not sin; do not let the sun go down on your anger, and do not give the devil an opportunity. Let him who steals steal no longer; but rather let him labor, performing with his own hands what is good, in order that he may have something to share with him who has need. Let no unwholesome word proceed from your mouth, but only such a word as is good for edification according to the need of the moment, that it may give grace to those who hear. And do not grieve the Holy Spirit of God, by whom you were sealed for the day of redemption. Let all bitterness and wrath and anger and clamor and slander be put away from you, along with all malice. And be kind to one another, tenderhearted, forgiving each other, just as God in Christ also has forgiven you. (4:17–32)

Stephen's life displayed God's grace and power because he was filled with obedient faith and with the Holy Spirit. Those traits marked him with a greatness so often overlooked. There is no other path to virtuous character and a spiritually influential life than the path Stephen exemplified.

HIS COURAGE

But some men from what was called the Synagogue of the Freedmen, including both Cyrenians and Alexandrians, and some from Cilicia and Asia, rose up and argued with Stephen. And yet they were unable to cope with the wisdom and the Spirit with which he was speaking. Then they secretly induced men to say, "We have heard him speak blasphemous words against Moses and against God." And they stirred up the people, the elders and the scribes, and they came upon him and dragged him away, and brought him before the Council. And they put forward false witnesses who said, "This man incessantly speaks against this holy place, and the Law; for we have heard him say that this Nazarene, Jesus, will destroy this place and alter the customs which Moses handed down to us." (6:9–14)

A man with the character of Stephen is a match for any attack—and a fierce one came. Alarmed by the power and effectiveness of Stephen's ministry, **some men from what was called the Synagogue of the Freedmen, including both Cyrenians and Alexandrians, and some from Cilicia and Asia, rose up and argued with Stephen.** The phrase **rose up** indicates not that they got out of their chairs but that they were stirred to action. Enraged by their hatred of the Lord Jesus and their love of self-righteous sin, these men went after this gifted man of God.

Commentators have discussed how many synagogues are in view here. The Greek text is not conclusive, but it seems likely that Luke has in mind three separate synagogues—**the Synagogue of the Freedmen,** another **including both Cyrenians and Alexandrians,** and a third composed of people **from Cilicia and Asia.** The cultural and linguistic differences between those groups make it unlikely that they all attended the same synagogue.

Synagogues were meeting places where the Jewish community assembled to read the Scriptures and worship. They originated as far back as the Babylonian Captivity, when the exiles were cut off from access to the temple. According to the Talmud, there were 480 synagogues in Jerusalem at this time (F. F. Bruce, *The Book of the Acts* [Grand Rapids: Eerdmans, 1971], 124; citing TJ *Megillah* 73 d), although that figure may be exaggerated. Many synagogues, like the three mentioned here, consisted of Hellenistic Jews. It is possible that Stephen was a member of one of these synagogues.

The **Freedmen** were the descendants of Jewish slaves captured by Pompey in 63 B.C. and taken to Rome. They were later granted their freedom and formed a Jewish community there. **Cyrenians and Alexandrians** were from two of the major cities of North Africa, Cyrene (home of the Simon who carried Jesus' cross [Luke 23:26]), and Alexandria. Both cities had large Jewish populations. **Cilicia and Asia** were Roman provinces in Asia Minor. Since Paul's hometown of Tarsus was located in Cilicia (Acts 21:39; 22:3), he likely attended their synagogue in Jerusalem. That he was present for the events surrounding Stephen's trial and execution is evident from 7:58 and 8:1. It is possible that, as a student of the great Rabban Gamaliel, he even participated in the debate with Stephen.

Men from all three synagogues came together and **argued with Stephen. Argued** is from *suzēteō*, which refers not to a quarrel but to a formal debate. Luke does not give us the content of the debate. Some of Stephen's arguments can be inferred from the charges brought against him (6:13–14) and his speech before the Sanhedrin. The debate no doubt centered on the death, resurrection, and messiahship of Jesus, and the inability of the Mosaic law and temple ritual to save.

Whatever the precise issues of the debate were, Stephen won. His opponents **were unable to cope with the wisdom and the Spirit with which he was speaking.** Their human reasoning was no match for Stephen's God-given **wisdom.** The phrase **the Spirit with which he was speaking** probably does not refer to the Holy Spirit but to the energy, zeal, sincerity, and fervency with which Stephen spoke. He thus had the two requirements for effective public speaking and triumphing in debate: unarguable truth and potent delivery. The impact of those two was more than his opponents could handle.

Unable to defeat Stephen in a fair debate, his opponents changed tactics. Resorting to an *ad hominem* argument, **they secretly induced men to say, "We have heard him speak blasphemous words against Moses and against God." Secretly induced** is from *hupoballō* and means "to suggest or prompt" with an evil motive. They recruited and coached false witnesses to accuse Stephen, the same tactic used at Jesus' trial (Matt. 26:59–61). Even the trumped-up charges of blasphemy were like those against his Lord.

The false witnesses accused Stephen of speaking **blasphemous words against Moses and against God.** Such was their zeal for the law that they mentioned Moses before God. Blasphemy, speaking evil of something God deems sacred, such as the law of Moses, the person of God, or His temple, was a very serious crime, punishable by death (Lev. 24:16). That his opponents accused Stephen of blaspheming Moses suggests he was denying the ability of the law to save. They charged him with blaspheming God by speaking against the temple (v. 14) where God's presence dwelt. That accusation no doubt also reflects Stephen's presentation of Christ as the embodiment of God (cf. John 10:36).

Since the people were fanatically zealous for Moses and God, they were easily **stirred up** by the false charges. Along with **the elders and the scribes** (some of whom were likely members of the Sanhedrin) the mob **came upon** Stephen and **dragged him away** for trial before **the Council** (the Sanhedrin). *Sunarpazō* (**dragged away**) means "to seize with violence." It is used in Luke 8:29 of a man seized by an evil spirit, while in Acts 19:29 it describes the seizure of Paul's companions by an unruly gang.

The fear of the people that had forced the authorities to arrest the apostles without violence (5:26) dissipated, and those same people violently seized Stephen. Stephen was popular when he healed the sick and performed signs and wonders. But like the fickle crowd that turned on Jesus so soon after hailing Him as the Messiah, these people were swayed to change their minds and attack the preacher. There is a fine line between hearing the gospel and hatred of the gospel—the line of apostasy. Those who cross it often turn violent.

Luke does not tell us how soon after Stephen's seizure that his trial began. It is unlikely that the Sanhedrin was assembled and waiting when he was seized. When the trial began, these Hellenists **put forward false witnesses.** These are undoubtedly the same ones referred to in verse 11. It was their false accusations that prompted Stephen's seizure.

The **false witnesses** repeated the charges that had stirred up the people, namely that Stephen **incessantly** spoke against the **holy place** (the temple), **and the Law.** They were false witnesses not because they put words in Stephen's mouth but because they twisted what he did say. F. F. Bruce writes,

> They are called "false witnesses," as those who brought similar testimony against Jesus are called (Matt. 26:59–61; Mark 14:55–59). But in both cases the falseness of their testimony consisted not in wholesale fabrication but in subtle and deadly misrepresentation of words actually spoken. (*The Book of the Acts*, 135)

Verse 14 gives an example of the slant they put on Stephen's words: **We have heard him say that this Nazarene, Jesus, will destroy this place and alter the customs which Moses handed down to us.** The phrase **this Nazarene** expresses their contempt for Jesus, since they believed nothing good could come from Nazareth (cf. John 1:46). Jesus had never claimed He would **destroy** the Jerusalem temple. He said to His adversaries, "Destroy this temple, and in three days I will raise it up" (John 2:19). As John 2:21 makes clear, "He was speaking of the temple of His body." Since that false accusation had succeeded in getting Jesus condemned, they were quick to use it against Stephen.

Another charge calculated to enrage the people was that Stephen taught that Jesus would **alter the customs which Moses handed down** to them. Stephen, like the apostles, had proclaimed Jesus as the fulfillment of all that the Old Covenant ritual typified. The New Covenant, prophesied by Jeremiah (cf. Jer. 31:31–34), had superseded the Old. The moral law had not changed, but the ceremonial law was done away with. Reality had replaced ritual. Stephen will show in his sermon that he had enormous respect for Moses and the law. Their choice of words, however, made him out to be a revolutionary, seeking to overturn the established divine order. They turned his positive proclamation into a negative attack.

Throughout this ordeal, Stephen's courage shines through. Despite the intense opposition he encountered, he never backed down or compromised. As his enemies complained, he incessantly reiterated the gospel message. Even while on trial for his life before the Sanhedrin, his courage did not waver. In Acts 7:51–53 he boldly rebuked them in the following words:

> You men who are stiff-necked and uncircumcised in heart and ears are always resisting the Holy Spirit; you are doing just as your fathers did. Which one of the prophets did your fathers not persecute? And they killed those who had previously announced the coming of the Righteous One, whose betrayers and murderers you have now become; you who received the law as ordained by angels, and yet did not keep it.

Stephen's courage stamped him with the mark of greatness.

His Countenance

And fixing their gaze on him, all who were sitting in the Council saw his face like the face of an angel. (6:15)

This scene presents a striking contrast. Stephen stood before the Sanhedrin accused of being an evil blasphemer of God, the temple, and the law. Yet when the members of that **Council** fixed **their gaze on**

him, they **saw his face like the face of an angel.** Far from being evil, Stephen radiated the holiness and glory of God.

God Himself answered their false charges by putting His glory on Stephen's face—something experienced by no other person in history except Moses (Ex. 34:27–35). He thus showed His approval of Stephen's teaching in exactly the same way He did that of Moses. Paul writes,

> If the ministry of death, in letters engraved on stones, came with glory, so that the sons of Israel could not look intently at the face of Moses because of the glory of his face, fading as it was, how shall the ministry of the Spirit fail to be even more with glory? For if the ministry of condemnation has glory, much more does the ministry of righteousness abound in glory. For indeed what had glory, in this case has no glory on account of the glory that surpasses it. For if that which fades away was with glory, much more that which remains is in glory. (2 Cor. 3:7–11)

By putting His glory on Stephen's face, God showed His approval of the New Covenant and its messenger.

Stephen's noble character and extraordinary courage reflect his greatness. The church's selection of him for high office shows their high regard for him. Most significant of all, Stephen was great in God's sight. By honoring him as He had Moses, God singled Stephen out as one of the greatest men who ever lived. And his life and testimony profoundly affected an even greater man—Saul of Tarsus.

Every believer should remember Stephen and imitate those qualities in his life that made him the man with the face of an angel. That would be his most fitting memorial.

In Defense of the Faith

16

And the high priest said, "Are these things so?" And he said, "Hear me, brethren and fathers! The God of glory appeared to our father Abraham when he was in Mesopotamia, before he lived in Haran, and said to him, 'Depart from your country and your relatives, and come into the land that I will show you.' Then he departed from the land of the Chaldeans, and settled in Haran. And from there, after his father died, God removed him into this country in which you are now living. And He gave him no inheritance in it, not even a foot of ground; and yet, even when he had no child, He promised that He would give it to him as a possession, and to his offspring after him. But God spoke to this effect, that his offspring would be aliens in a foreign land, and that they would be enslaved and mistreated for four hundred years. 'And whatever nation to which they shall be in bondage I Myself will judge,' said God, 'and after that they will come out and serve Me in this place.' And He gave him the covenant of circumcision; and so Abraham became the father of Isaac, and circumcised him on the eighth day; and Isaac became the father of Jacob, and Jacob of the twelve patriarchs. And the patriarchs became jealous of Joseph and sold him into Egypt. And yet God was with him, and rescued him from all his afflictions, and granted him favor and wisdom in the sight of Pharaoh, king of Egypt; and he made him governor over Egypt and all his household. Now a famine came over all Egypt and Canaan, and great affliction with it; and our fathers could find no food. But when Jacob heard that there was grain in Egypt, he sent our fathers there the first time. And on the second visit Joseph made himself known to his brothers, and Joseph's family was disclosed to Pharaoh. And Joseph sent word and invited Jacob his father and all his relatives to come to him, seventy-five persons in all. And Jacob went down to Egypt and there passed away, he and our fathers. And from there they were removed to Shechem, and laid in the tomb which Abraham had purchased for a sum of money from the sons of Hamor in Shechem. But as the time of the promise was approaching which God had assured to Abraham, the people increased and multiplied in Egypt, until there arose another king over Egypt who knew nothing about Joseph. It was he who took shrewd advantage of our race, and mistreated our fathers so that they would expose their infants and they would not survive. And it was at this time that Moses was born; and he was lovely in the sight of God; and he was nurtured three months in his father's home. And after he had been exposed, Pharaoh's daughter took him away, and nurtured him as her own son. And Moses was educated in all the learning of the Egyptians, and he was a man of power in words and deeds. But when he was approaching the age of forty, it entered his mind to visit his brethren, the sons of Israel. And when he saw one of them being treated unjustly, he defended him and took vengeance for the oppressed by striking down the Egyptian. And he supposed that his brethren understood that God was granting them deliverance through him; but they did not understand. And on the following day he appeared to them as they were fighting together, and he tried to reconcile them in peace, saying, 'Men, you are brethren, why do you injure one another?' But the one who was injuring his neighbor pushed him away, saying, 'Who made you a ruler and judge over us? You do not mean to kill me as you killed the Egyptian yesterday, do you?' And at this remark Moses fled, and became an alien in the land of Midian, where he became the father of two sons. And after forty years had passed, an angel appeared to him in the wilderness of Mount Sinai, in the flame of a burning thorn bush. And when Moses saw it, he began to marvel at the sight; and as he approached to look more closely, there came the voice of the Lord: 'I am the God of your fathers, the God of Abraham and Isaac and Jacob.' And Moses shook with fear and would not venture to look. But the Lord said to him, 'Take off the sandals from your feet, for the place on which you are standing is holy ground. I have certainly seen the oppression of My people in Egypt, and have heard their groans, and I have come down to deliver them; come now, and I will send you to Egypt.' This Moses whom they disowned, saying, 'Who made you a ruler and a judge?' is the one whom God sent to be both a ruler and a deliverer with the help of the angel who appeared to him in the thorn bush. This man led them out, performing wonders and signs in the land of Egypt and in the Red Sea and in the wilderness for forty years. This is the Moses who said to the sons of Israel, 'God shall raise up for you a prophet like me from your brethren.' This is the one who was in the congregation in the wilderness together with the angel who was speaking to him on Mount Sinai, and who was with our fathers; and he received living oracles to pass on to you. And our fathers were unwilling to be obedient to him, but repudiated him and in their hearts turned back to Egypt, saying to Aaron, 'Make for us gods who will go before us; for this Moses who led us out of the land of Egypt—we do not know what happened to him.' And at that time they made a calf and brought a sacrifice to the idol, and were rejoicing in the works of their hands. But God turned away and delivered them up to serve the host of heaven; as it is written in the book of the prophets, 'It was not to Me that you offered victims and sacrifices forty years in the wilderness, was it, O house of Israel? You also took along the tabernacle of Moloch and the star of the god Rompha, the images which you made to worship them. I also will remove you beyond Babylon.' Our fathers had the tabernacle of testimony in the wilderness, just as He who spoke to Moses directed him to make it according to the pattern which he had seen. And having received it in their turn, our fathers brought it in with Joshua upon dispossessing the nations whom God drove out before our fathers, until the time of David. And David found favor in God's sight, and asked that he might find a dwelling place for the God of Jacob. But it was Solomon who built a house for Him. However, the Most High does not dwell in houses made by human hands; as the prophet says: 'Heaven is My throne, And earth is the footstool of My feet; What kind of house will you build for Me?' says the Lord; 'Or what place is there for My repose? Was it not My hand which made all these things?' You men who are stiff-necked and uncircumcised in heart and ears are always resisting the Holy Spirit; you are doing just as your fathers did. Which one of the prophets did your fathers not persecute? And they killed those who had previously

announced the coming of the Righteous One, whose betrayers and murderers you have now become; you who received the law as ordained by angels, and yet did not keep it." (7:1–53)

To reach the world effectively with the gospel, believers must be able to defend their faith. When Paul instructed Titus to ordain as pastors men who were capable of "holding fast the faithful word which is in accordance with the teaching, that he may be able both to exhort in sound doctrine and to refute those who contradict" (Titus 1:9), it was not only to silence the rebellious, empty-talking deceivers (1:10–11), but also to teach the people so well that they could do the same. Peter instructed believers in general to "always [be] ready to make a defense to everyone who asks you to give an account for the hope that is in you, yet with gentleness and reverence" (1 Peter 3:15). Sadly, many Christians are unable to do that, having little or no understanding of why they believe. Lacking a solid foundation for their faith, they are easily "tossed here and there by waves, and carried about by every wind of doctrine, by the trickery of men, by craftiness in deceitful scheming" (Eph. 4:14). Tormented by doubt and ignorant of the faith, they are ineffective witnesses for the Lord Jesus Christ.

Apologetics is the study of the defense of the faith. The English word derives from the Greek word *apologia,* which means "a speech in defense of something." In Acts 25:16, it describes an accused person's defense at his trial. Paul gave an *apologia* to the angry mob in Jerusalem (Acts 22:1). To the Philippians he wrote, "I am appointed for the defense [*apologia*] of the gospel" (Phil. 1:16). In verse 7 of that chapter, Paul spoke of "the defense and confirmation of the gospel." That verse delineates the two sides of apologetics: defending the faith against attack, and presenting truth claims of Christianity to unbelievers.

Paul was not only adept at presenting the gospel but also one of its ablest defenders. Acts 17:2–3 describes Paul the apologist at work: "According to Paul's custom, he went to them [a synagogue in Thessalonica], and for three Sabbaths reasoned with them from the Scriptures, explaining and giving evidence that the Christ had to suffer and rise again from the dead, and saying, 'This Jesus whom I am proclaiming to you is the Christ.'" Like Paul, all believers are to "contend earnestly for the faith which was once for all delivered to the saints" (Jude 3).

There was a great defender of the faith before Paul, however, whose name was Stephen. Unable to best Stephen in open debate, his opponents trumped up false charges of blasphemy against him. They then seized him and hauled him before the Sanhedrin for trial (6:8–15). His defense was based solidly on the Old Testament Scriptures, which he often quoted verbatim. He knew he believed the truth and why he believed it. He ably defended the faith and showed his commitment to it with unflinching courage. So powerful was his polemic for the faith that his accusers sat spellbound until he finished. Then, beside themselves with rage, they stoned him.

As chapter 7 opens, his trial begins. The main part of the chapter consists of Stephen's defense against the false charges brought against him. He stood accused of blaspheming God, Moses, the law, and the temple, the most serious charges imaginable in Jewish society.

While the main thrust of Stephen's speech was to answer the charges of blasphemy, three other ideas are interwoven throughout. He knew he must capture and hold his audience's attention. He did that by reciting Israel's history as the groundwork for his defense. Since they were fiercely proud of their ancestry (cf. Rom. 2:17ff.; 9:4–5; Gal. 1:14) that was a topic they never tired of hearing about.

Another goal of Stephen's speech was to indict his hearers for rejecting the Messiah. Throughout his message, that indictment slowly builds until it reaches a devastating climax in verses 51–53. He shows them that by rejecting the Messiah, they were imitating their apostate fathers, who rejected Joseph, Moses, and even God Himself. Stephen was not the blasphemer, they were.

Finally, Stephen sought to present to them Jesus as the Messiah, using Joseph and Moses as types of Christ.

This passage presents Stephen's fourfold defense against the false charges of blasphemy brought against him. Any commentator is best served by not pursuing every possible lengthy discussion of the Old Testament references Stephen employs but by seeking to capture the dramatic themes and flow of this masterful message. Stephen's purpose is not to recite history but to establish that he is not guilty of blaspheming God, Moses, the law, or the temple. His accusers were, however, because they rejected the Messiah.

GOD

And the high priest said, "Are these things so?" And he said, "Hear me, brethren and fathers! The God of glory appeared to our father Abraham when he was in Mesopotamia, before he lived in Haran, and said to him, 'Depart from your country and your relatives, and come into the land that I will show you.' Then he departed from the land of the Chaldeans, and settled in Haran. And from there, after his father died, God removed him into this country in which you are now living. And He gave him no inheritance in it, not even a foot of ground; and yet, even when he had no child, He promised that He would give it to him as a possession, and to his offspring after him. But God spoke to this

effect, that his offspring would be aliens in a foreign land, and that they would be enslaved and mistreated for four hundred years. 'And whatever nation to which they shall be in bondage I Myself will judge,' said God, 'and after that they will come out and serve Me in this place.' And He gave him the covenant of circumcision; and so Abraham became the father of Isaac, and circumcised him on the eighth day; and Isaac became the father of Jacob, and Jacob of the twelve patriarchs. And the patriarchs became jealous of Joseph and sold him into Egypt. And yet God was with him, and rescued him from all his afflictions, and granted him favor and wisdom in the sight of Pharaoh, king of Egypt; and he made him governor over Egypt and all his household. Now a famine came over all Egypt and Canaan, and great affliction with it; and our fathers could find no food. But when Jacob heard that there was grain in Egypt, he sent our fathers there the first time. And on the second visit Joseph made himself known to his brothers, and Joseph's family was disclosed to Pharaoh. And Joseph sent word and invited Jacob his father and all his relatives to come to him, seventy-five persons in all. And Jacob went down to Egypt and there passed away, he and our fathers. And from there they were removed to Shechem, and laid in the tomb which Abraham had purchased for a sum of money from the sons of Hamor in Shechem. (7:1–16)

Stephen addresses the most serious crime first—the accusation of blasphemy against God. He establishes that he believes fully in the God of Israel, and that the Old Covenant is not abrogated but fulfilled in Christianity—and that is God's will.

The **high priest** (probably Caiaphas, who was in office until A.D. 36) began the proceedings by asking Stephen, **Are these things so?** He was asking, "How do you plead to the charges against you: Guilty or not guilty?" Stephen's reply does not appear at first glance to be a direct answer to that question. Richard Longenecker comments,

> The defense of Stephen before the Sanhedrin is hardly a defense in the sense of an explanation or apology calculated to win an acquittal. Rather, it is a proclamation of the Christian message in terms of the popular Judaism of the day and an indictment of the Jewish leaders for their failure to recognize Jesus of Nazareth as their Messiah or to appreciate the salvation provided in him. ("The Acts of the Apostles," in Frank E. Gaebelein, ed., *The Expositor's Bible Commentary,* vol. 9 [Grand Rapids: Zondervan, 1981], 337)

Stephen uses a lengthy historical summation to make his case. His style of reply had its roots in such Old Testament passages as Nehemiah 9:5ff.; Psalm 78, 105, 106. His purpose was to show that Christ and the Christian faith which he preached were the perfect fulfillment of the Old Testament. He traces the line of God's sovereign will from Abraham through Isaac, Jacob, Joseph, Moses, and David to our Lord—"the Righteous One" (v. 52).

Stephen began his historically derived response by appealing to them as **brethren,** showing his solidarity with them, and acknowledged them as **fathers,** showing his respect for them as the leaders of the Jewish people. The first person named is **the God of glory,** the One orchestrating all redemptive history. The title appears only here and in Psalm 29:3. It is the most rich, complete description of the almighty, holy, sovereign God, since His **glory** is the composite of all His attributes (cf. Ex. 33:18–19). After opening with the sovereign source of the whole plan, he turns to **our father Abraham,** the father of faith and of God's people. His opening line, then, established his belief in the sovereignty of the God of Abraham and acknowledged the fatherhood of Abraham over Israel. He was testifying that he was neither a blasphemer of God nor a traitor to his people. That amounted to a "not guilty" plea.

Stephen then affirmed his resolute belief in God's sovereign control of Israel's destiny. He began by describing the call of **Abraham when he was in Mesopotamia, before he lived in Haran.** There is an apparent historical discrepancy here. Abraham was originally from the city of Ur (Gen. 11:31). Stephen places his call while he still lived in that city **before he lived in Haran.** Genesis 12:1–4, however, appears to place God's call after Abraham had left Ur and settled in Haran. Since Stephen was fully controlled by the Holy Spirit (Acts 6:5, 15; 7:55) his facts must be correct and can be harmonized with other Scripture. Evidently, God originally called Abraham in Ur (Gen. 15:7; Neh. 9:7), then repeated that call in Haran. Both ancient writers Philo and Josephus give that obvious interpretation (F. F. Bruce, *The Book of the Acts* [Grand Rapids: Eerdmans, 1971], 146).

God commanded Abraham, **Depart from your country and your relatives, and come into the land that I will show you.** In obedience to that call Abraham **departed from the land of the Chaldeans, and settled in Haran.** Haran, located about 500 miles northwest of Ur, was noted for its moon worship. Abraham remained there until **his father died** (Gen. 11:32). This poses another interesting problem with an apparently contradictory text. Homer Kent, Jr.'s, comment is helpful:

The death of Abraham's father Terah is placed before Abraham's departure from Haran. A comparison of the data in Genesis (11:26, 32; 12:4) seems to indicate that Terah lived another 60 years *after* Abraham left. Genesis states that Terah was 70 when he fathered his oldest son, presumably Abraham (11:26). Since Abraham was 75 when he left Haran (12:4), Terah would have been 145. Yet Terah did not die till he was 205 (11:32). The best solution seems to be that Abraham was not the oldest son of Terah, but was named first because he was the most prominent (11:26). If Abraham was born when Terah was 130, the figures are harmonized. (*Jerusalem to Rome* [Grand Rapids: Baker, 1992], 68)

God then **removed him into this country** (Israel) in which they were **now living.** Abraham's obedience under God's sovereignty accomplished God's purpose for his life.

As Paul was later to do (cf. Rom. 4; Gal. 3), Stephen focuses on Abraham as a man of faith. Completely by faith he obeyed God's sovereign call and left his homeland, not knowing exactly where he was going. Even when he arrived in his new country, God **gave him no inheritance in it, not even a foot of ground.** The only land Abraham possessed was his burial plot (Gen. 23). All he received—and that **when he had no child**—was God's promise and pledge **that He would give** the land **to him as a possession, and to his offspring after him** (cf. Gen. 12:7; 13:15; 15:18; 17:8). The closest Abraham came to seeing such a grand promise fulfilled was the birth of Isaac.

Abraham's faith was further tested by God's revelation that **his offspring would be aliens in a foreign land, and that they would be enslaved and mistreated for four hundred years** (cf. Gen. 15:13). The exact length of Israel's stay in Egypt was 430 years (Ex. 12:40); Stephen gives a round figure from Genesis. Abraham believed God's promise that **whatever nation to which they shall be in bondage I Myself will judge.** God further promised that after their time in bondage, they would **come out and serve** Him **in this place** (the land of Israel; cf. Gen. 15:14).

Following the flow of salvation history, Stephen moved into the patriarchal period. God's sovereign control of Israel's destiny continued with the succeeding generations, as He reaffirmed the covenant to Abraham's descendants. The sign of God's **covenant** with Abraham was **circumcision.** After **Abraham became the father of Isaac,** he **circumcised him on the eighth day** in obedience to that covenant. Isaac then **became the father of Jacob, and Jacob of the twelve patriarchs**—the heads of the twelve tribes of Israel.

Stephen now was beginning to lay the groundwork for the blistering condemnation he would deliver in verses 51–53. The **twelve pa-**

triarchs, among the most revered men in Israel's history, **became jealous of Joseph and sold him into Egypt.** By so doing, Joseph's brothers rejected the very one God had set apart for special blessing (Gen. 37:5ff.; 1 Chron. 5:1). They were a graphic illustration of the nation's spiritual blindness manifested in the case of Jesus.

Despite his brothers' rejection, **God was with Joseph, and rescued him from all his afflictions, and granted him favor and wisdom in the sight of Pharaoh, king of Egypt; and he made him governor over Egypt and all his household.** Stephen makes inescapably clear that the twelve patriarchs were guilty of opposing God and His purpose. They sold Joseph, but God rescued him. The nation's rebellion against God thus began with the patriarchs themselves. The Hellenists were doing the very same thing that the founding fathers of the nation were guilty of doing and what they were falsely accusing Stephen of doing.

Although he waits until the conclusion of his sermon to openly declare that Jesus is the Messiah (v. 52), even in his historical summation Stephen gives glimpses of Christ. Joseph's life in many ways is analogous to Christ. Both were from the nation of Israel. Jesus, like Joseph, was delivered up out of envy (v. 9; cf. Mark 15:10). Jesus was condemned to death by the testimony of false witnesses; Joseph was imprisoned because of the false accusations of Potiphar's wife. Just as God freed Jesus from the prison of death and exalted Him, so also did He free Joseph from prison and exalted him to high office. As Joseph was able to deliver his sinful brothers from physical death, so Jesus delivers His brothers from spiritual death.

After Joseph's rejection by his brothers, Stephen reminds them, **a famine came over all Egypt and Canaan, and great affliction with it; and our fathers could find no food.** Similarly, Israel's rejection of Jesus plunged them into a spiritual famine—a famine that will last until that day "when all Israel will be saved" (Rom. 11:26).

Because of the severity of the famine, **when Jacob heard that there was grain in Egypt, he sent the fathers there the first time.** It was not until their **second visit,** however, that **Joseph made himself known to his brothers, and Joseph's family was disclosed to Pharaoh.** It is only just before Christ's second coming that Israel will recognize Him for who He is (cf. Zech. 12:10–13:1; 14).

After revealing himself to his brothers, **Joseph sent word and invited Jacob his father and all his relatives to come to him, seventy-five persons in all.** Genesis 46:26–27; Exodus 1:5; and Deuteronomy 10:22 say that seventy people went down to Egypt. However, the Septuagint text of Genesis 46:27 reads seventy-five. Stephen, being a Hellenist, would naturally have used the Septuagint's figure. The larger figure was apparently arrived at by including in the total Joseph's descendants born in Egypt. Gleason Archer writes,

> We therefore conclude that both totals [from the Hebrew Masoretic text and the Septuagint] are correct, though they were calculated differently. Jacob's own sons numbered twelve; his grandsons by them numbered fifty-two; there were already four great-grandsons born in Canaan by the time of the migration, for a total of sixty-six. Manasseh and Ephraim, born in Egypt, increased the total to sixty-eight; Jacob and his wife (whichever she was) brought it up to seventy. But the Septuagint added the seven grandsons of the prime minister [Joseph] and omitted Jacob and his wife from the tally.
>
> This brings us to the result that Stephen correctly reported the number seventy-five, according to the Septuagint in Genesis 46:27 and Exodus 1:5. Likewise, Genesis 46:27, Exodus 1:5, and Deuteronomy 10:22 in the Masoretic text are correct with their total of seventy. Either figure is correct, depending on whether Joseph's grandchildren are included. (Four great-grandchildren of Jacob were included even in the Masoretic text tally of seventy.) (*Encyclopedia of Bible Difficulties* [Grand Rapids: Zondervan, 1982], 379)

After **Jacob went down to Egypt,** he **passed away** in that nation, along with all the **fathers.** After their deaths, **they were removed to Shechem, and laid in the tomb which Abraham had purchased for a sum of money from the sons of Hamor in Shechem.** Verse 16 presents two difficulties. First, Jacob was not buried in **Shechem** but in Abraham's burial plot in Machpelah (Gen. 50:13). Because of that, the antecedent of **they** in verse 15 is to be restricted to the fathers (Joseph and his brothers) only, and does not include Jacob. According to Joshua 24:32, Joseph was buried at Shechem; Stephen here informs us that Jacob's other sons were also buried there.

A more serious difficulty lies in Stephen's statement that Abraham **purchased** the tomb **for a sum of money from the sons of Hamor in Shechem.** According to Joshua 24:32, it was Jacob who bought the plot at Shechem. Many explanations have been offered, but two seem most reasonable. First, it is entirely possible that Abraham made the original purchase **from the sons of Hamor** (the people, or tribe to which he belonged) **in Shechem.** He built an altar there (Gen. 12:6–7) and quite likely purchased the plot of ground on which he built it. Abraham did not settle there, however, and over time the site may have reverted to the occupying people of Hamor, thus necessitating Jacob's repurchase of it (Archer, *Encyclopedia of Bible Difficulties*, 379–81; W. Arndt, *Does the Bible Contradict Itself?* [reprint, St. Louis: Concordia, 1955], 14–17).

A second possible explanation is that Stephen telescopes the accounts of Abraham's purchase of the Machpelah site and Jacob's acquisition of the Shechem site. That would be consistent with his telescoping of the two calls of Abraham in verse 2 (Bruce, *The Book of the Acts*, 149 n. 39; Simon J. Kistemaker, *New Testament Commentary: Acts* [Grand Rapids: Baker, 1990], 249).

It would be rash to charge either Stephen or Luke with an error based on our limited knowledge. It is utterly inconceivable that someone as steeped in the Old Testament as Stephen would have made such an obvious historical blunder. Further, he may have had a definite purpose in mind in referring to Shechem, since in his day that city lay within the territory of the hated Samaritans. (For a discussion of Stephen's theological motives for mentioning Shechem, see Rex A. Koivisto, "Stephen's Speech: A Theology of Errors?" *Grace Theological Journal* 8 [Spring 1987]: 101–14.) Nor is it plausible that a careful and divinely inspired historian such as Luke (cf. Luke 1:1–4) would have erroneously recorded Stephen's speech.

To charge either Luke or Stephen with an error has serious implications for the doctrine of inspiration. To do so is either to affirm that the Spirit of Truth inspired error, or to deny that all the Bible is inspired. The former is absurd to the point of blasphemy; the latter contradicts 2 Timothy 3:16. And if all of Scripture is not inspired, who decides what is and is not inspired? Fallible human reason is certainly not qualified to sit in judgment on the Word of God. The problem, then, lies with the veracity of neither Stephen nor Luke, but only with our lack of complete information.

Stephen thus defends himself against the accusation that he blasphemed God. He does not but affirms the great covenant work of God through Abraham and the patriarchs.

MOSES

But as the time of the promise was approaching which God had assured to Abraham, the people increased and multiplied in Egypt, until there arose another king over Egypt who knew nothing about Joseph. It was he who took shrewd advantage of our race, and mistreated our fathers so that they would expose their infants and they would not survive. And it was at this time that Moses was born; and he was lovely in the sight of God; and he was nurtured three months in his father's home. And after he had been exposed, Pharaoh's daughter took him away, and nurtured him as her own son. And Moses was educated in all the learning of the Egyptians, and he was a man of power in words

and deeds. But when he was approaching the age of forty, it entered his mind to visit his brethren, the sons of Israel. And when he saw one of them being treated unjustly, he defended him and took vengeance for the oppressed by striking down the Egyptian. And he supposed that his brethren understood that God was granting them deliverance through him; but they did not understand. And on the following day he appeared to them as they were fighting together, and he tried to reconcile them in peace, saying, 'Men, you are brethren, why do you injure one another?' But the one who was injuring his neighbor pushed him away, saying, 'Who made you a ruler and judge over us? You do not mean to kill me as you killed the Egyptian yesterday, do you?' And at this remark Moses fled, and became an alien in the land of Midian, where he became the father of two sons. And after forty years had passed, an angel appeared to him in the wilderness of Mount Sinai, in the flame of a burning thorn bush. And when Moses saw it, he began to marvel at the sight; and as he approached to look more closely, there came the voice of the Lord: 'I am the God of your fathers, the God of Abraham and Isaac and Jacob.' And Moses shook with fear and would not venture to look. But the Lord said to him, 'Take off the sandals from your feet, for the place on which you are standing is holy ground. I have certainly seen the oppression of My people in Egypt, and have heard their groans, and I have come down to deliver them; come now, and I will send you to Egypt.' This Moses whom they disowned, saying, 'Who made you a ruler and a judge?' is the one whom God sent to be both a ruler and a deliverer with the help of the angel who appeared to him in the thorn bush. This man led them out, performing wonders and signs in the land of Egypt and in the Red Sea and in the wilderness for forty years. This is the Moses who said to the sons of Israel, 'God shall raise up for you a prophet like me from your brethren.' (7:17–37)

Having successfully defended himself against the charge of blaspheming God, Stephen now moves to the second accusation, rejection of Moses. He shows that just as he reveres God, so also does he honor Moses. Again, he pleads "not guilty." Stephen elucidates that defense by continuing his historical survey. In the first sixteen verses, he has covered the period from Abraham to Joseph, from the call of Abraham to the captivity of Israel in Egypt. Now he moves into the second great period of Israel's history, from Moses to the Babylonian captivity.

The **time of the promise** refers to the time when God would fulfill His promise to **Abraham.** That promise was that "He would give [the land] to him as a possession, and to his offspring after him" (Acts

7:5). By this time, the patriarchs were dead (cf. Heb. 11:13), and **the people** of Israel had **increased and multiplied in Egypt.** They were content there, and had not returned to the land God had promised them. The time for God's promise to be fulfilled had arrived, and He sovereignly orchestrated events to move Israel out of Egypt.

At this time, **there arose another king over Egypt who knew nothing about Joseph** (Ex. 1:8). This is another quote from the Old Testament that shows Stephen's knowledge of the text. Alarmed at the growing Israelite population, and fearing they might unite with an invader, this pharaoh began to oppress the children of Israel. He **took shrewd advantage of** the Jewish **race,** forcing them into slavery and hard labor (Ex. 1:13–14). He **mistreated** them, compelling them to **expose their infants** so that **they would not survive.** This infanticide by throwing babies out to be left to the elements was limited to male infants (Ex. 1:15–22).

God had prepared His deliverer, however. **It was at this** crucial **time** in Israel's history **that Moses was born.** The details of Moses' life and ministry were well known to the Sanhedrin, so Stephen merely summarizes them to make his point. Sensitive to the accusation that he had blasphemed Moses, Stephen makes a point of praising him, describing him as **lovely in the sight of God.**

Moses could not escape the peril of the time, and, after being **nurtured three months in his father's home,** he also was **exposed.** Like so many other infants, he was to be thrown into the Nile to drown (Ex. 1:22). His parents, however, placed him in a basket so he would not die. According to God's sovereign plan, **Pharaoh's daughter** found him, **took him away, and nurtured him as her own son** (Ex. 2:1–6). As the adopted grandson of the pharaoh, **Moses was educated in all the learning of the Egyptians.** Stephen continues to show his respect for Moses by describing him as **a man of power in words and deeds.** Moses was a remarkable man. His natural leadership qualities, coupled with the most comprehensive education in the ancient world, made him uniquely qualified for his task.

God's call came **when he was approaching the age of forty.** At that time, **it entered his mind to visit his brethren, the sons of Israel.** Although raised in Pharaoh's household, Moses had never forgotten his people. No doubt his mother instilled that into him during the years God had providentially arranged that she serve as his nurse (Ex. 2:7–9). He decided to help his beleaguered people. Seeing **one of them being treated unjustly, he defended him and took vengeance for the oppressed by striking down the Egyptian.** By taking that murderous action, **Moses supposed that his brethren understood that God was granting them deliverance through him.** His goal in visiting them was not to pay a social call but to deliver them from their oppressors. **They,** however, **did not understand.** Although Moses had shown his commitment to them by killing an Egyptian, they failed to recognize or acknowledge him as their deliverer.

On the following day he appeared to two of **them as they were fighting together, and he tried to reconcile them in peace, saying, "Men, you are brethren, why do you injure one another?"** Moses saw himself not only as the deliverer of the nation but also as a peacemaker among individuals. His efforts were not appreciated, however, and he was rejected. **The one who was injuring his neighbor pushed him away, saying** sarcastically, **"Who made you a ruler and judge over us?"** Then he added ominously, **"You do not mean to kill me as you killed the Egyptian yesterday, do you?"** (Ex. 2:14). Realizing his killing of the Egyptian had become widely known, **Moses fled, and became an alien in the land of Midian, where he became the father of two sons** (Ex. 2:15, 22). No doubt viewing him as the leader of a Jewish insurrectionist movement, Pharaoh sought unsuccessfully to execute him (Ex. 2:15). Israel's foolish rejection of Moses served to lengthen their time in bondage by forty years. That, too, is analogous to Israel's rejection of the messianic Deliverer and consequent lengthened forfeiture of blessing.

Moses lived among the Midianites for those **forty years.** At the end of that time, **an angel appeared to him in the wilderness of Mount Sinai, in the flame of a burning thorn bush** (Ex. 3:1ff.). The fire represented the presence of God. **When Moses saw it, he began to marvel at the sight; and as he approached to look more closely, there came the voice of the Lord: "I am the God of your fathers, the God of Abraham and Isaac and Jacob"** (Ex. 3:6). God was renewing the covenant, as the reference to **Abraham, Isaac,** and **Jacob** indicates. Unlike many today who gratuitously claim visions of God, **Moses shook with fear and would not venture to look.** God's presence called for reverential fear, not flippant familiarity. Therefore **the Lord said to him, "Take off the sandals from your feet, for the place on which you are standing is holy ground"** (Ex. 3:5). Like the Holy of Holies in the temple, the area around the burning bush was made holy by the presence of the Holy One of Israel.

After forty years in the desert, the time had come for Moses to lead the people to the Promised Land. **"I have certainly seen,"** God told him, **"the oppression of My people in Egypt, and have heard their groans, and I have come down to deliver them** (Ex. 3:7); **come now, and I will send you to Egypt"** (Ex. 3:10). Although His people were continually unfaithful to Him, God remained faithful to His covenant.

Stephen reaches his point. The very **Moses whom they disowned, saying, "Who made you a ruler and a judge?" is the one whom God sent to be both a ruler and a deliverer with the help of the angel who appeared to him in the thorn bush.** This is a constant pattern in Israel's history—spiritual pride coupled with spiritual ignorance that causes them to reject the deliverers God sends them. It is sometimes argued that Jesus could not have been the Messiah, or else Israel would have recognized Him. As Stephen points out, however, they rejected both Joseph and Moses. This was their typical response to those God sent to deliver them. Jesus spoke of this attitude in Matthew 21:33–46.

Moses accomplished his mission and **led them out, performing wonders and signs in the land of Egypt and in the Red Sea and in the wilderness for forty years.** Israel's further rebellion against God under Moses, in spite of the **wonders and signs** they had seen **in the land of Egypt and in the** parting of the **Red Sea and in the wilderness,** caused them another delay. Because of that rebellion, they wandered outside the Promised Land **for forty** more **years.**

From Stephen's discussion of Moses, it is obvious that he has the utmost respect for him. The charge of blaspheming Moses is as false as that of blaspheming God. Indeed, Stephen turned the tables on the Sanhedrin, showing that the nation itself had been guilty of rejecting Moses. The Jews' response to Moses' life, like their response to Joseph's, parallels their response to Christ.

Stephen reminds them that Moses predicted Messiah would come, prophesying to **the sons of Israel, "God shall raise up for you a prophet like me from your brethren."** That passage, taken from Deuteronomy 18:15, was well known to all of Stephen's contemporaries. In John 6:14, the crowd said of Jesus, "This is of a truth the Prophet who is to come into the world." They affirmed that He was the One Moses had promised would come, an affirmation with which these Jews would not agree. They were thus doing again what their fathers had done—rejecting the God-sent deliverer. Only this was more serious than all the others combined. This was the Messiah they were rejecting.

Had the Sanhedrin been willing to consider the facts, they could not have missed the parallels between their nation's history and their behavior toward Jesus. Nor could they have missed the parallels between Jesus and Moses. Moses humbled himself by leaving Pharaoh's palace; Jesus humbled Himself by becoming man (Phil. 2:7–8). Moses was rejected at first, so was Jesus (John 1:11). Moses was a shepherd; Jesus is the Good Shepherd (John 10:11, 14). Moses redeemed his people from bondage in Egypt; Jesus redeems men from bondage to sin. The history of Moses foreshadows the history of Jesus Christ.

THE LAW

This is the one who was in the congregation in the wilderness together with the angel who was speaking to him on Mount Sinai, and who was with our fathers; and he received living oracles to pass on to you. And our fathers were unwilling to be obedient to him, but repudiated him and in their hearts turned back to Egypt, saying to Aaron, 'Make for us gods who will go before us; for this Moses who led us out of the land of Egypt—we do not know what happened to him.' And at that time they made a calf and brought a sacrifice to the idol, and were rejoicing in the works of their hands. But God turned away and delivered them up to serve the host of heaven; as it is written in the book of the prophets, 'It was not to Me that you offered victims and sacrifices forty years in the wilderness, was it, O house of Israel? You also took along the tabernacle of Moloch and the star of the god Rompha, the images which you made to worship them. I also will remove you beyond Babylon.' (7:38–43)

It is an easy transition from Moses to the law, since the two of them are closely associated. While Moses was with **the congregation** of Israel **in the wilderness,** he received the law from **the angel who** spoke **to him on Mount Sinai and who was with our fathers.** That angels were involved in the giving of the law is evident from verse 53 (cf. Gal. 3:19; Heb. 2:2), though the nature of their involvement is not made clear in Scripture. The **living oracles** were the law, which, like the rest of Scripture, is "living and active and sharper than any two-edged sword" (Heb. 4:12). It is divine, authoritative revelation.

Stephen affirms his belief in the law, again making a "not guilty" plea. He declares that God was the author of the law, angels were its mediator, and Moses was its recipient. That certainly was not blasphemy, and the Sanhedrin knew it.

Having defended himself sufficiently and more, Stephen now goes on the offensive. **Our fathers,** he reminds them, **were unwilling to be obedient to him, but repudiated him and in their hearts turned back to Egypt.** It was not Stephen who disobeyed the law, but the very **fathers** the Sanhedrin revered. Stephen did not reject Moses, but those same **fathers repudiated** Moses and the law, **and in their hearts turned back to Egypt.** Incredibly, though they had been cruelly oppressed there, they looked back with longing at their time in Egypt (Num. 11:5).

While Moses was on Mount Sinai receiving the law from God, the people turned to Egyptian idolatry. They said **to Aaron, "Make for**

us gods who will go before us; for this Moses who led us out of
the land of Egypt—we do not know what happened to him" (Ex.
32:1, 23). Their rejection of Moses overlapped their rejection of the law.
Aaron obliged them and **made a calf,** and the Israelites **brought a sacrifice to the idol, and were rejoicing in the works of their hands.**
Calf worship was an integral part of Egyptian religion. Israel's penchant
for idolatry, which began at Sinai, contradicts the proud claims of the
Sanhedrin that Israel was the people of the law. Before it was even delivered to them, they had rejected it.

Although God had every right to destroy the nation, He remained
faithful to His covenant. Three thousand were executed (Ex. 32:28), but
the nation was spared. **God turned away** in judgment, however, **and
delivered them up to serve the host of heaven.** Just as He judicially
abandoned the Gentiles (Rom. 1:24, 26, 28), so also did God abandon
His people to idolatry (cf. Hos. 4:17). From the time of the wilderness
wandering through the Babylonian captivity, idolatry was a ceaseless
problem for Israel.

Stephen supports his point by quoting God's words, **written in
the book of the prophets: It was not to Me that you offered victims and sacrifices forty years in the wilderness, was it, O house
of Israel? You also took along the tabernacle of Moloch and the
star of the god Rompha, the images which you made to worship
them. I also will remove you beyond Babylon** (Amos 5:25–27). It
should be noted that Amos used the word "Damascus" where Stephen
uses **Babylon.** Both the Hebrew and the Septuagint say "Damascus."
Amos was prophesying the captivity of the northern kingdom at the
hands of Assyria—a deportation which took them beyond Damascus.
Later the southern kingdom was taken captive to Babylon. Stephen, led
by the inspiring Spirit, chooses to expand the text of Amos to embrace
the judgment of God on the whole nation. Stephen's use of that prophecy succinctly summarizes the sad, idolatrous history of Israel (cf. Deut.
17:3, 2 Kings 17:16; 21:3; Jer. 8:2; 19:13), which culminated in the Babylonian Captivity.

THE TEMPLE

**Our fathers had the tabernacle of testimony in the wilderness,
just as He who spoke to Moses directed him to make it according
to the pattern which he had seen. And having received it in their
turn, our fathers brought it in with Joshua upon dispossessing
the nations whom God drove out before our fathers, until the
time of David. And David found favor in God's sight, and asked
that he might find a dwelling place for the God of Jacob. But it**

was Solomon who built a house for Him. However, the Most High does not dwell in houses made by human hands; as the prophet says: 'Heaven is My throne, And earth is the footstool of My feet; What kind of house will you build for Me?' says the Lord; 'Or what place is there for My repose? Was it not My hand which made all these things?' You men who are stiff-necked and uncircumcised in heart and ears are always resisting the Holy Spirit; you are doing just as your fathers did. Which one of the prophets did your fathers not persecute? And they killed those who had previously announced the coming of the Righteous One, whose betrayers and murderers you have now become; you who received the law as ordained by angels, and yet did not keep it. (7:44–53)

In response to the accusation that he spoke against the Jewish house of worship, Stephen traces the history of the temple to show his respect for it because it was ordained by God. He begins before the temple with **the tabernacle of testimony in the wilderness.** The Lord God, says Stephen, **spoke to Moses and directed him to make it according to the pattern which he had seen** (Ex. 25:8, 9, 40). The wilderness generation could not plead ignorance of God's glory, since the **tabernacle** was in their midst. Nor could the later **fathers** who, **having received** the tabernacle **in their turn, brought it in with Joshua upon dispossessing the nations whom God drove out before** Israel (Josh. 3:14ff.; 18:1; 23:9; 24:18). From the time of the conquest **until the time of David,** Israel had the tabernacle—a constant symbol of God's holy presence. Yet they persisted in falling into idolatry. Again, Stephen points to the apostasy and rejection of the representatives of Himself that God sends.

After God gave **David** victory over all his enemies, he **asked that he might find a dwelling place for the God of Jacob** (2 Sam. 7). David's request was denied, however, and it was **Solomon who built a house for Him.** Stephen makes only a brief reference to Solomon's temple, since the Sanhedrin was very familiar with its history. Further, the current temple was not Solomon's, which had been destroyed by the Babylonians (Ezra 5:12). That temple had been replaced by one built by Zerubbabel (Ezra 5:2), which had also been destroyed. The current temple had been built by the non-Jew Herod. And within the lifetime of many of Stephen's hearers, in A.D. 70, that temple too would be destroyed.

The transitory nature of the temple leads to Stephen's point, namely that **the Most High does not dwell in houses made by human hands.** Solomon understood that truth. In his prayer at the dedication of the temple he asked rhetorically, "Will God indeed dwell on the earth? Behold, heaven and the highest heaven cannot contain Thee, how much less this house which I have built!" (1 Kings 8:27).

Stephen buttresses his point by quoting Isaiah **the prophet,** who wrote, **"Heaven is My throne, and earth is the footstool of My feet; what kind of house will you build for Me?" says the Lord; "Or what place is there for My repose? Was it not My hand which made all these things?"** (Isa. 66:1). Stephen was not guilty of blaspheming the temple. They were, for confining God to it. Instead, with Solomon and Isaiah, he argued that God was greater than any temple. The temple was the symbol of God's presence, not the prison of His essence.

Throughout Stephen's speech the tension must have been building. As he pointed out Israel's rejections and apostasies, the Sanhedrin must have become increasingly uneasy. They no doubt wondered what point he intended to make. Their wait was over as Stephen, having laid the historical foundation for it, hit them with a devastating indictment: They were just like their fathers in the days of Joseph, Moses, and David. They were **stiff-necked,** or obstinate, echoing God's evaluation of their predecessors (Ex. 32:9; 33:5). The term pictures a person who defiantly refuses to bow before the Lord. Because they prided themselves on their physical circumcision and ritual behavior, Stephen's description of them as **uncircumcised in heart and ears** was especially pointed. Their sin had never been forgiven. They were as unclean before God as uncircumcised Gentiles. That was the ultimate condemnation.

Their stubborn **resisting** of **the Holy Spirit** made them guilty of **doing just as** their **fathers did.** As their fathers had rejected Joseph and Moses and the tabernacle presence, so did they reject the Messiah. Stephen forcefully drives that point home by asking them, **Which one of the prophets did your fathers not persecute?** His words echo those of the Lord Jesus Christ:

> Woe to you! For you build the tombs of the prophets, and it was your fathers who killed them. Consequently, you are witnesses and approve the deeds of your fathers; because it was they who killed them, and you build their tombs. For this reason also the wisdom of God said, "I will send to them prophets and apostles, and some of them they will kill and some they will persecute, in order that the blood of all the prophets, shed since the foundation of the world, may be charged against this generation, from the blood of Abel to the blood of Zechariah, who perished between the altar and the house of God; yes, I tell you, it shall be charged against this generation." (Luke 11:47–51)

Stephen then draws the parallel to its bloody conclusion. As their fathers had **killed those who had previously announced the**

coming of the Righteous One, the Messiah, so had they become His **betrayers and murderers.** While priding themselves on having **received the law as ordained by angels,** they **did not keep it.** They were without excuse, since the law pointed to Christ (John 5:39). Stephen once again echoes the words of his Lord, who said to these same leaders, "If you believed Moses, you would believe Me; for he wrote of Me" (John 5:46). They had no real respect for Moses or the law or they never would have murdered the One Moses promised (Gen. 18:15) or the One of whom the law spoke.

Despite their proud boast that "if we had been living in the days of our fathers, we would not have been partners with them in shedding the blood of the prophets" (Matt. 23:30), they had done far worse. Their fathers had murdered God's prophets; they had murdered His Son, **the Righteous One** (a title used only here and in Acts 3:14 and 22:14). Now they were to commit yet another murder. Stephen would shortly become another in the long line of God's messengers killed by God's chosen nation, and the first killed for preaching the name of Christ.

That it resulted in his execution rather than his acquittal does not tarnish the brilliance of Stephen's defense and indictment. It will forever remain one of the greatest sermons ever uttered. The Sanhedrin should have heard it with their hearts and repented. Tragically, they did not.

The First
Christian Martyr

17

Now when they heard this, they were cut to the quick, and they began gnashing their teeth at him. But being full of the Holy Spirit, he gazed intently into heaven and saw the glory of God, and Jesus standing at the right hand of God; and he said, "Behold, I see the heavens opened up and the Son of Man standing at the right hand of God." But they cried out with a loud voice, and covered their ears, and they rushed upon him with one impulse. And when they had driven him out of the city, they began stoning him, and the witnesses laid aside their robes at the feet of a young man named Saul. And they went on stoning Stephen as he called upon the Lord and said, "Lord Jesus, receive my spirit!" And falling on his knees, he cried out with a loud voice, "Lord, do not hold this sin against them!" And having said this, he fell asleep. And Saul was in hearty agreement with putting him to death. (7:54–8:1a)

In the spring of 1521, a Roman Catholic monk and professor of theology was summoned to appear before Emperor Charles V and the Imperial Diet of the Holy Roman Empire. For the previous few years, Martin Luther had fearlessly criticized the abuses of the Roman Church.

His criticisms had fanned into flame the long-smoldering resentments of the German people toward Rome. Determined to put an end to the popular religious uprising Luther had sparked, the young Emperor summoned him to Worms, where the Diet would convene. There he would stand trial, and if convicted, he faced execution. Luther's friend Spalatin warned him against going to Worms, although he had a safe conduct pass from the Emperor. A century earlier, John Hus had been burned at the stake at the Council of Constance, his safe conduct pass notwithstanding. In reply, Luther wrote that he would enter Worms in spite of the "gates of hell and the powers of darkness," even if there were "as many devils in it as there were tiles on the roofs of the houses" (Harold J. Grimm, *The Reformation Era* [New York: Macmillan, 1954], 137). He appeared before the Diet and refused to recant what he had written. He would take back nothing, he asserted, that his accusers could not prove wrong from Scripture:

> Unless I am convinced by the testimony of the Scriptures or by clear reason (for I do not trust either in the pope or in councils alone, since it is well known that they have often erred and contradicted themselves), I am bound by the Scriptures I have quoted and my conscience is captive to the Word of God. I cannot and I will not retract anything, since it is neither safe nor right to go against conscience. I cannot do otherwise, here I stand, may God help me, Amen. (Lewis W. Spitz, *The Rise of Modern Europe: The Protestant Reformation* [New York: Harper & Row, 1985], 75)

Fifteen hundred years earlier, a miracle-working servant of Christ stood trial for his life. Like Luther, Stephen stood solidly on the rock of divine revelation. And like Luther, his bold stand was to change the course of history. His speech in his own defense was a masterful recounting of Israel's history. In it he ably defended himself, and by extension all Christians, against the false charges that he had blasphemed God, Moses, the law, and the temple. Faithful evangelist Stephen then went on the offensive, closing his speech with a blistering denunciation of the Sanhedrin's hypocrisy. By so doing, he turned the tables on his accusers. It was they, not him, who stood convicted of blasphemy.

The concluding verses of chapter 7 record the last moments of Stephen's life. For unlike Luther, who was spirited away to safety by Elector Frederick the Wise of Saxony, Stephen was to pay for his boldness with his life. It is a dramatic, moving passage. Although he was killed, Stephen was not the victim, he was the victor. Death merely ushered Stephen into the presence of his Lord. Most of the murdering mob (with the notable exception of young Saul of Tarsus), though they lived on, would perish eternally.

A stark contrast between Stephen and his murderers weaves its way through this brief passage. So extreme is the contrast that it can be said to symbolize the contrast between heaven and hell. That contrast may be viewed from four angles: It is the contrast between being filled with anger and being filled with the Spirit, between spiritual blindness and spiritual sight, between death and life, and between hate and love.

FILLED WITH ANGER VERSUS
FILLED WITH THE SPIRIT

Now when they heard this, they were cut to the quick, and they began gnashing their teeth at him. But being full of the Holy Spirit, (7:54–55a)

The Sanhedrin had no doubt listened to the earlier part of Stephen's speech with interest and agreement. After all, he was merely reciting the nation's history—a topic dear to their hearts. But as his drift became increasingly clear, they began to grow uncomfortable. And **when they heard** Stephen's outright castigation of them in verses 51–53, **they were cut to the quick.** *Diapriō* (**cut to the quick**) literally means "to saw in half." Stephen's words ripped apart the veneer of their false spirituality and exposed them for the blasphemous hypocrites they were.

Infuriated rather than broken in repentance by Stephen's words, **they began gnashing their teeth at him.** That act expressed their rage and frustration (cf. Pss. 35:16; 37:12), and reminds us of a generation of obstinate sinners to come. When the angels pour out the bowls of God's wrath and judgment during the Tribulation, sinners then will also stubbornly refuse to repent:

> And the fourth angel poured out his bowl upon the sun; and it was given to it to scorch men with fire. And men were scorched with fierce heat; and they blasphemed the name of God who has the power over these plagues; and they did not repent, so as to give Him glory. And the fifth angel poured out his bowl upon the throne of the beast; and his kingdom became darkened; and they gnawed their tongues because of pain, and they blasphemed the God of heaven because of their pains and their sores; and they did not repent of their deeds. . . . And the seventh angel poured out his bowl upon the air; and a loud voice came out of the temple from the throne, saying, "It is done." And there were flashes of lightning and sounds and peals of thunder; and there was a

great earthquake, such as there had not been since man came to be upon the earth, so great an earthquake was it, and so mighty. And the great city was split into three parts, and the cities of the nations fell. And Babylon the great was remembered before God, to give her the cup of the wine of His fierce wrath. And every island fled away, and the mountains were not found. And huge hailstones, about one hundred pounds each, came down from heaven upon men; and men blasphemed God because of the plague of the hail, because its plague was extremely severe. (Rev. 16:8–11, 17–21)

Even the severest judgments ever to hit the earth will not cause obstinate sinners to repent. Three times in the above passage they show their anger toward God by blaspheming Him.

Stephen's hearers seem just as resistant and callous toward the truth. This was at least the third time they had heard the gospel presented (cf. 4:8ff.; 5:27ff.), yet their anger escalated and they continued to harden their hearts. It is a sobering reality that when men persist in willfully hardening their hearts, God may step in and judicially harden them. The apostle Paul warned such people, "The Holy Spirit rightly spoke through Isaiah the prophet to your fathers, saying, 'Go to this people and say, "You will keep on hearing, but you will not understand; and you will keep on seeing, but you will not perceive"'" (Acts 28:25–26). Of Israel he wrote,

What then? That which Israel is seeking for, it has not obtained, but those who were chosen obtained it, and the rest were hardened; just as it is written, "God gave them a spirit of stupor, eyes to see not and ears to hear not, down to this very day." And David says, "Let their table become a snare and a trap, and a stumbling block and a retribution to them. Let their eyes be darkened to see not, and bend their backs forever." (Rom. 11:7–10)

Similarly, after Pharaoh repeatedly hardened his own heart, God hardened it (cf. Ex. 8:15, 19, 32; 9:7, 34 with Ex. 10:1; 11:10). Well does the writer of Hebrews warn,

Therefore, just as the Holy Spirit says, "Today if you hear His voice, do not harden your hearts as when they provoked Me, as in the day of trial in the wilderness, where your fathers tried Me by testing Me, and saw My works for forty years. Therefore I was angry with this generation, and said, 'They always go astray in their heart; and they did not know My ways'; As I swore in My wrath, 'They shall not enter My rest.'" Take care, brethren, lest there should be in any one of you an evil, unbelieving heart, in falling away from the living God. (3:7–12)

The Sanhedrin had heard the truth. They had heard Jesus' teaching and witnessed His miracles. They also had heard the preaching of the apostles and seen the miracles they performed. Because of their continual rejection, Stephen did not give them another invitation but an indictment—one that filled them with rage. They gnashed their teeth that day, and perhaps most of them are doing that same thing today in hell. Their action previewed what they would be doing through all eternity. Jesus repeatedly described hell as a place where there is gnashing of teeth. In Matthew 13:41–42 He warned that "the Son of Man will send forth His angels, and they will gather out of His kingdom all stumbling blocks, and those who commit lawlessness, and will cast them into the furnace of fire; in that place there shall be weeping and gnashing of teeth." He warned the unbelieving Jews that "many shall come from east and west, and recline at the table with Abraham, and Isaac, and Jacob, in the kingdom of heaven; but the sons of the kingdom shall be cast out into the outer darkness; in that place there shall be weeping and gnashing of teeth" (Matt. 8:11–12; cf. Matt. 13:50; 22:13; 24:51; 25:30; Luke 13:28). The suffering of hell will include the endless anger and frustration of those people who will forever feel both intense conviction for their damning sin and anger toward God. People who reject God's grace and love will not feel remorse under His judgment. In fact, that will only make them angrier.

In sharp contrast, Stephen was **full of the Holy Spirit.** Amid the storm of fury that howled around him, Stephen remained calm, totally yielded to the Spirit's control. *Huparchō* (**being**) "properly [expresses] continuance of an antecedent state or condition" (G. Abbott-Smith, *A Manual Greek Lexicon of the New Testament* [Edinburgh: T. & T. Clark, 1977], 457), a meaning reinforced by its use here in the present tense. Being filled with the Spirit was a way of life for Stephen (cf. 6:3, 5; Eph. 5:18). Consequently, he didn't have to make any adjustments in his life when his time came to face death.

The Spirit produces the fruit of godly living in believers' daily lives. But, as He did for Stephen, He also does provide special grace and strength in times of crisis. "When they bring you before the synagogues and the rulers and the authorities," Jesus told His followers, "do not become anxious about how or what you should speak in your defense, or what you should say; for the Holy Spirit will teach you in that very hour what you ought to say" (Luke 12:11–12). Peter wrote, "If you are reviled for the name of Christ, you are blessed, because the Spirit of glory and of God rests upon you" (1 Peter 4:14). The Spirit grants grace to persecuted believers, enabling them to glorify God in their deaths. Stephen was the prototype for countless thousands of Christian martyrs whose deaths have confirmed that truth.

Christians, then, must not shy away from difficult situations. Like Paul, they can say, "I am well content with weaknesses, with insults, with distresses, with persecutions, with difficulties, for Christ's sake; for when I am weak, then I am strong" (2 Cor. 12:10). They must boldly communicate Christ in all circumstances, knowing that the Holy Spirit will grant them the grace to face the consequences triumphantly and with joy and peace.

SPIRITUAL BLINDNESS AND SPIRITUAL SIGHT

he gazed intently into heaven and saw the glory of God, and Jesus standing at the right hand of God; and he said, "Behold, I see the heavens opened up and the Son of Man standing at the right hand of God." But they cried out with a loud voice, and covered their ears, and they rushed upon him with one impulse. (7:55b–57)

A Spirit-filled believer keeps "seeking the things above, where Christ is, seated at the right hand of God" (Col. 3:1). In the midst of his circumstances, Stephen **gazed intently into heaven.** He was looking for Jesus (cf. 1:10, 11), and he did not look in vain. **He saw the glory of God, and Jesus standing at the right hand of God.** Stephen was one of the few in Scripture blessed with a glimpse into heaven, along with Isaiah (Isa. 6:1–3), Ezekiel (Ezek. 1:26–28), Paul (2 Cor. 12:2–4), and John (Rev. 4:1ff.). God opened Stephen's eyes to see the blazing Shekinah **glory** that revealed the presence of God the Father, with **Jesus standing at** His **right hand.** To him was granted the privilege of being the first to see Jesus (before Paul and John) in His glorified state after His ascension.

Elsewhere in the New Testament, Jesus is described as being seated at the right hand of God (Matt. 22:44; 24:64; Luke 22:69; Acts 2:34; Eph. 1:20; Col. 3:1; Heb. 1:3; 8:1; 10:11–12; 12:2). He is seated in terms of His redemptive work, which is forever completed (Heb. 10:12). Stephen sees Jesus standing to show His concern for him. He also stands to welcome Stephen into heaven.

So enthralled was Stephen with his beatific vision that he burst out, **Behold, I see the heavens opened up and the Son of Man standing at the right hand of God.** For the Sanhedrin, such a statement was the last straw, their tolerance for this blasphemer was exhausted. Stephen's use of the phrase **Son of Man** may have been the sharpest dagger, because it took them back to the trial of another prisoner. Like Stephen, Jesus was accused of blasphemy by false witnesses, yet He kept silent. Finally, in frustration, the high priest demanded that

He speak: "'I adjure You by the living God, that You tell us whether You are the Christ, the Son of God.' Jesus said to him, 'You have said it yourself; nevertheless I tell you, hereafter you shall see the Son of Man sitting at the right hand of Power, and coming on the clouds of heaven'" (Matt. 26:63–64). For that so-called blasphemy of claiming to be the Son of God and Son of Man who would sit on God's right hand, they had executed Jesus. Stephen's vision and words describing who he saw throws that claim Jesus made right back in their faces. Jesus claimed He would be at the right hand of God; Stephen now asserts that He is there! They must either execute Stephen too or admit they were wrong when they had Jesus murdered.

The Sanhedrin chose to silence the truth by killing Stephen. Crying **out with a loud voice,** they **covered their ears** (so as not to hear any further blasphemy) and **rushed upon** Stephen **with one impulse.** Thus did they prove true the Lord Jesus Christ's description of them as "blind guides of the blind" (Matt. 15:14; cf. Matt. 23:16, 24). They continued in the sorry tradition of their fathers by rejecting yet another of God's messengers to them. And having rejected and killed the Messiah, it is not surprising that they reject and kill one of His most faithful heralds.

Luke's choice of *hormaō* (**rushed**) vividly portrays the Sanhedrin's fury. It is the word used to describe the mad rush of the herd of demon-possessed swine into the Sea of Galilee (Mark 5:13; Matt. 8:32). It is also used in Acts 19:29 to describe the frenzied mob that rushed into the theater at Ephesus. To put it in terms of modern English vernacular, they lost it. Casting aside dignity and propriety, the highest court in Israel was reduced to a howling, murderous mob.

Death and Life

And when they had driven him out of the city, they began stoning him, and the witnesses laid aside their robes at the feet of a young man named Saul. And they went on stoning Stephen as he called upon the Lord and said, "Lord Jesus, receive my spirit!" (7:58–59)

Commentators disagree over whether Stephen was slaughtered by mob violence or legally executed. The scene lends itself to the former interpretation, as does the Sanhedrin's lack of authority to carry out death sentences (John 18:31). The details of Stephen's death, however, show they attempted to hold on to some features of legality. They did not stone Stephen until **they had driven him out of the city.** That was in keeping with the injunction of Leviticus 24:14. Further, stoning was the punishment for blasphemy according to Leviticus 24:16. Before **they**

began stoning Stephen, **the witnesses laid aside their robes at the feet of a young man named Saul.** Deuteronomy 17:7 commanded that the witnesses be the first to throw stones at the accused. Perhaps the false witnesses did.

Despite their anger, the Sanhedrin apparently tried to give Stephen's death the appearance of formal justice. It is true that the Romans reserved the right of capital punishment for themselves. Pilate, however, was still governor, and the Sanhedrin knew they had nothing to fear from him. He had proved his vacillating weakness in permitting the execution of Jesus, whom he knew was innocent. But he had Him killed anyway, because he feared the Jews would cause him to lose his position as governor (cf. John 19:1–18). In spite of his efforts, he was in serious trouble with Rome, which would shortly recall him as governor. Also, he normally lived in Caesarea, not Jerusalem, and hence was probably nowhere near this scene.

It is doubtful, however, that the full procedure for execution by stoning prescribed in the *Mishna* was carried out in Stephen's case. That procedure called for the victim to be pushed off a ten-foot high parapet. If that did not kill him, the first witness dropped a large stone on his heart. In the unlikely event that he survived that, the second witness then dropped another stone on him. It is highly unlikely that Stephen would have been in any condition to speak if that had been done in his case (cf. vv. 59–60). More likely is the scene of uncontrollable angry people pushing, shoving, and throwing rocks at random at Stephen. It should be noted from Acts 8:2 that they did not follow the legally prescribed manner of burial given in the Talmud, adding more evidence that the whole affair was illegal.

The mention of **a young man named Saul** marks a major turning point in salvation history. This, of course, was the man more commonly known to history as Paul the apostle. He makes here his first appearance in Acts and becomes the dominant figure from chapter 13 to the end of the book. For now, however, he has only a cameo role, keeping watch over the clothes of Stephen's executioners. His position up front where the action was suggests he was deeply involved in the whole wicked affair. In any case, Stephen's profound and powerful sermon, as well as his calmness and forgiving love for his killers, made a lasting impression on Saul (cf. Acts 22:30). Seeds of his own startling conversion were surely planted that day.

The mob went on with the grisly work of **stoning Stephen.** As death approached, **he called upon the Lord and said, "Lord Jesus, receive my spirit!"** His cry echoed that of our Lord on the cross, "Father, into Thy hands I commit my spirit" (Luke 23:46), with one major exception: Jesus committed Himself to the Father, Stephen to the Lord

Jesus. That he did so testifies to the deity of Christ, whom he obviously regarded as equal to the Father.

This confession of Stephen indicates that he expected to enter the Lord's presence as soon as he died. The Bible does not teach any delay at all between life here and in heaven, either some holding place such as purgatory or some unconscious state called soul-sleep. Instead, Scripture teaches that believers enter Christ's presence immediately following death (2 Cor. 5:8; Phil. 1:23). Our Lord promised the thief on the cross that He would take him to Paradise (the abode of God and the righteous) that very day (Luke 23:43). His parable of the rich man and Lazarus (Luke 16:19–31) taught that the dead are never unconscious or unaware of their circumstances. Revelation 6:9–11 describes the Tribulation martyrs as awake in divine presence and able to plead with the Lord for vengeance on their murderers.

Stephen's confident prayer was answered. Upon his death, he was ushered immediately into the presence of the Lord he had so faithfully served.

HATE AND LOVE

And falling on his knees, he cried out with a loud voice, "Lord, do not hold this sin against them!" And having said this, he fell asleep. And Saul was in hearty agreement with putting him to death. (7:60–8:1a)

The mob poured out their hatred on Stephen by stoning him mercilessly. His heart, in contrast, was filled only with love for them. Amid the flying stones, Stephen fell **on his knees** and **cried out with a loud voice, "Lord, do not hold this sin against them!"** As had his beloved Lord before him, Stephen pleaded for God's forgiveness on behalf of his executioners. He was praying for their salvation, since that is the only way God forgives sin. The death of the prophet Zechariah, the son of Jehoiada, provides an instructive comparison. Second Chronicles 24:20–22 describes his murder:

> Then the Spirit of God came on Zechariah the son of Jehoiada the priest; and he stood above the people and said to them, "Thus God has said, 'Why do you transgress the commandments of the Lord and do not prosper? Because you have forsaken the Lord, He has also forsaken you.'" So they conspired against him and at the command of the king they stoned him to death in the court of the house of the Lord. Thus Joash the king did not remember the kindness which his father

225

Jehoiada had shown him, but he murdered his son. And as he died he said, "May the Lord see and avenge!"

Like Stephen, Zechariah was unjustly put to death. Unlike Stephen, however, his dying prayer was for justice and vengeance, not forgiveness.

Only Christians can love as Stephen did, "because the love of God has been poured out within our hearts through the Holy Spirit who was given to us" (Rom. 5:5).

Having finished his petition, Stephen **fell asleep.** Peacefully, calmly he slipped into the presence of his Lord. Unquestionably, his Master said to him, "Well done, good and faithful slave . . . enter into the joy of your master" (Matt. 25:21). Sleep is a lovely way to describe the death of a believer. It is painless and temporary and takes one from the experience of weariness, work, and consciousness of all the problems of life to the freshness of a new day (cf. John 11:11–12; 1 Cor. 11:30; 15:20, 51; 1 Thess. 4:14; 5:10).

Luke closes his account of Stephen's life with a very important footnote. He reminds us again of Saul's presence, noting that **Saul was in hearty agreement with putting** Stephen **to death.** By his own confession Saul was "the chief of sinners" with murderous intent toward all believers in Jesus Christ (1 Tim. 1:13–15). That murderous hate was evident here. As already noted, Stephen's bold preaching, and especially his calm courage and forgiving love in the face of death, profoundly affected Saul as his later testimony in Acts 22:20 acknowledges. From Stephen's influence came Paul, and from death-dealing Saul God made Paul, whose life-bringing gospel penetrated the entire Roman world, forever altering the course of history. As Augustine put it, "If Stephen had not prayed, the church would not have had Paul."

Both in life and in death, Stephen was so much like his Lord. Jesus was filled with the Spirit, so was Stephen. Jesus was full of grace, so was Stephen. Jesus boldly confronted the religious establishment of his day, so did Stephen. Jesus was convicted by lying witnesses, so was Stephen. Jesus had a mock trial, so did Stephen. Jesus was executed though innocent of any crime, so was Stephen. Both were accused of blasphemy. Both died outside the city and were buried by sympathizers. And as already noted, both prayed for the salvation of their executioners. Was there ever a man more like Jesus?

The Persecuted Church Reaches Out

18

And on that day a great persecution arose against the church in Jerusalem; and they were all scattered throughout the regions of Judea and Samaria, except the apostles. And some devout men buried Stephen, and made loud lamentation over him. But Saul began ravaging the church, entering house after house; and dragging off men and women, he would put them in prison. Therefore, those who had been scattered went about preaching the word. And Philip went down to the city of Samaria and began proclaiming Christ to them. And the multitudes with one accord were giving attention to what was said by Philip, as they heard and saw the signs which he was performing. For in the case of many who had unclean spirits, they were coming out of them shouting with a loud voice; and many who had been paralyzed and lame were healed. And there was much rejoicing in that city. (8:1b–8)

On Sunday, January 8, 1956, on the shore of a lonely river deep in the Ecuadorian jungle, five missionaries were murdered by primitive Auca Indians. News of the massacre shocked the world. To some, their deaths seemed a senseless tragedy. Many decried the promising missionary careers cut short, the five young wives bereft of their husbands, the children left fatherless.

Those with deeper spiritual insight saw things differently. Nate Saint, one of the five martyrs, had written,

> As we weigh the future and seek the will of God, does it seem right that we should hazard our lives for just a few savages? As we ask ourselves this question, we realize that it is not the call of the needy thousands, rather it is the simple intimation of the prophetic Word that there shall be some from every tribe in His presence in the last day and in our hearts we feel that it is pleasing to Him that we should interest ourselves in making an opening into the Auca prison for Christ. (Elisabeth Elliot, *Through Gates of Splendor* [Wheaton, Ill.: Tyndale, 1981], 176)

Elisabeth Elliot, widow of another of the martyrs, Jim Elliot, commented,

> To the world at large this was a sad waste of five young lives. But God has His plan and purpose in all things. There were those whose lives were changed by what happened on Palm Beach. In Brazil, a group of Indians at a mission station deep in the Mato Grosso, upon hearing the news, dropped to their knees and cried out to God for forgiveness for their own lack of concern for fellow Indians who did not know of Jesus Christ. From Rome, an American official wrote to one of the widows, "I knew your husband. He was to me the ideal of what a Christian should be." An Air Force Major stationed in England, with many hours of jet flying, immediately began making plans to join the Missionary Aviation Fellowship. A missionary in Africa wrote: "Our work will never be the same. We knew two of the men. Their lives have left their mark on ours."
>
> Off the coast of Italy, an American naval officer was involved in an accident at sea. As he floated alone on a raft, he recalled Jim Elliot's words (which he had read in a news report): "When it comes time to die, make sure that all you have to do is die." He prayed that he might be saved, knowing that he had more to do than die. He was not ready. God answered his prayer, and he was rescued. In Des Moines, Iowa, an eighteen-year-old boy prayed for a week in his room, then announced to his parents: "I'm turning my life over completely to the Lord. I want to try to take the place of one of those five." (p. 253)

At first glance, Stephen's death may also seem pointless. Here was another promising career cut short. He was a powerful, miraculous preacher, with a deep knowledge of the Old Testament. Such was the godly character of his life that he was one of the seven chosen by the church to oversee its daily affairs. Why was it necessary that one so gifted have such a brief ministry?

Further, his ministry seemed to have ended in failure. Not only was he killed as a heretic, but his death also triggered the first persecution against the entire church. That persecution, spearheaded by Saul of Tarsus, scattered the Jerusalem fellowship. Such a skewed view of Stephen's death, however, betrays a lack of understanding of the way the Holy Spirit works. The persecution, which seemed to be a negative, was in reality a positive factor. It led to the first great missionary outreach by the early church. Satan's attempt to stamp out the church's fire merely scattered the embers and started new fires around the world. In the words of the early church Father Tertullian, the blood of the martyrs became the seed of the church.

The church's first missionary effort, beginning in this chapter, was foreshadowed in chapter 5, when people from the cities near Jerusalem brought their sick for the apostles to heal (5:16). Stephen's outreach to the Hellenistic Jews, those from foreign lands, was a step toward world evangelism. In chapter 8, the church is seen reaching out to Judea, Samaria, and even to a Gentile. They were carrying out their Lord's mandate to "be My witnesses both in Jerusalem, and in all Judea and Samaria, and even to the remotest part of the earth" (Acts 1:8).

This chapter marks another turning point. Jerusalem, which has dominated the story up to this point, begins to settle into the background, illustrating the truth that opportunity ignored is opportunity lost. The church there continues, but the explosive days of apostolic miracles and exponential growth fade. Paul wrote that the gospel came "to the Jew first" and then "to the Greek" (Rom. 1:16). The murder of Stephen almost surely fixed a point of the gospel's final rejection by the Jewish leaders, and God's design for the gospel to move out into new territory began.

In the opening verses of this critical chapter three progressive features describing the initial expansion stand out: persecution, which led to preaching, which led to productivity.

PERSECUTION

And on that day a great persecution arose against the church in Jerusalem; and they were all scattered throughout the regions of Judea and Samaria, except the apostles. And some devout men buried Stephen, and made loud lamentation over him. But Saul began ravaging the church, entering house after house; and dragging off men and women, he would put them in prison. (8:1b-3)

The persecution the church had faced up to this point had been directed at the apostles and their associates who were proclaiming the risen Jesus. Peter and John had encountered opposition from the Jewish authorities, and Stephen had died a martyr's death. As of yet, however, no persecution had been aimed at the members of the church. That was to change quickly.

On the very **day** of Stephen's death, **a great persecution arose against the church in Jerusalem.** That persecution, detonated by the murder of Stephen, was led by a Hellenist Jew named Saul of Tarsus. He was a brilliant student of the revered rabbi Gamaliel, "advancing in Judaism beyond many of [his] contemporaries among [his] countrymen, being more extremely zealous for [his] ancestral traditions" (Gal. 1:14). His own testimony was that he was "a Hebrew of Hebrews; as to the Law, a Pharisee; as to zeal, a persecutor of the church; as to the righteousness which is in the Law, found blameless" (Phil. 3:5–6). His commitment and zeal were turned toward the elimination of the church. (For further biographical information on Paul, see *Romans 1–8*, MacArthur New Testament Commentary [Chicago: Moody, 1991], xiii–xvii.)

Ironically, this same Saul who consented to Stephen's death would later suffer far more for the cause of Christ than did Stephen. The very first physical persecution Stephen encountered killed him, while Paul was repeatedly battered (cf. 2 Cor. 11:23ff.) until finally killed. As the Lord Jesus Christ said about him, "I will show him how much he must suffer for My name's sake" (Acts 9:16). He endured the emotion of facing death many times (2 Cor. 4:8–12).

Paul's ministry was in many ways to parallel that of Stephen. Stephen preached Christ in the synagogues, so did Paul (Acts 17:1–2). The Jewish people rejected Stephen's message, as they did Paul's (Acts 18:5–6). Stephen was accused of speaking against Moses, the law, and the temple, so was Paul (Acts 21:28; 24:6; 25:8; 28:17). Stephen was stoned, so was Paul (although he did not die) (Acts 14:19–20). Both were tried before the Sanhedrin (Acts 6:12ff.; 22:30ff.). Finally, both died as martyrs.

Stephen's death, then, was the catalyst for the storm of persecution, led by Saul, that broke on the church. The predictions of the Lord Jesus Christ were coming true: "If they persecuted Me, they will also persecute you" (John 15:20); "they will make you outcasts from the synagogue, but an hour is coming for everyone who kills you to think that he is offering service to God" (John 16:2).

Because of the persecution, the believers **were all scattered throughout the regions of Judea and Samaria, except the apostles.** "All" does not mean every individual Christian, except the apostles, left Jerusalem. That the Jerusalem church continued to exist is clear from Acts 9:26; 11:2, 22; 15:4; and 21:17. What it does mean is that the church was broken up, and many of its members forced to flee. Acts 11:19–20 suggests that those who fled were primarily Hellenists. Further, "from this time onward the Jerusalem church appears to have consisted almost entirely of 'Hebrews'" (F. F. Bruce, *The Book of the Acts* [Grand Rapids: Eerdmans, 1971], 174). It was only natural that the Hellenists of which Stephen was likely one would bear the brunt of the persecution.

Like faithful watchmen, the **apostles** remained at their posts. They remained in the city out of devotion to their Lord and the desire to shepherd the flock in Jerusalem. An additional reason appears in verse 2: Jerusalem was still a mission field. The **devout men** who **buried Stephen, and made loud lamentation over him,** may not have been believers. Luke uses the term **devout** elsewhere to speak of pious Jews (cf. Luke 2:25; Acts 2:5). Perhaps they were friends of Stephen's from the Hellenist synagogue he attended. Their **loud lamentation**—forbidden by the *Mishna* in the case of an executed criminal—amounted to a public protest of Stephen's death. Despite its rejection by the leaders, there were still people like these whose hearts might be open to the gospel. The apostles remained behind in part to continue their evangelistic efforts.

Meanwhile, the storm of persecution continued unabated, as **Saul began ravaging the church.** Armed with "authority from the chief priests" (Acts 26:10), he began **entering house after house** in search of Christians. **Dragging off men and women** alike, **he would put them in prison.** Not content to harass the saints in Jerusalem, he "persecuted this Way to the death, binding and putting both men and women into prisons" (Acts 22:4). He "kept pursuing them even to foreign cities" (Acts 26:11) with the permission of the Jewish leaders (Acts 22:5). Ironically, it was on one of those missions that he was converted (Acts 9:1ff.). In his zeal for his beliefs (cf. Gal. 1:13), he fulfilled the Lord's prediction recorded in John 16:2. He sincerely thought he was serving God by incarcerating and executing believers. And only a direct confrontation with the Lord Jesus Christ would persuade him otherwise.

The effects of Saul's persecution were devastating. *Lumainomai* (**ravaging**) appears only here in the New Testament. It means "to destroy," "to ruin," or "to damage." In extrabiblical writings, it was used to describe the destruction of a city (Walter Bauer, William Arndt, and F. Wilbur Gingrich, *A Greek-English Lexicon of the New Testament and Other Early Christian Literature* [Chicago: Univ. of Chicago Press, 1979], 481) and mangling by a wild beast (Fritz Rienecker and Cleon L. Rogers, Jr., *Linguistic Key to the Greek New Testament* [Grand Rapids: Zondervan, 1982], 278). Saul literally tore the church apart—an act that would haunt him for the rest of his life so that he felt utterly unworthy to be called an apostle (cf. Acts 22:3–5, 19–20; 26:9ff.; Gal. 1:13; 1 Cor. 15:9; 1 Tim. 1:13).

The persecution resulted in the scattering of the church. But God used the wrath of men for His gospel purposes.

PREACHING

Therefore, those who had been scattered went about preaching the word. And Philip went down to the city of Samaria and began proclaiming Christ to them. And the multitudes with one accord were giving attention to what was said by Philip, as they heard and saw the signs which he was performing. For in the case of many who had unclean spirits, they were coming out of them shouting with a loud voice; and many who had been paralyzed and lame were healed. (8:4–7)

Therefore, in spite of the persecution, those believers **who had been scattered** were not cowering somewhere in fear but **went about preaching the word.** They had been doing so before the outbreak of the persecution, and after being **scattered** they continued to preach. **Went about** is from *dierchomai,* a word used frequently in Acts of missionary endeavors (8:40; 9:32; 13:6; 14:24; 15:3, 41; 16:6; 18:23; 19:1, 21; 20:2).

Preaching is from *euangelizō,* which refers to proclaiming the gospel. All the scattered believers were involved in evangelism. Although some are specially gifted as evangelists (Acts 21:8; Eph. 4:11; 2 Tim. 4:5), all Christians are called to proclaim Christ. Satan's persecution promoted the very thing it was designed to destroy. It fired the believers with new zeal to proclaim the gospel in new areas.

In verse 5, the Holy Spirit focuses on one man as an example of faithful evangelism. **Philip,** the first missionary named in Scripture, becomes the key figure for the rest of the chapter. This is not the apostle Philip, who would have stayed in Jerusalem, but one of the seven chosen to serve the needs of the Hellenist widows (Acts 6:5). Like Stephen, his faithfulness to that task led God to use him in a wider ministry (cf. Matt. 25:23). Although Paul later instructed Timothy to "do the work of an evangelist" (2 Tim. 4:5), Philip is the only man in Scripture actually given the title "evangelist" (Acts 21:8). That is a fitting honor in light of his pioneering work in spreading the gospel.

Beginning his evangelistic work, **Philip went down** from the high plateau of Jerusalem **to the city of Samaria,** located some forty miles north of Jerusalem. It was the ancient capital of the Northern Kingdom of Israel, founded by Omri (1 Kings 16:24), who moved the capital there from Tirzah. After nearly a century and a half of idolatry and rebellion against God, the city fell to the Assyrians under Shalmaneser V in 722 B.C. (2 Kings 17:1–6; 18:9–12). Samaria's downfall marked the end of the Northern Kingdom. Many of its people were resettled in other lands by the Assyrians (2 Kings 17:6), who also located people from other nations in that region (2 Kings 17:24ff.). The resulting mix of Jews and Gentile peoples became known as the Samaritans. Second Kings 17:33 records their religious syncretism: "They feared the Lord and served their own gods according to the custom of the nations from among whom they had been carried away into exile."

Friction soon developed between the Samaritans and the Israelites. When some Samaritans offered to help rebuild the temple, they were contemptuously rejected—despite their claims to be worshipers of the true God (Ezra 4:1–3). Hostility between Jews and Samaritans grew during the intertestamental period and was evident during New Testament times (cf. Luke 9:52–53; John 4:9; 8:48).

The Lord had defied conventional opinion by announcing his messiahship to a Samaritan woman, setting an example of His commitment to the world and to sinners (cf. John 4:4ff.). His express command in Acts 1:8 was initially fulfilled by Philip, who **began proclaiming Christ** to the Samaritans. **Proclaiming** is from *kērussō,* which means "to proclaim publicly," or "herald." By New Testament times, the Samaritans had shed their idolatry. They now worshiped the true God—although after their own confused fashion, which Jesus described as "worshiping that which you do not know" (cf. John 4:20–24). The Samaritans, like the Jews, looked for the coming of the Messiah (John 4:25). Given that foundation of belief, Stephen could simply proclaim Jesus as the long-awaited Messiah. With some we need to spend time in pre-evangelism, tearing down their false system of belief and proving the truth of Christianity. Only then will they be prepared to understand the gospel message. Others, like these Samaritans, already have that background. They are ready to hear the gospel.

The Holy Spirit had prepared their hearts to respond to Philip's message. As a result, his preaching resulted in a wholesale spiritual awakening, as **the multitudes with one accord were giving attention to what was said by** him. **The signs which** Philip **was performing** authenticated him as a true messenger of God (cf. Acts 2:43; 4:30; 5:12–16; 6:8; 14:3; 15:12, and the discussion in chapter 13 of this volume).

Verse 7 gives some samples of the miracles performed by Philip: **In the case of many who had unclean spirits, they were coming out of them shouting with a loud voice; and many who had been paralyzed and lame were healed.** Luke notes that those possessed by **unclean spirits,** or demons, were freed from their bondage. Jesus had frequently encountered and healed demon-possessed individuals (cf. Matt. 4:24; 8:16, 28; 9:32–34; 12:22–28; etc.), as Satan mustered all his forces in a futile effort to oppose Him. Jesus was still healing the demon-possessed through this associate of the apostles.

Such demon-indwelt people exist in our own day, although they may not be as commonly manifest in Western culture as in third-world cultures. As C. S. Lewis notes, Satan and his demons adapt themselves to whatever world view prevails in a given society. They are equally at home with Western materialists and third-world magicians (*The Screwtape Letters* [New York: Macmillan, 1961], 3). Many are controlled by demons who give no outward sign of it. That is especially true of those involved in promoting false religion. (For a discussion of whether Christians can be demon-possessed, see my book *How to Meet the Enemy* [Wheaton, Ill.: Victor, 1992].)

Despite the claims of those in the so-called "spiritual warfare" movement, believers today do not have the authority or ability to command or to directly cast out demons. I have elsewhere noted that the temporary sign gift of miracles was the power (*dunamis*) to cast out demons (*1 Corinthians,* MacArthur New Testament Commentary [Chicago: Moody, 1984], 302). Like the other sign gifts, that gift no longer operates today. As with physical healing, however, we can pray for God to intercede.

Nowhere in Scripture are believers told to "bind Satan" or exercise authority over demons. Satan will not be bound until a holy angel does so in the future (Rev. 20:1–3). And those who attempt to assert their authority over demons risk winding up like the Jewish exorcists, the sons of Sceva, of Acts 19:13–16. It is dangerous to claim for ourselves authority God has not granted us. The biblical instruction for conducting spiritual warfare is laid out in Ephesians 6:10–18.

Unable to resist Philip's God-given power, the **unclean spirits were coming out** of their victims, **shouting with a loud voice.** Demons often cried out when they were cast out of an individual (cf. Mark 1:23, 26; 3:11; 5:7; Luke 4:33, 41), perhaps in rage and protestation.

Besides casting out demons, Philip also healed **many who had been paralyzed and lame.** Such healings of serious physical ailments made the power of God evident. It is no wonder, then, that the people paid close attention to the truth in Philip's preaching.

PRODUCTIVITY

And there was much rejoicing in that city. (8:8)

The powerful miracles and preaching of Philip resulted, as it had in Jerusalem, in the salvation of many Samaritans. But as true bibli-

cal preaching inevitably does, it produced another vastly different response. Some accepted the gospel, believing and reacting with **much
rejoicing.** They were the true believers, the wheat. Their joy came not
just from physical deliverance from diseases, or spiritual deliverance
from demons, but from complete deliverance from sin through the Messiah, the Lord Jesus Christ. Others, however, were false believers, or
tares. Such a man was Simon Magus, the subject of the following narrative.

The Faith That Does Not Save

19

Now there was a certain man named Simon, who formerly was practicing magic in the city, and astonishing the people of Samaria, claiming to be someone great; and they all, from smallest to greatest, were giving attention to him, saying, "This man is what is called the Great Power of God." And they were giving him attention because he had for a long time astonished them with his magic arts. But when they believed Philip preaching the good news about the kingdom of God and the name of Jesus Christ, they were being baptized, men and women alike. And even Simon himself believed; and after being baptized, he continued on with Philip; and as he observed signs and great miracles taking place, he was constantly amazed. Now when the apostles in Jerusalem heard that Samaria had received the word of God, they sent them Peter and John, who came down and prayed for them, that they might receive the Holy Spirit. For He had not yet fallen upon any of them; they had simply been baptized in the name of the Lord Jesus. Then they began laying their hands on them, and they were receiving the Holy Spirit. Now when Simon saw that the Spirit was bestowed through the laying on of the apostles' hands, he offered them money, saying, "Give

this authority to me as well, so that everyone on whom I lay my hands may receive the Holy Spirit." But Peter said to him, "May your silver perish with you, because you thought you could obtain the gift of God with money! You have no part or portion in this matter, for your heart is not right before God. Therefore repent of this wickedness of yours, and pray the Lord that if possible, the intention of your heart may be forgiven you. For I see that you are in the gall of bitterness and in the bondage of iniquity." But Simon answered and said, "Pray to the Lord for me yourselves, so that nothing of what you have said may come upon me." (8:9–24)

One of the most fearful realities in all of Scripture is that some who think they are saved will be eternally lost. Thinking they are on the narrow way of saving truth that leads to heaven, they are in reality on the broad way of religion that leads to destruction (cf. Matt. 7:13–14). They will one day hear from the Lord Jesus Christ the most shocking, terrifying words any human could ever hear: "I never knew you; depart from Me, you who practice lawlessness" (Matt. 7:23). To their horror, they will discover too late that there is an entrance to hell at the edge of the very gates of heaven.

Whenever the gospel is preached, it will inevitably produce both genuine saving faith and false faith. The seed of the Word will fall on good soil and bad soil. There will be branches who abide in the vine, and those that are cut off and burned. There will be those with working faith and those with demon faith. There will be those to whom Jesus discloses Himself and those to whom He does not entrust Himself. There are those who "have faith to the preserving of the soul" and those who "shrink back to destruction" (Heb. 10:39). There will be wheat and there will be tares.

In Matthew 13:24–30, Jesus told a parable illustrating that truth:

He presented another parable to them, saying, "The kingdom of heaven may be compared to a man who sowed good seed in his field. But while men were sleeping, his enemy came and sowed tares also among the wheat, and went away. But when the wheat sprang up and bore grain, then the tares became evident also. And the slaves of the landowner came and said to him, 'Sir, did you not sow good seed in your field? How then does it have tares?' And he said to them, 'An enemy has done this!' And the slaves said to him, 'Do you want us, then, to go and gather them up?' But he said, 'No; lest while you are gathering up the tares, you may root up the wheat with them. Allow both to grow together until the harvest; and in the time of the harvest I will say to the

> reapers, 'First gather up the tares and bind them in bundles to burn them up; but gather the wheat into my barn.'"

As often happened, the disciples missed the point, and requested an explanation:

> Then He left the multitudes, and went into the house. And His disciples came to Him, saying, "Explain to us the parable of the tares of the field." And He answered and said, "The one who sows the good seed is the Son of Man, and the field is the world; and as for the good seed, these are the sons of the kingdom; and the tares are the sons of the evil one; and the enemy who sowed them is the devil, and the harvest is the end of the age; and the reapers are angels. Therefore just as the tares are gathered up and burned with fire, so shall it be at the end of the age. The Son of Man will send forth His angels, and they will gather out of His kingdom all stumbling blocks, and those who commit lawlessness, and will cast them into the furnace of fire; in that place there shall be weeping and gnashing of teeth. Then the righteous will shine forth as the sun in the kingdom of their Father. He who has ears, let him hear." (Matt. 13:36–43)

This text presents an example of genuine saving faith, the Ethiopian eunuch. But first it presents the first known satanic attempt to sow a tare in the church, Simon Magus. Simon appeared to be a genuine believer; even one as discerning as Philip accepted him as such and baptized him. Simon even "continued on with Philip" (verse 13). He thus manifested three marks of a genuine believer: he believed, he was obedient in baptism, and he continued with Philip. He illustrates the difficulty of telling the wheat from the tares. It was not until he attempted to buy the authority to confer the Holy Spirit that he was unmasked.

Where did Simon go wrong? How did one who came so close miss out on true salvation? Faith must be grounded in the truth, and his was not. This passage reveals four glaring, massive faults in Simon's theology: He had a wrong view of self, salvation, the Spirit, and sin. Those faults kept him from genuine faith and left him in the position to perish eternally.

A Wrong View of Self

Now there was a certain man named Simon, who formerly was practicing magic in the city, and astonishing the people of Samaria, claiming to be someone great; and they all, from smallest

to greatest, were giving attention to him, saying, "This man is what is called the Great Power of God." And they were giving him attention because he had for a long time astonished them with his magic arts. (8:9–11)

A faulty view of man keeps myriads out of the kingdom. The view that man is essentially good is as pervasive as it is damning. It lulls its victims into a false sense of security, causing them to think that God applauds their good deeds. In reality, He views the supposed good works with which they clothe themselves as "a filthy garment" (Isa. 64:6). Any view of man as basically good and capable of earning acceptance with God deadens people to the reality of God's impending judgment and blinds them to their need of a Savior. Those who fail to see themselves as sinners will see no need for a Savior.

Simon had an egotistical view of himself. **Practicing magic in the city, and astonishing the people of Samaria** led him to claim **to be someone great.** He saw in Philip's teaching a means to gain more greatness for himself. **Magic** referred originally to the lore of the magi— the priests of the Medo-Persians. It was a mix of science and superstition, combining astrology, divination, and occultic practices with history, mathematics, and agriculture. It could be trickery or demonic. (For further information on the magi, see *Matthew 1–8*, MacArthur New Testament Commentary [Chicago: Moody, 1985], 26–28.)

Simon's hold on the people of Samaria was complete. **All** of them, **from smallest to greatest, were giving attention to him.** Impressed by his occult powers, they exclaimed, **This man is what is called the Great Power of God.** That title shows that Simon claimed deity for himself (cf. Mark 14:62). That Simon viewed himself as God betrays the most heretical view of self imaginable. The early church Fathers reported that Simon was one of the founders of Gnosticism and that he viewed himself as God incarnate:

> The first two teachers to propagate gnostic ideas within Christian circles were Simon and his successor Menander. Unlike later and more famous representatives of Gnosticism, both Simon and Menander claimed divinity for themselves. According to Acts 8:9–11, Simon called himself the "great power of God." The Greek term he used, dunamis, was used by later, more orthodox theologians in reference to both the Son and the Holy Spirit. . . . Justin Martyr also reports Simon's messianic claim. (Harold O. J. Brown, *Heresies* [Garden City, N.Y.: Doubleday, 1984], 50)

Simon's perverted view of himself gave Satan an opening to use him to spread false doctrine through the church. His false teaching, later elaborated into full-blown Gnosticism, was to threaten and embattle the church from Paul onward for centuries.

Like many charlatan magicians of his day (cf. Acts 13:6), Simon probably believed in his powers. That he may not have been a conscious fraud rendered him even more dangerous and believable. It is not surprising, then, that the Samaritans **were giving him attention because he had for a long time astonished them with his magic arts.** After all, they believed in God and had messianic hopes. That made them especially vulnerable to someone like Simon. Sadly, people in our supposedly sophisticated age are equally vulnerable to charlatans who claim to be miracle-workers in the name of God.

As long as Simon believed he was God, or nearly God, he could not come to a proper sense of himself. People must see themselves as lost, weak, and helpless without God before they can be saved. Simon, locked firmly in pride's grip, did not.

Pride is a universal and deadly sin. It is the most characteristic and controlling sin in all human fallenness. Pride is an easy sin to indulge in, since it does not entail the loss of public reputation, prestige, health, or wealth associated with other socially unacceptable sins. Pride, in fact, has been redefined as a virtue. Sinful pride often masquerades under seemingly upright motives. In Herod, it masked itself as integrity and beheaded John the Baptist. In the Pharisees, it masked itself as holiness and rejected the Holy One. Among the Jewish authorities, it masked itself as zeal for God and executed the Son of God.

Pride cost man Eden, and the fallen angels heaven. It doomed Sodom and Gomorrah. It cost Nebuchadnezzar his reason, Rehoboam his kingdom, Uzziah his health, and Haman his life.

The Bible has much to say about the evil of pride. Job 35:12 says, "They cry out, but He does not answer because of the pride of evil men." The psalmist points out that "the wicked, in the haughtiness of his countenance, does not seek Him. All his thoughts are, 'There is no God'" (Ps. 10:4); and he implores the Lord to "cut off all flattering lips, the tongue that speaks great things" (Ps. 12:3). Proverbs 6:16–19 describes seven things the Lord hates. Heading the list is "haughty eyes." Proverbs 8:13 reads, "The fear of the Lord is to hate evil; pride and arrogance and the evil way," while Proverbs 16:5 cautions that "everyone who is proud in heart is an abomination to the Lord; assuredly, he will not be unpunished." The familiar words of Proverbs 16:18 warn that "pride goes before destruction, and a haughty spirit before stumbling," while Proverbs 21:4 states plainly that "haughty eyes and a proud heart . . . [are] sin." Paul advises that "if anyone thinks he is something when he is nothing, he deceives himself" (Gal. 6:3). No one can be saved while clinging to their pride, because "God is opposed to the proud, but gives grace to the humble" (James 4:6).

In Luke 18:9–14, the Lord Jesus Christ told a parable teaching that the proud cannot be saved:

> And He also told this parable to certain ones who trusted in themselves that they were righteous, and viewed others with contempt: "Two men went up into the temple to pray, one a Pharisee, and the other a tax-gatherer. The Pharisee stood and was praying thus to himself, 'God, I thank Thee that I am not like other people: swindlers, unjust, adulterers, or even like this tax-gatherer. I fast twice a week; I pay tithes of all that I get.' But the tax-gatherer, standing some distance away, was even unwilling to lift up his eyes to heaven, but was beating his breast, saying, 'God, be merciful to me, the sinner!' I tell you, this man went down to his house justified rather than the other; for everyone who exalts himself shall be humbled, but he who humbles himself shall be exalted."

It is only those with the humility of little children who are fit to enter the kingdom (Matt. 18:2–4). In one of the most powerful invitations to sinners, James wrote,

> But He gives a greater grace. Therefore it says, "God is opposed to the proud, but gives grace to the humble." Submit therefore to God. Resist the devil and he will flee from you. Draw near to God and He will draw near to you. Cleanse your hands, you sinners; and purify your hearts, you double-minded. Be miserable and mourn and weep; let your laughter be turned into mourning, and your joy to gloom. Humble yourselves in the presence of the Lord, and He will exalt you. (James 4:6–10)

Only the humble, aware of their inadequacies and shortcomings, have that sense of lostness that drives them to God. It is the poor in spirit, not the proud in heart, who experience saving faith (Matt. 5:3). Nothing short of a true estimate of one's wretchedness, and a broken and contrite heart coupled with longing for forgiveness, prepare the soul for salvation.

A Wrong View of Salvation

But when they believed Philip preaching the good news about the kingdom of God and the name of Jesus Christ, they were being baptized, men and women alike. And even Simon himself believed; and after being baptized, he continued on with Philip; and as he observed signs and great miracles taking place, he was constantly amazed. (8:12–13)

Simon's magical arts were no match for Philip's Spirit-given power (vv. 6–7). Through Philip's ministry, a revival broke out in the city. **When** the people **believed Philip preaching the good news about the kingdom of God and the name of Jesus Christ, they were being baptized, men and women alike.** Philip's message consisted of two parts. **The kingdom of God** refers to God's sovereign rule over the sphere of salvation that is entered by those who belong to Him through faith in His Son. **The name of Jesus Christ** symbolizes all that He is. Philip preached to them about the realm of the saved and then zeroed in on the truths about the Lord Jesus Christ, who alone provides entrance into that realm.

Because of Philip's preaching, the people **believed** and **were being baptized, men and women alike.** As more people believed, Simon saw his following dwindle. His declining popularity, a desire to be associated with God and the Messiah, and a desire to learn what he perceived to be Philip's power, motivated **Simon himself** to believe. **After being baptized, he continued on with Philip,** for at least three perceivable reasons. First, he wanted to sustain contact with the people following the preacher. By joining Philip's movement, he went where the action was and kept his opportunity for influence alive. Second, **as he observed signs and great miracles taking place, he was constantly amazed.** He had, so to speak, a professional interest in finding out the source of Philip's amazing powers. Third, as his later conduct shows, he wanted to figure out how to acquire that power for himself. Magicians often sold each other their tricks and incantations.

It becomes clear soon that Simon's baptism did not save him. Baptism has no power to take away sin. It is important, however, and commanded of all believers following salvation, though it plays no part in it. (For a further discussion of this point see the discussion of Acts 2:38 in chapter 6.)

Simon viewed salvation as a purely ritualistic, external matter, an additional act in his life instead of the total transformation of his whole person on the inside (2 Cor. 5:17). Faith that does not transform the life is not saving faith. James wrote, "What use is it, my brethren, if a man says he has faith, but he has no works? Can that faith save him? Even so faith, if it has no works, is dead, being by itself. But someone may well say, 'You have faith, and I have works; show me your faith without works, and I will show you my faith by my works'" (James 2:14, 17–18). The demons have faith (James 2:19), but are not saved. They believe, and even tremble, but do not love righteousness and hate sin— the evidence of salvation. Nor were those described in John 2:23–25 saved by their shallow faith: "Now when He was in Jerusalem at the Passover, during the feast, many believed in His name, beholding His signs which He was doing. But Jesus, on His part, was not entrusting Himself to them, for He knew all men, and because He did not need anyone to bear witness concerning man for He Himself knew what was in man. Simon believed in the signs but not in the One whose power was behind them. True salvation is not mere profession or ritual act. It is the divine transformation of the soul from love of self to love of God, from love of sin to love of holiness.

A Wrong View of the Spirit

Now when the apostles in Jerusalem heard that Samaria had received the word of God, they sent them Peter and John, who came down and prayed for them, that they might receive the Holy Spirit. For He had not yet fallen upon any of them; they had simply been baptized in the name of the Lord Jesus. Then they began laying their hands on them, and they were receiving the Holy Spirit. Now when Simon saw that the Spirit was bestowed through the laying on of the apostles' hands, he offered them money, saying, "Give this authority to me as well, so that everyone on whom I lay my hands may receive the Holy Spirit." (8:14–19)

Word of the amazing success of Philip's ministry reached **the apostles in Jerusalem.** When they **heard that Samaria had received the word of God, they sent Peter and John** to check it out. That Samaritans were included in the kingdom was shocking to devout Jews, who despised them as half-breed outcasts. Peter and John's mission was threefold: First, they came to help Philip with the spiritual harvest. The response of the Samaritans was too great for one man to handle. Second, they came to give apostolic sanction and blessing to Philip's work among the Samaritans. The apostles were the leaders of the church and maintained that position even after the church spread from Jerusalem. Finally, they **came down** from Jerusalem **and prayed** for the Samaritans **that they might receive the Holy Spirit.** Although they had believed and been baptized, the Spirit **had not yet fallen upon any of them; they had simply been baptized in the name of the Lord Jesus.**

Many who teach that Christians receive the Spirit subsequent to salvation appeal to this and similar passages for support. Here is a clear example, they argue, of people who were saved, yet did not have the Holy Spirit. Such teaching ignores the transitional nature of Acts. (For further discussion of the transitional nature of Acts and the issue of subsequence regarding the coming of the Spirit, see my book *Charismatic*

Chaos [Grand Rapids: Zondervan, 1992].) It also flies in the face of the plain teaching of Scripture that "if anyone does not have the Spirit of Christ, he does not belong to Him" (Rom. 8:9). There is no such thing as a Christian who does not yet have the Holy Spirit, since "by one Spirit we were all baptized into one body" at conversion (1 Cor. 12:13).

Why did the Samaritans (and later the Gentiles) have to wait for the apostles before receiving the Spirit? For centuries, the Samaritans and the Jews had been bitter rivals. If the Samaritans had received the Spirit independent of the Jerusalem church, that rift would have been perpetuated. There could well have been two separate churches, a Jewish church and a Samaritan church. But God had designed one church, in which "there is neither Jew nor Greek, there is neither slave nor free man, there is neither male nor female," but "all [are] one in Christ Jesus" (Gal. 3:28).

By delaying the Spirit's coming until Peter and John arrived, God preserved the unity of the church. The apostles needed to see for themselves, and give firsthand testimony to the Jerusalem church, that the Spirit came upon the Samaritans. The Samaritans also needed to learn that they were subject to apostolic authority. The Jewish believers and the Samaritans were thus linked together into one body.

Today, believers receive the Spirit at salvation (cf. 1 Cor. 12:13). There was no need for delay after Jews, Gentiles, Samaritans, and Old Testament saints were already included in the church.

When they arrived, Peter and John **began laying their hands on** the Samaritan believers, **and they were receiving the Holy Spirit.** That was too much for Simon. When he **saw that the Spirit was bestowed through the laying on of the apostles' hands, he offered them money.** Evidently, the believers were speaking in tongues as on the Day of Pentecost so that there was a perceivable sign of this great reality sufficient to arouse Simon's interest. Philip had impressed him, but Peter and John overwhelmed him. Simon asked them brashly and excitedly, **"Give this authority to me as well, so that everyone on whom I lay my hands may receive the Holy Spirit."** He treated the two apostles as though they were fellow practitioners of magic, and was ready to negotiate the price to buy the secret of their power. By this act, Simon gave his name to the term "simony," which through history has referred to the buying and selling of ecclesiastical offices.

Nothing God has, however, is for sale—certainly not the Holy Spirit! Indeed, there is nothing sinful men have to offer Him. Salvation and spiritual blessing He pours out freely to His children. In Isaiah 55:1 God cries out, "Ho! Every one who thirsts, come to the waters; and you who have no money come, buy and eat. Come, buy wine and milk without money and without cost." Yet countless thousands, ignorant of that fact, are striving desperately and futilely to buy God's blessing.

Peter unhesitatingly reacted with outrage at Simon's attempt. With his characteristic bluntness, he **said to him, "May your silver perish with you, because you thought you could obtain the gift of God with money! You have no part or portion in this matter, for your heart is not right before God."** Peter was irate, as his inflammatory prose indicates. The literal meaning of the Greek text has been softened by most translations. J. B. Phillips's rendering, "To hell with you and your money!" conveys the actual sense of Peter's words. Simon's view of the Spirit as a commodity to be bought and added to his repertoire was utterly and blasphemously wrong, and betrayed his lost condition.

A Wrong View of Sin

"Therefore repent of this wickedness of yours, and pray the Lord that if possible, the intention of your heart may be forgiven you. For I see that you are in the gall of bitterness and in the bondage of iniquity." But Simon answered and said, "Pray to the Lord for me yourselves, so that nothing of what you have said may come upon me." (8:22–24)

Peter follows his condemnation of Simon with a call for his repentance. He commands Simon to **repent of this wickedness of yours, and pray the Lord that if possible, the intention of your heart may be forgiven you.** He challenges Simon to have a correct view of his heinous sin—one that sees it for what is and turns from it. As noted in chapters 6 and 10 of this volume, *metanoeō* (**repent**) involves turning from sin to God. If Simon did so, **the intention of** his **heart** to do evil would **be forgiven him.** Peter, using Old Testament expressions for the most serious offenses against God (cf. Deut. 19:18–20), warns Simon of the seriousness of his situation: **"I see that you are in the gall of bitterness and in the bondage of iniquity."** The phrase **gall of bitterness** is very strong. *Cholē* (**gall**) refers to a bitter ingredient or bile. Coupled with *pikria* (**bitterness**), it conveys an extremely bitter, harsh, and distasteful condition. It vividly pictures the reality of one **in the bondage of iniquity.** Sin is a harsh taskmaster. Proverbs 5:22 warns that "his own iniquities will capture the wicked, and he will be held with the cords of his sin."

Simon, however, was not persuaded. Although shaken and afraid, he refused to ask the Lord for forgiveness. Instead, he said to the apostles, **"Pray to the Lord for me yourselves, so that nothing of what you have said may come upon me."** His only concern was to escape the temporal consequences of his sin. True repentance, however, consists of more than mere sorrow for sin. Paul writes in 2 Corinthians 7:9–10,

> I now rejoice, not that you were made sorrowful, but that you were made sorrowful to the point of repentance; for you were made sorrowful according to the will of God, in order that you might not suffer loss in anything through us. For the sorrow that is according to the will of God produces a repentance without regret, leading to salvation; but the sorrow of the world produces death.

Simon had a wrong view of self, of salvation, of the Spirit, and of sin. All that added up to a faith that did not save.

The Faith
That Does Save

20

And so, when they had solemnly testified and spoken the word of the Lord, they started back to Jerusalem, and were preaching the gospel to many villages of the Samaritans. But an angel of the Lord spoke to Philip saying, "Arise and go south to the road that descends from Jerusalem to Gaza." (This is a desert road.) And he arose and went; and behold, there was an Ethiopian eunuch, a court official of Candace, queen of the Ethiopians, who was in charge of all her treasure; and he had come to Jerusalem to worship. And he was returning and sitting in his chariot, and was reading the prophet Isaiah. And the Spirit said to Philip, "Go up and join this chariot." And when Philip had run up, he heard him reading Isaiah the prophet, and said, "Do you understand what you are reading?" And he said, "Well, how could I, unless someone guides me?" And he invited Philip to come up and sit with him. Now the passage of Scripture which he was reading was this: "He was led as a sheep to slaughter; and as a lamb before its shearer is silent, so He does not open His mouth. In humiliation His judgment was taken away; who shall relate His generation? For His life is removed from the earth." And the eunuch answered Philip and said, "Please tell me, of whom does the prophet say this? Of himself, or of someone else?" And Philip opened his mouth, and beginning from this Scripture he preached Jesus to him. And as they went along the road they came to some water; and the eunuch said, "Look! Water! What prevents me from being baptized?" [And Philip said, "If you believe with all your heart, you may." And he answered and said, "I believe that Jesus Christ is the Son of God."] And he ordered the chariot to stop; and they both went down into the water, Philip as well as the eunuch; and he baptized him. And when they came up out of the water, the Spirit of the Lord snatched Philip away; and the eunuch saw him no more, but went on his way rejoicing. But Philip found himself at Azotus; and as he passed through he kept preaching the gospel to all the cities, until he came to Caesarea. (8:25–40)

Throughout redemptive history, God has poured out His blessings to mankind through the channel of His covenant people. God never intended Israel to be a reservoir, storing up divine blessings for themselves. Instead, they were to be a funnel through which those blessings could be dispersed to a lost world. In Isaiah 42:6 God identified them as a lamp lighting the darkness around them. He said to Israel, "I am the Lord, I have called you in righteousness, I will also hold you by the hand and watch over you, and I will appoint you as a covenant to the people, as a light to the nations."

Israel largely failed in her mission. She tended toward two extremes, both of which blocked the channel of God's blessings. First was a separatistic nationalism that wanted no contact with the Gentile nations. Jonah typifies such an attitude. Commanded to preach to the hated Assyrians, he instead took off in the opposite direction. Only after spending three days in the stomach of a large fish would he reluctantly agree to go to Nineveh. Then, instead of rejoicing when Nineveh repented, he became extremely upset:

> But [Nineveh's repentance] greatly displeased Jonah, and he became angry. And he prayed to the Lord and said, "Please Lord, was not this what I said while I was still in my own country? Therefore, in order to forestall this I fled to Tarshish, for I knew that Thou art a gracious and compassionate God, slow to anger and abundant in lovingkindness, and one who relents concerning calamity. Therefore now, O Lord, please take my life from me, for death is better to me than life." (Jonah 4:1–3)

The other extreme was that of compromise. Influenced by the surrounding nations, Israel frequently fell into pagan idolatry. An idolatrous Israel had no message to give to the idolatrous Gentile nations around her. By the time of Jesus, the worship of pagan idols was gone, disappearing for the most part after the Babylonian Captivity. It was replaced, however, by a corrupted form of Judaism that advocated salvation by works.

Because of Israel's failure, God cut a new channel through which His blessings could reach the world—the church. Unlike national Israel, the church would embrace all nations. Beginning on Pentecost and in Jerusalem as an exclusively Jewish group, the church soon reached out to the half–breed Samaritans. Another milestone was reached as Philip presented Jesus Christ to a Gentile. Through this man, a high official in the court of the Ethiopian queen, the gospel would first penetrate the souls of the great African continent. In contrast to Simon, his faith was genuine, resulting in salvation. That genuine faith required three elements: the proper preparation, the proper presentation, and the proper response.

The Proper Preparation

And so, when they had solemnly testified and spoken the word of the Lord, they started back to Jerusalem, and were preaching the gospel to many villages of the Samaritans. But an angel of the Lord spoke to Philip saying, "Arise and go south to the road that descends from Jerusalem to Gaza." (This is a desert road.) And he arose and went; and behold, there was an Ethiopian eunuch, a court official of Candace, queen of the Ethiopians, who was in charge of all her treasure; and he had come to Jerusalem to worship. And he was returning and sitting in his chariot, and was reading the prophet Isaiah. (8:25–28)

Genuine saving faith demands the proper preparation. In the parable of the sower, only the good, properly prepared soil brought forth the fruits of salvation. The text indicates four features which prepared the soil of the eunuch's heart.

THE SOVEREIGN WORK OF THE SPIRIT

And so, when they had solemnly testified and spoken the word of the Lord, they started back to Jerusalem, and were preaching the gospel to many villages of the Samaritans. But an angel of the Lord spoke to Philip saying, "Arise and go south to the road

that descends from Jerusalem to Gaza." (This is a desert road.)
(8:25–26)

Salvation, both in its eternal planning and its temporal outworking, is totally God's work. Salvation originates in the sovereign will of
God (Acts 13:48; Rom. 8:29ff.; Eph. 1:3–7) and is implemented by His
grace (Eph. 2:8–9; 2 Thess. 2:13; 2 Tim. 2:10; Titus 1:1; 1 Peter 1:1).

Two insurmountable barriers keep man from grasping God's salvation by his own efforts. First, men are spiritually dead and therefore
unable to respond to God. Ephesians 2:1 says simply and directly, "You
were dead in your trespasses and sins." To be physically dead means to
be unable to respond to physical stimuli, and to be spiritually dead
means to be unable to respond to spiritual stimuli. As the saying goes,
"Dead men don't believe!"

Our Lord was equally blunt in John 6:44: "No one can come to
Me, unless the Father who sent Me draws him." Paul explains in 1 Corinthians 2:14 that "a natural man [rebellious, sinful man apart from God]
does not accept the things of the Spirit of God; for they are foolishness
to him, and he cannot understand them, because they are spiritually ap-
praised." Consequently, the preaching of the gospel, apart from the
quickening work of the Spirit, is perceived as nothing but a "stumbling
block," and "foolishness" (1 Cor. 1:23).

As if man's spiritual deadness were not enough, a second factor
keeps him from God. Paul writes, "If our gospel is veiled, it is veiled to
those who are perishing, in whose case the god of this world has blinded the minds of the unbelieving, that they might not see the light of the
gospel of the glory of Christ, who is the image of God" (2 Cor. 4:3–4).
Satan and his demon hosts are also actively involved in keeping men
from finding God's truth. Like the birds in the parable of the sower, they
snatch away from fallen men the truth of the gospel. As a result, "when
anyone hears the word of the kingdom, and does not understand it, the
evil one comes and snatches away what has been sown in his heart"
(Matt. 13:19).

In light of those truths, it is ludicrous to assume that anyone,
apart from the work of the Holy Spirit in his or her lifeless soul, could
ever come to saving faith in Christ. Man cannot climb the barriers separat-
ating him from God. Sovereignly, God, in His love and mercy, must
reach out to man. If He did not do so, no one could ever be saved.

The Spirit began his preparatory work by maneuvering Philip
into a strategic position. After Peter and John **had solemnly testified
and spoken the word of the Lord, they started back to Jerusalem.**
On their return trip, **they were preaching the gospel to many villages of the Samaritans,** carrying on the evangelistic work begun by
Philip. **But an angel of the Lord spoke to Philip saying, "Arise and**

**go south to the road that descends from Jerusalem to Gaza."
(This is a desert road.)** The circumstances that were to lead to the
eunuch's salvation were sovereignly and specifically arranged by the
Spirit.

Gaza was one of the five chief cities of the Philistines, along
with Ashdod, Ashkelon, Ekron, and Gath. Old Gaza had been destroyed
early in the first century b.c. and a new city was built nearer the coast. A
road from **Jerusalem** to Egypt, however, still ran through the ruins of
old Gaza. Luke's footnote that **this is a desert road** underscores the
strangeness of the Spirit's command to Philip. There were two roads
from Jerusalem to Gaza, and the Spirit commands Philip to take the one
that was seldom used (Simon J. Kistemaker, *New Testament Commentary: Acts* [Grand Rapids: Baker, 1990], 311). It is also possible to trans-
late the Greek phrase *kata mesēmbrian* (toward the **south**) "at noon"
(I. Howard Marshall, *The Acts of the Apostles* [Grand Rapids: Eerdmans,
1984], 161). That rendering would "make the divine command to Philip
all the more unusual and perplexing: at noon the road would be deserted of travelers because of the heat" (Marshall, *Acts,* 161).

This was no mere chance encounter and certainly not the result
of clever human ingenuity. Apart from the Spirit's orchestration of
events, it would have never taken place at all. That emphasizes again
the sovereign work of the Spirit in salvation.

THE SUBMISSIVE WILL OF PHILIP

And he arose and went; (8:27a)

God often accomplishes His sovereign work through human instruments (cf. Acts 2:4, 14; 4:8, 31; 6:3–8; 7:55; 8:17; 10:1–48;
16:25–34). Like a master sculptor, He takes otherwise useless and in-
consequential tools and uses them to create a masterpiece. There is a
prerequisite, however, for being used by God. Paul writes, "Now in a
large house there are not only gold and silver vessels, but also vessels of
wood and of earthenware, and some to honor and some to dishonor.
Therefore, if a man cleanses himself from these things, he will be a ves-
sel for honor, sanctified, useful to the Master, prepared for every good
work" (2 Tim. 2:20–21). God uses holy tools to do His work.

Philip was such an instrument. When ordered to go on what
must have seemed an illogical journey, **he arose and went.** He did not
struggle with the irrationality of the command before obeying, nor did
he question God. To leave the thriving work in Samaria for a deserted
road might seem absurd to many but not to the man of God who has just

been visited by an angel of the Lord. By willing obedience he became the means by which God saved the eunuch.

and behold, there was an Ethiopian eunuch, a court official of Candace, queen of the Ethiopians, who was in charge of all her treasure; and he had come to Jerusalem to worship. (8:27b)

The **Ethiopian eunuch** was a seeker after the true God, as shown by his long journey **to Jerusalem to worship.** How he came into contact with Judaism is not told, but there was a large Jewish colony at Alexandria. He was a high ranking official in his country, a **court official of Candace, queen of the Ethiopians.** Ethiopia in that day was a large kingdom located south of Egypt. To the Greeks and Romans, it represented the outer limits of the known world (John B. Polhill, *The New American Commentary: Acts* [Nashville: Broadman, 1992], 223). Its kings were believed to be incarnations of the sun god, and the everyday affairs of government were held to be beneath them. Real power lay with the queen mothers, known by the hereditary title **Candace** (which is not a proper name, but an official title, like Pharaoh or Caesar). This man **was in charge of all her treasure.** In modern terms, he was the Minister of Finance, or Secretary of the Treasury.

Despite his power and prestige, he had a vast emptiness in his soul. He made a long, arduous journey from his homeland to Jerusalem, searching for the true God. Unfortunately, given the state of contemporary Judaism, he probably went away still empty. It is not certain whether he was physically a eunuch. The term was also used to speak of government officials who had not been emasculated (such as Potiphar [Gen. 39:1 LXX], who was married). He likely was an actual eunuch, though, since Luke uses both **eunuch** and **court official** to describe him. If that were true, he would have been denied access to the temple (Deut. 23:1) and therefore been unable to participate fully in the Jewish worship services. Further, he would not have been allowed to become a full proselyte to Judaism (Polhill, *Acts,* 224). He would have been limited to the status of a God-fearer—one who attended the synagogues and read the Scriptures but stopped short of becoming a full proselyte. The Gentile Cornelius was an example of such a God-fearer (Acts 10:1–2).

God's sovereignty in salvation does not obviate man's responsibility. That God rewards the seeking heart is the clear teaching of Scripture. In Jeremiah 29:13 God said, "You will seek Me and find Me, when you search for Me with all your heart," while in John 7:17 the Lord Jesus Christ said, "If any man is willing to do His will, he shall know of the teaching, whether it is of God, or whether I speak from Myself." The eunuch is a classic example of one who lived up to the light he had. God then gave him the full revelation of Jesus Christ through Philip's ministry.

THE SCRIPTURAL WORD OF TRUTH

And he was returning and sitting in his chariot, and was reading the prophet Isaiah. (8:28)

While returning to his own country, the eunuch was **sitting in his chariot, and was reading the prophet Isaiah.** He had a desire to know God and was aware that He was to be known through the Scripture. He was indeed an eager seeker. He had no doubt paid a great price in Jerusalem for that scroll, which would have been difficult for a Gentile to acquire. Perhaps **Isaiah** had special meaning to him, since the book speaks encouragingly to eunuchs (Isa. 56:3–5).

While God's existence, and some of His attributes, can be discerned from nature (Rom. 1:20), saving knowledge of Him comes only through the Scriptures. Jesus said in John 5:39, "You search the Scriptures, because you think that in them you have eternal life; and it is these that bear witness of Me." In verse 46 He added, "If you believed Moses, you would believe Me; for he wrote of Me." Encountering two of his followers after His resurrection, he chided them for their obtuseness: 'O foolish men and slow of heart to believe in all that the prophets have spoken! Was it not necessary for the Christ to suffer these things and to enter into His glory?' And beginning with Moses and with all the prophets, He explained to them the things concerning Himself in all the Scriptures" (Luke 24:25–27).

Paul's grand words to the Romans serve to enrich the understanding of this account:

> For there is no distinction between Jew and Greek; for the same Lord is Lord of all, abounding in riches for all who call upon Him; for "Whoever will call upon the name of the Lord will be saved." How then shall they call upon Him in whom they have not believed? And how shall they believe in Him whom they have not heard? And how shall they hear without a preacher? And how shall they preach unless they are sent? Just as it is written, "How beautiful are the feet of those who bring glad tidings of good things!" (Rom. 10:12–15)

All the essentials were in place; the Spirit's work of preparation was complete. Philip had obeyed the Spirit's call and was in place to meet the man. The eunuch's heart was seeking, prepared by reading the Scriptures. All was set for the next step.

The Proper Presentation

And the Spirit said to Philip, "Go up and join this chariot." And when Philip had run up, he heard him reading Isaiah the prophet, and said, "Do you understand what you are reading?" And he said, "Well, how could I, unless someone guides me?" And he invited Philip to come up and sit with him. Now the passage of Scripture which he was reading was this: "He was led as a sheep to slaughter; and as a lamb before its shearer is silent, so He does not open His mouth. In humiliation His judgment was taken away; who shall relate His generation? For His life is removed from the earth." And the eunuch answered Philip and said, "Please tell me, of whom does the prophet say this? Of himself, or of someone else?" And Philip opened his mouth, and beginning from this Scripture he preached Jesus to him. (8:29–35)

When **the Spirit said to Philip, "Go up and join this chariot,"** he instantly obeyed. Although the eunuch's entourage must have been impressive, Philip was not intimidated. Boldness belongs to Spirit-filled people (Acts 4:31). We can discern in Philip's words the essence of an effective presentation of the gospel.

IT MUST CENTER ON SCRIPTURE

And when Philip had run up, he heard him reading Isaiah the prophet, and said, "Do you understand what you are reading?" And he said, "Well, how could I, unless someone guides me?" And he invited Philip to come up and sit with him. Now the passage of Scripture which he was reading was this: "He was led as a sheep to slaughter; and as a lamb before its shearer is silent, so He does not open His mouth. In humiliation His judgment was taken away; who shall relate His generation? For His life is removed from the earth." And the eunuch answered Philip and said, "Please tell me, of whom does the prophet say this? Of himself, or of someone else?" (8:30–34)

Apparently without the benefit of a formal introduction normally required for an audience with such an exalted leader, and demonstrating his eagerness by having **run up,** Philip **heard him reading Isaiah the prophet.** The ancient custom of reading aloud provided an opening for Philip, who, though a complete stranger, boldly asked, **"Do you understand what you are reading?"** The man was so perplexed by the passage he had been reading that he seems not to have cared who Philip was or why he was in his presence. The eunuch just exclaimed, **"Well, how could I, unless someone guides me?"** Amazingly, he then **invited Philip to come up and sit with him.** The evangelist's heart must have been rejoicing in the confidence that God had so prepared this man. That the official invited Philip to explain the Scriptures to him speaks of the eunuch's seeking, humble, and teachable spirit (cf. Isa. 55:6–7).

The **passage of Scripture** the eunuch **was reading was this: "He was led as a sheep to slaughter; and as a lamb before its shearer is silent, so He does not open His mouth. In humiliation His judgment was taken away; who shall relate His generation? For His life is removed from the earth."** That passage, taken from Isaiah 53:7–8, puzzled the eunuch. **"Please tell me,"** he asked Philip, **"of whom does the prophet say this? Of himself, or of someone else?"** His confusion was understandable, since contemporary Jewish thought was divided on the interpretation of this passage. Some held that the slaughtered sheep represented the nation, others that Isaiah spoke of himself, still others that he referred to the Messiah. There was no doubt in Philip's mind, however, of whom Isaiah wrote.

Like his Lord (John 3:1ff.; 4:5ff.), Paul (1 Cor. 9:22), Apollos (Acts 18:24), and Stephen (Acts 7:2ff.), Philip was knowledgeable enough in the Scriptures to meet the eunuch where he was. Every believer should strive to be proficient in the Scriptures so that we, too, can meet people at the point of their perplexity and lead them to the Savior. In the words of Peter, we are to "always [be] ready to make a defense to everyone who asks [us] to give an account for the hope that is in [us]" (1 Peter 3:15).

An effective presentation of the gospel must be based solidly on Scripture. The use of personal testimony, stories, tracts, and other tools is no substitute. For Scripture alone is "the power of God for salvation to everyone who believes, to the Jew first and also to the Greek" (Rom. 1:16). The power is in the Word.

IT MUST CENTER ON JESUS CHRIST

And Philip opened his mouth, and beginning from this Scripture he preached Jesus to him. (8:35)

Philip was ready. **Beginning from** the very **Scripture** the eunuch had been reading, **he preached Jesus to him.** He showed the eunuch that the Lamb of which the passage spoke was none other than the Messiah, who would be the ultimate and final sacrifice for sin. He then presented evidence that Jesus was that Messiah.

Any gospel presentation, to be effective, must clearly and comprehensively present the Person and work of Jesus Christ. Perhaps the reason some reject Jesus is that He has not been presented well enough for them to understand who He is and what He has accomplished. To proclaim to others what Christ has done in our lives is important, but the biblical truth about Jesus Christ is the essential message the sinner must hear. As Paul wrote to the Romans, "Faith comes from hearing . . . the word of Christ" (10:17).

THE PROPER RESPONSE

And as they went along the road they came to some water; and the eunuch said, "Look! Water! What prevents me from being baptized?" [And Philip said, "If you believe with all your heart, you may." And he answered and said, "I believe that Jesus Christ is the Son of God."] And he ordered the chariot to stop; and they both went down into the water, Philip as well as the eunuch; and he baptized him. And when they came up out of the water, the Spirit of the Lord snatched Philip away; and the eunuch saw him no more, but went on his way rejoicing. But Philip found himself at Azotus; and as he passed through he kept preaching the gospel to all the cities, until he came to Caesarea. (8:36–40)

The Spirit's preparation and Philip's presentation combined to produce the proper response on the eunuch's part. That response was threefold: faith, confession, and rejoicing.

FAITH

And as they went along the road they came to some water; and the eunuch said, "Look! Water! What prevents me from being baptized?" (8:36)

At some point as **they went along the road** the eunuch was granted saving faith and was instructed about baptism. That is implied by his reaction when **they came to some water. The eunuch said** to

Philip, **"Look! Water! What prevents me from being baptized?"** They came across a pool or stream in the desert at just the appropriate moment for the man to publicly testify to his saving faith by being obedient to the ordinance of immersion. That is yet another example of the sovereign Spirit's control of events.

CONFESSION

[And Philip said, "If you believe with all your heart, you may." And he answered and said, "I believe that Jesus Christ is the Son of God."] And he ordered the chariot to stop; and they both went down into the water, Philip as well as the eunuch; and he baptized him. (8:37–38)

The oldest and most reliable manuscripts do not contain verse 37, which should be omitted from the text. Still, something like that confession must have occurred. Coming to the water, the eunuch **ordered the chariot to stop; and they both went down into the water, Philip as well as the eunuch; and he baptized him.** As noted in the discussion of Acts 2:38 in chapter 6, baptism is the public confession of faith expected of all believers. The eunuch not only confessed his faith personally to Philip but openly in front of his entire entourage. That both he and Philip **went down into the water** indicates that his baptism was by immersion. So does the word *baptizō*, which means "to dip" or "to immerse."

REJOICING

And when they came up out of the water, the Spirit of the Lord snatched Philip away; and the eunuch saw him no more, but went on his way rejoicing. But Philip found himself at Azotus; and as he passed through he kept preaching the gospel to all the cities, until he came to Caesarea. (8:39–40)

After **they came up out of the water, the Spirit of the Lord snatched Philip away; and the eunuch saw him no more.** Elijah (1 Kings 18:12; 2 Kings 2:16) and Ezekiel (Ezek. 3:12, 14; 8:3) were also miraculously snatched away. By performing this startling miracle, the Holy Spirit confirmed to the entire caravan that Philip was indeed His spokesman. As for the eunuch, **he went on his way** home **rejoicing.** Joy is a mark of a true believer (John 15:11; 17:13; Acts 13:52; Rom. 12:12; 14:17; 15:13; Gal. 5:22; Phil. 1:25; 1 Thess. 1:6; 1 Peter 1:8; Jude 24).

Philip, meanwhile, **found himself at Azotus. Azotus,** twenty miles north of Gaza, was the current name for the ancient Philistine city of Ashdod. As **he passed through** the coastal region, **he kept preaching the gospel to all the cities.** No matter where he was, Philip had only one thing on his mind. As he made his way north toward **Caesarea,** where he and his family apparently made their home (Acts 21:9), he preached in the cities (such as Joppa and Lydda, which Peter would shortly visit) as he traveled.

Luke does not give us the subsequent history of the Ethiopian eunuch. According to the church Father Irenaeus, he became a missionary to the Ethiopians (Richard N. Longenecker, "The Acts of the Apostles," in Frank E. Gaebelein, ed., *The Expositor's Bible Commentary*, vol. 9 [Grand Rapids: Zondervan, 1981], 366). What is clear is that the Spirit's preparation, coupled with Philip's presentation, produced in him the faith that does save.

The
Transformed
Life

21

Now Saul, still breathing threats and murder against the disciples of the Lord, went to the high priest, and asked for letters from him to the synagogues at Damascus, so that if he found any belonging to the Way, both men and women, he might bring them bound to Jerusalem. And it came about that as he journeyed, he was approaching Damascus, and suddenly a light from heaven flashed around him; and he fell to the ground, and heard a voice saying to him, "Saul, Saul, why are you persecuting Me?" And he said, "Who art Thou, Lord?" And He said, "I am Jesus whom you are persecuting, but rise, and enter the city, and it shall be told you what you must do." And the men who traveled with him stood speechless, hearing the voice, but seeing no one. And Saul got up from the ground, and though his eyes were open, he could see nothing; and leading him by the hand, they brought him into Damascus. And he was three days without sight, and neither ate nor drank. Now there was a certain disciple at Damascus, named Ananias; and the Lord said to him in a vision, "Ananias." And he said, "Behold, here am I, Lord." And the Lord said to him, "Arise and go to the street called Straight, and inquire at the house of Judas for a man from Tarsus named

Saul, for behold, he is praying, and he has seen in a vision a man named Ananias come in and lay his hands on him, so that he might regain his sight." But Ananias answered, "Lord, I have heard from many about this man, how much harm he did to Thy saints at Jerusalem; and here he has authority from the chief priests to bind all who call upon Thy name." But the Lord said to him, "Go, for he is a chosen instrument of Mine, to bear My name before the Gentiles and kings and the sons of Israel; for I will show him how much he must suffer for My name's sake." And Ananias departed and entered the house, and after laying his hands on him said, "Brother Saul, the Lord Jesus, who appeared to you on the road by which you were coming, has sent me so that you may regain your sight, and be filled with the Holy Spirit." And immediately there fell from his eyes something like scales, and he regained his sight, and he arose and was baptized; and he took food and was strengthened. Now for several days he was with the disciples who were at Damascus, and immediately he began to proclaim Jesus in the synagogues, saying, "He is the Son of God." And all those hearing him continued to be amazed, and were saying, "Is this not he who in Jerusalem destroyed those who called on this name, and who had come here for the purpose of bringing them bound before the chief priests?" But Saul kept increasing in strength and confounding the Jews who lived at Damascus by proving that this Jesus is the Christ. And when many days had elapsed, the Jews plotted together to do away with him, but their plot became known to Saul. And they were also watching the gates day and night so that they might put him to death; but his disciples took him by night, and let him down through an opening in the wall, lowering him in a large basket. And when he had come to Jerusalem, he was trying to associate with the disciples; and they were all afraid of him, not believing that he was a disciple. But Barnabas took hold of him and brought him to the apostles and described to them how he had seen the Lord on the road, and that He had talked to him, and how at Damascus he had spoken out boldly in the name of Jesus. And he was with them moving about freely in Jerusalem, speaking out boldly in the name of the Lord. And he was talking and arguing with the Hellenistic Jews; but they were attempting to put him to death. But when the brethren learned of it, they brought him down to Caesarea and sent him away to Tarsus. So the church throughout all Judea and Galilee and Samaria enjoyed peace, being built up; and, going on in the fear of the Lord and in the comfort of the Holy Spirit, it continued to increase. (9:1–31)

At a young age, John Newton went to sea. Like most sailors of his day, he lived a life of rebellion and debauchery. For several years, he worked on slave ships, capturing slaves for sale to the plantations of the New World. So low did he sink that at one point he became a slave himself, captive of another slave trader. Eventually, he became the captain of his own slave ship. The combination of a frightening storm at sea, coupled with his reading of Thomas á Kempis's classic *Imitation of Christ*, planted the seeds that resulted in his conversion. He went on to become a leader in the evangelical movement in eighteenth-century England, along with such men as John and Charles Wesley, George Whitefield, and William Wilberforce. On his tombstone is inscribed the following epitaph, written by Newton himself: "John Newton, clerk, once an infidel and Libertine, a servant of slavers in Africa, was, by the rich mercy of our Lord and Savior Jesus Christ, preserved, restored, pardoned, and appointed to preach the Faith he had long labored to destroy" (Kenneth W. Osbeck, *101 Hymn Stories* [Grand Rapids: Kregel, 1982], 28). When he penned the beloved hymn "Amazing Grace," he knew firsthand the truths it proclaimed.

Mel Trotter was a barber by profession and a drunkard by perversion. So debauched had he become that when his young daughter died, he stole the shoes she was to be buried in and pawned them for money to buy more drinks. One night he staggered into the Pacific Garden Mission in Chicago and was marvelously saved. Burdened for the men of skid row, he opened a rescue mission in Grand Rapids, Michigan. He went on to found more than sixty more missions and became supervisor of a chain of them stretching from Boston to San Francisco (Elgin S. Moyer, *Who Was Who in Church History* [New Canaan, Conn.: Keats, 1974], 411).

One day in August 386, a professor of rhetoric named Aurelius Augustine sat despondently in his garden. Although the son of a Christian mother, he had abandoned his mother's faith in favor of the Persian religion known as Manichaeism. He also took a mistress, with whom he lived for thirteen years. Abandoning Manichaeism as unsatisfactory, he continued a futile search for truth. Through the preaching of the church Father Ambrose, he became intellectually convinced of the truth of Christianity. Yet he held back, "prevented from accepting the faith by weakness in dealing with sexual temptation" (R. S. Pine-Coffin, "Introduction," to *Saint Augustine: Confessions* [New York: Penguin, 1978], 11). Now, in the midst of his turmoil, he heard a child's voice singing in Latin *tolle lege* ("take and read"). In his *Confessions,* he describes what happened next:

> I stemmed my flood of tears and stood up, telling myself that this could
> only be a divine command to open my book of Scripture and read the

first passage on which my eyes should fall. . . . So I hurried back to the place where [his friend] Alypius was sitting, for when I stood up to move away I had put down the book containing Paul's Epistles. I seized it and opened it, and in silence I read the first passage on which my eyes fell: *Not in revelling and drunkenness, not in lust and wantonness, not in quarrels and rivalries. Rather, arm yourselves with the Lord Jesus Christ; spend no more thought on nature and nature's appetites* [Rom. 13:13–14]. I had no wish to read more and no need to do so. For in an instant, as I came to the end of the sentence, it was as though the light of confidence flooded into my heart and all the darkness of doubt was dispelled. (*Confessions* VIII, 12, translated by R. S. Pine-Coffin [New York: Penguin, 1978])

Delivered from a life of sin and confusion, Augustine went on to become the greatest theologian the church had known since the apostle Paul.

Church history is replete with accounts such as these, which highlight the marvelous power of the gospel to transform sinners. But no transformation is as remarkable, or has had such far-reaching implications for history, as the conversion of Saul of Tarsus. So significant an event was his conversion that Scripture records it no less than three times (cf. Acts 22:1–16; 26:4–18).

It is fitting that such a unique individual would have a unique conversion. Saul was by birth a Jew, by citizenship a Roman, by education a Greek, and purely by the grace of God a Christian (cf. Phil. 3:4–9). He was a missionary, theologian, evangelist, pastor, organizer, leader, thinker, fighter for truth, and lover of souls. Never has a more godly man lived, except our Lord Himself.

Saul was born in Tarsus, an important city (Acts 21:39) in the Roman province of Cilicia. Tarsus was located near where Asia Minor and Syria meet, not far from Antioch. It was famous for its university, which ranked with those of Athens and Alexandria as among the most honored in the Roman world. Saul's father must have been a Roman citizen, since Saul was himself a citizen of Rome by birth (Acts 22:28). His Jewish credentials were equally impeccable. Like his father before him, he was a Pharisee (Acts 23:6), who studied in Jerusalem under the most respected rabbi of his day, Gamaliel (Acts 22:3). Since he had apparently never met Jesus, he must have returned to Tarsus to live after completing his studies.

Saul makes his first appearance in Scripture in connection with Stephen. As noted in the discussion of Acts 6:9 in chapter 15, Saul may have been one of the Hellenists who unsuccessfully debated him. When Stephen was executed, Saul guarded the robes of those involved in the stoning. His position so close to the action suggests he was deeply involved with the whole affair.

There is no question as to Saul's role in the persecution that broke out after Stephen's death—he was its mastermind and ringleader. As noted in the discussion of Acts 8:1–3 in chapter 18, Saul was terrifyingly adept at persecuting believers. The Jerusalem fellowship broke up under the force of his attacks. Many of the Hellenist believers, who apparently bore the brunt of the persecution, fled Jerusalem. As the events of this chapter unfold, Saul is hot on the trail of those who fled to Damascus. In his testimony to Agrippa (Acts 26:9–11) he articulated the fierceness of his assault:

> So then, I thought to myself that I had to do many things hostile to the name of Jesus of Nazareth. And this is just what I did in Jerusalem; not only did I lock up many of the saints in prisons, having received authority from the chief priests, but also when they were being put to death I cast my vote against them. And as I punished them often in all the synagogues, I tried to force them to blaspheme; and being furiously enraged at them, I kept pursuing them even to foreign cities.

After the interlude of chapter 8, which describes the ministry of Philip, the scene shifts back to Jerusalem. **Saul,** Luke notes, **was still breathing threats and murder against the disciples of the Lord.** Persecuting Christians consumed him; it had become his whole life. The very air he was **breathing** was that of **threats and murder against the disciples of the Lord.** The term **disciples** refers to all believers, not merely the twelve apostles. Every Christian is a follower of and learner from the Lord Jesus Christ. Saul wanted every one he could lay his hands on.

Hearing of a group of Christians in Damascus, Saul driven by deadly ambition and twisted religious zeal, **went to the high priest, and asked for letters from him to the synagogues at Damascus, so that if he found any belonging to the Way, both men and women, he might bring them bound to Jerusalem. The high priest,** in his capacity as president of the Sanhedrin, was viewed by the Romans as head of the Jewish state. He thus had authority over Jewish internal matters such as this one. Accordingly, Saul needed **letters from him to the synagogues at Damascus** to have authority to apprehend Christians. He intended, **if he found any belonging to the Way** (whether **men** or **women**), to **bring them bound to Jerusalem.**

Damascus, the ancient capital of Syria, had a large Jewish population. That is evidenced by the massacre of some ten to twenty thousand Jews in A.D. 66 (F. F. Bruce, *The Book of the Acts* [Grand Rapids:

Eerdmans, 1971], 194). Given the size of the Jewish population, there would have been several synagogues.

The description of Christianity as **the Way** appears several times in Acts (19:9, 23; 22:4; 24:14, 22). It apparently derives from Jesus' description of Himself as "the way, and the truth, and the life" (John 14:6). **The Way** is an apropos title for Christianity, since it is the way of God (Acts 18:26), the way into the Holy Place (Heb. 10:19–20), and the way of truth (2 Peter 2:2).

Having obtained the necessary papers, Saul and his entourage set out for Damascus. The normal route north and east would cause them to pass through Samaria. The revival there, led by Philip, Peter, and John, may have infuriated Saul all the more. With intense hostility he approached Damascus and the encounter that would turn his world upside down.

From the dramatic story of Saul's conversion emerge seven features of the transformed life: faith in the Savior, fervency in supplication, faithfulness in service, the filling of the Spirit, fellowship with the saints, fervency in speaking, and fearlessness in suffering.

Faith in the Savior

And it came about that as he journeyed, he was approaching Damascus, and suddenly a light from heaven flashed around him; and he fell to the ground, and heard a voice saying to him, "Saul, Saul, why are you persecuting Me?" And he said, "Who art Thou, Lord?" And He said, "I am Jesus whom you are persecuting, but rise, and enter the city, and it shall be told you what you must do." And the men who traveled with him stood speechless, hearing the voice, but seeing no one. And Saul got up from the ground, and though his eyes were open, he could see nothing; and leading him by the hand, they brought him into Damascus. And he was three days without sight, and neither ate nor drank. (9:3–9)

The remarkable conversion of Saul, in which he put his faith in the Savior he had been so viciously persecuting, unfolds in five phases: contact, conviction, conversion, consecration, and communion.

CONTACT

And it came about that as he journeyed, he was approaching Damascus, and suddenly a light from heaven flashed around him; (9:3)

Saul was still charging full speed for **Damascus** when he was **suddenly** stopped dead in his tracks. **A light from heaven flashed around him,** and Saul and his companions fell into the dirt (Acts 26:14).

Confronted with the appearance of the blazing glory of Jesus Christ, Saul, the hardened persecutor of Christians, was speechless with terror. Luke's other accounts of this event (Acts 22, 26) fill in more of the details. From Acts 22:6 we learn that the encounter took place about noon. The **light from heaven** was not anything from the material creation, since it transcended in brilliance even the bright Middle Eastern sun (26:13). Those who traveled with Saul heard the voice of the Lord as he did, yet did not understand the words spoken (cf. v. 7 with 22:9; John 12:29), because the Lord's words were for Saul's ears only. Saul actually saw Jesus in glorious brilliance as he repeatedly testifies (Acts 9:17, 27; 22:14; 26:16; 1 Cor. 9:1; 15:8) while his co-persecutors saw only the light (Acts 22:9).

Ironically, the last person till then to have seen the resurrected, glorified Christ was Stephen. Here is yet another connection between the ministries of Stephen and Paul (cf. chapter 15 of this commentary). It is a testimony to the power of God's grace that the man involved in Stephen's death would be the next to see Jesus Christ.

Although He does not do it so dramatically, God always initiates the contact in salvation (cf. John 6:37, 44; 10:27–29; 17:2, 6, 9, 11, 24; 2 Cor. 4:6; Phil. 1:29; James 1:18). As noted in chapter 20 of this volume, the Holy Spirit sovereignly arranged the circumstances leading to the Ethiopian eunuch's conversion. That was, and is, necessary, since unbelieving men, being dead in their trespasses and sins (Eph. 2:1), cannot come to God on their own (cf. Rom. 3:10–12; 1 Cor. 2:14; Eph. 2:4–10; Col. 2:13).

That salvation is initiated by God is nowhere more powerfully stated than by Paul to Titus:

> For we also once were foolish ourselves, disobedient, deceived, enslaved to various lusts and pleasures, spending our life in malice and envy, hateful, hating one another. But when the kindness of God our Savior and His love for mankind appeared, He saved us, not on the basis of deeds which we have done in righteousness, but according to His mercy, by the washing of regeneration and renewing by the Holy Spirit. (Titus 3:3–5)

CONVICTION

and he fell to the ground, and heard a voice saying to him, "Saul, Saul, why are you persecuting Me?" (9:4)

Prostrate on **the ground,** Saul **heard a voice saying to him, "Saul, Saul, why are you persecuting Me?"** The repetition is emphatic, as elsewhere in Luke's writings (cf. Luke 10:41; 13:34; 22:31). Here it marks a rebuke of Saul, intended to bring anguish of soul, so Saul would realize how wrong he had been, and guilt would overwhelm him. He was one who had hated Jesus Christ without cause (John 15:25).

Our Lord's words **"Why are you persecuting Me?"** reflect the inseparable link between Himself, as head of the body, and its members. No blow struck on earth goes unfelt in heaven by our sympathetic High Priest. By persecuting Christians, Saul inflicted blows directly on their Lord.

Saul, who had been so violent, was violently brought face to face with the enormity of his crimes—not against Christians but against Christ. Those who go to hell do so ultimately because of their rejection of the Savior. Even those who don't persecute believers, but simply live apart from Jesus Christ, are as guilty of crimes against Him as was Saul. As Saul himself was later to write, "If anyone does not love the Lord, let him be accursed" (1 Cor. 16:22). Jesus said the Holy Spirit would convict men "concerning sin, because they do not believe in Me" (John 16:9). The crime of all crimes for which men will be eternally damned is to refuse to love and follow the Lord Jesus Christ.

True salvation must include conviction of this damning sin, since it is this very sin and no other that finally separates man from God. Saul knew enough about the Christian faith to hate it and persecute it. He knew the claims of Jesus and the true history of God's redemption as Stephen had preached it. He knew the apostles and their associates Stephen and Philip had miraculous power over disease and demons. All that the Spirit had laid as the groundwork in Saul's life. When Jesus confronted Saul, the conviction must have been overwhelming. He knew about the truth; here he was crushed into the dust and made to believe it.

CONVERSION

And he said "Who art Thou, Lord?" And He said, "I am Jesus whom you are persecuting, (9:5)

Saul's immediate response, **"Who art Thou, Lord?"** was a recognition of deity—he knew it was the Lord. The whole Christian gospel filled his mind (negatively) all the time as he pursued his passion of persecuting believers. It is not hard to believe that he already knew the answer to this question as he asked it—if not by faith, then by fear. His worst imaginable nightmare would have been to discover that Jesus was the Messiah, Christianity was true, the gospel was God's truth, and he had been fighting God. When Saul heard the words **"I am Jesus whom you are persecuting,"** the light of truth was confirmed in his soul and the gospel became positive. The Christian message he knew well, having debated it with Stephen. Jesus, whom he had believed dead, was obviously alive and obviously who He claimed to be. And the Lord reminded him at that moment how pointless and painful his efforts against Him were. In Acts 26:14, the Lord said to him, "Saul, Saul, why are you persecuting Me? It is hard for you to kick against the goads [sharp, pointed sticks]." Saul's resistance was crushed at that moment and his heart, broken by repentance, was healed by faith. Philippians 3:4–11 describes the mental change that occurred in his soul at this moment:

> . . . although I myself might have confidence even in the flesh. If anyone else has a mind to put confidence in the flesh, I far more: circumcised the eighth day, of the nation of Israel, of the tribe of Benjamin, a Hebrew of Hebrews; as to the Law, a Pharisee; as to zeal, a persecutor of the church; as to the righteousness which is in the Law, found blameless. But whatever things were gain to me, those things I have counted as loss for the sake of Christ. More than that, I count all things to be loss in view of the surpassing value of knowing Christ Jesus my Lord, for whom I have suffered the loss of all things, and count them but rubbish in order that I may gain Christ, and may be found in Him, not having a righteousness of my own derived from the Law, but that which is through faith in Christ, the righteousness which comes from God on the basis of faith, that I may know Him, and the power of His resurrection and the fellowship of His sufferings, being conformed to His death; in order that I may attain to the resurrection from the dead.

Some have foolishly attempted to explain away Saul's experience as the result of an epileptic seizure. That explanation is inadequate, even granting the dubious assumption that Saul was an epileptic. No such seizure could account for the complete about-face Saul's life took. Nor does it account for the fact that Saul's traveling companions saw the light and heard the voice. For the rest of his life Saul offered only one explanation—he had in fact seen the risen, glorified Lord Jesus Christ.

This miraculous conversion, without human involvement at its occurrence, is an example of the extent and power of saving, sovereign grace. Paul testifies to that grace in 1 Timothy 1:13–17:

> . . . even though I was formerly a blasphemer and a persecutor and a violent aggressor. And yet I was shown mercy, because I acted ignor-

antly in unbelief; and the grace of our Lord was more than abundant, with the faith and love which are found in Christ Jesus. It is a trustworthy statement, deserving full acceptance, that Christ Jesus came into the world to save sinners, among whom I am foremost of all. And yet for this reason I found mercy, in order that in me as the foremost, Jesus Christ might demonstrate His perfect patience, as an example for those who would believe in Him for eternal life. Now to the King eternal, immortal, invisible, the only God, be honor and glory forever and ever. Amen.

CONSECRATION

"but rise, and enter the city, and it shall be told you what you must do." And the men who traveled with him stood speechless, hearing the voice, but seeing no one. And Saul got up from the ground, and though his eyes were open, he could see nothing; and leading him by the hand, they brought him into Damascus. (9:6–8)

The genuineness of Saul's conversion immediately became evident. From Acts 22:10, we learn that he asked, "What shall I do, Lord?" Saul's surrender was complete, as he humbly submitted himself to the will of the Lord he had hated. In contrast to the teaching of many today, Saul knew nothing of accepting Christ as Savior, then (hopefully) making him Lord later. The plain teaching of Scripture is that Jesus is Lord (cf. Rom. 10:9–10), independent of any human response. The question in salvation is not whether Jesus is Lord, but whether we are submissive to His lordship. Saul was, from the moment of his conversion to the end of his life.

In response to Saul's inquiry, Jesus told him to **rise and enter the city** of Damascus, **and it shall be told you what you must do.** Luke notes that **the men who traveled with him stood speechless, hearing the voice, but seeing no one.** This incident was no subjective projection of Saul's mind but an actual historical occurrence. **Saul got up from the ground, and though his eyes were open, he could see nothing; and leading him by the hand, they brought him into Damascus.** His entry into the city was very different than he had anticipated. Instead of barging in as the conquering hero, the scourge of Christians, he entered helplessly blinded, being led by the hand.

God crushed Saul, bringing him to the point of total consecration. From the ashes of Saul's old life would arise the noblest and most useful man of God the church has ever known.

COMMUNION

And he was three days without sight, and neither ate nor drank. (9:9)

So startling and sudden had been his placing of faith in the Savior that Saul needed time to reflect on the transformation of every aspect of his life. During his **three days without sight,** when he **neither ate nor drank,** God led him through the process of reconstructing everything he was and did. Although salvation is an instantaneous transformation from death to life, darkness to light, it takes time to plumb the depths of its meaning and richness. Saul began that process.

Now there was a certain disciple at Damascus, named Ananias; and the Lord said to him in a vision, "Ananias." And he said, "Behold, here am I, Lord." And the Lord said to him, "Arise and go to the street called Straight, and inquire at the house of Judas for a man from Tarsus named Saul, for behold, he is praying, and he has seen in a vision a man named Ananias come in and lay his hands on him, so that he might regain his sight." (9:10–12)

While Saul waited, blinded and fasting, thinking deeply about what had occurred, God was dealing with another man. The **certain disciple at Damascus named Ananias** was obviously not the same Ananias executed by God in chapter 5. Acts 22:12 describes him as "devout" and "well spoken of by all the Jews who lived" in Damascus. He was likely one of the spiritual leaders of the Damascus church. If so, he also, ironically, would have been one of Saul's main targets. **The Lord** told **him in a vision** to **arise and go to the street called Straight and inquire at the house of Judas for a man from Tarsus named Saul.** That was a severe test of Ananias's faith, since Saul's fearsome reputation was widely known (cf. vv. 13–14). Ananias would have had no way of knowing of Saul's conversion, since the Lord did not reveal it to him.

The footnote **for behold, he is praying** informs us of what Saul did during his three days without sight. Prayer is the spontaneous response of the believing heart to God. Those truly transformed by Jesus Christ find themselves lost in the wonder and joy of communion with Him. Prayer is as natural for the Christian as breathing. Paul became a man of unceasing prayer.

While he waited for Ananias, God gave Saul a **vision** that Ananias would **come** and **lay his hands on him, so that he might regain his sight.** God, in His tender kindness to this persecutor, did not want him to be in any unnecessary sorrow, so He gave Saul hope for receiving his sight. A pair of visions were about to bring together two men who had been poles apart.

FAITHFULNESS IN SERVICE

But Ananias answered, "Lord, I have heard from many about this man, how much harm he did to Thy saints at Jerusalem; and here he has authority from the chief priests to bind all who call upon Thy name." But the Lord said to him, "Go, for he is a chosen instrument of Mine, to bear My name before the Gentiles and kings and the sons of Israel; for I will show him how much he must suffer for My name's sake." And Ananias departed and entered the house, and after laying his hands on him said, "Brother Saul, the Lord Jesus, who appeared to you on the road by which you were coming, has sent me so that you may regain your sight," (9:13–17a)

In answer to Saul's prayer, God directed Ananias to go to him. As already noted, that command provided a severe test for Ananias's courage. Understandably, he balked at going, protesting, **"Lord, I have heard from many about this man, how much harm he did to Thy saints at Jerusalem; and here he has authority from the chief priests to bind all who call upon Thy name."** Since the word from the believers in Jerusalem had arrived before Saul, the church at Damascus knew he was coming and why. So Ananias said in effect, "Lord, do You know what You are asking?" The request no doubt appeared to him to be suicidal. His life was at stake, and so was the ministry he had in the church. He was asking if the Lord really meant to end both.

Ananias's protest was overruled, as God explained **to him, "Go, for he is a chosen instrument of Mine, to bear My name before the Gentiles and kings and the sons of Israel."** The call to the ministry is not based on the whims of men but on the sovereign choice of God. Ananias understood that truth clearly, and so did Saul. In Galatians 1:1 he wrote, "Paul, an apostle (not sent from men, nor through the agency of man, but through Jesus Christ, and God the Father, who raised Him from the dead)" (cf. 1 Tim. 2:7; 2 Tim. 1:11). To the Colossian church he said, "I was made a minister," and that "by the stewardship of God bestowed on me" (1:23, 25). He also understood that though he often preached to the Jews first (Acts 13:14; 14:1; 17:1, 10;

18:4; 19:8), his primary calling was to minister to the **Gentiles** (Rom. 11:13; 15:16). Further, he was privileged to **bear** witness to his Lord **before kings,** such as Agrippa (Acts 25:23ff.), and, most likely, Caesar (cf. 2 Tim. 4:16–17).

Those trials were only a small portion of **how much** Saul would **suffer for** Jesus' **name's sake.** First Corinthians 4:9–13, 2 Corinthians 11:23–29, and 12:7–10 catalog the suffering Saul endured for the sake of His Lord. And his suffering, which never stopped until an ax severed his devout head from his faithful body, didn't wait long to begin—only a few days.

Strengthened by the direct word from the Lord, and overcoming his fears, Ananias **departed and entered the house** of Judas, **and after laying his hands on him said, "Brother Saul, the Lord Jesus, who appeared to you on the road by which you were coming, has sent me so that you may regain your sight."** As Acts 22:14–15 reveals, this was Saul's commissioning for service: "And [Ananias] said, 'The God of our fathers has appointed you to know His will, and to see the Righteous One, and to hear an utterance from His mouth. For you will be a witness for Him to all men of what you have seen and heard.'"

The stories of both Ananias and Saul illustrate the truth that the transformed life demands service to Christ. As Saul was later to write, "Let a man regard us in this manner, as servants of Christ, and stewards of the mysteries of God" (1 Cor. 4:1).

THE FILLING OF THE SPIRIT

and be filled with the Holy Spirit. (9:17b)

Ananias was the bearer of far more important news to Saul than that he would regain his sight. Far more wonderfully, he would also **be filled with the Holy Spirit.** The Spirit was already active in Saul's life, convicting him of sin (John 16:9), convincing him of the lordship of Jesus (1 Cor. 12:3), converting him (John 3:5; Titus 3:5), placing him into Christ's body, the church, and indwelling him permanently (1 Cor. 12:13). Beyond all that, he was to be filled with the Spirit in a way that uniquely empowered him for service (cf. 2:4, 14; 4:8, 31; 6:5, 8). (For a further discussion of the filling of the Spirit, see *Ephesians,* MacArthur New Testament Commentary [Chicago: Moody, 1986], 245ff.)

It is significant that unlike the Jews (Acts 2:1–4), the Samaritans (Acts 8:14–17), and soon the Gentiles (Acts 10:44–46), Saul had received the Spirit and his commissioning to service with no apostles present. Saul was a Jew, so there was no need to repeat the initial coming of the Spirit that occurred at Pentecost. Also, he was an apostle in his own right and did not derive his authority from the other apostles (Gal. 1:1; cf. 1 Cor. 9:1; 2 Cor. 11:5; 12:11; Gal. 1:15–17), nor was he subject to their authority. Like them, he was chosen personally by the Lord Jesus Christ and received the Spirit for his commissioning and power directly from Him.

The Spirit transformed Saul in two fundamental ways. First, He took Saul's natural strengths and refined them. Saul was a gifted natural leader, with strong will power. He was a man of strong convictions, a self-starter, bold, a master at using his time and talents, a motivated individual, and a profoundly gifted thinker and speaker.

The Holy Spirit also eliminated undesirable characteristics and replaced them with desirable ones. He replaced Saul's cruel hatred with love; his restless, aggressive spirit with peace; his rough, hard-nosed treatment of people with gentleness; his pride with humility.

Only the Spirit of God can so thoroughly sanctify a life. Saul later expressed that truth to the Corinthians: "But we all, with unveiled face beholding as in a mirror the glory of the Lord, are being transformed into the same image from glory to glory, just as from the Lord, the Spirit" (2 Cor. 3:18).

FELLOWSHIP WITH THE SAINTS

And immediately there fell from his eyes something like scales, and he regained his sight, and he arose and was baptized; and he took food and was strengthened. Now for several days he was with the disciples who were at Damascus, (9:18–19)

Immediately after Ananias's words, **there fell from** Saul's **eyes something like scales, and he regained his sight.** In response to Ananias's exhortation (cf. Acts 22:16), Saul arose and was baptized. By that act he openly united with the very people he had hated and persecuted. His hated enemies became his friends, while his former friends instantly became his enemies (cf. v. 23). In keeping with the consistent pattern of believers' testimonies in Acts, Saul's baptism followed his conversion.

Saul enjoyed his first taste of Christian fellowship as **he took food and was strengthened.** He remained **for several days with the disciples who were at Damascus,** allowing them to celebrate his conversion with him and minister to his needs. One can imagine the overwhelming joy of those days and the incessant praise to God.

One sure mark of a transformed life is the desire to be with fellow Christians. First John 3:14 reads, "We know that we have passed out of death into life, because we love the brethren. He who does not love abides in death." Believers are those who do "not walk in the counsel of the wicked, nor stand in the path of sinners, nor sit in the seat of scoffers" (Ps. 1:1). They can say with the psalmist, "I am a companion of all those who fear Thee, and of those who keep Thy precepts" (Ps. 119:63).

That does not mean, of course, that Christians are to have no contact with unbelievers (1 Cor. 5:9–10). But a professing Christian who prefers the company of the people of the world is probably still one of them.

FERVENCY IN SPEAKING

and immediately he began to proclaim Jesus in the synagogues, saying, "He is the Son of God." And all those hearing him continued to be amazed, and were saying, "Is this not he who in Jerusalem destroyed those who called on this name, and who had come here for the purpose of bringing them bound before the chief priests?" But Saul kept increasing in strength and confounding the Jews who lived at Damascus by proving that this Jesus is the Christ. (9:20–22)

Those transformed by the saving grace of God cannot stop speaking about it (Acts 4:20), and Saul was no exception. After a few days of fellowship with the saints, he **immediately began to proclaim Jesus in the synagogues.** To the shocked Christians, surprised by his conversion, can be added the shocked Jews, who were expecting him to take Christians prisoner, not preach Jesus Christ in their synagogues. From the beginning he felt that courageous compulsion that later caused him to exclaim, "Woe is me if I do not preach the gospel" (1 Cor. 9:16).

In the very **synagogues** to which he had come with warrants for the arrest of Christians, Saul now **began to proclaim Jesus.** The content of that preaching was that Jesus is the Son of God, a title for our Lord that speaks of His deity (cf. John 10:31–36). (For a discussion of the issue of the sonship of Jesus Christ, see *Hebrews*, MacArthur New Testament Commentary [Chicago: Moody, 1983], 26ff.)

The shock and consternation Saul's preaching produced is inconceivable for us. The most zealous defender of Judaism now became the most zealous evangelist for Christianity. Not surprisingly, **all those hearing him continued to be amazed, and were saying, "Is this not he who in Jerusalem destroyed those who called on this name, and who had come here for the purpose of bringing them bound before the chief priests?"** They could not comprehend the drastic change in Saul.

Far from wilting under the pressure of confusion turning into hostility, **Saul kept increasing in strength and confounding the Jews who lived at Damascus by proving that this Jesus is the Christ.** Like Stephen before him, he met the Jews in open debate about the deity and messiahship of Jesus. Saving faith "comes from hearing, and hearing by the word of Christ" (Rom. 10:17).

That Saul was **confounding the Jews** in this dialogue should surprise no one. He had the finest education first-century Judaism could offer, and they could not hope to match his knowledge of the Scripture. Once he understood who Jesus was, he had the key that unlocked the whole Old Testament. He was then able to use his vast knowledge of those Scriptures and his Spirit-controlled brilliance, as well as the truth of Jesus' miracles, words, death, and resurrection, to prove **that this Jesus** was indeed the long-awaited Messiah.

FEARLESSNESS IN SUFFERING

And when many days had elapsed, the Jews plotted together to do away with him, but their plot became known to Saul. And they were also watching the gates day and night so that they might put him to death; but his disciples took him by night, and let him down through an opening in the wall, lowering him in a large basket. And when he had come to Jerusalem, he was trying to associate with the disciples; and they were all afraid of him, not believing that he was a disciple. But Barnabas took hold of him and brought him to the apostles and described to them how he had seen the Lord on the road, and that He had talked to him, and how at Damascus he had spoken out boldly in the name of Jesus. And he was with them moving about freely in Jerusalem, speaking out boldly in the name of the Lord. And he was talking and arguing with the Hellenistic Jews; but they were attempting to put him to death. But when the brethren learned of it, they brought him down to Caesarea and sent him away to Tarsus. So the church throughout all Judea and Galilee and Samaria enjoyed peace, being built up; and, going on in the fear of the Lord and in the comfort of the Holy Spirit, it continued to increase. (9:23–31)

Luke's phrase **when many days had elapsed** marked out a time period that is more specifically defined in the statement of Galatians 1:17–18: "Nor did I go up to Jerusalem to those who were apostles before me; but I went away to Arabia, and returned once more to Damascus. Then three years later I went up to Jerusalem to become acquainted with Cephas, and stayed with him fifteen days." In actuality, three years elapsed between verses 22 and 23. It is implied that Saul spent those years learning from the Lord in the kingdom of Nabatean Arabia. (This is an area not to be confused with the territory of modern Arabia, but located from nearby Damascus south to the Sinai peninsula. Some historians say that a colony of Nabateans lived in Damascus.) He returned and began preaching in Damascus more powerfully than ever, thoroughly exasperating the **Jews** who **plotted together to do away with him.** In God's providence, **their plot became known to Saul.** He noted in 2 Corinthians 11:32 that "in Damascus the ethnarch under Aretas the king was guarding the city of the Damascenes in order to seize me." Apparently the Jews were not the only ones Saul had irritated. During his three years in Nabatean Arabia, he had thoroughly preached the gospel and had worn out his welcome with both the Jews and the Arabs.

United in their desire to kill Saul, **they were watching the gates day and night so that they might put him to death.** The city was surrounded by a wall, and the only exit was through the gates. The Christians, however, found another way out. One of them evidently had access to a house on the city wall, so Saul's **disciples took him by night, and let him down through an opening in the wall, lowering him in a large basket.**

Having made good his escape, Saul went immediately to **Jerusalem,** and began **trying to associate with the disciples.** They, understandably, **were all afraid of him, not believing that he was a disciple.** Saul must have seemed to them to be the quintessential wolf in sheep's clothing, now trying to destroy from within what he had previously tried to destroy from without.

How long this impasse lasted is unknown, but the imperfect tense of the verb translated **was trying** suggests that repeated attempts by Saul to join the fellowship were rebuffed. Finally, **Barnabas** (called "Son of Encouragement" in Acts 4:36) **took hold of him and brought him to the apostles and described to them how he had seen the Lord on the road, and that He had talked to him, and how at Damascus he had spoken out boldly in the name of Jesus.** With the highly regarded Barnabas to vouch for him, Saul was finally accepted.

Having at last gained acceptance, Saul began **moving about freely in Jerusalem, speaking out boldly in the name of the Lord.** Picking up where Stephen had left off, **he was talking and arguing with the Hellenistic Jews.** Because of the intolerant attitude that he himself had done so much to initiate (cf. Acts 8:1), they turned on him immediately and **began attempting to put him to death.** The ways in which they attempted this action are not stated.

The church soon discovered that it was almost as bad having Saul with them as against them. He quickly stirred up a hornet's nest, and, no doubt in the minds of some, as much for their own good as his, they decided to send him home. According to Galatians 1:18, his stay lasted a mere fifteen days. **The brethren learned of** the Hellenists' plot, probably from Saul's own vision recorded in Acts 22:17–21:

> And it came about when I returned to Jerusalem and was praying in the temple, that I fell into a trance, and I saw Him saying to me, "Make haste, and get out of Jerusalem quickly, because they will not accept your testimony about Me." And I said, "Lord, they themselves understand that in one synagogue after another I used to imprison and beat those who believed in Thee. And when the blood of Thy witness Stephen was being shed, I also was standing by approving, and watching out for the cloaks of those who were slaying him." And He said to me, "Go! For I will send you far away to the Gentiles."

For his own safety, **they brought** Saul **down to Caesarea** (the seaport on the Mediterranean) **and sent him away to Tarsus,** his hometown in Cilicia.

Thus did Saul disappear from the scene for a few years. During that period, however, he was far from idle. Between this time and the time when Barnabas found him in Tarsus and brought him to Antioch (11:25–26), he was aggressively doing what the Lord had called him to do. According to Galatians 1:21, he "went into the regions of Syria and Cilicia." At least some of the churches of that region mentioned in Acts 15:23 must have been founded by him in those years.

With Saul the firebrand gone from the scene, both as the persecutor of the church and the chief target of the Christ-haters, things quieted down in Palestine. Luke again summarizes the progress of the church by stating that **the church throughout all Judea and Galilee and Samaria enjoyed peace, being built up; and, going on in the fear of the Lord and in the comfort of the Holy Spirit, it continued to increase.** Besides Saul's departure, political changes contributed to the church's temporary respite. The ouster of the compliant Pilate as governor, coupled with the expansion of Herod Agrippa's authority, restricted the Jews' freedom of action. They were thus less able to carry out drastic measures against the church.

Saul's life was dramatically and totally transformed that day on the road near Damascus. And from that moment, so was the history of the world, as we shall see when he returns to center stage in chapter 13.

Marks of an Effective Personal Ministry

22

Now it came about that as Peter was traveling through all those parts, he came down also to the saints who lived at Lydda. And there he found a certain man named Aeneas, who had been bed-ridden eight years, for he was paralyzed. And Peter said to him, "Aeneas, Jesus Christ heals you; arise, and make your bed." And immediately he arose. And all who lived at Lydda and Sharon saw him, and they turned to the Lord. Now in Joppa there was a certain disciple named Tabitha (which translated in Greek is called Dorcas); this woman was abounding with deeds of kindness and charity, which she continually did. And it came about at that time that she fell sick and died; and when they had washed her body, they laid it in an upper room. And since Lydda was near Joppa, the disciples, having heard that Peter was there, sent two men to him, entreating him, "Do not delay to come to us." And Peter arose and went with them. And when he had come, they brought him into the upper room; and all the widows stood beside him weeping, and showing all the tunics and garments that Dorcas used to make while she was with them. But Peter sent them all out and knelt down and prayed, and turning to the body, he said, "Tabitha, arise." And she opened her eyes,

and when she saw Peter, she sat up. And he gave her his hand and raised her up; and calling the saints and widows, he presented her alive. And it became known all over Joppa, and many believed in the Lord. And it came about that he stayed many days in Joppa with a certain tanner, Simon. (9:32–43)

No matter how large their ministries may have been, God's noblest servants have always taken the time to minister to individuals. Moses nearly wore himself out doing that, until his father-in-law rebuked him for mismanaging his time and told him to delegate (Ex. 18:14ff.). Despite the crowds that thronged Him constantly, the Lord Jesus Christ always had concern and time for individuals (cf. Matt. 9:19–22). Stephen had been engaged in the personal care of widows (Acts 6:1–6). Paul, though consumed with reaching cities and nations, endeared himself to people whose names are all through his letters. The great apostle shared his life and labor with them (cf. Rom. 16). The busy Reformers Luther and Calvin did not neglect their pastoral duties. The idea of a man of God who ministers only to the large crowds is foreign to Scripture. God expects all Christians, leaders included, to pour their lives into others (2 Tim. 2:2).

The apostle Peter knew what it was to preach to the masses. From the day of Pentecost on he spoke to huge crowds in Jerusalem. He also preached twice before the Sanhedrin (Acts 4, 5). This passage reveals the other side of Peter's ministry, his personal service to individuals. Six elements of that service are implied, not from Peter's direct teaching but indirectly from his actions. Peter was effective with individuals because he was involved, Christ-exalting, available, powerful, fruitful, and free from prejudice.

PETER WAS INVOLVED

Now it came about that as Peter was traveling through all those parts, he came down also to the saints who lived at Lydda. And there he found a certain man named Aeneas, who had been bedridden eight years, for he was paralyzed. (9:32–33)

The scene shifts from Paul back to Peter, who will again be the central figure in the narrative for the next three chapters. Paul has been converted and has boldly proclaimed his newfound faith both in Damascus and Jerusalem. His preaching so aggravated his opponents that first in Damascus, then in Jerusalem, they sought to kill him. He has by now fled Jerusalem for his home city of Tarsus. Several years later, as recorded in chapter 13, Paul's ministry will dominate the rest of the record of Acts.

The continued expansion of the church outside Jerusalem (assisted by the persecution noted in Acts 8:1–2) required movement on Peter's part. The statement **it came about that as Peter was traveling** shows the ceaseless itinerant character of Peter's ministry at that time. On one of his trips, **he came down** to visit **the saints who lived at Lydda.** Peter was not set in some hierarchical office but was moving, which made it easy for God to direct him. Those actively involved in ministry are usually the ones to whom God grants the most ministry opportunities. God has always seemed to entrust His richest ministries to His busiest saints. Just being wholeheartedly active in ministry places one in strategic opportunities.

Lydda, known in the Old Testament as Lod, was located about ten miles southeast of the seacoast city of Joppa. It was an important place, since the roads from Egypt to Syria and from Joppa to Jerusalem passed through it. Today it is the location of Israel's international airport. When Peter arrived there, **he found a certain man named Aeneas, who had been bedridden eight years, for he was paralyzed.** The use of the term **a certain man** to describe him, when contrasted with the description of Dorcas as "a certain disciple," suggests he was not a believer. There are no examples in the New Testament of believers being healed (though Lazarus, Dorcas, and Eutychus were raised from the dead).

Luke does not say whether **Aeneas** was **paralyzed** due to a stroke, an illness such as polio, or an injury. In any case, his paralysis was beyond the abilities of the limited medical knowledge of that day. He had already **been bedridden eight years,** and faced that prospect for the rest of his life.

Peter's availability because he was involved gave him an open door for ministry. The miracle, besides its obvious impact in the life of Aeneas, was to be used by God to bring large numbers of people in the surrounding region to faith in Jesus Christ.

Peter Was Christ-Exalting

And Peter said to him, "Aeneas, Jesus Christ heals you; arise, and make your bed." And immediately he arose. And all who lived at Lydda and Sharon saw him, and they turned to the Lord. (9:34–35)

Those who would minister effectively for Jesus Christ must seek to exalt Him, not promote themselves. Peter understood his role perfectly (cf. Acts 10:25–26). Coming to Aeneas, **Peter said to him, "Aeneas, Jesus Christ** (not Peter) **heals you"** (cf. Acts 3:6). Peter's selfless humility stands in sharp contrast to the many in the ministry today who seek their own fame (and fortune), instead of seeking to exalt the Name of the Lord Jesus Christ.

Peter took our Lord's words, spoken in John 15:4–5, to heart: "Abide in Me, and I in you. As the branch cannot bear fruit of itself, unless it abides in the vine, so neither can you, unless you abide in Me. I am the vine, you are the branches; he who abides in Me, and I in him, he bears much fruit; for apart from Me you can do nothing." In his first epistle, he echoed those words: "Whoever speaks, let him speak, as it were, the utterances of God; whoever serves, let him do so as by the strength which God supplies; so that in all things God may be glorified through Jesus Christ, to whom belongs the glory and dominion forever and ever. Amen" (1 Peter 4:11).

Paul also understood that principle. To the Ephesians he wrote, "Now to Him who is able to do exceeding abundantly beyond all that we ask or think, according to the power that works within us, to Him be the glory in the church and in Christ Jesus to all generations forever and ever. Amen" (Eph. 3:20–21). Of his ministry he wrote, "Therefore in Christ Jesus I have found reason for boasting in things pertaining to God. For I will not presume to speak of anything except what Christ has accomplished through me, resulting in the obedience of the Gentiles by word and deed" (Rom. 15:17–18).

Then Peter commanding Aeneas to respond to the healing said, **arise, and make your bed.** Aeneas **immediately arose,** with no paralysis. Since Aeneas's cure was complete, and he would no longer be confined to it, Peter commanded him to **make** his **bed.** As noted in the discussion of Acts 3:8 in chapter 8, the healings performed by Jesus Christ and the apostles were instantaneous and total. The New Testament knows nothing of "progressive healings," where someone has been "healed," and is now gradually getting better. (For a discussion of the gift of healing, see my book *Charismatic Chaos* [Grand Rapids: Zondervan, 1992].)

Peter's healing of Aeneas had widespread and dramatic repercussions. **All who lived at Lydda and Sharon saw him, and they turned to the Lord. All** may shock the reader, but such was the power and grace of God through Peter in that area that **all** believed. Not only in Aeneas's home city of **Lydda,** but also in the surrounding plain of Sharon, the people came to faith in the Lord. Peter's willingness to be involved with people and his desire to glorify his Lord made him a useful instrument by which the Lord could gather a rich harvest for His kingdom. The phrase **turned to the Lord** employs the verb *epistrephō*, "to turn around" (cf. its use in Acts 3:19; 11:21; 14:15; 15:19; 26:18, 20, and in 2 Cor. 3:16 and 1 Thess. 1:9), which describes salvation as more than a change of mind; indeed it is a change of life direction. Conversion is an about-face from one belief and behavior to a completely opposite commitment.

Peter Was Available

Now in Joppa there was a certain disciple named Tabitha (which translated in Greek is called Dorcas); this woman was abounding with deeds of kindness and charity, which she continually did. And it came about at that time that she fell sick and died; and when they had washed her body, they laid it in an upper room. And since Lydda was near Joppa, the disciples, having heard that Peter was there, sent two men to him, entreating him, "Do not delay to come to us." And Peter arose and went with them. And when he had come, they brought him into the upper room; and all the widows stood beside him weeping, and showing all the tunics and garments that Dorcas used to make while she was with them. (9:36–39)

Peter's availability led to an even more astounding opportunity. Aeneas was healed, but Dorcas was raised from the dead.

While Peter was at Lydda, tragedy struck the church at nearby **Joppa.** One of the most beloved members was **a certain disciple named Tabitha** (more commonly known by her **Greek** name of **Dorcas;** both names mean "gazelle"). The epitaph on this lovely lady was that **this woman was abounding with deeds of kindness and charity, which she continually did.** Specifically, as verse 39 shows, she made clothes for the poor and needy. In contrast to Aeneas, she is specifically called a **disciple.** *Mathētria* (**disciple**), the feminine form of *mathētēs* ("disciple"), appears only here in the New Testament. Dorcas was certainly an appropriate model for what a Christian woman should be. She fulfilled her calling as a disciple, as described by Paul in Ephesians 2:10: "For we are His workmanship, created in Christ Jesus for good works, which God prepared beforehand, that we should walk in them"; and Colossians 1:10, "That you may walk in a manner worthy of the Lord, to please Him in all respects, bearing fruit in every good work and increasing in the knowledge of God." She was a New Testament example of a Proverbs 31 woman, one who "extends her hand to the poor; and . . . stretches out her hands to the needy" (Prov. 31:20).

Naturally when **at that time she fell sick and died,** it was a serious blow to the believers in Joppa. **They washed her body** in preparation for burial, as was customary. However, instead of burying her immediately, as was also customary (cf. Acts 5:6, 10), **they laid** her body **in an upper room.** Evidently, they had something else in mind.

What that was becomes immediately apparent. **Lydda was near Joppa,** and **the disciples heard that Peter was there.** No doubt they had also heard of his healing of Aeneas, which gave them an idea. They **sent two men** to Peter, **entreating him** urgently, **"Do not delay to come to us."**

Despite his consuming duties among the masses confessing Jesus as Lord, **Peter arose and went with them.** He was never too busy with the crowds to be available to help in time of need. **When he had come** to Joppa, **they brought him into the upper room** where they had laid Dorcas's body.

Peter saw firsthand how loved Dorcas was and what a loss her death was for the church at Joppa. **All the widows** of the church **stood beside him weeping, and showing all the tunics and garments that Dorcas used to make while she was with them.** The church's responsibility to care for widows, though often neglected today, was taken seriously in the early church (cf. Acts 6:1ff.; 1 Tim. 5:1ff.). Employment opportunities for women were severely limited, and widows without family to care for them were often left destitute (cf. Mark 12:41–44; Luke 7:11–15). The loss of Dorcas, therefore, was a serious blow to these **widows.**

Many believe that to deny women leadership roles in the church is to deny them the opportunity to minister. Nothing could be further from the truth. Dorcas neither preached nor led the newlyborn church, yet her ministry in the Joppa church was so crucial as to endear her to all.

PETER WAS PRAYERFUL

But Peter sent them all out and knelt down and prayed, and turning to the body, he said, "Tabitha, arise." And she opened her eyes, and when she saw Peter, she sat up. And he gave her his hand and raised her up; and calling the saints and widows, he presented her alive. (9:40–41)

As he had seen the Lord do when He raised Jairus's daughter (Mark 5:40), **Peter sent them all out** of the room where Dorcas's body lay. He would not put on a display before the crowd that would draw all attention to him, and wanted a quiet place to pray.

Some might think that Peter, who had been involved in countless healings (cf. Acts 5:12–16), should have simply commanded Dorcas to rise. He knew, however, the source of his power and presumed nothing about the will of God. Accordingly, he **knelt down and prayed.**

Essential to all successful ministry, prayer acknowledges dependence on God. Prayer realizes that God is "able to do exceeding abundantly beyond all that we ask or think, according to [His] power that works within us" (Eph. 3:20). Peter had learned the importance of prayer from His Lord, having seen and heard Him many times in communion with His Father (cf. Matt. 14:23; Luke 6:12–13).

Many years ago five young college students made their way to London to hear Charles Haddon Spurgeon preach. Arriving early at the Metropolitan Tabernacle, they found the doors still locked. While they waited on the steps, a man approached them. "Would you like to see the heating apparatus of this church?" he asked. That was not what they had come for, but they agreed to go with him. He led them into the building, down a long flight of stairs, and into a hallway. At the end of the hallway he opened a door into a large room filled with seven hundred people on their knees praying. "That," said their guide (who was none other than Spurgeon himself), "is the heating apparatus of this church."

Having finished praying, Peter turned to Dorcas's **body** and said, **"Tabitha, arise." And she opened her eyes, and when she saw Peter, she sat up. And he gave her his hand and raised her up; and calling the saints and widows, he presented her alive.** For those who loved her the joy must have been inexpressible. That God did not raise her solely for their benefit, however, will soon become evident.

Peter Was Fruitful

And it became known all over Joppa, and many believed in the Lord. (9:42)

God's greater purpose for raising Dorcas now became clear as word of her return to life **became known all over Joppa.** As noted in chapters 8 and 13 of this volume, God used miracles as confirming signs that the gospel is true. He also used them to authenticate the apostles as His messengers. God used the raising of Dorcas as the spark for the salvation throughout the city.

As with the healing of Aeneas, Peter's ministry bore much fruit. Because of Dorcas's resurrection, **many** in Joppa **believed in the Lord.** It may be affirmed that turning to the Lord (v. 35), a phrase commonly used in Acts, is synonymous with believing in the Lord (cf. Acts 11:21). There is no saving faith without conversion, no true belief without repentance and transformation. Again Peter's God-empowered ministry, both in Lydda and Joppa, caused many souls to be added to the kingdom.

PETER WAS FREE FROM PREJUDICE

And it came about that he stayed many days in Joppa with a certain tanner, Simon. (9:43)

This footnote serves as a bridge between this passage and the following account of Cornelius's conversion. Peter decided to remain **in Joppa** and **stayed many days with a certain tanner** named **Simon.** These were challenging days for Peter, as the walls of his lifelong prejudices tumbled down. First came the conversion and Spirit-filling of the Samaritans, with whom no self-respecting Jew had any dealings. Yet Peter had been forced to welcome them as brothers in Christ. Soon will come an even greater shock, as Gentiles enter the church.

In this seemingly insignificant footnote, yet another wall comes down, as Peter stays with a **tanner.** Tanners were despised in first-century Jewish society, since they dealt with the skins of dead animals. Tanning was thus considered an unclean occupation, and Simon would have been shunned by the local synagogue.

Prejudice is devastating to any ministry. In far too many Christian circles, those who do not fit the mold are rejected. Any bigotry is a blight on the cause of God, who "is not one to show partiality" (Acts 10:34). There is no place in an effective personal ministry for prejudice. The zealous Jewish nationalist Paul learned that lesson. To the Corinthians he wrote,

> For though I am free from all men, I have made myself a slave to all, that I might win the more. And to the Jews I became as a Jew, that I might win Jews; to those who are under the Law, as under the Law, though not being myself under the Law, that I might win those who are under the Law; to those who are without law, as without law, though not being without the law of God but under the law of Christ, that I might win those who are without law. To the weak I became weak, that I might win the weak; I have become all things to all men, that I may by all means save some. (1 Cor. 9:19–22)

Peter knew the principles for an effective personal ministry, and lived them out. Because of that, the Lord blessed his ministry to individuals as much as his ministry before the huge crowds. In fact, one led to the other. And it would be through his ministry to another individual, Cornelius, that the final barrier would be thrown down, and Gentiles would be admitted to the church.

Salvation
Reaches Out

23

Now there was a certain man at Caesarea named Cornelius, a centurion of what was called the Italian cohort, a devout man, and one who feared God with all his household, and gave many alms to the Jewish people, and prayed to God continually. About the ninth hour of the day he clearly saw in a vision an angel of God who had just come in to him, and said to him, "Cornelius!" And fixing his gaze upon him and being much alarmed, he said, "What is it, Lord?" And he said to him, "Your prayers and alms have ascended as a memorial before God. And now dispatch some men to Joppa, and send for a man named Simon, who is also called Peter; he is staying with a certain tanner named Simon, whose house is by the sea." And when the angel who was speaking to him had departed, he summoned two of his servants and a devout soldier of those who were in constant attendance upon him, and after he had explained everything to them, he sent them to Joppa. And on the next day, as they were on their way, and approaching the city, Peter went up on the housetop about the sixth hour to pray. And he became hungry, and was desiring to eat; but while they were making preparations, he fell into a trance; and he beheld the sky opened up, and a certain ob-

ject like a great sheet coming down, lowered by four corners to
the ground, and there were in it all kinds of four-footed animals
and crawling creatures of the earth and birds of the air. And a
voice came to him, "Arise, Peter, kill and eat!" But Peter said,
"By no means, Lord, for I have never eaten anything unholy and
unclean." And again a voice came to him a second time, "What
God has cleansed, no longer consider unholy." And this happened three times; and immediately the object was taken up into
the sky. Now while Peter was greatly perplexed in mind as to
what the vision which he had seen might be, behold, the men
who had been sent by Cornelius, having asked directions for Simon's house, appeared at the gate; and calling out, they were
asking whether Simon, who was also called Peter, was staying
there. And while Peter was reflecting on the vision, the Spirit
said to him, "Behold, three men are looking for you. But arise,
go downstairs, and accompany them without misgivings; for I
have sent them Myself." And Peter went down to the men and
said, "Behold, I am the one you are looking for; what is the reason for which you have come?" And they said, "Cornelius, a centurion, a righteous and God-fearing man well spoken of by the
entire nation of the Jews, was divinely directed by a holy angel
to send for you to come to his house and hear a message from
you." And so he invited them in and gave them lodging. And on
the next day he arose and went away with them, and some of the
brethren from Joppa accompanied him. And on the following
day he entered Caesarea. Now Cornelius was waiting for them,
and had called together his relatives and close friends. And
when it came about that Peter entered, Cornelius met him, and
fell at his feet and worshiped him. But Peter raised him up, saying, "Stand up; I too am just a man." And as he talked with him,
he entered, and found many people assembled. And he said to
them, "You yourselves know how unlawful it is for a man who is
a Jew to associate with a foreigner or to visit him; and yet God
has shown me that I should not call any man unholy or unclean.
That is why I came without even raising any objection when I was
sent for. And so I ask for what reason you have sent for me." And
Cornelius said, "Four days ago to this hour, I was praying in my
house during the ninth hour; and behold, a man stood before me
in shining garments, and he said, 'Cornelius, your prayer has
been heard and your alms have been remembered before God.
Send therefore to Joppa and invite Simon, who is also called Peter, to come to you; he is staying at the house of Simon the tanner by the sea.' And so I sent to you immediately, and you have
been kind enough to come. Now then, we are all here present be-

fore God to hear all that you have been commanded by the Lord." And opening his mouth, Peter said: "I most certainly understand now that God is not one to show partiality, but in every nation the man who fears Him and does what is right, is welcome to Him. The word which He sent to the sons of Israel, preaching peace through Jesus Christ (He is Lord of all)—you yourselves know the thing which took place throughout all Judea, starting from Galilee, after the baptism which John proclaimed. You know of Jesus of Nazareth, how God anointed Him with the Holy Spirit and with power, and how He went about doing good, and healing all who were oppressed by the devil; for God was with Him. And we are witnesses of all the things He did both in the land of the Jews and in Jerusalem. And they also put Him to death by hanging Him on a cross. God raised Him up on the third day, and granted that He should become visible, not to all the people, but to witnesses who were chosen beforehand by God, that is, to us, who ate and drank with Him after He arose from the dead. And He ordered us to preach to the people, and solemnly to testify that this is the One who has been appointed by God as Judge of the living and the dead. Of Him all the prophets bear witness that through His name everyone who believes in Him receives forgiveness of sins." While Peter was still speaking these words, the Holy Spirit fell upon all those who were listening to the message. And all the circumcised believers who had come with Peter were amazed, because the gift of the Holy Spirit had been poured out upon the Gentiles also. For they were hearing them speaking with tongues and exalting God. Then Peter answered, "Surely no one can refuse the water for these to be baptized who have received the Holy Spirit just as we did, can he?" And he ordered them to be baptized in the name of Jesus Christ. Then they asked him to stay on for a few days. (10:1–48)

Mark Twain's classic novel *The Adventures of Tom Sawyer* records the following exchange between Tom and his friend Huck Finn. Tom has just informed Huck that he is not welcome in Tom's gang. Huck protests, "Now Tom, hain't you always been friendly to me? You wouldn't shet me out, would you, Tom?" Tom replies, "Huck, I wouldn't want to, and I don't want to—but what would people say? Why they'd say, 'Mph! Tom Sawyer's Gang! pretty low characters in it!' They'd mean you, Huck. You wouldn't like that, and I wouldn't" ([Chicago: Fountain, 1949], 215).

Children are not the only ones who play such cruel games with each other; adults are quite prone to it as well. We are quick to exclude from our group those we deem undesirable—those who fail to flatter us, support our opinions, reinforce our prejudices, boost our pride, or feed our egos, or whose style of life is significantly different. The world in general expresses its intolerance and bigotry in conflicts at every level, from silent prejudice to outright war.

Even the church is not immune to this tendency. Those of another culture, skin color, social status, educational group, or income level often find themselves as unwelcome in the church as Huck Finn was in Tom Sawyer's gang. Such intolerant exclusivism grieves the heart of the Lord Jesus Christ, whose purpose and prayer was that believers "may all be one; even as Thou, Father, art in Me, and I in Thee, that they also may be in Us; that the world may believe that Thou didst send Me" (John 17:21). In the church, "there is neither Jew nor Greek, there is neither slave nor free man, there is neither male nor female; for you are all one in Christ Jesus" (Gal. 3:28).

The cultural barriers were no less deep-seated and rigid in the ancient world than in our own day. If the church was not to forever remain a small sect of Judaism, those barriers would have to be crossed. Already in Acts, the barrier separating the Jews and Samaritans had been breached, through the ministry of Philip, Peter, and John, which resulted in numbers of Samaritan converts. The delay in their receiving the Spirit until Peter and John arrived emphasized to both sides that Samaritans and Jews were endowed by the same Spirit of God and placed into the church.

But an even more formidable barrier loomed. The Jews' distaste for the Samaritans paled in comparison to their hatred of the Gentiles (cf. Jonah 3:10–4:4, which shows the prophet's anger over God's saving Gentiles). Before the gospel could be preached to all nations and embrace all nations (Matt. 28:19–20), this final barrier to unity had to be torn down. A small crack in the wall had already been made through the conversion of the Ethiopian eunuch (8:26–40). He, however, returned to his distant land and did not remain to fellowship with the Jewish believers. In God's providence, the time had come to reconcile Jews and Gentiles in the church.

It is fitting that Peter, the leader of the Twelve, should be the one who opened the door to the uncircumcised. It was Peter who preached on the day of Pentecost and to the crowd at Solomon's Portico. Peter was also the point man in the ongoing battle with the Sanhedrin. Nor, as already noted, were the Samaritans added to the church apart from his ministry.

For Peter to take such a drastic step required some preparation. Already, he had become increasingly emancipated from the prejudices he was raised with. He had accepted Samaritans as brothers in Christ and equals in the church. As chapter 10 unfolds, he is staying with a tanner—a trade despised by the devout Jews. But accepting Gentiles as equals before the Lord was an entirely different matter. Strict Jews would have nothing at all to do with Gentiles. They would not be guests in Gentile homes (cf. v. 28) or invite Gentiles to their homes. Dirt from a Gentile country was considered defiled, and a Jew would shake it off his sandals before entering Israel (from which practice the expression "shake the dust off" [Matt. 10:14; Mark 6:11; Luke 9:5; Acts 13:51] came). Jews would not eat food prepared by Gentile hands. Cooking utensils purchased from a Gentile had to be purified before being used. In short, Gentiles were considered unclean and their presence defiling.

The theological foundation for the unity of Jews and Gentiles in the church had already been laid. In Ephesians 2:11–22, Paul pointed out that through Christ's one, comprehensive sacrificial death He "made both groups into one, and broke down the barrier of the dividing wall" (Eph. 2:14). Luke here chronicles the historical realization of that spiritual truth.

But this chapter is more than just the story of the introduction of Gentiles into the church; it is also the account of one man's salvation. The sequence of events leading to Cornelius's salvation presents a timeless pattern of how salvation unfolds. From the text six elements may be discerned: sovereign preparation, submissive will, salvation presentation, spiritual power, symbolic confession, and sweet fellowship.

Sovereign Preparation

Now there was a certain man at Caesarea named Cornelius, a centurion of what was called the Italian cohort, a devout man, and one who feared God with all his household, and gave many alms to the Jewish people, and prayed to God continually. About the ninth hour of the day he clearly saw in a vision an angel of God who had just come in to him, and said to him, "Cornelius!" And fixing his gaze upon him and being much alarmed, he said, "What is it, Lord?" And he said to him, "Your prayers and alms have ascended as a memorial before God. And now dispatch some men to Joppa, and send for a man named Simon, who is also called Peter; he is staying with a certain tanner named Simon, whose house is by the sea." And when the angel who was speaking to him had departed, he summoned two of his servants and a devout soldier of those who were in constant attendance upon him, and after he had explained everything to them, he sent them to Joppa. And on the next day, as they were on their way, and approaching the city, Peter went up on the housetop about the sixth hour to pray. And he became hungry, and was desiring to eat; but while they were making preparations, he fell

into a trance; and he beheld the sky opened up, and a certain object like a great sheet coming down, lowered by four corners to the ground, and there were in it all kinds of four-footed animals and crawling creatures of the earth and birds of the air. And a voice came to him, "Arise, Peter, kill and eat!" But Peter said, "By no means, Lord, for I have never eaten anything unholy and unclean." And again a voice came to him a second time, "What God has cleansed, no longer consider unholy." And this happened three times; and immediately the object was taken up into the sky. Now while Peter was greatly perplexed in mind as to what the vision which he had seen might be, behold, the men who had been sent by Cornelius, having asked directions for Simon's house, appeared at the gate; and calling out, they were asking whether Simon, who was also called Peter, was staying there. And while Peter was reflecting on the vision, the Spirit said to him, "Behold, three men are looking for you. But arise, go downstairs, and accompany them without misgivings; for I have sent them Myself." (10:1–20)

The momentous events of Gentile inclusion in the church and Cornelius's salvation required sovereign preparation. Both the convert, Cornelius, and the preacher, Peter, received visions from God preparing them for what was to follow.

THE PREPARATION OF CORNELIUS

Now there was a certain man at Caesarea named Cornelius, a centurion of what was called the Italian cohort, a devout man, and one who feared God with all his household, and gave many alms to the Jewish people, and prayed to God continually. About the ninth hour of the day he clearly saw in a vision an angel of God who had just come in to him, and said to him, "Cornelius!" And fixing his gaze upon him and being much alarmed, he said, "What is it, Lord?" And he said to him, "Your prayers and alms have ascended as a memorial before God. And now dispatch some men to Joppa, and send for a man named Simon, who is also called Peter; he is staying with a certain tanner named Simon, whose house is by the sea." And when the angel who was speaking to him had departed, he summoned two of his servants and a devout soldier of those who were in constant attendance upon him, and after he had explained everything to them, he sent them to Joppa. (10:1–8)

Since man is dead in sin (Eph. 2:1–4), salvation cannot and does not begin with him (cf. John 1:12–13; 6:37; Eph. 1:4; Acts 13:48). One such dead man, Cornelius, whom God was about to save, lived in **Caesarea,** an important city located on the coast roughly thirty miles north of Joppa. It was the capital of the Roman province of Judea, and the residence of its procurator. Naturally, a large Roman garrison was stationed there. Among them was Cornelius, **a centurion of what was called the Italian cohort.** A Roman legion at full strength consisted of 6,000 men, and was divided into ten cohorts of 600 men each. A centurion commanded 100 of these men, and each legion therefore had 60 centurions, who were considered the backbone of the Roman army. The Roman historian Polybius described centurions as "not so much venturesome daredevils as natural leaders of a steady and sedate spirit, not so much men who will initiate attacks and open the battle as men who will hold their ground when worsted and hard pressed and be ready to die at their posts" (*Histories* vi. xix–xlii, cited in Naphtali Lewis and Meyer Reinhold, eds., *Roman Civilization: Sourcebook 1: The Republic* [New York: Harper & Row, 1966], 435). Like the other centurions mentioned in the New Testament, Cornelius had reached his rank by proving to be a strong, responsible, reliable man.

More than a good soldier, however, Cornelius was **a devout man, and one who feared God with all his household, and gave many alms to the Jewish people, and prayed to God continually.** His was a seeking heart; he had lived up to the light he had, and God was about to give him more. This is the necessary balance to divine election, that God responds to the seeking, willing heart (cf. Isa. 55:6–7; Jer. 29:13; John 7:17). Divine election and human responsibility are both the clear teaching of Scripture. Salvation is both accomplished by God and commanded of sinners. Although our limited comprehension does not allow us to harmonize them, there is no conflict in the mind of God.

Cornelius was a God-fearer. The Lord had moved on his dark soul so that he had abandoned his pagan religion and was worshiping Jehovah God. That devotion expressed itself in his giving of **many alms to the Jewish people,** and by the fact that he **prayed to God continually.** He had stopped short, however, of becoming a full proselyte to Judaism through circumcision.

Because of His sovereign election of Cornelius, and in response to his seeking heart, God moved to prepare him. **About the ninth hour** (3:00 P.M.) **of the day he clearly saw in a vision an angel of God who had just come in to him, and said to him, "Cornelius!"** The **ninth hour** was the most important time of prayer in the Jewish day (Acts 3:1). God responded to his prayer by sending the angelic messenger.

The appearance of angels in Scripture produced terror and awe (Judg. 6:22; 13:20; 1 Chron. 21:16; Dan. 10:4–9; Matt. 28:2–5; Luke 1:11–13, 30; 2:9–10)—very different from the casual flippancy with which many today treat their supposed encounters with them. Understandably, the veteran soldier Cornelius was terrified. **Fixing his gaze upon** the angel **and being much alarmed, he said, "What is it, Lord?"**

The angel was quick to reassure Cornelius, saying to him, **"Your prayers and alms have ascended as a memorial before God."** God knew Cornelius's heart, that he was a devout man, worshiping Him to the best of his knowledge. Despite Cornelius's sincerity, and devotion to the true God, he could not be saved apart from a correct understanding of the gospel of Jesus Christ (Acts 4:12). God was arranging to provide him with that knowledge. Specifically, the angel instructed him to **"dispatch some men to Joppa, and send for a man named Simon, who is also called Peter; he is staying with a certain tanner named Simon, whose house is by the sea."**

Cornelius responded immediately. When **the angel who was speaking to him had departed, he summoned two of his servants and a devout soldier of those who were in constant attendance upon him, and after he had explained everything to them, he sent them to Joppa.**

At first glance, there seems to be no reason for this delay. Certainly the angel was quite capable of delivering the gospel message to Cornelius. Although an angel will proclaim the gospel in the future (Rev. 14:6), God has chosen to work through human instruments. God also wanted Peter there to observe firsthand Cornelius's salvation. Only then would he be fully prepared to accept Gentiles into the church.

THE PREPARATION OF PETER

And on the next day, as they were on their way, and approaching the city, Peter went up on the housetop about the sixth hour to pray. And he became hungry, and was desiring to eat; but while they were making preparations, he fell into a trance; and he beheld the sky opened up, and a certain object like a great sheet coming down, lowered by four corners to the ground, and there were in it all kinds of four-footed animals and crawling creatures of the earth and birds of the air. And a voice came to him, "Arise, Peter, kill and eat!" But Peter said, "By no means, Lord, for I have never eaten anything unholy and unclean." And again a voice came to him a second time, "What God has cleansed, no longer consider unholy." And this happened three times; and

immediately the object was taken up into the sky. Now while Peter was greatly perplexed in mind as to what the vision which he had seen might be, behold, the men who had been sent by Cornelius, having asked directions for Simon's house, appeared at the gate; and calling out, they were asking whether Simon, who was also called Peter, was staying there. And while Peter was reflecting on the vision, the Spirit said to him, "Behold, three men are looking for you. But arise, go downstairs, and accompany them without misgivings; for I have sent them Myself." (10:9–20)

Meanwhile, back at Joppa, God was preparing the preacher for this monumental encounter. **On the next day,** as the men sent by Cornelius **were on their way, and approaching** Joppa, Peter received a divine vision. **He went up on the housetop about the sixth hour** (noon) **to pray.** It was mealtime, **and he became hungry, and was desiring to eat.** There was to be an unexpected delay in his meal, however. While his hosts **were making preparations** for the meal, Peter **fell into a trance.** God not only sovereignly called Cornelius to salvation but also prepared Peter as the means, humanly speaking, to accomplish that. God's sovereign call of individuals for special service is well-documented in Scripture (cf. Isa. 49:1; Jer. 1:5; John 15:16; Gal. 1:1).

In his trance, Peter **beheld the sky opened up, and a certain object like a great sheet coming down, lowered by four corners to the ground, and there were in it all kinds of four-footed animals and crawling creatures of the earth and birds of the air.** Appropriately enough, since he was hungry, Peter's vision involved eating. That the sheet contained both clean and unclean animals reflects the Old Testament instruction in which God laid down certain dietary restrictions for Israel (cf. Lev. 11). Leviticus 20:25–26 describes His reason for giving those restrictions:

> You are therefore to make a distinction between the clean animal and the unclean, and between the unclean bird and the clean; and you shall not make yourselves detestable by animal or by bird or by anything that creeps on the ground, which I have separated for you as unclean. Thus you are to be holy to Me, for I the Lord am holy; and I have set you apart from the peoples to be Mine.

It was imperative that Israel be kept separate from her idolatrous neighbors, and such restrictions would hinder social intercourse with them.

Since the coming of the New Covenant and the calling of a new people (the church), the day of those restrictions was over, as Peter soon discovered. In his vision, God commanded him to **arise, kill and eat.** As any devout Jew would have been, Peter was horrified. He protested immediately, **"By no means, Lord, for I have never eaten anything unholy and unclean."** He had zealously kept the dietary laws all his life, believing such "kosher" commitment was required by the Lord. His strict adherence reflected his devotion to pleasing God. How could he immediately throw all that aside without assaulting his conscience, so sensitive to dietary duty?

Peter resisted strongly the message, so the **voice came to him a second time, "What God has cleansed, no longer consider unholy."** So ingrained were the dietary regulations into his life that he still could not comprehend what was happening. Finally, after this scenario was repeated **three times, immediately the object was taken up into the sky.**

The vision left **Peter greatly perplexed in mind as to what the vision which he had seen** might signify. That meaning was twofold. On the negative side, it signified the abolishing of the Old Testament dietary restrictions (cf. Mark 7:14–23; Rom. 14:1–3; Col. 2:16–17; 1 Tim. 4:1–5). Such separating features were now counterproductive, since God was bringing Jews and Gentiles together in the church, not keeping them apart. On the positive side, the vision pictured the inclusion of both the Gentiles, symbolized by the unclean animals, and the Jews, symbolized by the clean ones, into one body.

Peter's perplexity was short-lived. At that very moment, **the men who had been sent by Cornelius, having asked directions for Simon's house, appeared at the gate; and calling out, they were asking whether Simon, who was also called Peter, was staying there.** They arrived **while Peter was reflecting on the vision,** still trying to figure out what the Lord was saying. The time had come for the encounter that would clear up Peter's confusion, so **the Spirit said to him, "Behold, three men are looking for you. But arise, go downstairs, and accompany them without misgivings; for I have sent them Myself."** God not only sovereignly prepared Cornelius and Peter but also sovereignly determined and arranged the timing of bringing them together.

SUBMISSIVE WILL

And Peter went down to the men and said, "Behold, I am the one you are looking for; what is the reason for which you have come?" And they said, "Cornelius, a centurion, a righteous and God-fearing man well spoken of by the entire nation of the Jews, was divinely directed by a holy angel to send for you to come to

his house and hear a message from you." And so he invited them in and gave them lodging. And on the next day he arose and went away with them, and some of the brethren from Joppa accompanied him. And on the following day he entered Caesarea. Now Cornelius was waiting for them, and had called together his relatives and close friends. And when it came about that Peter entered, Cornelius met him, and fell at his feet and worshiped him. But Peter raised him up, saying, "Stand up; I too am just a man." And as he talked with him, he entered, and found many people assembled. And he said to them, "You yourselves know how unlawful it is for a man who is a Jew to associate with a foreigner or to visit him; and yet God has shown me that I should not call any man unholy or unclean. That is why I came without even raising any objection when I was sent for. And so I ask for what reason you have sent for me." And Cornelius said, "Four days ago to this hour, I was praying in my house during the ninth hour; and behold, a man stood before me in shining garments, and he said, 'Cornelius, your prayer has been heard and your alms have been remembered before God. Send therefore to Joppa and invite Simon, who is also called Peter, to come to you; he is staying at the house of Simon the tanner by the sea.' And so I sent to you immediately, and you have been kind enough to come. Now then, we are all here present before God to hear all that you have been commanded by the Lord." (10:11–33)

Peter and Cornelius model the obedience God demands—both at the point of salvation and throughout the Christian life. The Bible repeatedly teaches that obedience accompanies true faith (cf. Matt. 7:21–23; 21:28–32; Luke 9:23, 57–62; John 8:30–31; 14:15, 21, 23; 15:10, 14; Acts 6:7; Rom. 1:5; 16:26; James 2:14–26; 1 John 2:3–4, 19). (For further discussion of this vital point, see my books *The Gospel According to Jesus*, rev. ed. [Grand Rapids: Zondervan, 1994], and *Faith Works* [Dallas: Word, 1993].)

As had Cornelius, Peter obeyed, though he probably still did not fully understand what was happening. He **went down to the men** (the soldier and two servants sent by Cornelius) **and said, "Behold, I am the one you are looking for; what is the reason for which you have come?"** Their reply, which must have astonished Peter even more, was that **"Cornelius, a centurion, a righteous and God-fearing man well spoken of by the entire nation of the Jews, was divinely directed by a holy angel to send for you to come to his house and hear a message from you."**

It was now Peter's turn to do something astonishing as he **invited** the men **in and gave them lodging.** It was too late for them to return to Caesarea that day, so Peter **invited** them to spend the night there.

Here was a further crack in the barrier dividing Jew and Gentile. No self-respecting Jew would have given lodging to Gentiles—especially to a soldier of the hated Roman occupation army. **Lodging** is from *xenizō,* which means "to entertain as a guest." It is used in Hebrews 13:2 to speak of entertaining angels. Peter gave his unexpected guests the red carpet treatment, showing the work of God in his heart had broken down the typical Jewish prejudice. Because of that, he knew the difference between the Old Testament law, which was binding, and the human tradition, which was not. He had a hard time letting the dietary law go but had no animosity in his heart toward Gentiles, so the hospitality was easy.

On the next day Peter **arose and went away with them, and some of the brethren from Joppa accompanied him.** In obedience to the command he received in his vision, Peter returned with Cornelius's messengers to Caesarea. Although not commanded to do so, he took with him six (Acts 11:12) **of the brethren from Joppa.** This seemingly insignificant decision on Peter's part becomes important later in the story. Since Peter had no divine instruction to do this, it illustrates how God leads believers through their desires (cf. Ps. 37:4).

After spending the night en route, **on the following day** they **entered Caesarea.** Two worlds were about to collide, as seven devout, orthodox Jews were about to meet a houseful of eager Gentiles. A milestone in the history of the church had been reached.

Meanwhile **Cornelius was waiting for them,** and he had not been idle. Eagerly anticipating what Peter had to share with him, he **had called together his relatives and close friends.** When Peter entered his house, **Cornelius met him.** Overwhelmed, Cornelius **fell at his feet and worshiped him.** Peter's immediate, emphatic response should give pause to those advocating worship of the saints. **Peter raised** Cornelius **up, saying, "Stand up; I too am just a man."** In Acts 14:11–15, Paul and Barnabas were similarly horrified when the pagan multitudes at Lystra attempted to worship them. Even angels disavow such misguided worship (Rev. 22:8–9).

When Peter **entered,** he **found many people assembled.** God had not commanded Cornelius to assemble these people, yet their presence was a crucial arrangement of divine providence using the will of Cornelius. If only Cornelius were saved, the Jerusalem church may have considered him an aberration. If a group of Gentiles were saved, however, they would have to accept that God was including Gentiles into the church.

Addressing this group of non-Jews, Peter said to them, **"You yourselves know how unlawful it is for a man who is a Jew to as-**

sociate with a foreigner or to visit him; and yet God has shown me that I should not call any man unholy or unclean. That is why I came without even raising any objection when I was sent for. And so I ask for what reason you have sent for me." Peter begins by telling them that he should not be there, since it is **unlawful for a man who is a Jew to associate with a foreigner or to visit him** (cf. John 4:9; 18:28; Acts 11:2–3; 22:21–22; Gal. 2:12). By that standard Peter had lived his life. God, however, had taught him, and he had accepted that he was no longer to consider Gentiles **unclean. That is why he came without even raising any objection when he was sent for.** He still was not sure why he was present in this house, however, so he asked **for what reason** they **had sent for** him.

Cornelius replied by relating the specifics of his vision: **"Four days ago to this hour, I was praying in my house during the ninth hour; and behold, a man stood before me in shining garments, and he said, 'Cornelius, your prayer has been heard and your alms have been remembered before God. Send therefore to Joppa and invite Simon, who is also called Peter, to come to you; he is staying at the house of Simon the tanner by the sea.' And so I sent to you immediately, and you have been kind enough to come. Now then, we are all here present before God to hear all that you have been commanded by the Lord."** The soldier uses a military term, *prostassō* (**commanded**), referring to a military order. He understood that when the Lord spoke it was a command demanding obedience. He was ready to receive his orders from the Lord.

So Peter and Cornelius both had been sovereignly prepared by God and had responded obediently to His directions. All was ready for Peter's gospel presentation, which would result in the salvation of Cornelius and the others.

SALVATION PRESENTATION

And opening his mouth, Peter said: "I most certainly understand now that God is not one to show partiality, but in every nation the man who fears Him and does what is right, is welcome to Him. The word which He sent to the sons of Israel, preaching peace through Jesus Christ (He is Lord of all)—you yourselves know the thing which took place throughout all Judea, starting from Galilee, after the baptism which John proclaimed. You know of Jesus of Nazareth, how God anointed Him with the Holy Spirit and with power, and how He went about doing good, and healing all who were oppressed by the devil; for God was with Him. And we are witnesses of all the things He did both in the land of the Jews and in Jerusalem. And they also put Him to death by hanging Him on a cross. God raised Him up on the third day, and granted that He should become visible, not to all the people, but to witnesses who were chosen beforehand by God, that is, to us, who ate and drank with Him after He arose from the dead. And He ordered us to preach to the people, and solemnly to testify that this is the One who has been appointed by God as Judge of the living and the dead. Of Him all the prophets bear witness that through His name everyone who believes in Him receives forgiveness of sins." (10:34–43)

In contrast to his indicting sermons on the Day of Pentecost and at Solomon's portico, and his bold defenses before the Sanhedrin, Peter here is led by the Spirit to give a simple gospel presentation. Some situations call for a detailed apologetic and historic presentation before the hearers can understand the gospel message. Others, with divinely plowed hearts, require only the simple truths of the gospel. Cornelius and the other Gentiles gathered with him were such divinely prepared individuals.

The phrase **opening his mouth** is a colloquial Greek expression marking the speech that follows as important. Looking around at his improbable audience, Peter began by shattering what remained of the barrier separating the two groups with his fresh insight: **"I most certainly understand now that God is not one to show partiality, but in every nation the man who fears Him and does what is right, is welcome to Him."** With one stroke, Peter cuts to the heart of the issue and rivets their attention on him.

Saying **I . . . understand** is an admission that this is really new for him, and that only now, at long last, was he beginning to **understand** that the church was to include men from **every nation.** The truth of Jesus' words "I have other sheep, which are not of this fold" (John 10:16) was dawning. The meaning of the vision was clear. Actually, because this was not new truth, Peter and his Jewish companions should have already known that **God is not one to show partiality.** That is clearly taught in the Old Testament (Deut. 10:17; 2 Chron. 19:7; Job 34:19).

Paul elaborated on that truth. To the Romans he wrote, "Is God the God of Jews only? Is He not the God of Gentiles also? Yes, of Gentiles also, since indeed God who will justify the circumcised by faith and the uncircumcised through faith is one" (Rom. 3:29–30; cf. 2:11; Eph. 6:9).

Peter then expanded that thought, explaining that **in every nation the man who fears Him and does what is right is welcome to**

Him. Some have misunderstood this verse to be teaching universalism, that God accepts all who are sincere on the basis of their works. That view is obviously inconsistent with biblical teaching and absurd. If Cornelius and the others were already saved, what was Peter doing there preaching that only through the name of Jesus can souls be saved (v. 43)? Further, that they were not yet saved is clearly stated in Acts 11:14. There are some who would deny that there is any pre-salvation work on the part of the sinner, leading to salvation. This, too, is absurd, since the text clearly states that salvation comes to those who fear God and do what is right. Is this salvation by works? Of course not. Peter is simply expressing the reality that there is a Spirit work in the heart of the sinner (cf. John 16:8–11; Acts 11:18; 2 Tim. 2:25). That work produces a person **who fears** or reverences God **and does what is right,** and who **is welcome** or acceptable (*dektos*) to God. That word means "marked by a favorable manifestation of the divine pleasure," as used in 2 Corinthians 6:2, "'At the acceptable time I listened to you, and on the day of salvation I helped you'; behold, now is 'the acceptable time', behold, now is 'the day of salvation.'" This text shows that the welcome or acceptable time is the time of salvation. No matter what the age, race, sex, or social strata, when the heart hungers for God and for righteousness (Matt. 5:6), it is the welcome time for salvation. Commenting on this verse, Everett Harrison remarks, "The meaning is not that such persons are thereby saved (cf. Acts 11:14) but rather that they are suitable candidates for salvation. Such preparation betokens a spiritual earnestness that will result in faith as the gospel is heard and received (*Interpreting Acts: The Expanding Church* [Grand Rapids: Zondervan, 1986], 182).

Cornelius responded to the work of God in his soul, yet it must not be thought that he did that on his own, apart from the grace of God. The truth is that no one, whether Gentile (cf. Rom. 1:18ff.) or Jew (cf. Rom. 2:1ff.) does that (Rom. 3:10–18). God had worked in Cornelius's heart so that he sought to know and obey God, and when he heard the saving truth of the gospel, he eagerly responded.

Peter introduced his message by assuring them that salvation was available to the prepared heart. Yet it was not enough for them merely to know of its availability; they needed to know how to appropriate the forgiveness of sin and deliverance from judgment. Peter turns, then, to the main theme of the gospel, namely that salvation comes through Jesus Christ to anyone from any nation. In the words of the hymn "The Church's One Foundation," the church is

> Elect from ev'ry nation,
> Yet one o'er all the earth.

The **word** of God containing the message of salvation came first **to the sons of Israel** (cf. Rom. 1:16). It was the glorious message of **peace through Jesus Christ.** All people are fallen and are enemies who are at war with God (cf. Rom. 5:10). The sacrificial death of the Lord Jesus Christ ended that hostility and brought peace between man and God by paying the price for sin. In the words of the apostle Paul, "God was in Christ reconciling the world to Himself, not counting their trespasses against them" (2 Cor. 5:19), and has "made peace through the blood of His cross" (Col. 1:20). Salvation is offered to all because Jesus **is Lord of all.**

As already noted, Caesarea was the seat of the Roman government in Judea. Consequently, Peter can affirm to Cornelius and the others that **you yourselves know the thing which took place throughout all Judea, starting from Galilee, after the baptism which John proclaimed.** They were aware **of Jesus of Nazareth, how God anointed Him with the Holy Spirit and with power, and how He went about doing good, and healing all who were oppressed by the devil; for God was with Him.**

The **baptism which John proclaimed** was a baptism signifying an attitude of repentance and longing for the reign of righteousness. It prepared the nation for the Messiah, who was **Jesus of Nazareth.** As He began His ministry, **God anointed Him with the Holy Spirit and with power** (cf. Matt. 3:13–17; Luke 3:21–22). Peter describes that ministry as going **about doing good,** then lists as an example His **healing** of **all who were oppressed by the devil.** That phrase encompasses the whole gamut of human ailments, from direct demon oppression to disease to spiritual darkness. "The Son of God," wrote the apostle John, "appeared for this purpose, that He might destroy the works of the devil" (1 John 3:8). Jesus Christ's complete overpowering of Satan and his demons left no doubt that **God was with Him.**

All they had heard about Jesus' ministry was true, Peter affirms. He adds the apostolic corroboration that **we are witnesses of all the things He did both in the land of the Jews and in Jerusalem,** and then comes quickly to the significant event saying, **And they also put Him to death by hanging Him on a cross. God raised Him up on the third day, and granted that He should become visible, not to all the people, but to witnesses who were chosen beforehand by God, that is, to us, who ate and drank with Him after He arose from the dead.** That religious men would lead the effort to **put to death** the One who went about doing good and overruling the work of Satan illustrates the depths of human depravity—even when it is masked with religion. **God,** however, overturned the world and hell, vindicating Jesus by raising **Him up on the third day.**

The significance of Peter's statement that Jesus became visible should not be overlooked. Countless heretics, from apostolic times to the present, have denied the truth of Christ's physical resurrection. That fact is central to Christianity, however. Paul points out in 1 Corinthians 15:12–19 the serious consequences of denying the resurrection. If "Christ has not been raised, [our] faith is worthless; [we] are still in [our] sins" (1 Cor. 15:17). Those who deny Christ's literal resurrection destroy the only bridge spanning the gulf separating them from God. For the record, Paul has left us the inspired fact that the risen Jesus appeared to Peter, then the Twelve, more than 500 believers at one time, then to James, all the apostles, and finally to himself (1 Cor. 15:5–8).

Not everyone had the privilege of witnessing the resurrected Christ, however. He appeared, Peter declares, **not to all the people, but to witnesses who were chosen beforehand by God, that is, to us, who ate and drank with Him after He arose from the dead.** God chose only a few to bear testimony to the world that Jesus Christ had risen from the dead, and all of them were believers. Peter's reference to those **who ate and drank with Him after He arose from the dead** offers further proof of His bodily resurrection, since in Jewish thought spirit beings were incapable of such actions.

Verse 42 relates the warning that was essential to the apostolic witness. They were **ordered** (commanded) **to preach to the people, and solemnly to testify that this is the One who has been appointed by God as Judge of the living and the dead** (cf. John 5:21–29; Acts 17:30–31; 2 Thess. 1:7–10; 2 Tim. 4:8; Rev. 19:11ff.). Jesus Christ will be to every person either deliverer or judge.

The apostles were not the only witnesses of Jesus Christ; so also were the **prophets.** They bore **witness that through His name** (by His power and authority) **everyone who believes in Him receives forgiveness of sins.** Isaiah (Isa. 53:11), Jeremiah (Jer. 31:34), and Zechariah (Zech. 13:1) were among those who spoke of the forgiveness Messiah would bring. All that Jesus is and did is the culmination of divine promises made centuries earlier. The last recorded line of Peter's message, **everyone who believes in Him receives forgiveness of sins,** is essential. Every component is critical to the gospel. **Everyone** indicates the universal offer of saving grace (cf. Acts 2:39; 13:39; Rom. 9:33; 10:11; 1 Tim. 2:4; 2 Peter 3:9; Rev. 22:17). **Who believes in Him** indicates the means of receiving saving grace—by faith in Christ alone (Acts 9:42; 11:17; 13:39; 14:23; 15:9; 16:31; 19:4; cf. John 3:14–17; 6:69; Rom. 10:11; Gal. 3:22; Eph. 2:8–9). **Receives forgiveness of sins** indicates the marvelous, unspeakable privilege conferred by saving grace (Acts 2:38; 13:38–39; cf. Matt. 26:28; Eph. 1:7; Col. 1:14).

SPIRITUAL POWER

While Peter was still speaking these words, the Holy Spirit fell upon all those who were listening to the message. And all the circumcised believers who had come with Peter were amazed, because the gift of the Holy Spirit had been poured out upon the Gentiles also. For they were hearing them speaking with tongues and exalting God. (10:44–46a)

While Peter was still speaking these words his sermon was suddenly and dramatically interrupted. Without the text saying so, it is apparent that when Cornelius and the other Gentiles heard that forgiveness was available through Jesus Christ (v. 43), they believed. In immediate response to their faith, **the Holy Spirit fell upon all those who were listening to the message.** Saving faith results in the indwelling of the Holy Spirit (cf. Rom. 8:9; 1 Cor. 12:13), and to be "devoid of the Spirit" characterizes unbelievers (Jude 19). It is true that the Spirit's coming was delayed for the Samaritans. Although they were saved through Philip's preaching, they had to wait until the arrival of Peter and John. As noted in the discussion of Acts 8:14–19 in chapter 19, however, that was to emphasize the unity of Samaritans and Jews in the church. No such delay was needed here, since the apostle Peter was already present.

Acts 8 does not establish the norm for receiving the Spirit. If believers were always to be saved and then later to receive the Spirit, why did Cornelius and the others receive the Spirit the moment they were saved? The view of some that they were already saved and merely received the Spirit here runs afoul of 11:14. Further, if they were already saved and this were simply the occasion of their receiving the Spirit, why did Peter preach the gospel? Why did he not instead give them teaching on how to receive the Spirit? The Spirit's coming required no petition, no confession, no water baptism, and no laying on of hands. He came as they listened and believed. That is clear from Peter's inspired testimony in Acts 11:17 that God had given them the Holy Spirit, "after believing in the Lord Jesus Christ."

There can be no such thing as a Christian without the Holy Spirit, since He is essential to the Christian life. The Holy Spirit grants power to witness (Acts 1:8) and pray (Rom. 8:26). Through His ministry comes assurance of salvation (Rom. 8:16), since by Him believers are "sealed for the day of redemption" (Eph. 4:30; cf. Eph. 1:13). He is the "pledge of our inheritance" (Eph. 1:14) and also our teacher (1 John 2:27).

Peter was no doubt startled by what happened, though he had previously seen the same reality with the Samaritans. But **all the cir-**

cumcised believers who had come with Peter were amazed, because the gift of the Holy Spirit had been poured out upon the
Gentiles also. For they were hearing them speaking with tongues
and exalting God. These six brethren Peter brought with him from Joppa were astonished that the Gentiles were saved and received the Spirit.
That the church was not to be exclusively Jewish must have come as
quite a shock to them. Yet they could hardly deny what was happening,
since they were **hearing** the Gentiles **speaking with tongues and exalting God.**

This passage does not teach that speaking in tongues is normally to be expected with the coming of the Spirit. The Spirit granted it on
this occasion as visible proof that He indwelt these Gentiles. He knew
that the Jewish brethren with Peter would be hard to convince, so He
granted the same manifestation experienced by Jewish Christians at
Pentecost. It should be noted that here, as throughout Acts, speaking in
tongues is a group, not an individual, phenomenon. (For a discussion
of speaking in tongues, see chapter 3 of this commentary, my book
Charismatic Chaos [Grand Rapids: Zondervan, 1992], and *1 Corinthians,* MacArthur New Testament Commentary [Chicago: Moody, 1984].)

Symbolic Confession

**Then Peter answered, "Surely no one can refuse the water for
these to be baptized who have received the Holy Spirit just as we
did, can he?" And he ordered them to be baptized in the name of
Jesus Christ.** (10:46b–48a)

Here, as always in the New Testament, baptism follows salvation. Indeed, Peter's entire argument for baptizing Cornelius and the
others rests on the fact that they had **received the Holy Spirit,** and
therefore were saved. Baptism thus plays no part in salvation. Through
it, believers publicly confess in symbolic fashion the inner transformation of salvation. Rather than do it himself, Peter wisely **ordered them
to be baptized in the name of Jesus Christ** by the Jewish Christians
who accompanied him. He thus involved the Jews in this momentous
reality, knowing they would then be even more willing to support it. Peter could anticipate the reaction when he reported back to Jerusalem,
and wanted all the support he could muster.

Sweet Fellowship

Then they asked him to stay on for a few days. (10:48b)

Since the joy of fellowship with those of like precious faith, and the opportunity to learn from the noble apostle all they could about their Lord and salvation was so precious, Cornelius and his fellow converts **asked** Peter **to stay on for a few days.** The desire for Christian fellowship and learning they expressed is a mark of genuine saving faith. Lydia (Acts 16:15) expressed a similar desire after her conversion.

This epochal chapter has witnessed the inclusion of Gentiles as equals in the church. The last barrier has fallen. Peter later described this great experience in Acts 15:7–8: "Brethren, you know that in the early days God made a choice among you, that by my mouth the Gentiles should hear the word of the gospel and believe. And God, who knows the heart, bore witness to them, giving them the Holy Spirit, just as He also did to us." The way was thus opened for the spread of Christianity throughout the Roman world through the tireless missionary efforts of the early church.

The
Gentile
Church

24

Now the apostles and the brethren who were throughout Judea heard that the Gentiles also had received the word of God. And when Peter came up to Jerusalem, those who were circumcised took issue with him, saying, "You went to uncircumcised men and ate with them." But Peter began speaking and proceeded to explain to them in orderly sequence, saying, "I was in the city of Joppa praying; and in a trance I saw a vision, a certain object coming down like a great sheet lowered by four corners from the sky; and it came right down to me, and when I had fixed my gaze upon it and was observing it I saw the four-footed animals of the earth and the wild beasts and the crawling creatures and the birds of the air. And I also heard a voice saying to me, 'Arise, Peter; kill and eat.' But I said, 'By no means, Lord, for nothing unholy or unclean has ever entered my mouth.' But a voice from heaven answered a second time, 'What God has cleansed, no longer consider unholy.' And this happened three times, and everything was drawn back up into the sky. And behold, at that moment three men appeared before the house in which we were staying, having been sent to me from Caesarea. And the Spirit told me to go with them without misgivings. And these six brethren also went with me, and we entered the man's house. And he reported to us how he had seen the angel standing in his house, and saying, 'Send to Joppa, and have Simon, who is also called Peter, brought here; and he shall speak words to you by which you will be saved, you and all your household.' And as I began to speak, the Holy Spirit fell upon them, just as He did upon us at the beginning. And I remembered the word of the Lord, how He used to say, 'John baptized with water, but you shall be baptized with the Holy Spirit.' If God therefore gave to them the same gift as He gave to us also after believing in the Lord Jesus Christ, who was I that I could stand in God's way?" And when they heard this, they quieted down, and glorified God, saying, "Well then, God has granted to the Gentiles also the repentance that leads to life." So then those who were scattered because of the persecution that arose in connection with Stephen made their way to Phoenicia and Cyprus and Antioch, speaking the word to no one except to Jews alone. But there were some of them, men of Cyprus and Cyrene, who came to Antioch and began speaking to the Greeks also, preaching the Lord Jesus. And the hand of the Lord was with them, and a large number who believed turned to the Lord. And the news about them reached the ears of the church at Jerusalem, and they sent Barnabas off to Antioch. Then when he had come and witnessed the grace of God, he rejoiced and began to encourage them all with resolute heart to remain true to the Lord; for he was a good man, and full of the Holy Spirit and of faith. And considerable numbers were brought to the Lord. And he left for Tarsus to look for Saul; and when he had found him, he brought him to Antioch. And it came about that for an entire year they met with the church, and taught considerable numbers; and the disciples were first called Christians in Antioch. Now at this time some prophets came down from Jerusalem to Antioch. And one of them named Agabus stood up and began to indicate by the Spirit that there would certainly be a great famine all over the world. And this took place in the reign of Claudius. And in the proportion that any of the disciples had means, each of them determined to send a contribution for the relief of the brethren living in Judea. And this they did, sending it in charge of Barnabas and Saul to the elders. (11:1–30)

The news that the hated Gentiles were included in the church reached Jerusalem before Peter did, since he remained in Caesarea for a few days (Acts 10:48). That news sent shock waves through the Hebrew Christian community. So significant was it that Luke, moved by the inspiring Holy Spirit, repeats the account of their conversion in this chapter as well.

That unusual repetition marks the event as one of unique significance. Christianity was not to become merely another sect of Judaism. Had that happened, the Lord Jesus Christ's great commission (Matt. 28:19–20) would never have been carried out. Unlike Israel before her, the church would not fail to channel the blessings of God's grace and forgiveness to the world.

The church's outreach to the Gentiles was thus a crucial step in the outworking of God's redemptive plan. That outreach, which began with Peter's ministry to Cornelius and his household, now continues with the founding of the first Gentile church. Having moved from Jerusalem to Judea to Samaria, the gospel was about to take its final, yet still ongoing, step to the "remotest part of the earth" (Acts 1:8).

The founding of this first Gentile congregation unfolds in four stages: the groundwork, the genesis, the growth, and the generosity.

THE GROUNDWORK

Now the apostles and the brethren who were throughout Judea heard that the Gentiles also had received the word of God. And when Peter came up to Jerusalem, those who were circumcised took issue with him, saying, "You went to uncircumcised men and ate with them." But Peter began speaking and proceeded to explain to them in orderly sequence, saying, "I was in the city of Joppa praying; and in a trance I saw a vision, a certain object coming down like a great sheet lowered by four corners from the sky; and it came right down to me, and when I had fixed my gaze upon it and was observing it I saw the four-footed animals of the earth and the wild beasts and the crawling creatures and the birds of the air. And I also heard a voice saying to me, 'Arise, Peter; kill and eat.' But I said, 'By no means, Lord, for nothing unholy or unclean has ever entered my mouth.' But a voice from heaven answered a second time, 'What God has cleansed, no longer consider unholy.' And this happened three times, and everything was drawn back up into the sky. And behold, at that moment three men appeared before the house in which we were staying, having been sent to me from Caesarea. And the Spirit told me to go with them without misgivings. And these six brethren also went with me, and we entered the man's house. And he reported to us how he had seen the angel standing in his house, and saying, 'Send to Joppa, and have Simon, who is also called Peter, brought here; and he shall speak words to you by which

you will be saved, you and all your household.' And as I began to speak, the Holy Spirit fell upon them, just as He did upon us at the beginning. And I remembered the word of the Lord, how He used to say, 'John baptized with water, but you shall be baptized with the Holy Spirit.' If God therefore gave to them the same gift as He gave to us also after believing in the Lord Jesus Christ, who was I that I could stand in God's way?" And when they heard this, they quieted down, and glorified God, saying, "Well then, God has granted to the Gentiles also the repentance that leads to life." (11:1–18)

While Peter was still ministering in Caesarea, word of the remarkable events that had taken place reached the Jerusalem fellowship. Luke informs us that the rest of **the apostles and the brethren who were throughout Judea heard that the Gentiles also had received the word of God.** Consequently **when Peter came up to Jerusalem, those who were circumcised took issue with him, saying, "You went to uncircumcised men and ate with them."** The phrase **those who were circumcised** appears to describe the believing Jews who made up the Jerusalem fellowship (cf. Acts 10:45). Startled by the obvious social implications, many no doubt held that if Gentiles were really to live as Christians, they would first have to become Jewish proselytes (cf. Acts 15:5). Many were still zealous for the law and Jewish customs. The temple was their main meeting place. Not surprisingly, they **took issue with** Peter, **saying** indignantly, **"You went to uncircumcised men and ate with them."** Even though they were believers in Jesus Christ, such an obvious breach of Jewish custom outraged them. Acknowledging that Jesus was their Messiah and Lord was one thing, accepting that He was equally the Lord of Gentiles another.

Instead of entering into a heated rebuke of their prejudice, Peter simply recounted the remarkable events leading to the Gentile's conversion (Acts 10:1–48). He **began speaking and proceeded to explain to them in orderly sequence, saying, "I was in the city of Joppa praying; and in a trance I saw a vision, a certain object coming down like a great sheet lowered by four corners from the sky; and it came right down to me, and when I had fixed my gaze upon it and was observing it I saw the four-footed animals of the earth and the wild beasts and the crawling creatures and the birds of the air. And I also heard a voice saying to me, 'Arise, Peter; kill and eat.' But I said, 'By no means, Lord, for nothing unholy or unclean has ever entered my mouth.' But a voice from heaven answered a second time, 'What God has cleansed, no longer consider unholy.' And this happened three times, and everything was drawn back up into the sky. And behold, at that** moment three men appeared before the house in which we were staying, having been sent to me from Caesarea. And the Spirit told me to go with them without misgivings. And these six brethren also went with me, and we entered the man's house. And he reported to us how he had seen the angel standing in his house, and saying, 'Send to Joppa, and have Simon, who is also called Peter, brought here; and he shall speak words to you by which you will be saved, you and all your household.' And as I began to speak, the Holy Spirit fell upon them, just as He did upon us at the beginning. And I remembered the word of the Lord, how He used to say, 'John baptized with water, but you shall be baptized with the Holy Spirit.'"

He then wrapped up his reiteration and summary (v. 17) with the pointed observation that **"if God therefore gave to them the same gift as He gave to us also after believing in the Lord Jesus Christ, who was I that I could stand in God's way?"** Who wants to argue with what the Lord has done? It was unarguably God saving the Gentiles, as evidenced by the coming of the Holy Spirit with the very same attendant phenomena as at Pentecost. In his recounting of the events, they should have noted two more key points. First, he did not act alone but took with him **six brethren** from the Joppa church. Their testimony, added to his, made the case even more convincing. Second, what happened at Cornelius's house squared with Scripture. Peter reminded his accusers of **the word of the Lord, how He used to say, "John baptized with water, but you shall be baptized with the Holy Spirit."** The Scripture was being fulfilled, just as the greatest prophet of all had said (cf. Acts 1:5). Miraculous phenomena signaling the arrival of the Holy Spirit, corroborating testimony by unsympathetic but trustworthy witnesses, and the promise of Scripture spoken by the Lord Himself was enough evidence to squelch the protests.

When Peter's accusers **heard this, they quieted down.** They could hardly argue with the Holy Spirit, the testimony of seven witnesses, or the Scriptures. That they would come to the admission that **God** had **granted to the Gentiles also the repentance that leads to life** was one of the most shocking admissions in the annals of Jewish history. For until the Hebrew Christians came to that realization, they would never begin the task of evangelizing the Gentiles.

This was the beginning of the divine effort to lay the groundwork for the first Gentile church. At least seven years elapsed from Pentecost until the founding of that church at Antioch. There were several reasons for that delay. First, apostolic authority had to be established. It took time for the believers to become grounded in the apostles' teaching (cf. Acts 2:42) and for the development of leaders. During those seven years, the apostles laid the doctrinal foundation for the church. Second, individual believers needed to be brought to a sufficient level of maturity before they could be sent out. Immature believers would not make effective missionaries. Third, it took time to tear down the long-established walls of prejudice. That was starting to be achieved (cf. Gal. 2:11–14), so the time was right to give birth to the church in a Gentile land and to move to the last phase of our Lord's plan for evangelism—"to the remotest part of the earth" (Acts 1:8).

THE GENESIS

So then those who were scattered because of the persecution that arose in connection with Stephen made their way to Phoenicia and Cyprus and Antioch, speaking the word to no one except to Jews alone. But there were some of them, men of Cyprus and Cyrene, who came to Antioch and began speaking to the Greeks also, preaching the Lord Jesus. And the hand of the Lord was with them, and a large number who believed turned to the Lord. (11:19–21)

This passage picks up where 8:4 left off, discussing the effect of **the persecution that arose in connection with Stephen.** That persecution, led by Saul of Tarsus, **scattered** the Jerusalem fellowship all over. While some went to Samaria (8:5, 25) and Caesarea (8:40; 10:24ff.), Damascus (9:10), Lydda, Joppa, and Sharon (9:35–36), at the same time in the far north a church was being planted among Gentiles. Some of the displaced Jews **made their way to Phoenicia and Cyprus and Antioch. Phoenicia** was the coastal region immediately north of Judea, where the cities of Tyre and Sidon were located. From there they could take ship for the major island of **Cyprus,** some sixty miles offshore. They could also continue up the coast to **Antioch,** approximately 200 miles north of Sidon.

Wherever they went, the refugees from Jerusalem were **speaking the word to no one except to Jews alone.** They could not have known that the gospel had spread to the Gentiles, since they fled Jerusalem before that happened. Lacking knowledge of that precedent, they still assumed the gospel was for the Jewish people alone.

Eventually, however, that mold for the church was broken. **Some of them** (Hellenists), **men of Cyprus and Cyrene, came to Antioch and began speaking to the Greeks also, preaching the Lord Jesus.** Being Greek-speaking Jews, from predominantly Gentile areas, they were more open to preaching to Gentiles than the native Palestinian Jews. Through their efforts, the first Gentile church was born.

Antioch was a major ancient metropolis. It was the third largest in the Empire, behind only Rome and Alexandria. **Antioch** was noted for its culture and commerce since many Roman trade routes passed through it. The Roman author Cicero described it as a place of learned men and liberal studies. It was also a vile place, full of pagan worship and sexual immorality. When the Roman satirist Juvenal wanted to aim a barb at Rome, he wrote that the Orontes River (near Antioch) emptied its garbage into the Tiber River (near Rome). The debauched prostitution of the temple of Daphne was only five miles away.

That the Hellenists were **preaching the Lord Jesus,** the facts of His life, death, and resurrection, as Peter had to Cornelius and his household, seems obvious. To have presented Him as the Jewish Messiah would have had little meaning to predominantly Gentile audiences.

In the Old Testament the phrase **the hand of the Lord** meant two things. First, it spoke of God's power expressed in judgment (cf. Ex. 9:33; Deut. 2:15; Josh. 4:24; 1 Sam. 5:6; 7:13). It also referred to God's power expressed in blessing (Ezra 7:9; 8:18; Neh. 2:8, 18). In this case it was related to God's blessing, so that **a large number who believed turned to the Lord.** Again, as in almost all places where Jesus Christ was being preached, the response was great (cf. Acts 2:47; 4:4; 5:14; 6:1, 7; 9:31, 35, 42; 11:24; 14:1, 21; 16:5; 17:12). People not only **believed** intellectually but also **turned** from their sins **to the Lord** (cf. 1 Thess. 1:9). As always, believing is inseparable from repentance manifested in a changed life.

THE GROWTH

And the news about them reached the ears of the church at Jerusalem, and they sent Barnabas off to Antioch. Then when he had come and witnessed the grace of God, he rejoiced and began to encourage them all with resolute heart to remain true to the Lord; for he was a good man, and full of the Holy Spirit and of faith. And considerable numbers were brought to the Lord. And he left for Tarsus to look for Saul; and when he had found him, he brought him to Antioch. And it came about that for an entire year they met with the church, and taught considerable numbers; and the disciples were first called Christians in Antioch. (11:22–26)

Neither the salvation of the Ethiopian eunuch nor that of Cornelius and his household prepared the Jerusalem believers for the widespread Gentile conversions in Antioch. When **the news about them reached the ears of the church at Jerusalem,** they decided to send a representative to investigate. Accordingly, **they sent Barnabas off to Antioch.** Barnabas first appeared in chapter 4, when he sold some property to meet the needs of other believers. Through his influence, Paul was finally accepted by the Jerusalem church (Acts 9:27). He was a leading teacher in the church and a loving, gentle, generous man, in keeping with his name, which means "son of encouragement."

The choice of a representative was crucial. Sending a rigidly legalistic individual could have spelled disaster. Barnabas, however, had the qualifications needed for the job. Verse 24 further describes him as **a good man, and full of the Holy Spirit and of faith.** He possessed the necessary spiritual qualities for one who was to discern what was happening.

Barnabas was also the right man to send because, like some of the founders of the Antioch church, he was a Cypriot Jew (4:36–37). He would not be perceived as an outsider but as one of them.

The grace of God may be invisible, but its effects are readily seen. When Barnabas arrived in Antioch and **witnessed the grace of God** by which they were saved, **he rejoiced.** Other Jews may have been upset at the conversion of Gentiles, but not Barnabas. To see lost Gentile souls added to the kingdom brought him immeasurable joy.

He then **began to encourage them all with resolute heart** determination **to remain true to the Lord.** That exhortation reflects the concern that every pastor feels for new converts, that they continue in the faith. In Acts 13:43, Paul and Barnabas exhorted new believers to "continue in the grace of God." In 14:22, they exhorted the Christians of Lystra, Iconium, and Antioch to "continue in the faith." The only way **to remain true to the Lord** is to continue in His Word, where He reveals Himself to the believer. The apostle John wrote, "Let that abide in you which you heard from the beginning. If what you heard from the beginning abides in you, you also will abide in the Son and in the Father" (1 John 2:24). "If you abide in My word," Jesus said, "then you are truly disciples of Mine" (John 8:31). It is through the Word that the Holy Spirit, the resident truth teacher (1 John 2:27), instructs believers.

Again, Luke chronicles the progress of the ever-expanding church by updating its growth. Through the ongoing ministry in Antioch, **considerable numbers were brought to the Lord.** The harvest was too vast for Barnabas to handle alone, so he went for help. He immediately thought of the best possible man for the job, so **he left for Tarsus to look for Saul.** Finding him was no easy task, however. Several years had passed since Saul fled Jerusalem for his home in Tarsus (Acts 9:30). He had apparently been disinherited for his Christian beliefs (Phil. 3:8) and forced to move from his home. *Anazēteō* (**to look for**) suggests a laborious search on Barnabas's part. The Greek lexicographers Moulton and Milligan said *anazēteō* is used "specially of searching for human beings with an implication of difficulty" (cited in G. Abbott-Smith, *A Manual Greek Lexicon of the New Testament* [Edinburgh: T. & T. Clark, 1977], 29).

Eventually, Barnabas caught up with Saul, **and when he had found him, he brought him to Antioch.** These two gifted men formed a powerful ministry team. They faced the daunting task of shepherding a large number of new believers in a hostile pagan environment. Their solution was **for an entire year** to meet **with the church,** during which time **they taught considerable numbers.** Unlike many in today's church, they knew the most urgent need of those new Christians was to be taught the Word of God. In mass meetings of the Antioch believers, Barnabas and Saul did just that.

Their example is an important one for the contemporary church to follow. Teaching the Word of God is at the heart of the church's ministry. The apostles in Acts 6 made clear that teaching the Word is the highest priority of church leaders. Barnabas and Saul did their job well. The leaders of the church at Antioch mentioned in chapter 13 were probably their disciples.

Luke then adds the historical footnote that **the disciples were first called Christians in Antioch.** The term means "of the party of Christ" and was used in derision. Peter encouraged those who suffered "as a Christian," to "not feel ashamed, but in that name [to] glorify God" (1 Peter 4:16). What was a term of derision, though, soon became a badge of honor to the early church. The historian Eusebius relates the account of the martyr Sanctus, who replied to all his torturers' questions simply, "I am a Christian" (*Ecclesiastical History* V, I [Grand Rapids: Baker, 1973], 172).

THE GENEROSITY

Now at this time some prophets came down from Jerusalem to Antioch. And one of them named Agabus stood up and began to indicate by the Spirit that there would certainly be a great famine all over the world. And this took place in the reign of Claudius. And in the proportion that any of the disciples had means, each of them determined to send a contribution for the relief of the brethren living in Judea. And this they did, sending it in charge of Barnabas and Saul to the elders. (11:27–32)

The first Gentile church was not only sound in doctrine but also strong in love. **At this time some prophets came down from Jerusalem to Antioch** bearing disturbing news. The term **prophet** refers not to an Old Testament figure such as Isaiah or John the Baptist but to the preachers of the New Testament (cf. 1 Cor. 14:32; Eph. 2:20). **One of them named Agabus stood up and began to indicate by the Spirit that there would certainly be a great famine all over the world.** Like the apostles, the prophets were not a permanent order. Having fulfilled their foundational purpose, they gradually faded from the scene, to be replaced by the evangelists and pastor-teachers (Eph. 4:11).

The prophecy of Agabus came to pass **in the reign of Claudius** (A.D. 41–54). The years A.D. 45–46 saw great famines in Israel. Several ancient writers attest to that fact, including Tacitus (*Annals* XI.43), Josephus (*Antiquities* XX.ii.5), and Suetonius (*Claudius* 18).

The response of the Antioch church to the request for money to help the Judean believers was immediate. **In the proportion that any of the disciples had means, each of them determined to send a contribution for the relief of the brethren living in Judea.** Determined to help the mother church in Jerusalem, the Christians at Antioch collected relief supplies for them. Much like the generosity of the church in Jerusalem (Acts 4:34–35) was this expression of love by their Gentile brothers. Each gave **in proportion** to his **means,** and the church sent the contribution back to Jerusalem **in charge** of their two best men—**Barnabas and Saul.** Their return to Jerusalem is noted in Acts 12:25.

The final stage in the Lord's command recorded in Acts 1:8 had been reached. The church, originally Jewish, had expanded from Jerusalem and Judea to Samaria and to the Gentiles in the remotest part of the earth. The church at Antioch, begun in this chapter, was to play a leading role for several centuries. But of all its honors, one stands out: it was the church that the apostle Paul pastored and from which he was called by the Spirit to launch his missionary journeys (Acts 13:1ff.).

The Folly
of Fighting God

25

Now about that time Herod the king laid hands on some who belonged to the church, in order to mistreat them. And he had James the brother of John put to death with a sword. And when he saw that it pleased the Jews, he proceeded to arrest Peter also. Now it was during the days of Unleavened Bread. And when he had seized him, he put him in prison, delivering him to four squads of soldiers to guard him, intending after the Passover to bring him out before the people. So Peter was kept in the prison, but prayer for him was being made fervently by the church to God. And on the very night when Herod was about to bring him forward, Peter was sleeping between two soldiers, bound with two chains; and guards in front of the door were watching over the prison. And behold, an angel of the Lord suddenly appeared, and a light shone in the cell; and he struck Peter's side and roused him, saying, "Get up quickly." And his chains fell off his hands. And the angel said to him, "Gird yourself and put on your sandals." And he did so. And he said to him, "Wrap your cloak around you and follow me." And he went out and continued to follow, and he did not know that what was being done by the angel was real, but thought he was seeing a vision. And when they

had passed the first and second guard, they came to the iron gate
that leads into the city, which opened for them by itself; and they
went out and went along one street; and immediately the angel
departed from him. And when Peter came to himself, he said,
"Now I know for sure that the Lord has sent forth His angel and
rescued me from the hand of Herod and from all that the Jewish
people were expecting." And when he realized this, he went to
the house of Mary, the mother of John who was also called Mark,
where many were gathered together and were praying. And
when he knocked at the door of the gate, a servant-girl named
Rhoda came to answer. And when she recognized Peter's voice,
because of her joy she did not open the gate, but ran in and announced that Peter was standing in front of the gate. And they
said to her, "You are out of your mind!" But she kept insisting
that it was so. And they kept saying, "It is his angel." But Peter
continued knocking; and when they had opened the door, they
saw him and were amazed. But motioning to them with his hand
to be silent, he described to them how the Lord had led him out
of the prison. And he said, "Report these things to James and the
brethren." And he departed and went to another place. Now
when day came, there was no small disturbance among the soldiers as to what could have become of Peter. And when Herod
had searched for him and had not found him, he examined the
guards and ordered that they be led away to execution. And he
went down from Judea to Caesarea and was spending time
there. Now he was very angry with the people of Tyre and Sidon;
and with one accord they came to him, and having won over
Blastus the king's chamberlain, they were asking for peace, because their country was fed by the king's country. And on an appointed day Herod, having put on his royal apparel, took his seat
on the rostrum and began delivering an address to them. And the
people kept crying out, "The voice of a god and not of a man!"
And immediately an angel of the Lord struck him because he did
not give God the glory, and he was eaten by worms and died. But
the word of the Lord continued to grow and to be multiplied. And
Barnabas and Saul returned from Jerusalem when they had fulfilled their mission, taking along with them John, who was also
called Mark. (12:1–25)

Throughout the universe, war rages on every front. God, the holy
angels, and elect men battle Satan, his demonic hosts, and fallen men.
Although the outcome of the war has never been in doubt, the battles
are no less real.

The war began on the angelic level when Lucifer, highest of all created beings, rebelled against his Creator. Lucifer, more commonly known as Satan ("adversary"), was cast from heaven, taking with him one-third of the angels (Rev. 12:4). From that moment until the present, war has raged between Satan and God, engulfing angels and men.

On the human front, the battle began when Adam and Eve rebelled against God in Eden. When they sampled the forbidden fruit (at the instigation of Satan) the war of the ages spread to the human realm. Through the centuries since then, men have shaken their fists in defiance at God. And though the folly of fighting Him is self-evident, that does not stop each succeeding generation from trying. They pit their impotence against His omnipotence, shattering themselves like raw eggs thrown against granite.

Solomon well expressed the hopelessness of fighting God when he wrote, "There is no wisdom and no understanding and no counsel against the Lord" (Prov. 21:30). Though sinful men often hail those who fight against God as wise, in reality they are fools. True wisdom lies in being on God's side.

History is strewn with the wreckage of the broken lives of those foolish enough to fight God. The nineteenth-century German philosopher Friedrich Nietzsche despised Christianity as the religion of weaklings. Fighting God eventually pushed him over the brink, and he spent the last several years of his life insane.

Novelist Sinclair Lewis, winner of the 1930 Nobel Prize for literature, also thought he could fight God. His novel *Elmer Gantry* mocked Christianity. Its leading character was an evangelist who was also an alcoholic and an unceasing fornicator. Lewis's fight against God cost him his sobriety, and he died a hopeless alcoholic in a clinic near Rome.

Another Nobel-Prize-winning author, Ernest Hemingway, considered himself living proof that one could successfully fight God. He boasted of fighting in revolutions, tumbling women, and leading a life of sin without apparent consequences. His sins eventually found him out, however, and he put a shotgun to his head and killed himself. Fighting God cost him his life.

In biblical times, just as in our own, there were those who tried vainly to battle God. Many of them were kings or other rulers, whose immense earthly power deceived them into thinking they could successfully oppose heaven. In reality, they and their kingdoms "are like a drop from a bucket, and are regarded as a speck of dust on the scales; behold, He lifts up the islands like fine dust. All the nations are as nothing before Him, they are regarded by Him as less than nothing and meaningless" (Isa. 40:15, 17).

One of the first in the long line of rulers who fought God was the pharaoh who ruled Egypt at the time of the Exodus. Fighting God cost him and his people dearly as horrible plagues, culminating in the death of every firstborn Egyptian male, lashed their land. Still Pharaoh fought on, until his army drowned in the Red Sea. The Canaanite king of Arad's part in the war against God resulted in the destruction of his people and their cities (Num. 21:1–3). Sihon of the Amorites (Num. 21:21–31) and Og of Bashan (Num. 21:33–35) suffered similar fates. Balak, king of Moab, was clever enough to avoid a direct frontal assault. Instead he used that prophet-for-hire Balaam in an attempt to curse Israel (Num. 22–24). Balak's strategy backfired, however, as God intervened and had Balaam bless Israel instead. The king of Ai fought God and was hanged for his trouble (Josh. 8:29). The thirty-one Canaanite kings listed in Joshua 12:7–24 suffered similar defeats. Sennacherib, proud leader of the feared and powerful Assyrian army, saw that army decimated in battle against God (2 Kings 19:35). Soon afterward, he himself was dead, murdered by two of his own sons (Isa. 37:38).

Sadly, even many leaders of God's own people fought Him. Every one of the kings of Israel, and many of those of Judah, opposed God. The result was the destruction of the northern kingdom by Assyria and the southern kingdom by Babylon. God does not tolerate rebellion even among the ranks of His own people.

In the New Testament era one family of rulers stands out in the battle against God: the Herods. The patriarch of the family was known in all modesty as Herod the Great. He ruled Judea from 47 B.C. to 37 B.C. Then, having been dubbed "King of the Jews" by Antony, Octavius, and the Roman Senate, he ruled all of Palestine from 37 B.C. until his death shortly after Christ's birth (Matt. 2:15).

Herod the Great was a particularly bloodthirsty ruler. He executed one of his wives, Mariamne, her mother, and three of his sons (the last one five days before his own death). Shortly before his death, he lured prominent Jewish leaders to Jericho where he imprisoned them. Knowing the people would not mourn his death, he ordered that these leaders be executed after he died. That way, he reasoned, there would at least be mourning going on at the time of his death. Fortunately, his mad scheme was not carried out. Most barbaric of all was Herod's slaughter of all the innocent young male children near Bethlehem (Matt. 2:16). He sought vainly by this cruel act to kill the true King of the Jews, who was safely in Egypt with His parents.

The **Herod the king** of this chapter was Herod Agrippa I, who reigned from A.D. 37 to A.D. 44. He was the grandson of Herod the Great, who had murdered his father, Aristobulus. The apostle Paul would one day stand trial before his son, Herod Agrippa II. Despite being raised and educated in Rome, Agrippa I was always on shaky ground with the Romans. He ran up numerous debts in Rome, then fled to Palestine, leaving angry creditors behind him. Unwise comments he made got back to the Roman emperor Tiberius, who promptly imprisoned him. Released from prison following Tiberius's death, he was made ruler of northern Palestine (Luke 3:1), to which Judea and Samaria were eventually added in A.D. 41. He ruled the largest territory of Palestine since Herod the Great nearly fifty years earlier. Because of his tenuous relationship with Rome, it was imperative that he maintain the loyalty of his Jewish subjects.

One way to win favor with the resident Jewish authorities was to persecute the hated sect of the Christians, especially the apostles. Accordingly, **about the time** of the famine mentioned in chapter 11, Agrippa **laid hands on some who belonged to the church in order to mistreat them.** One of those was the beloved apostle **James the brother of John,** whom Agrippa ordered **put to death with a sword.** James thus became the first of the apostles to suffer martyrdom. That he was executed **with a sword** suggests the charges against him included leading the people astray after false gods (cf. Deut. 13:12–15). As his Lord had predicted, he drank of the same cup as did Jesus (Matt. 20:23). He was the first apostle to die (apart from Judas), and the only one whose death is recorded in the New Testament.

Agrippa's ploy was a resounding success. **When he saw that** James's arrest and execution **pleased the Jews,** he decided to go all out. He reasoned that the arrest and execution of Peter, the acknowledged leader of the Christians, would forever endear him to his Jewish subjects. Therefore, **during the days of Unleavened Bread,** the weekly feast following Passover, Agrippa **proceeded to arrest Peter** (for the third time, cf. 4:3; 5:18). He cunningly chose the Passover season, when Jerusalem would be thronged with devout Jewish pilgrims. That would ensure his act maximum coverage.

Having **seized** Peter, Agrippa **put him in prison, delivering him to four squads of soldiers, intending after the Passover to bring him out before the people.** Agrippa knew that during Passover itself the people would be busy. He therefore intended to wait until **after the Passover to bring him out before the people.** He would have his showy public trial of Peter after the busyness of the holiday ended but before the crowds left Jerusalem.

Meanwhile, Peter remained in prison, securely guarded by **four squads of soldiers,** likely because someone remembered that the last time he escaped (5:19). These squads, consisting of four soldiers each, rotated the watch on Peter. At any given time, two were in the cell with him, chained to him, and two more were stationed outside the cell door (v. 6). Peter was definitely in the maximum security wing of Agrippa's prison.

Like so many before him, Agrippa was to learn the hard way the folly of fighting God. He would have been wise to heed Gamaliel's warning to the Sanhedrin not to be "found fighting against God" (Acts 5:39). Such a foolhardy course of action is dangerous, if not fatal and eternally terrible, because God fights back. In Jeremiah 21:5, God warns His enemies that "I Myself shall war against you with an outstretched hand and a mighty arm, even in anger and wrath and great indignation." He warned the hypocrites in the church at Pergamum, "Repent therefore; or else I am coming to you quickly, and I will make war against [you] with the sword of My mouth" (Rev. 2:16).

Three reasons for not fighting God stand out in Acts 12: God's power cannot be contested, His punishment cannot be avoided, and His purposes cannot be frustrated.

God's Power Cannot Be Contested

So Peter was kept in the prison, but prayer for him was being made fervently by the church to God. And on the very night when Herod was about to bring him forward, Peter was sleeping between two soldiers, bound with two chains; and guards in front of the door were watching over the prison. And behold, an angel of the Lord suddenly appeared, and a light shone in the cell; and he struck Peter's side and roused him, saying, "Get up quickly." And his chains fell off his hands. And the angel said to him, "Gird yourself and put on your sandals." And he did so. And he said to him, "Wrap your cloak around you and follow me." And he went out and continued to follow, and he did not know that what was being done by the angel was real, but thought he was seeing a vision. And when they had passed the first and second guard, they came to the iron gate that leads into the city, which opened for them by itself; and they went out and went along one street; and immediately the angel departed from him. And when Peter came to himself, he said, "Now I know for sure that the Lord has sent forth His angel and rescued me from the hand of Herod and from all that the Jewish people were expecting." And when he realized this, he went to the house of Mary, the mother of John who was also called Mark, where many were gathered together and were praying. And when he knocked at the door of the gate, a servant-girl named Rhoda came to answer. And when she recognized Peter's voice, because of her joy she did not open the gate, but ran in and announced that Peter was standing in front of the gate. And they said to her, "You are out of your mind!" But she kept insisting that it was so. And they kept saying, "It is his angel." But Peter continued knocking; and when they had opened the door, they saw him and were amazed. But

motioning to them with his hand to be silent, he described to
them how the Lord had led him out of the prison. And he said,
"Report these things to James and the brethren." And he departed and went to another place. Now when day came, there was no
small disturbance among the soldiers as to what could have become of Peter. And when Herod had searched for him and had
not found him, he examined the guards and ordered that they be
led away to execution. And he went down from Judea to Caesarea and was spending time there. (12:5–19)

While **Peter was kept in the prison,** the church responded as
they usually did when facing persecution: **prayer for him was being
made fervently by the church to God** (cf. 4:23–31). They knew only
God had the power to release Peter. The adverb *ektenōs* (**fervently**) is
related to *ektenēs,* a medical term describing the stretching of a muscle
to its limits. *Ektenōs* is used in Luke 22:44 to describe our Lord's prayer
in Gethsemane, when "being in agony He was praying very fervently;
and His sweat became like drops of blood, falling down upon the
ground." The church poured the maximum effort they were capable of
into their prayers for Peter. They knew the truth James was later to express, that "the effective prayer of a righteous man can accomplish
much" (James 5:16). The *ektenēs* word group describes three essential
elements of the Christian life: love (1 Peter 4:8), service (Acts 26:7), and,
in the present passage, prayer.

Herod thought he had the situation well in hand. God had other
plans, however. **On the very night when Herod was about to bring
him forward, Peter was sleeping between two soldiers, bound
with two chains; and guards in front of the door were watching
over the prison.** Despite his appalling circumstances, Peter was
sound asleep. Neither the presence of the guards, the hardness of the
cell floor, the wretchedness of the prison, nor the imminent threat of execution could disturb his rest. In fact, so soundly was he sleeping that
the angel had to prod him to wake him up.

Our sleeping pill and tranquilizer saturated society could take a
lesson from Peter on how to trust God. First, he trusted in the Lord Jesus's promise to him that he would die later, when he was old (John
21:18). Since he was not yet an old man, he had nothing to fear. Further,
each time he had been in jail before, he had been released. God had a
perfect track record. All this enabled Peter to advise believers to cast
"all your anxiety upon Him, because He cares for you" (1 Peter 5:7). Believers who learn, like Peter, to trust God's promises and past perfor-
mance, usually sleep soundly.

In Herod's plans to curry favor with the Jewish people there was
a major, fatal flaw—he neglected to consider what God might do. God

had more ministry for Peter and did not want him executed yet. Therefore **an angel of the Lord suddenly appeared, and a light shone in the cell; and he struck Peter's side and roused him, saying, "Get up quickly."** As already noted, Peter was sound asleep. Not even the brilliant **light** that **shone in the cell** aroused him. Finally, the angel **struck Peter's side and roused him, saying, "Get up quickly."**

As Peter finally woke up, **his chains fell off his hands.** Still half asleep and not knowing what to make of the situation, Peter had to be reminded that if he was leaving, he needed to get dressed. The angel commanded Peter, **"Gird yourself and put on your sandals." And he did so.** The angel then said to Peter, **"Wrap your cloak around you and follow me."**

Peter obediently **went out** of the cell after the angel **and continued to follow** him. Still groggy, however, **he did not know that what was being done by the angel was real, but thought he was seeing a vision.** In a series of wonderful miracles, they made their way past **the first and second guard,** and **came to the iron gate that leads into the city, which opened for them by itself; and they went out and went along one street.** Having seen Peter out of the cell and then out of the prison and safely away, **immediately the angel departed from him.** His duty was done (cf. Heb. 1:14). Herod learned the same truth as had the Sanhedrin before him (cf. Acts 5:17ff.), that no prison can hold those whom God wants out.

Only then did Peter fully realize what was happening. He finally **came to himself** and exclaimed, **"Now I know for sure that the Lord has sent forth His angel and rescued me from the hand of Herod and from all that the Jewish people were expecting,"** namely his execution. This was not a dream; he really was free.

It suddenly dawned on Peter that it was not wise for a well-known, easily recognizable escaped prisoner to remain standing there in the street. **When he realized this, he went to the house of Mary, the mother of John who was also called Mark, where many were gathered together and were praying.** He went to be with the believers and to inform them of his freedom. Peter encouraged them that they were also safe because God was still in control and had answered their zealous prayers.

The house of Mary, the mother of Peter's companion **John Mark,** was **where many** of the believers **were gathered together praying** for Peter's release. She was evidently a wealthy woman, since she had servants (v. 13), and her house was large enough to accommodate all the believers present. Before going into hiding, Peter made his way to her house. That he knew to go there suggests that believers gathered there regularly.

When Peter got to Mary's house, **he knocked at the door of the gate and a servant-girl named Rhoda came to answer.** She, naturally, asked who was there at that hour of the night. Peter identified himself, but instead of opening the gate for him, **when she recognized Peter's voice, because of her joy she did not open the gate, but ran in and announced that Peter was standing in front of the gate.** Mustering up all the faith behind their prayers, they said to her, "You are out of your mind!" They knew perfectly well that Peter was still in jail! Undaunted, **she kept insisting that it was so.** Despite her insistence, they still were not ready to accept the fact that God had answered their prayers. If Rhoda had not taken leave of her senses, then perhaps what she had heard was Peter's **angel,** someone suggested. In Jewish thought, each person had a guardian angel who could assume the form of that person.

Meanwhile, the real Peter was left in an awkward and dangerous position. With no other option, he **continued knocking,** hoping he did not attract attention to himself and get arrested again. Finally, Rhoda was able to persuade the others to come and see for themselves. **When they** finally **opened the door** (much to Peter's relief), **they saw him and were amazed.** His inability to enter without their opening may show something of the fear of arrest that gripped these believers.

The noise made by the overjoyed believers threatened to do what Peter's knocking had not: to arouse the neighbors and get Peter recaptured. Hurriedly **motioning to them with his hand to be silent, he described to them how the Lord had led him out of the prison. And he said, "Report these things to James and the brethren." And he departed and went to another place.** Peter quickly told the amazing story of his escape, which no doubt greatly encouraged his listeners. Peter then commanded them to report the news to James (not the martyred apostle but the Lord's brother, Matt. 13:55). From Acts 15 we learn that he was the head of the Jerusalem church at this time. Having done that, Peter prudently **departed and went to another place.** He didn't want to put all his fellow believers in jeopardy, and he knew Agrippa would soon be looking for him. Luke does not tell us where he went. The suggestion of those who want to identify him as the first pope, that he went to Rome at this early date, is not likely, especially since Acts 15 finds him back in Jerusalem after Agrippa's death.

Regardless of where he went, Peter fades from the scene as far as the record of Acts is concerned. Apart from his brief appearance at the Jerusalem council (Acts 15), this is the last we see of Peter. From here on out, the story revolves around Paul and his ministry.

Peter's sudden, mysterious disappearance from a securely guarded cell caused an uproar among the guard force. **When** the next **day came,** Luke informs us, **there was no small disturbance among**

the soldiers as to what could have become of Peter. They frantically turned the prison upside down searching for him, since they knew all too well what fate awaited a soldier who lost a prisoner (cf. 16:27; 27:42).

They could not find Peter, however, and eventually were forced to report that to Herod. Their worst fears were realized, for **Herod,** having **searched for** Peter unsuccessfully, turned his fury on the hapless guards. He **examined the guards and ordered that they be led away to execution.** Herod was a suspicious man, and the guards could have proffered no reasonable explanation for Peter's escape.

After court martialing and executing the offending guards, Herod in a huff **went down from Judea to Caesarea and was spending time there.** His plan had blown up in his face, and he needed a vacation to pull himself together. Unfortunately for him, he still failed to learn that he could not fight God. That mistake, which cost him Peter and his prestige with the Jews, was shortly to cost him his life.

GOD'S PUNISHMENT CANNOT BE AVOIDED

Now he was very angry with the people of Tyre and Sidon; and with one accord they came to him, and having won over Blastus the king's chamberlain, they were asking for peace, because their country was fed by the king's country. And on an appointed day Herod, having put on his royal apparel, took his seat on the rostrum and began delivering an address to them. And the people kept crying out, "The voice of a god and not of a man!" And immediately an angel of the Lord struck him because he did not give God the glory, and he was eaten by worms and died. (12:20–23)

Several months had passed since Peter's escape when, for reasons unknown to us, Herod became **very angry with the people of Tyre and Sidon.** They were outside Herod's jurisdiction, but since Old Testament times **their country** had been **fed** by the region ruled by Herod (cf. 1 Kings 5:11; Ezra 3:7; Ezek. 27:17).

Realizing the danger of having Herod irate with them, **with one accord they came to him, and having won over Blastus the king's chamberlain, they were asking for peace.** Herod's economic blockade was crippling them, and they needed to make **peace** with him quickly. They persuaded (possibly with money) **Blastus the king's chamberlain** to act as an intermediary.

Herod agreed to terms, but to further demonstrate his prowess, he subjected the ambassadors from the two cities to a spectacle. **On an**

appointed day (according to the Jewish historian Josephus the occasion was a feast in honor of Herod's patron, the Roman Emperor Claudius), **Herod, having put on his royal apparel, took his seat on the rostrum and began delivering an address to them.** They met in the amphitheater built by Agrippa's grandfather, Herod the Great. Josephus describes the scene: "[Herod] put on a garment made wholly of silver, and of a contexture truly wonderful, and came into the theatre early in the morning; at which time the silver of his garment being illuminated by the fresh reflection of the sun's rays upon it, shone out after a surprising manner" (*Antiquities* XIX, vii, 2).

Overwhelmed by his splendor (or, more likely, seeking to flatter him), **the people kept crying out, "The voice of a god and not of a man!"** Josephus notes that Herod "did neither rebuke them, nor reject their impious flattery" (*Antiquities* XIX, vii, 2).

God's response was swift. **Immediately an angel of the Lord struck him because he did not give God the glory, and he was eaten by worms and died.** Dr. Jean Sloat Morton comments,

> The phrase "eaten of worms," in Greek is *skolakobrotos.* The root word *skolax* means "a specific head structure of a tapeworm." Since the word *scolex* (plural *scolices*) is applied to the head of tapeworms, Herod's death was almost certainly due to the rupture of a cyst formed by a tapeworm. There are several kinds of tapeworms, but one of the most common ones found in sheep-growing countries is the dog tape, *Echinococcus granulosus.* The heaviest infections come from areas where sheep and cattle are raised. Sheep and cattle serve as intermediate hosts for the parasite. The dog eats the infected meat, then man gets the eggs from the dog, usually by fecal contamination of hair.
>
> The disease is characterized by the formation of cysts, generally on the right lobe of the liver; these may extend down into the abdominal cavity. The rupture of such a cyst may release as many as two million scolices. The developing worms inside of the cysts are called scolices, because the anterior region constitutes the major part of development at this stage. When the cyst ruptures, the entrance of cellular debris along with the scolices may cause sudden death.
>
> The use of the word *scolex* is not limited to this reference about Herod; the term also appears in Mark 9:44. A literal translation of the phrase in Mark 9:44 would read, "where their scolex dieth not." This usage is very interesting because the tapeworm keeps propagating itself. Each section of the worm is a self-contained unit which has both male and female parts. The posterior part matures and forms hundreds of worm eggs. The word *scolex* in this text portrays a biological description of permanence which the text demands for the comparison. (*Science in the Bible* [Chicago: Moody, 1978], 261–62)

According to Josephus, Herod lingered on for five days, in terrible pain. Amid all his pomp and majesty, he suffered an ignominious and shameful death. So ended the reign and life of the man who had dared to touch two of God's apostles. His crime for which he was executed (A.D. 44) was that **he did not give God the glory,** the very crime for which all the unregenerate who reject God will be condemned (Rom. 1:18–23).

God's Purposes Cannot Be Frustrated

But the word of the Lord continued to grow and to be multiplied. And Barnabas and Saul returned from Jerusalem when they had fulfilled their mission, taking along with them John, who was also called Mark. (12:24–25)

Again Luke keeps us on track with the church's growth by reporting that despite the furious opposition of men, **the word of the Lord continued to grow and to be multiplied.** They could no more stop its spread than King Canute could stop the tide from coming in.

After stating the fact that God's purposes cannot be frustrated, Luke cites as an example **Barnabas and Saul,** who **returned from Jerusalem when they had fulfilled their mission.** They had completed their mission of bringing famine relief to the Jerusalem church (11:30). That mission took place after Herod's death. He died, but the church he persecuted lived on.

Luke notes that **John, who was also called Mark,** accompanied them. From Colossians 4:10 we learn that he was Barnabas's cousin. As he accompanied them on their relief mission to Jerusalem, so he would accompany them on their first missionary journey (13:5). His defection during that journey (13:13) would eventually lead to a rift between Paul and Barnabas (15:36–40).

Verses 24–25 mark an important transition in Acts. They introduce again the apostle Paul, with whose ministry the rest of the book will be primarily concerned.

Indexes

Index of Greek Words

martūrēs, 21
matanoeō, 73, 246
mathētēs, 283
mathētria, 283

ōdinas, 65

pais, 106
peitharcheō, 169
phobos, 86
pikria, 246
plērēs, 189
poieō, 190

proginoskein, 63
prognōsis, 63
proorizō, 141
prostassō, 299

sēmeion, 61
skolios, 76
sozō, 135
stratēgos, 128
sunarpazō, 194
suzēteō, 193

trapeza, 179

Index of Scripture

Index of Subjects

New Testament Commentary Series by Dr. John F. MacArthur, Jr.

Matthew 1-7
Matthew 8-15
Matthew 16-23
Matthew 24-28
Acts 1-12
Acts 13-28
Romans 1-8
Romans 9-16
First Corinthians
Galatians
Philippians
Colossians and Philemon
First and Second Thessalonians
First Timothy
Second Timothy
Titus
Hebrews
James
Revelation 1-11
Revelation 12-22

SINCE 1894, Moody Publishers has been dedicated to equip and motivate people to advance the cause of Christ by publishing evangelical Christian literature and other media for all ages, around the world. Because we are a ministry of the Moody Bible Institute of Chicago, a portion of the proceeds from the sale of this book go to train the next generation of Christian leaders.

If we may serve you in any way in your spiritual journey toward understanding Christ and the Christian life, please contact us at www.moodypublishers.com.

"All Scripture is God-breathed and is useful for teaching, rebuking, correcting and training in righteousness, so that the man of God may be thoroughly equipped for every good work."
—2 TIMOTHY 3:16, 17

MOODY
PUBLISHERS

THE NAME YOU CAN TRUST®